# PARAGRAPHS AND THEMES

**D. C. Heath and Company**
*Lexington, Massachusetts    Toronto*

# PARAGRAPHS and

# THEMES *Fourth Edition*

*P. Joseph Canavan*

*Mount San Antonio College*

Published simultaneously in Canada.

Printed in the United States of America.

International Standard Book Number: 0-669-05273-6

Library of Congress Catalog Card Number: 82-81608

# ACKNOWLEDGMENTS

Mortimer J. Adler   From *How to Read a Book* (New York: Simon & Schuster, 1940).

George K. Anderson and Robert Warnock   From *The World in Literature*, Vol. IV (Glenview, Ill.: Scott, Foresman and Company, 1951).

Thomas A. Bailey and David M. Kennedy   From *The American Pageant*, 6th ed. (Lexington, Mass.: D.C. Heath and Company, 1979). © 1979 by D.C. Heath and Company. Reprinted by permission.

Sharon Begley and Mary Lord   "At Last, The Face of Venus," *Newsweek* (June 9, 1980). Copyright 1980, by Newsweek, Inc. All rights reserved. Reprinted by permission.

Caroline Bird and Sara Welles Briller   From *Born Female*, rev. ed. (New York: David McKay Company, Inc., 1968, 1970). Reprinted by permission.

Ron Butler   "Cantinflas: Mexico's Prince of Comedy," *Américas* (April 1981). Reprinted by permission from *Américas* magazine, published by the General Secretariat of the Organization of American States in English and Spanish.

Don G. Campbell   "New York: Revisit to a Shady Lady," *Los Angeles Times* (June 7, 1981). Copyright 1981, *Los Angeles Times*. Reprinted by permission.

Glenn R. Capp   From *How to Communicate Orally*, 2nd ed. Copyright © 1961, 1966. Reprinted by permission of Prentice-Hall, Inc., Englewood Cliffs, N.J.

Rachel Carson   From *The Edge of the Sea* by Rachel Carson. Copyright © 1955 by Rachel L. Carson. Reprinted by permission of Houghton Mifflin Company. Also from *The Sea Around Us* by Rachel L. Carson. Copyright © 1950, 1951, 1961 by Rachel Carson, renewed 1979 by Roger Christie. Reprinted by permission of Oxford University Press, Inc. Also from *Silent Spring* by Rachel Carson. Copyright © 1962 by Rachel L. Carson. Reprinted by permission of Houghton Mifflin Company.

Changing Times   "Big Money in Pro Sports," *Changing Times* (June 1981). Reprinted with permission from *Changing Times* magazine, © 1981 Kiplinger Washington Editors, Inc. June, 1981.

Anton Chekhov   "A Chorus Girl," in *The Chorus Girl and Other Stories* translated from the Russian by Constance Garnett. Reprinted with permission of Macmillan Publishing Co., Inc., from *The Chorus Girl and Other Stories* by Anton Chekhov. Copyright 1920 by Macmillan Publishing Co., Inc., renewed 1948 by David Garnett. Also by permission of the Estate of Constance Garnett and Chatto & Windus Ltd.

Thelma Clarke   From *Fables of Tewa Indian Dances*, as recorded by Regina DeCata of San Juan, by Thelma Clarke, Clarke Industries, 533 Dakota Ave., S.E., Albuquerque, N.M. 87108.

Samuel Clemens   Specified material from *Life on the Mississippi* by Mark Twain. Harper & Row. Reprinted by permission of Harper & Row, Publishers, Inc. Also from pp. 98–99, 108–109, 110–111 in *Mark Twain's Autobiography*, Vol. I. Copyright 1924 by Clara Gabrilowitsch; renewed 1952 by Clara Clemens Samossoud. Reprinted by permission of Harper & Row, Publishers, Inc.

Shepherd Clough et al.   From *European History in a World Perspective: 1715 to the Present*, 3rd ed. © 1976 by D.C. Heath and Company. Reprinted by permission.

Barry Commoner   "The Killing of a Great Lake," excerpted from *The World Book Year Book*. © 1968 Field Enterprises Educational Corporation. Reprinted by permission.

Joseph Conrad   Excerpts from *Heart of Darkness* and *Typhoon* by Joseph Conrad from *A Conrad Argosy*, copyright 1942 by Doubleday & Company, Inc. Reprinted by permission of the publisher and the Trustees of the Joseph Conrad Estate. Also excerpt from "The Lagoon" from the book *Tales of Unrest* by Joseph Conrad. Reprinted by permission of Doubleday & Company, Inc. and the Trustees of the Joseph Conrad Estate. Also from "Typhoon" from the book *Typhoon* by Joseph Conrad. Reprinted by permission of Doubleday & Company, Inc., and the Trustees of the Joseph Conrad Estate.

Aaron Copland   From *What to Listen for in Music*, rev. ed. (New York: McGraw Hill, Inc., 1957).

Stephen Crane   Reprinted from *The Red Badge of Courage* by Stephen Crane, by permission of W.W. Norton & Company, Inc. A Norton Critical Edition, Edited by Sculley Bradley, Richmond Croom Beatty, E. Hudson Long, and Donald Pizer. Copyright © 1976, 1962 by W.W. Norton & Company, Inc.

Michael Cusak  From "The American Dream: Past . . . and Future." Reprinted by permission of Scholastic, Inc., from *Senior Scholastic* magazine (January 23, 1981). Copyright © 1981 by Scholastic, Inc.

Robert H. Dalton  From *Personality and Social Interactions* (Lexington, Mass.: D.C. Heath and Company, 1961).

Lester del Rey  From *Mysterious Sky.* Copyright © 1964 by Lester del Rey. Reprinted by permission of Chilton Book Company.

John Dewey  From *How We Think* (Lexington, Mass.: D.C. Heath and Company, 1939).

Anita Wilkes Dore  From *The Emerging Woman: Quest for Equality* (New York: Globe Book Company, Inc., 1974).

Howard S. Dye, John R. Moore, and J. Fred Holly  From *Economics: Principles, Problems, and Perspectives* (Boston: Allyn and Bacon, Inc., 1962).

A.J. Eardley  From *General College Geology* (New York: Harper & Row, Publishers, Inc., 1965).

*Economist*  "Cows to the Rescue" by a correspondent in India, *The Economist* (November 1981). Reprinted by permission of *The Economist*, London.

Lawrence Elliott  "Trapped in Mid-Air." Reprinted with permission from the May 1981 *Reader's Digest.* Copyright © 1981 by The Reader's Digest Assn., Inc.

William D. Ellis  From "Solve That Problem With Humor." Reprinted with permission from the May 1973 *Reader's Digest.* Copyright © 1973 by The Reader's Digest Assn., Inc.

Leonard Engel  From *The Sea. Life Nature Library / The Sea* by Leonard Engel and the Editors of Time-Life Books. © 1961, 1980 Time Inc. Reprinted by permission.

Amitai Etzioni  From "The Women's Movement — Token vs. Objectives," *Saturday Review* (May 20, 1972). © 1972. Reprinted by permission of the *Saturday Review.*

Peter Farb  From *The Insects. Life Nature Library / The Insects* by Peter Farb and the Editors of Time-Life Books. Copyright 1962. Reprinted by permission.

Dennis B. Farrell  "The Harvey Girls" by Dennis B. Farrell. From *Arizona Highways* magazine (April 1981). Reprinted by permission of the author.

Susan K. Fletcher  "Holding Court for Canines," *American Way* (August 1981). Reprinted by permission of *American Way*, inflight magazine of American Airlines. Copyright 1981 by American Airlines.

C.S. Forester  From *Beat to Quarters* by C.S. Forester. Copyright 1937 by C.S. Forester; © renewed 1964 by C.S. Forester. Reprinted by permission of Little, Brown and Company and A.D. Peters & Co., Ltd. Also from *Lord Hornblower* by C.S. Forester, Copyright 1946 by The Curtis Publishing Company; Copyright 1946 by C.S. Forester; © renewed 1974 by Dorothy Ellen Forester. Reprinted by permission of Little, Brown and Company and the Harold Matson Company, Inc.

Michael Fox  From "What Is Your Pet Trying to Tell You?" Excerpted from *The World Book Year Book.* © 1981 World Book-Childcraft International, Inc. Reprinted by permission.

Ira Henry Freeman  Reprinted from *Out of the Burning* by Ira Henry Freeman. © 1960 by Ira Henry Freeman. By permission of Crown Publishers, Inc.

Francis L. and Roberta B. Fugate  From "Erle Stanley Gardner: Love of the West Led Him to the Best-Seller List," *American West*, May / June 1981. Quoted with permission.

Robert Furneaux  From *Krakatoa* by Robert Furneaux. © 1964 by Robert Furneaux. Published by Prentice-Hall, Inc., Englewood Cliffs, N.J. 07632. Reprinted by permission.

Frank Gibney  From "The A-bomb and Its Japanese Victims," *Los Angeles Times* (December 6, 1981). Reprinted by permission.

Robert L. Heilbroner  From *The Worldly Philosophers.* Copyright © 1953, 1961, 1972 by Robert L. Heilbroner. Reprinted by permission of Simon & Schuster, a Division of Gulf & Western Corporation.

Herodotus  "The Art of Embalming," from *The Histories of Herodotus of Halicarnassus*, Vol. I, Book 2. Translated by Harry Varter. (New York: The Heritage Press, 1958).

Eric Hoffer  From "A Time for Juveniles." Copyright © 1965 by *Harper's Magazine.* All rights reserved. Reprinted from the June 1965 issue by special permission.

Alma Boice Holland  From "Second Thoughts About Readers," *The Writer's Digest* (July 1967). Reprinted by permission.

R.W. Horton and H.W. Edwards    From *Backgrounds of American Literary Thought*, 2nd ed. (Englewood Cliffs, N.J.: Prentice-Hall, Inc., 1952).

Jane Jacobs    From *The Death and the Life of Great American Cities* (New York: Random House, 1961). Copyright © 1961 by Jane Jacobs.

James Jeans    From *The Mysterious Universe* (London: Macmillan, 1930). Reprinted by permission of Cambridge University Press. Also from "Why the Sky Looks Blue" in *The Stars in Their Courses* by Sir James Jeans. © 1954 by Cambridge University Press. Reprinted by permission of Cambridge University Press.

Peter M. Jones    From "Socialism in Economic Terms." Reprinted by permission of Scholastic, Inc., from *Senior Scholastic* magazine (April 17, 1981). Copyright © 1981 by Scholastic, Inc.

Helen Keller    Excerpt from *The Story of My Life* by Helen Keller (New York: Dell Publishing Co., Inc., 1905, 1954, 1961). Reprinted by permission of Doubleday & Company, Inc.

Joseph Wood Krutch    Excerpt from *The Desert Year* by Joseph Wood Krutch. Copyright 1952 by Joseph Wood Krutch. By permission of William Morrow & Company. Also from *The Voice of the Desert* by Joseph Wood Krutch. Copyright 1954 by Joseph Wood Krutch. By permission of William Morrow & Company.

Norman Lewis    From *How to Read Better and Faster* (New York: Thomas Y. Crowell Company, 1951)

Sam Lowe    From "The American Nile: Saga of the Colorado River," *Arizona Highways* (October 1980). Reprinted by permission of the author.

James Maurer    From "Adobe: Mud for Castles and Hovels," *American West*, November / December 1980. Quoted with permission.

Robert M. McCorkle    From "Excelsior Hotel," *American West*, January / February 1981. Quoted with permission.

William B. Mean    From "Seems To Me," *American Way* (August 1981). Reprinted by permission of *American Way*, inflight magazine of American Airlines. Copyright 1981 by American Airlines. Also by permission of the author.

Strand Mikkelsen    From "How to Ski," *Popular Science Monthly* (January 1931). Reprinted courtesy of *Popular Science Monthly*. © 1930 by Popular Science Publishing Co., Inc.

Robert S. Morison    From "The Faces in the Lecture Room," *Daedalus* (1966). Reprinted by permission of the American Academy of Arts and Sciences.

Paul Mussen, Mark R. Rosenzweig, and Elliot Aronson    From *Psychology: An Introduction* (Lexington, Mass.: D.C. Heath and Company, 1973).

*Newsweek*    "The Graying of America," condensed from *Newsweek* (February 28, 1977). Copyright 1977 by Newsweek, Inc. All rights reserved. Reprinted by permission.

Charles Nordhoff and James N. Hall    From *Mutiny on the Bounty* by Charles Nordhoff and James Norman Hall. Copyright 1932 by Little, Brown and Company; © renewed 1960 by Mrs. Laura W.G. Nordhoff and Sarah M. Hall. By permission of Little, Brown and Company in association with the Atlantic Monthly Press.

Lynn Norment    From "Why Women Get Depressed," *Ebony* (April 1981). Reprinted by permission of *Ebony* magazine, copyright, 1981 by Johnson Publishing Company, Inc.

Orville Palmer    From "What To Do When Children Cheat," *Parents' Magazine* (January 1966). Reprinted by permission of *Parents' Magazine*.

James W.W. Pennington    From "The Fugitive Blacksmith: or, Events in the History of James W.C. Pennington, Pastor of a Presbyterian Church, New York, Formerly a Slave in the State of Maryland," in *Great Slave Narratives*, edited by Arna Botemps (Boston: Beacon Press, 1969).

Elizabeth Pierce    From "Guiding Lights," *American Way* (August 1981). Reprinted by permission of *American Way*, inflight magazine of American Airlines. Copyright 1981 by American Airlines.

Robert C. Pooley    From *The Teaching of English Usage* (Urbana, Ill.: National Council of Teachers of English, 1974).

Dudley Pope    From *Ramage* (Philadelphia: Lippincott Company, 1965).

W.H. Prescott    From *History of the Reign of Ferdinand and Isabella*, Vol. II. New and revised edition edited by John Foster Kirt (Philadelphia: J.B. Lippincott Company, 1973).

J.B. Priestley    From "An Englishman's Outrageous View of Texas Football," in *Journey*

*Down a Rainbow* by J.B. Priestley and Jacquetta Hawkes (London: William Heinemann, Ltd., 1955). Copyright © 1955 by J.B. Priestley and Jacquetta Hawkes. Reprinted by permission of A.D. Peters & Co. Ltd.

Judith Ramsey   From "Guide to Recognizing and Handling Mental Illness," *Family Circle* (October 1974). Reprinted by permission of the author.

David Riesman   From *The Lonely Crowd*, in collaboration with Revel Denney and Nathan Glazer (New Haven, Conn.: Yale University Press, 1950).

Sigurd Rislov   From "The Community College," *Atlantic Monthly* (June 1957). Copyright 1957 by Sigurd Rislov. Reprinted by permission.

Nicholas Rose   From "Ice Age Pioneers: How the East Was Won," *Oceans* (July / August 1979).

Carl Sandburg   Excerpted from *Abraham Lincoln: The Prairie Years*, One-Volume Edition, copyright 1954 by Carl Sandburg. Reprinted by permission of Harcourt Brace Jovanovich, Inc.

Science Digest   From "Young Men Lead in Science Discovery," *Science Digest* (January 1961). Reprinted with permission of *Science Digest*. © The Hearst Corporation.

Richard W. Slatta   From "Cowboys and Gauchos," *Américas* (March 1981). Reprinted by permission from *Américas* magazine, published by the General Secretariat of the Organization of American States in English and Spanish.

Gary Smith   "Holmes on the Range," *The New York Daily News* (as it appeared in *Scholastic Coach*, February 1981). Copyright 1980 by New York News, Inc. Reprinted by permission.

Theodore C. Sorensen   From *Kennedy* by Theodore C. Sorensen. Copyright © 1965 by Theodore C. Sorensen. Reprinted by permission of Harper & Row, Publishers, Inc.

Ian Stevenson, M.D.   From "How Children Learn Prejudice" from "People Aren't Born Prejudiced," *Parents' Magazine* (February 1960). Copyright © 1960 Parents' Magazine Enterprises. Reprinted by permission.

Ann and Myron Sutton   From *Nature on the Rampage* (Philadelphia: J.B. Lippincott Company, 1962). Copyright © 1962 by Ann and Myron Sutton.

A.J.P. Taylor   From *English History 1914–1945* (New York: Oxford University Press, 1965)

Morris Tepper   From "Tornados" by Morris Tepper, *Scientific American* (May 1958), p. 34. Copyright © 1958 by Scientific American, Inc. All rights reserved. Reprinted by permission.

Leo Tolstoy   From *The Death of Ivan Ilych and Hadji Murad and Other Stories*, translated by Louise and Aylmer Maude (Oxford, England: Oxford University Press). Reprinted by permission.

Arnold Toynbee   From *East to West: A Journey Round the World* by Arnold J. Toynbee. Copyright © 1958 by Oxford University Press, Inc. Reprinted by permission.

Peter Truel   From "The Ambitions of the Rich," edited by Tim Hindle. *The Economist* (November 1981).

Wallace Tucker   From "Dinosaurs Whodunit." This article originally appeared in *Science Digest*, May 1981. Reprinted by permission.

Mark Twain (See *Samuel Clemens*).

U.S. News and World Report   "Exploding Volcano: Full Impact Yet to Come," *U.S. News and World Report* (June 2, 1980). Reprinted by permission from *U.S. News & World Report*. Copyright 1980, U.S. News and World Report, Inc.

Karl von Frisch   Excerpted from *Man and the Living World* by Karl von Frisch; copyright © 1949 by Deutscher Verlag, Berlin. English translation by Elasa B. Lowenstein, copyright © 1962 by Oliver and Boyd. Reprinted by permission of Harcourt Brace Jovanovich, Inc. and Oliver and Boyd.

T. Walter Wallbank et al.   From *Civilization: Past and Present*, Vol. I (Glenview, Ill.: Scott, Foresman and Company, 1969).

Robert Warnock and George Anderson   From *The World in Literature*, Vol. I (Glenview, Ill.: Scott, Foresman and Company, 1950).

Kenneth F. Weaver   From "Have We Solved the Mysteries of the Moon?" *National Geographic*, September 1973. Reprinted by permission.

Robert F. Weaver   From "The Cancer Puzzle," *National Geographic*, September 1976. Reprinted by permission.

Walter Prescott Webb   From "Ended: 400 Year Boom," Copyright © 1951 by *Harper's Magazine.* All rights reserved. Reprinted from the October 1951 issue by special permission.

Webster's Seventh New Collegiate Dictionary   Extracts reprinted by permission. From *Webster's Seventh New Collegiate Dictionary* © 1967 by G. & C. Merriam Co., Publishers of the Merriam-Webster Dictionaries.

David Wechsler   From "Measuring the I.Q. Test," *The New York Times Magazine* (January 20, 1957). © 1957 by The New York Times Company. Reprinted by permission.

Don Wharton   From "They're Saving America's Priceless Seashore." Reprinted with permission from the August 1966 *Reader's Digest.* Copyright © 1966 by The Reader's Digest Assn., Inc.

Carl G. Wilgus   From "Conserving Energy As You Ski," *Skiing* (February 1981). Reprinted by permission.

William Carlos Williams   "The Use of Force," from *The Farmer's Daughters.* Copyright 1938 by William Carlos Williams. Reprinted by permission of New Directions Publishing Corporation.

James Q. Wilson   From *American Government: Institutions and Policies.* © 1980 by D.C. Heath and Company. Reprinted by permission.

Mary Ann Frese Witt, Ronald Witt, and Charlotte Vestal Brown   From *The Humanities: Cultural Roots and Continuities,* Vol. I (Lexington, Mass.: D.C. Heath and Company, 1980).

*The World Book Encyclopedia*   From the articles "Star" and "Leaf." Excerpted from *The World Book Encyclopedia.* © 1982 by World Book-Childcraft International, Inc. Reprinted by permission.

# Preface

The fourth edition of *Paragraphs and Themes* incorporates several changes based on suggestions from instructors and students who used previous editions. Many of the model paragraphs, paragraph units, and essays have been replaced with recent, interesting, and popular selections. The material of the book is now organized into nine rather than eight chapters. Chapter 7 treats analysis by structure, function, and process. Analysis by causes and effects is the sole subject of Chapter 8. This new arrangement of material will allow students to concentrate on the individual methods, master the various techniques of development, and spend more time on the separate writing assignments. Other significant changes include additional material on the types of contrast and simplified and expanded presentation of vocabulary lists, quizzes, and tests.

The pattern of *Paragraphs and Themes* best reveals its purpose. It begins with an overall view of the short theme and the longer piece of writing. The function of this structural preview is to give students an understanding of the kinds of writing they will be doing most frequently in their college studies and to stress the relationship of the separate parts to the whole piece of writing. The discussion moves through a detailed treatment of the different kinds of paragraphs, emphasizing the ways of achieving unity, completeness, order, and coherence. It explains the nature and importance of the paragraph unit — a series of paragraphs that are organized around and develop a single main idea or fulfill a single function, such as introducing or concluding a theme, composition, or essay.

Because of the importance of prewriting to the writing process, a chapter is devoted to planning the paper. Students are shown the value of expressing clear and cogent main ideas for paragraphs and of formulating concise thesis statements for essays that inform and explain. They are advised to list possible supporting material, prepare a preliminary plan, and complete other steps that help the inexperienced writer think through the subject before placing thoughts on paper. The remaining pages — the major part of the book — discuss the techniques of organizing and structuring thought by narration, description, and exposition.

The book stresses writing to explain and inform. Considerable space is thus given to expository narration, expository description, and the various techniques of expository writing, such as comparison, contrast, analogy, analysis, classification, definition, and a combination of these methods. Argumentation (persuasion) is not covered. If students are conditioned to organize and develop expository papers effectively, the transition to the argumentation paper will not be difficult. Although narration, description, and exposition are treated as separate forms of discourse for the purpose of explaining each form, the book emphasizes that a writer's thought is more frequently organized and developed by a combination of methods, with one dominant method determined by the writer's purpose.

The numerous models of paragraphs, paragraph units, and essays by experienced writers that appear throughout *Paragraphs and Themes* have been selected to stimulate classroom analysis and discussion, to illustrate the basic rhetorical concerns, and to serve as ideas for written assignments. Included in this material are a number of short essays preceded or followed by an organizational and structural analysis, so that students may see the relationship of the parts to the whole and become aware of the writing skills and techniques employed by experienced writers. Every effort has been made to select models that are strong representatives of the kind of organization and development they illustrate and that provide students with interesting and exciting reading experiences. Moderately difficult models are balanced with less difficult ones. Contemporary selections with popular appeal have replaced many of the older, literary models.

Vocabulary Match-Up quizzes and Vocabulary Tests are still a key element of the text. Vocabulary items taken from readings are placed in a Vocabulary Preview before the material rather than after the paragraphs and essays as in the previous edition. This vocabulary-building material is designed to be self-teaching, helping students to gain a better understanding of the selections while increasing their command of language.

The exercises are also a very important part of the book. They provide students with an opportunity to review what they have learned about a particular method of thought development and to test themselves on what they are learning. In addition, the exercises offer teachers and students the opportunity to discuss the ways in which experienced writers structure their thoughts. Answers to some of the exercises are placed in the textbook to give students a model for their responses. Answers to 25 vocabulary Match-Up quizzes and Vocabulary Tests are also included. An instructor's manual that contains answers to the remaining exercises, 28 vocabulary review tests, answers to the review tests, and information concerning the writer's purpose accompanies the text.

P. J. C.

# Contents

## 9    EXPLAINING AND INFORMING — CLASSIFYING, DEFINING, AND COMBINING   441

*PARAGRAPHS AND THEMES*

# 1

## Viewing
## the Whole

This book treats three forms of discourse: *exposition, description,* and *narration.* In most writing, however, the different forms shade so smoothly one into another that the reader is seldom aware which form dominates. A writer's purpose largely determines the form he uses.

*A writer of exposition,* for example, usually gives information or explains his subject. In order to help with understanding, he addresses himself to the reader's intellect with logical explanations and valid support. He may be giving facts and specifics to explain an event like the invasion of France, the roles that society forces one to play, or the dangers of a certain action. He may be informing in order to explain how an event happened, such as a revolution or an earthquake. He may be instructing his reader on how to do something or how something is done — a process, for instance, like making steel.

*In description*, a writer appeals to a reader's imagination and perceptive senses. He wishes his reader to see, hear, taste, smell, and feel as he presents a vivid word picture of the subject. He may be describing a sunset, a sinking ship, an individual, or a dying elephant. Whatever the subject, a writer's purpose in description is the same: to appeal to the imagination, the emotions, and the senses.

*The writer of narration* tells a story; he writes about an incident or a series of incidents in which action dominates.

Effectiveness in structuring thought in these kinds of writing, especially exposition, is essential for the college student if he is going to be successful in the college program of studies. He will be required by various instructors to write essay examinations, research papers, book reports, laboratory assignments, compositions or themes, and many other types of written work that supplement the lectures, class discussions, and textbook information. Most of these written assignments will be relatively short papers, ranging from one to two paragraphs in length (100 to 200 words) to five to ten paragraphs (500 to 1000 words). In the writing class this paper is called a theme, essay, or composition.

### VOCABULARY PREVIEW

On certain pages of this chapter and subsequent chapters of the book, you will find a list of words taken from the model essays and paragraphs in the chapters. Begin compiling a vocabulary notebook by looking up the meaning of each word. In the chapters, you will find a variety of vocabulary tests on the same words. This work with vocabulary building will enable you to read the essays and paragraphs with better understanding and increase your own vocabulary so that you can bring your speaking, reading, and writing skills to higher levels of comprehension and communication. Each vocabulary word will be marked in the text in the following way: *entrepreneur*.° The answers to the vocabulary tests will be placed at the end of the chapter.

| | | |
|---|---|---|
| entrepreneur | corporate | realistic |
| maneuvers | grande dames | incompatible |
| surreptitiously | stratosphere | perspectives |
| clairvoyance | literally | depreciate |

## Structure of the Short Paper

Read the following essay — a model for the short paper.

▶ THE HARVEY GIRLS
**Dennis B. Farrell**

[1]The Harvey Girls. Somehow the name suggests a bouquet of lovely young women like those created with pen and ink by Charles Dana Gibson in the two decades before the turn of the last century. But the Harvey Girls, who made their debut as waitresses at El Tovar and other Harvey House restaurants along the route of the Sante Fe railroad, were no paper dolls.

[2]Although they were pretty, too, they were real and they endured into the 20th century as well as into legend. Actually, they had to play down their beauty, but it must have shone through because they have been romanticized in prose, poetry, and even a movie — and always as beautiful women.

[3]Certainly those young ladies must have had a strong spirit of adventure to come out to work in the wild and woolly West of the late 19th century. But come out they did, by the thousands. One estimate is that more than 20,000 young women from places like Kansas City, Chicago, New York, Boston, and Philadelphia became Harvey Girls and went west to seek their fortunes.

[4]The reason there were so many was that there was such a high turnover — and the reason for the high turnover was that so many of them quit to marry — miners, ranchers, men from all walks of life. They founded the West's first families.

[5]Some said their boss, Fred Harvey, the English-born entrepreneur° of the food business, might as well have set up a matrimonial bureau because so many of his employees left his hire to "get hitched." Despite a requirement that each Harvey Girl sign a one-year contract, in which she agreed not to marry before the end of that period, the turnover still was tremendous. The very qualities Harvey sought in his employees seemed to be the same ones men wanted in their wives.

[6]Girls who made it through the first six months without Cupid interfering were congratulated personally by Harvey, and often they would continue for another year or more with the restaurant chain.

[7]Nevertheless, proposals must have been routine events in their daily lives, and many a man was moved to wax poetic

over the young girls, as was John Moore, writing in the *Amarillo Globe.* ". . . All dressed in spotless linen, her hair all in a curl, so purely sweetly winning, is the happy Harvey Girl."

[8]Recruiting advertisements in Eastern newspapers called for "Young women of good character, attractive and intelligent, 18 to 30." No experience was required. A special training corps of Harvey employees taught the girls personal grooming and drilled them to perfection on how to set a table and serve food with a touch of elegance.

[9]One of the most important tableside maneuvers° they learned was the famous Harvey "code" for arranging cups for beverages. The young woman who took the orders surreptitiously° arranged cups to indicate different customer choices.

The girl who followed unerringly poured the right beverage into the right cup without asking a single question, suggesting a touch of clairvoyance° to the patrons.

[10]The requirement of "good character" meant just that with Fred Harvey. While some young women might have joined his staff to get away from heavy authority at home, they soon found they had to live with a matron who also had a rigid set of rules. At El Tovar and other Harvey operations, matrons were older employees who had come up the corporate° ladder. Like top sergeants, they inspected their recruits' dress and general appearance. And they made sure they observed the 10 p.m. curfew, which was lifted only on the most special occasions.

[11]The Harvey Girl uniform certainly should have done nothing to inflame men's passions. It was a black dress that buttoned high up the neck and had a white collar. They were allowed a white hair ribbon, but no fancy hairdos or makeup. Their shoes were black, too.

[12]But obviously this didn't deter their many suitors, and their very presence must have had a powerful effect on them.

[13]At El Tovar, as well as at other Harvey installations, the girls continued to meet, fall in love with, and marry the men they served in the dining rooms and the lunch counters.

It has been reported that something like 4000 male infants born of these marriages were named either Fred or Harvey or both, in honor of the famous restaurateur, and many of the biggest names in the West can trace their lineage to a Harvey Girl. The early training in manners and social graces that these young women received in their homes in the East, and the experience they had at meeting the public as Harvey Girls served them well in later life as hostesses and grande dames° of the manor.

[14]As their husbands tamed the West and carved out empires

in a rugged, beautiful land, their Harvey Girl wives marched beside them every step of the way.

In this short essay, Dennis B. Farrell has presented an interesting account of "The Harvey Girls." But he has also fulfilled the more important purpose of showing that his girls were not the paper dolls created by Charles Dana Gibson. They were real women who played a very vital role in the history of the West.

He accomplished his objective with a simple but very effective organizational plan and development. In the first paragraph he presents the necessary background material for reader understanding by identifying the girls as waitresses in the Harvey House restaurants along the Sante Fe railroad, and he states clearly his central thought (thesis statement): these girls "were no paper dolls."

In paragraphs 2 and 3, Farrell expands on this idea by saying that the Harvey Girls were real women with a strong spirit of adventure, not merely the beautiful women of romanticized literature and the film. They were the women who "founded the West's first families."

In the body of the essay (paragraphs 5–13), Mr. Farrell gives reasons why men wanted to marry them. The qualities that Harvey wanted in his girls were the same ones that "men wanted in their wives." These young women were of good character, trained in manners and social graces, and disciplined through adherence to a rigid set of rules of conduct that prepared them to be the hostesses and grande dames of the Western manor.

In the final paragraph, Farrell repeats in slightly different words the central idea stated in the first paragraph: the Harvey Girls were real women who helped their husbands tame the West and carve out empires "in a rugged, beautiful land."

Because Dennis B. Farrell wished to emphasize the central idea stated in the first paragraph, he developed his flowing thought in a *thesis-support-thesis* paper. In structuring this kind of paper, a writer states the thesis in the first paragraph or paragraphs, follows with the necessary supporting material, and restates the thesis in slightly different words in the final paragraph. A common modification of this pattern is the *thesis-support* paper. As the name implies, the writer of this paper states the thesis in the opening paragraph and moves onward through the support.

A caution, however, is necessary at this time. You must be aware that the model essays in the first chapters of this book will illustrate the most basic and common methods of developing thought. Two other common methods of development are found in the *question-answer* paper and the *support-thesis* paper. The *question-answer* paper is popular and effective because of its simple organization. The writer begins with a question and follows with the answer; the reader can readily discern the writer's purpose and follow easily the developing thought. A more difficult method of organizing and developing thought is the *support-thesis* paper. By using this kind of development, a writer can clue the reader to the central thought in the first paragraph by suggesting the thesis, make it clearer as he or she moves onward through the support, and state the thesis most emphatically as a conclusion in the final paragraph.

## Structure of the Longer Paper

The longer paper, as it is arbitrarily defined in this book, is an essay developing a single central thought (thesis) in more than 500 words. Longer papers may be developed with the same methods as the short papers. However, the *thesis-support-thesis* paper is a popular and effective kind of longer paper. In what way, then, do the short paper and the longer paper differ? The longer paper will often include paragraphs with particular functions, such as introductory, support, and conclusion purposes. The longer paper may be broken down, therefore, into three separate but related parts: an introduction, a body or middle, and a conclusion. As you read the following essay, which was selected to illustrate the structure of the longer paper, keep these questions in mind as they will help you in analyzing its structure.

I. Title
   A. Does the title gain reader interest?
   B. Is the title limited enough to give the reader an idea of what the paper is about?
II. Beginning
   A. How does the writer begin his paper? Does he simply state the thesis in the first sentence and move at once into the supporting material as we saw with the short paper?
   B. Is the beginning more formally organized into a paragraph or paragraphs whose special function is chiefly to introduce the topic and gain reader interest?
   C. How many of these functions does the introductory paragraph or paragraphs perform?
      1. State the thesis.
      2. Define terms or expressions.
      3. Gain reader interest.
      4. Present necessary background material so that the reader may better understand the discussion that follows.

      5. Indicate the organizational plan of the subsequent paragraphs.

      6. Lead the reader smoothly into the body of the paper.

III. Middle or body of the paper

   A. Does the writer leave you with the feeling that he has adequately explained and supported his thesis?

   B. Do the paragraphs and paragraph units (a series of paragraphs revolving around and developing a single main idea) develop the thesis completely enough by presenting a new and related aspect of that central thought?

   C. Is each paragraph or paragraph unit itself sufficiently developed with material related to and developing its main idea?

IV. Ending

   A. Does the writer leave the reader with a feeling that he has said all that he wishes to say about the subject?

   B. Does the writer end his paper with a formal conclusion, or does he feel that what he has already said is clear enough without additional comments?

   C. How many functions do the concluding paragraph or paragraphs perform?

      1. Restate the thesis in slightly different words.

      2. Summarize the main points developed in the middle paragraphs.

      3. Recommend some kind of future action.

      4. Emphasize the significance of the findings of the paper.

      5. Offer a solution to the problem.

      6. Close the paper with an anecdote or quotation that emphasizes the writer's purpose.

▶ BIG MONEY IN PRO SPORTS

**Changing Times**

[1]Dave Winfield, who is 29 years old, took a new job this year at an annual salary of about $2,000,000 in pay and fringes — quite a jump from the $350,000 a year his previous employer was paying him. His new employer is the New York Yankees baseball club. And he isn't the only professional athlete in the salary stratosphere°. Here are the most recent annual earnings of some other top sports pros:

[2]Tennis stars Bjorn Borg $1,019,345, John McEnroe $1,005,238, Martina Navratilova $747,548, Chris Evert-Lloyd $564,398, Tracy Austin $541,676; baseball players Nolan Ryan, Phil Niekro and George Brett, $1,000,000 each; basket-

ball players Moses Malone $1,000,000, Kareem Abdul-Jabbar over $700,000; hockey player Marcel Dionne $600,000; golfers Tom Watson $462,636, Nancy Lopez $215,987; football players Walter Payton $450,000, Archie Manning $379,000, Lee Roy Selmon $218,000; race car driver Carl Yarborough $431,842; soccer star Giorgio Chinaglia $283,000; bowler Mark Roth $124,517; rodeo champion Tom Ferguson $117,222.

[3]Not every professional athlete fares as well as the superstars. But even little-known pros don't do badly, especially now that players' unions in the major team sports are organized. The minimum player salary in major league baseball is $32,500; the average salary is $143,756. In the National Football League the minimum player salary is $25,000; the average is $78,650. In the National Basketball Association the minimum is $35,000; the average is $180,000. Players on teams in those sports also receive medical, life insurance and pension benefits.

[4]The leaflet that the office of the baseball commissioner sends to youngsters who inquire about a career in professional baseball describes it as "truly the best of all possible worlds. Professional baseball represents much more, of course, than the opportunity to be a hero in the eyes of the fans. It is also the rare opportunity to provide a lifetime of security — and thus satisfaction — while doing the only thing literally° millions of youngsters from all walks of life enjoy most. Playing Baseball."

[5]Baseball commissioner Bowie Kuhn says, "The financial rewards, added to the enjoyment of the total baseball experience, make our game an extremely attractive career for any young man with the necessary ability. The complete retirement package, including an outstanding pension program, is among the very best." It pays a player who retires at age 45 with four years in the majors $419 a month for life. A player with 20 years in the league can at age 65 draw a $4,824-a-month pension.

[6]The career literature of the National Football League is almost as lyrical: "Working conditions are first class, excellent in every way (housing, food, equipment, etc.) except possibly the weather, over which the employer has no control. . . . A pro football player, unlike most professional athletes, has to do relatively little traveling. He may make two or three overnight trips during the preseason and a maximum of eight during the regular season. . . . [He] is normally off on Monday and puts in about a seven-hour day, Tuesday through Friday, leaving plenty of free time for keeping up business contacts."

[7]Indeed, the greatest advantage of playing pro football, says the NFL, "is the entree it provides to business and professional opportunities. The professional football player is a highly respected, highly sought after athlete and can make tremendous strides in a relatively short period of time if he properly uses his college training and the entree he receives."

**The bumpy road to big bucks.**   [8]A professional athlete's life is not all fan acclaim and megabuck paychecks. And the path to a job as a pro can discourage all but the most committed and talented. The long trail begins on sandlots and blacktop courts, in community clubs and on playing fields, where 7- and 8-year-old youngsters learn to play in Little League, Pop Warner and other kiddie sports leagues.

[9]To have a realistic° chance of becoming a major league professional, a player must be the standout performer on every team he's on, from Little League through high school and college, if he goes to college. And the more time he spends playing this game, the better his odds of someday making the pros. That's why players who live in warm weather regions, where they can practice and play the game year-round, have an advantage.

[10]Though most professional baseball players are still recruited from among high school graduates, the professional football and basketball leagues stress the importance of college in the development of their pro players. College teams, like baseball's farm teams, serve as incubators for young athletes heading for the pro leagues. In football and basketball a player normally is not eligible to be drafted by a pro team until an age at which he would no longer be eligible to play on a college team. NBA teams can draft younger men who have renounced college team eligibility in writing.

[11]Playing on a college team for four years and getting a college degree are frequently incompatible.° Though its draft concentrates on college players, less than 33% of the players in the NFL have college degrees. As one union official says, college athletes looking forward to a pro career often end up majoring in playing ball.

[12]A rookie player signed to a contract by a professional baseball club will normally spend one to four years on the club's minor league farm team, where he must continue to demonstrate exceptional ability in order to get his crack at making it into the majors. Of 4,000 minor league baseball players, 2,500 drop out each year.

[13]Of all players of all sports who enter the minors on a professional contract, only 3% to 5% ever make the roster of a major league team. Only 210 to 230 rookies, including players from college teams, military teams and tryout camps, are picked each year by the NFL's 28 teams, and fewer survive training camp.

[14]A glance at the number of jobs for players in major league team sports reveals why the chances are so slim. There are only 650 player slots in major league baseball, 25 on each of the 26 teams (another 15 players per team are posted in the minors). The total number of positions on the NFL's 28 teams is about 1,400, and there are 276 on the NBA's 23 teams.

[15]As Peter Rose of the Major League Baseball Players Association will pointedly remind you, "On a major league team, the worst player — if there is such a thing — was probably the best who ever played on all the teams he played for on his way to the pros."

**Not all fun and games.**   [16]Perspectives° on big pay in big-time sports are different in the stands from what they are on the playing field. "The road to the pros is tough," says Frank Woschitz of the NFL Players Association. "That's why we think players should make a lot of money right from the start. But fans resent big player salaries." Star players, however, see their pay as fully earned, as Babe Ruth did: When asked how he felt about making more money than the President of the United States, the Babe explained, "I had a better year than he did."

[17]But the fact is that a big-league athlete may have fewer good years at a high salary than a President has in the White House. In baseball, Peter Rose observes, "a player may play ten years before he gets the big bucks, and then his career might be almost finished."

The average career in major league team sports ranges from three and a half years in basketball to five years in baseball. And the trend on many pro teams toward more use of younger players is shortening the span. Also, the snap of a bone can end a pro sports career abruptly.

[18]How much a player makes above the minimum salary depends not only on his ability, performance and good luck in avoiding injury but also on what position he plays and what team he plays for. In football, running backs and quarterbacks tend to be the highest paid — and running backs have the shortest average playing careers. In both the National and the

American baseball leagues, first base tends to be the best-paid position to play, and outfielders (usually the big hitters) earn almost as much.

[19]Average salaries for the Yankees, Phillies, Pirates and Angels are over $190,000, but the average is well under $100,000 on six of the 26 teams in the major leagues. The lowest salary average, on the Oakland A's, is $54,994.

Despite the players' financial gains from the fairly recent and still threatened system of free agency, in which veteran players can shop for the best deal from any team, most pro players have little control of their playing careers. To a team owner, players are chattel. They can be traded to another club for cash or other players or sent back to the minor leagues without consultation or consent. For tax purposes club owners depreciate° the players just as other employers write off machinery in a plant. At any time in a player's career — and probably more than once — he may have to adjust to a new team, new home city, new working conditions.

[20]The level at which professional athletes are expected to perform can diminish the joy of the game. Getting "up" for a game isn't easy when you are living out of a suitcase and playing when your body doesn't want to. There are always plenty of younger players eager for their chance, too, so playing hurt is something many veterans think they have to do to keep their job.

***The pros who go it alone.***   [21]Some professionals are entrepreneurs rather than hired help. In professional golf, bowling, tennis, racing, rodeo and other individual sports, players must independently prepare themselves for professional careers. The big paychecks in these sports come from contest purses, and the pros who compete for the prize money must cover their own expenses, from coaching and training to insurance and travel.

[22]Take professional golf, one of the highest-paying individual sports. Of the 13,000 professional golfers, the vast majority make a modest living working for golf and country clubs as teachers and operators of pro shops, where equipment and clothing are sold. Probably less than 3% of them participate in the big-money golf tournaments.

[23]Training for a career as a tournament pro can start with one or two rounds of golf a week at age 7. It usually includes playing for high school and college teams and in as many amateur tournaments as possible to become accustomed to the pressure

of competition. An amateur golfer with a handicap of 1 might be ready to try to go professional.

[24]To become a touring pro, a golfer must earn an eligibility card through the qualifying school of the Professional Golf Association or the Ladies Professional Golf Association. Of the 1,200 golfers who apply to the PGA each year, only about 50 survive the qualifying tests and play. Of the 220 LPGA applicants, 24 to 30 earn cards. In addition, about four cards are issued to winners of open qualifying rounds held prior to most major golf tournaments.

[25]Once they become touring pros, golfers must consistently perform well to retain their eligibility, since tournaments limit entries to 100 to 150 of the best golfers, and newly qualified pros are always waiting to emerge from the back of the pack to overtake wavering veterans.

*O those golden extras!*  [26]The superstars of professional sports — the Namaths, Borgs, Nicklauses, Merediths — are often able to parlay their celebrity during and after their playing days into more money than they can make at playing their game. They endorse products, perform in advertisements, give lectures, make movies and become sportscasters.

[27]According to David Harrop in *Paychecks: Who Makes What?* (Harper Colophon; $5.95 paperback), O.J. Simpson, who retired from pro football at the end of the 1979 season, "has made more than $200,000 for every movie he played in and has a five-year sportscasting and jack-of-all-trades contract with NBC-TV. He continues to make money by hurdling for Hertz; advertising and sharing in the profits of the Tree Sweet orange juice company; plugging Shindana toys (Shindana makes an O.J. Simpson doll); recommending Dingo boots; and promoting Wilson Sporting Goods and Hyde Spot-Bilt athletic shoes."

[28]On the court Bjorn Borg is an expensive billboard. In 1978 his tennis outfit alone (Tuborg headband, Fila clothes, Tretorn shoes, SAS shoulder patch) earned him over $300,000, and he picked up $100,000 for using Bancroft rackets, $2,000 for having them strung with VS gut. And grandfatherly golf pro Arnold Palmer, a familiar figure in business, advertising and tournament golf, does even better than Simpson or Borg.

[29]Is a pro sports career worthwhile? An official of a professional players' association answers that it is "wishful thinking for a youngster to plan on a pro sports career. Realistically, it is not something you could consider a career. Pro players who don't have solid career alternatives can end up with tragic

problems once they leave the pay bracket and limelight of professional sports."

The writer of this model essay for the longer paper selects a title that gains reader interest and tells what the paper is about. He begins his discussion with an introduction — a paragraph unit of seven paragraphs.* In these paragraphs, he presents evidence from various professional sports, such as baseball, tennis, and football, to support the view that these sports offer a young man or woman not only financial security but other benefits as well.

In paragraph 8 the writer states the thesis: "the path to a job as a pro can discourage all but the most committed and talented." Paragraphs 8 through 28 make up the body of the essay, presenting supporting material for the thesis statement. "The bumpy road to big bucks" is a paragraph unit, consisting of paragraphs 8 through 15, that emphasizes the years of training, the nature of the competition, and the athlete's slim chance of reaching the professional level.

In supporting the main idea that professional sport is not all fun and games (paragraphs 16 through 20), the writer points out that the professional athlete has a short career, has little control over his playing career, finds it difficult to "get up" for every game, and often plays hurt in order to keep his job.

In paragraphs 21 through 25, the writer discusses the problems of professionals who "go it alone," especially the professional golfer. The paragraph unit consisting of paragraphs 26 through 28 treats the "golden extras" — those benefits that are usually bonuses for the superstars.

In the final paragraph, the writer asks the question: "Is a pro sports career worthwhile?" He repeats his thesis statement in slightly different words in answering this question: "Realistically, it is not something you could consider a career."

The long paper, then, is organized and developed in much the same ways as the short paper. Both may be organized in one of the four patterns. Both consist of a series of paragraphs or paragraph units revolving around and developing the thesis statement. The long paper, however, will usually have more than one introductory paragraph and more paragraphs and paragraph units as supporting material. Conclusions are also more common in the long than in the short paper.

---

* A paragraph unit consists of more than one paragraph organized around and developing a single main idea or fulfilling a single function, such as introducing or concluding a theme, composition, or essay.

## VOCABULARY TEST ONE

Four words are lined up below each of twelve words taken from the two essays. Select the one that matches best and write its letter in the blank to the right. Answers are at the end of the chapter.

1. entrepreneur       _____
   (a) employer   (b) capitalist   (c) nobleman   (d) elder

2. maneuvers       _____
   (a) manners   (b) customs   (c) planned actions
   (d) rules

3. surreptitiously      _____
   (a) secretively   (b) quietly   (c) quickly   (d) carefully

4. clairvoyance      _____
   (a) ability to create a mystery   (b) air of elegance
   (c) act of kindness   (d) ability to see beyond natural vision

5. corporate       _____
   (a) business   (b) competitive   (c) short   (d) tall

6. grande dames      _____
   (a) fat women   (b) great ladies of high society
   (c) grandmothers   (d) foreign ladies

7. stratosphere      _____
   (a) struggle   (b) upper regions   (c) a balloon
   (d) dispute

8. literally       _____
   (a) forcefully   (b) imaginary   (c) in the true sense
   (d) joyfully

9. realistic       _____
   (a) sure   (b) possible   (c) graphic   (d) practical

10. incompatible      _____
    (a) harmful   (b) impossible   (c) unharmonious
    (d) rude

11. perspectives      _____
    (a) discussion   (b) arguments   (c) insights
    (d) mental views

12. depreciate       _____
    (a) use   (b) lessen in value   (c) increase in value
    (d) slander one's reputation

## The Parts of the Whole

From the analysis of the two model essays illustrating common ways of structuring thought for written communication, you have learned that a piece of writing, whatever its length, has a beginning, a middle, and an end. You have learned that thought, especially in exposition, is most effective when it is organized around a central idea called the *thesis*. In short papers this unifying idea is usually stated in the first sentence and followed at once by material (the middle or body of the paper) supporting that broad and general statement and by an occasional transitional paragraph carrying the reader smoothly from one stage of the developing thought to another. Longer papers may be more formally organized around the thesis statement into three parts: an *introduction*, a *middle*, and a *conclusion* along with occasional transitional paragraphs.

Structurally, then, a piece of writing may be viewed as a cluster of paragraphs with particular functions that revolve around and develop a stated thesis (a central thought) or statement of purpose.

## Recognizing the Parts

In the previous discussion you learned that a piece of writing consists of a number of paragraphs revolving around and developing a central thought — the thesis. You learned also that you can classify paragraphs on the basis of their function into four kinds: introductory, concluding, transitional, and *middle paragraphs*. Introductory, concluding, and transitional are called *special paragraphs* because they perform functions that differ from those of the more numerous middle paragraphs, which support, develop, and revolve around the central thought of the paper. Let us now treat each of the special paragraphs in some detail.

### Introductory Paragraph

An introductory paragraph or paragraph unit (a number of paragraphs at the beginning of the essay whose function is to introduce the subject) functions to gain reader interest, to indicate the thesis, and to lead the reader smoothly into the middle paragraphs. Introductions may be as varied as the ability of the writer and the length of the paper. Some writers, as we have already noted, begin with a statement of the thesis and move directly into the support. Other writers may present background material, define terms, or open with an anecdote or quotation relevant to the central thought. Still other writers begin with an unusual happening or shocking statement to capture reader interest before stating the thesis and presenting the support. Experienced writers, you will discover, do not limit themselves to beginning their discussion with one kind of introduction. Some effective introductions are the following.

## VOCABULARY PREVIEW

| | | |
|---|---|---|
| importuning | patronizingly | pampa |
| sustenance | postures | assignation |
| conflagration | vituperation | pouty |
| | | surly |

### MODEL 1 — A PANORAMA

▶ It is a melancholy object to those who walk through this great town or travel in the country, when they see the streets, the roads, and cabin-doors crowded with beggars of the female sex, followed by three, four, or six children, all in rags, and importuning° every passenger for an alms. These mothers, instead of being able to work for their honest livelihood, are forced to employ all their time in strolling to beg sustenance° for their helpless infants, who, as they grow up either turn thieves for want of work, or leave their dear native country, to fight for the Pretender in Spain, or sell themselves to the Barbadoes.

Jonathan Swift
"A Modest Proposal"

### MODEL 2 — AN EVENT

▶ The earthquake shook down in San Francisco hundreds of thousands of dollars' worth of walls and chimneys. But the conflagration° that followed burned up hundreds of millions of dollars' worth of property. There is no estimating within hundreds of millions the actual damage wrought. Not in history has a modern imperial city been so completely destroyed. San Francisco is gone. Nothing remains of it but memories and a fringe of dwelling-houses on its outskirts. Its industrial section is wiped out. Its business section is wiped out. The factories and warehouses, the great stores and newspaper buildings, the hotels and the palaces of the nabobs, are all gone. Remains only the fringe of dwelling-houses on the outskirts of what was once San Francisco.

Within an hour after the earthquake shock the smoke of San Francisco's burning was a lurid tower visible a hundred miles away. And for three days and nights this lurid tower swayed in the sky, reddening the sun, darkening the day, and filling the land with smoke.

Jack London
"The San Francisco Earthquake"

### MODEL 3 — SERIES OF QUESTIONS

▶ Are you a reader? Then how do you evaluate writers and the material they publish? If you are a concerned citizen, what do you make of today's authors? What will be their effect on our nation and society? It is a controversial and confusing subject because readers may also be writers, and you can be sure that all writers are readers.

Alma Boice Holland
"Second Thoughts About Readers"

### MODEL 4 — DIRECT STATEMENT OF THE THESIS

▶ Most of the important discoveries which bring about revolutionary advances in science are made by men under 35. Young men are the ones who have taken giant strides on which human advancement is made.

"Young Men Lead in Science Discovery"
*Science Digest*

The exercises that follow are first in a series of exercises designed to give you practice in structural analysis and to test what you have been learning. The answers to a few of the exercises will be given at the end of the chapter in which the exercise appeared so that you will have a model to follow in structuring your own answers.

## EXERCISE 1     **Introductions**

Read the introductory paragraphs below excerpted from an essay titled "What Is Your Pet Trying To Tell You?" Answer the questions that follow. Answers are at the end of the chapter.

▶ When I come home from work in the evening, I sometimes like to relax by playing my flute while my dog, Benji, and wolf, Tiny, enjoy a good howl. Neighbors who might glimpse me harmonizing with my companions sometimes smile patronizingly.° Few know that, by joining in this canine duet, I am actually communicating with my animals and deepening my friendship with them. For, although our dogs and cats share our homes and affections, most of us know very little about communicating with them.

As a veterinarian trained in animal psychology, I have studied cats and dogs for almost 20 years, trying to learn how they communicate, to better understand their wants and needs. I am convinced that we could respond to their needs more readily and could control them more successfully if, by learning to recognize and interpret their expressions and postures,° we could learn how to communicate with them more effectively. In short, we could develop deeper, more satisfying relationships with them.

Michael W. Fox
"What Is Your Pet Trying To Tell You?"

1. How does the writer gain reader interest?

2. How soon does the writer move into the subject?

3. What is the thesis statement?

4. What is the function of the last sentence in paragraph 2?

## EXERCISE 2   Introductions

Read the following paragraph. Answer the questions that follow.

▶ Horsemen have excited awe, admiration, fear, and vitupera-
tion° in plains regions around the world. The man on horseback — whether cowboy or Cossack, Gaucho or *llanero, vaquero* or *boiadeiro* — has elicited wide comment and inspired
a lively body of folklore and literature. Equestrian subcultures
that developed in grasslands, particularly in North and South
America, appear to share many common traits and values;
there are also frequently overlooked but fundamental differences. The Gauchos of the Argentine pampa° and the cowboys
of the U.S. West offer a fascinating comparison.

Richard W. Slatta
"Cowboys and Gauchos"

1. What information necessary for reader understanding does the
   writer present?

2. State the thesis sentence.

3. Does the writer tell the reader how he will organize and develop his
   flowing thought? What is the method?

## EXERCISE 3   **Introductions**

Read the following paragraph unit. Answer the questions that follow.

▶ New York — Coming back to New York City, where you have once lived and worked, after an interval of several years, is a little like making an assignation° with a lover you haven't seen in a decade.

There's the dread that the two of you have grown so far apart, that you'll end up spending the afternoon in the lobby of the Algonquin exchanging snapshots of the kiddies.

Not to fear. What outsiders always forget is that New York City never really changes — face lift after face lift she's the same pouty,° surly° sexpot who drove you up the wall, and out of her life, many years ago.

Don G. Campbell
"New York: Revisit to a Shady Lady"

1. What is the function of the first two paragraphs?

2. Write the thesis sentence or central thought.

3. Write a good title for this essay.

**VOCABULARY TEST TWO**

Four words are lined up below each of ten words taken from the essays and paragraphs. Select the one that matches best and write its letter in the blank to the right. Answers are at the end of the chapter.

1. importuning                                                                  *A*
   (a) begging urgently     (b) demanding of
   (c) asking     (d) disturbing

2. sustenance                                                                   *C*
   (a) money     (b) care     (c) nourishment     (d) clothes

3. conflagration                                                                *D*
   (a) tremor     (b) big wind     (c) sandstorn     (d) great fire

4. patronizingly                                                                *A*
   (a) condescendingly     (b) doubtfully     (c) orderly
   (d) knowledgeably

5. postures                                                                     *A*
   (a) attitudes, poses     (b) feelings     (c) moods
   (d) needs

6. vituperation                                                                 *B*
   (a) envy     (b) verbal abuse     (c) contempt
   (d) pleasure

7. pampa(s)                                                                     *D*
   (a) ranches     (b) slopes     (c) mountain ranges
   (d) grassy plains

8. assignation                                                                  *D*
   (a) secret pledge     (b) compact     (c) excuse
   (d) secret meeting, rendezvous

9. pouty                                                                        *C*
   (a) proud     (b) cold     (c) showing displeasure with the lips
   (d) anxious

10. surly                                                                       *A*
   (a) bad-tempered     (b) powerful     (c) persistent
   (d) gross

## Concluding Paragraph

The concluding paragraph or paragraphs give the reader the feeling that the writer has said all that he wants to say about the subject. Like the introductory paragraphs, the conclusion may be as varied and as effective as the ability of the writer. Some effective ways of concluding a paper are the following:

1. A final paragraph or sentence that is a logical part of the body of the paper; that is, it functions as part of the support. In this case the paper requires no formal conclusion.
2. With a statement of the thesis for the first time.
3. With a restatement of the thesis in slightly different words.
4. With a final question or statement that leaves the subject open for further thought because this is the only course of action.
5. With a review of the main points of the discussion — a kind of summary.
6. With an anecdote related to the thesis.
7. With a quotation related to the thesis.

Some ineffective ways of concluding a paper are the following:

1. With an apology. For example: "I am really not qualified to write on so controversial a subject."
2. With a summary when a summary is unnecessary.
3. With a complaint. For example: "I find it difficult to discuss such a broad subject as religion in 500 words."
4. With a trite quotation or an anecdote that does not relate to the thesis.
5. With an afterthought — that is, the writer adds something that he forgot to discuss in the body of the paper.
6. With an obvious conclusion — for example, he uses the phrases, *in conclusion, to conclude, I would like to conclude this discussion* and so on.
7. With a conclusion that raises additional problems that should have been settled during the discussion.

Answer the questions in the exercises that follow. They are designed to give you a review of the concluding paragraph. These concluding paragraphs were excerpted from the essays that you read for the exercises on introductions. To see the relationship of the parts to the whole paper, you should read each essay again.

**VOCABULARY PREVIEW**

| | | | |
|---|---|---|---|
| depict | bigoted | synonymous | flouting |
| divergences | blatantly | exposition | |
| disparate | seductively | paradoxes | |

## EXERCISE 4     **Conclusions**

Read the model conclusion below. Answer the questions that follow.
Answers are at the end of the chapter.

▶ As you can see, the body language and facial expressions of
dogs and cats are remarkably similar to those of humans, and
they depict° a similar range of emotions. The more we understand our pets' behavior, emotions, and intentions, the better
our relationships with them will be. Above all, through understanding their ways, we can better appreciate them as sensitive, intelligent beings. We can then treat them with the respect that all of the creatures great and small under our
stewardship deserve.

Michael W. Fox
"What Is Your Pet Trying To Tell You?"

1. What conclusion does the writer reach?

2. Do you think that a conclusion was necessary for the thesis stated
in the introduction?

## EXERCISE 5    Conclusions

Read the model conclusion below. Answer the questions that follow.

▶ The broad outlines of cowboy and Gaucho life and culture parallel one another, but deeper probing reveals major divergences° in their development. These differences merit attention because they illuminate the larger forces, movements, and social interaction that shaped Argentina and the western United States during the nineteenth century. Fascinating in his own right, the dashing "half man, half horse" of the Argentine pampa and the U.S. plains also provides a lens to focus the disparate° historical paths of their respective nations.

Richard W. Slatta
"Cowboys and Gauchos"

1. For what purpose does the writer develop his paper by showing differences as well as likenesses between the cowboys and Gauchos?

2. Do you think a conclusion was necessary for the thesis stated in the introduction? Why or why not?

## EXERCISE 6    Conclusions

Read the model conclusion below. Answer the questions that follow.

▶ Until, a few days before Christmas, another envelope surfaced in his mailbox: "Merry Christmas from Your Apartment Staff, Second Notice."

Greedy, pushy, self-centered, uncaring, snobbish, bigoted° and vicious. All come easily to mind as you lie, 3,000 miles away, on a California beach, soaking up the sun and recalling that it's been weeks since anyone blatantly° demanded a tip from you — longer than that since a cab has deliberately swerved three feet out of the line of traffic to splatter you with mud. New York? Who needs it?

But then you fly back to her and, sure enough, she's had another face lift but she's leaning against the same old lamp-post with the same short skirt slit seductively° up on her hips and the sultry, come-hither smile is as dazzling as ever.

And never mind that the polish doesn't quite cover the dirt under the nails.

Don G. Campbell<br>
"New York: Revisit to a Shady Lady"

1. What is the function of the first two paragraphs?

## Transitional Paragraph

The transitional paragraph is usually a short paragraph, sometimes only a sentence, that leads the reader smoothly from one phase of the writer's developing thought onward to another. It may also emphasize, summarize, or repeat a crucial point or points in the previous discussion.

Study the model transitional paragraphs that follow. Notice how the writer frequently carries the reader back to the previous discussion and then moves him forward to what will come in the next paragraphs.

MODEL 1

▶ Before attempting to answer these questions, let me discuss the achievements of the movement [Women's Liberation] thus far.

Amitai Etzioni
"The Women's Movement — Tokens vs. Objectives"

MODEL 2

▶ In our discussion so far we have seen that the biography of Freud is largely the story of the origin of Freudian psychology. We have followed fairly closely the early chronology of his life to show something of his cultural origins and brilliance of his contribution to his chosen field. Indeed, the impact of Freud on "mental science," as it was still called in his day, has been such that in the popular mind Freudianism and psychology are synonymous.° Before proceeding further, it will be necessary to map out the Freudian concept of the psychological organization of man. For the remainder of this part of the discussion we shall present briefly the characteristic points of the Freudian concept of the human psychological makeup or, as Freud termed it, the psyche.

Rod W. Horton and Herbert W. Edwards
*Backgrounds of American Literary Thought*

MODEL 3

▶ Since this theory of social evolution contains so much that reflects the influence of Hegel on Marx's thinking, it is necessary to introduce at this point some exposition° of Hegelianism.

Rod W. Horton and Herbert W. Edwards
*Backgrounds of American Literary Thought*

MODEL 4

▶ It is beyond the scope of the present chapter to offer in detail the complicated historical data preceding and attending Russia's formal acceptance of communism after 1917. However, before turning to a consideration of the introduction of Marxist ideology from Germany after 1848, it will perhaps be illuminating to call attention to some paradoxes° in the inception and working out of the "great experiment."

Rod Horton and Herbert W. Edwards
*Backgrounds of American Literary Thought*

## Middle Paragraphs (The Body of the Paper)

It is very easy to recognize the middle paragraph on the printed page; it consists of a number of sentences with the first line indented and with the last line not always ending at the right margin. In this respect, it is like the special paragraphs. But the middle paragraph has a different function from those other paragraphs and a different structure. A middle paragraph consists of a cluster of sentences, each with its own structural pattern, that revolve around and develop a single main idea. This main idea is usually stated clearly in a complete sentence known as the *topic* sentence. The main idea unifies the cluster of sentences that revolve around it, and the entire unit develops a new aspect of the central thought of the whole piece of writing. The cluster of sentences that develop the main idea is called the *support* or *supporting material.* The model paragraph that follows consists simply of a topic sentence with supporting statements.

Topic
Sentence

*[italics
mine]*

Support

Support

Support

▶ *There were times in the early days when the Indians were suspicious of unexpected visitors who might attempt to spy upon their secret dances.* It was their custom, at those times, to place spies about a mile away from their villages to guard against the approach of such strangers. It was also their usual custom to string ropes from house to house across the streets near the Plaza where their ceremonial house was located to prevent strangers from coming in and to secure quiet for their ceremonies.

Thelma Clarke
*Fables of Tewa Indian Dances*

## VOCABULARY TEST THREE

Four words are lined up below each of ten words taken from the model paragraphs and essays. Select the one that matches best and write its letter in the blank to the right. Answers are at the end of the chapter.

1. depict          *C*
   (a) obey    (b) prove    (c) portray, reproduce
   (d) indicate, hint

2. exposition          *A*
   (a) explanation    (b) discussion    (c) history
   (d) highlights

3. divergences          *B*
   (a) highways    (b) differences    (c) likenesses    (d) roots

4. disparate          *D*
   (a) varied    (b) deep    (c) disjointed    (d) dissimilar

5. bigoted          *A*
   (a) intolerant, biased    (b) tarnished    (c) unruly
   (d) alert

6. blatantly          *C*
   (a) hopefully    (b) quietly    (c) offensively noisy
   (d) slyly

7. seductively          *B*
   (a) carelessly    (b) temptingly, alluringly    (c) diligently
   (d) enthusiastically

8. synonymous          *D*
   (a) profound    (b) theoretical    (c) debatable
   (d) having the same meaning, equal

9. paradoxes          *B*
   (a) confusions    (b) apparent contradictions
   (c) obvious failures    (d) subtle differences

10. flouting          *A*
    (a) scorning, insulting    (b) disobeying    (c) following
    (d) supporting

Some writers, especially in developing thought for narration and description, organize their ideas around an implied main idea. Thus, the writer lets his reader infer the unifying idea from the material he presents. In the model paragraph that follows, the writer feels that the material will suggest the unifying idea: *reasons for cheating.*

▶ A good deal of cheating, therefore — but not all — is done to get good grades. There are also the "anything for kicks" youngsters who cheat for somewhat the same reasons that they drag race cars, shoplift, or wreck property — because they have nothing more constructive they want to do or can do, and because such flouting° of rules is considered smart by their friends. Generally, those who consider it smart to cheat will voice as a defense, "Everybody does it, why shouldn't I?"

Orville Palmer
"What to Do When Children Cheat"

***Function of the Middle Paragraph.***   Paragraphing enables a writer to organize and develop a single important idea. Frequently, a writer will express this main idea in the form of a generalization known as a *topic sentence* or *statement sentence.* Occasionally, he lets the reader infer the main idea from the contents of the paragraph. He develops his main idea by a number of sentences known as the *support.*

Paragraphing also enables a writer to develop the thesis of a longer piece of writing effectively. Just as a group of sentences relate to one another and to the main idea, so a group of paragraphs relate to one another and to the thesis of the essay, theme, or composition. Just as sentences develop the main idea of a paragraph, so paragraphs develop the thesis around which they are organized. A paragraph or group of paragraphs can serve as one link in a chain of thought. Each paragraph must contribute something directly to the central thought of the whole paper; otherwise, it is a digression and should be eliminated.

**VOCABULARY PREVIEW**

| | | |
|---|---|---|
| deteriorated | curtailed | tributaries |
| abounded | murky | |

Let us consider this dual role of paragraphing by studying the structure of another piece of writing, an excerpt from a longer article.

▶ THE KILLING OF A GREAT LAKE
**Barry Commoner**

[1]The Great Lakes, the huge inland seas that lie on the boundary between the United States and

*Thesis Statement*

Canada, have long provided man with wealth and beauty. *But now, because of man's folly, one of them — Lake Erie — is becoming a wasteland.* Listless waves lap along its shore, sucking in and out among the slimy green rocks, deserted beaches, and oily pilings of seldom-used piers.

*Main Idea*

*Effects/ Causes*

[2]*In recent years, Lake Erie has deteriorated° so badly* that the game fish that once abounded° there are almost entirely gone, and beaches are open only occasionally. Swimming is often curtailed° because of high bacterial counts in the water and the revolting stench of rotting algae and dead fish on the beaches. Boat owners are hesitant to take their craft into areas where oily material will cling to the hull.

*Topic Sentence*

*Effect/ Cause*

[3]*In some parts of the lake, the waters are murky° green from algae that thrive on the wastes dumped into the water.* During the summer months, the western basin of Lake Erie contains a mass of algae that sometimes covers 800 square miles and has a thickness of two feet.

*Repetition of Thesis*

*Topic Sentence*

*Causes of Pollution*

[4]The variety of floating and rotting wastes is a constant reminder that man can indeed kill a lake. *Much of the pollution comes from the large industrial cities near and along its southern and western shores.* Detroit dumps in wastes from its automotive, chemical, paper, and steel plants, as well as from its petroleum refineries. Toledo adds wastes from glass industries and more automotive, petroleum, and steel plants. Cleveland also pours in acids, oils, cyanides, and phenols from automotive, chemical, and steel industries, while Erie throws in pulp and paper wastes. Buffalo contributes pollution from flour mills and from chemical, portland cement, and steel plants. Added to all this is the common refuse of every urban center — treated and untreated human sewage — and fertilizers, insecticides, and weed-killers in the run-off water from the surrounding farmlands.

*Repetition of Thesis*

[5]*The lake is threatened with death.* It is slowly choking from its heavily polluted tributaries° and shoreline. Water experts warn there is little relief in sight. Some even say the lake is dying so fast it

> will soon be an aquatic desert — America's Dead
> Sea.

Barry Commoner's purpose is to tell the reader that, through man's folly, one of the Great Lakes is becoming a wasteland. He develops his thesis with three middle paragraphs — paragraphs 2, 3, and 4. His first paragraph of the discussion is a brief introductory paragraph that states clearly his thesis: "But now, because of man's folly, one of them — Lake Erie — is becoming a wasteland." He concludes the discussion (paragraph 5) with a cogent statement repeating the central thought — "The lake is threatened with death."

Each of the middle paragraphs revolves around and develops a single main idea that relates to and develops his central thought.

> In recent years, Lake Erie has deteriorated so badly . . . (paragraph 2, sentence 1).
>
> In some parts of the lake, the waters are a murky green from algae that thrive on the wastes dumped into the water (paragraph 3, sentence 1).
>
> Much of the pollution comes from the large industrial cities near and along its southern and western shores (paragraph 4, sentence 2).

Each of these main ideas relates to the thesis by stating that man's folly is killing the lake. Each main idea is developed in turn with a number of sentences explaining the causes of the destruction and showing the effects of that pollution.

---

**MATCH-UP ONE**

Match the definitions in column 2 with the words in column 1 taken from the essay "The Killing of a Great Lake" by placing the letter of the word in the blank at the right. Answers are at the end of the chapter.

| | | |
|---|---|---|
| a. deteriorated | 1. dark, gloomy | _D_ _____ |
| b. abounded | 2. reduced, cut off | _C_ _____ |
| c. curtailed | 3. became worse | _A_ _____ |
| d. murky | 4. streams and rivers | _E_ _____ |
| e. tributaries | 5. was plentiful | _B_ _____ |

---

## Answers: Chapter 1

### Exercise 1

1. The writer presents an interesting account of his playing the flute while his dog and wolf enjoy a good howl. He adds humor to the incident by mentioning his neighbor's reaction — a superior smile.
2. He leads immediately into his subject after the incident of the neighbor's reaction by explaining that through the canine duet he is actually communicating with his animals and deepening their friendship and respect for him.
3. The thesis statement in paragraph 2 reads: "I am convinced that we could respond to their needs more readily and could control them more successfully if, by learning to recognize and interpret their expressions and postures, we could learn to communicate with them more effectively."
4. It is a summarizing statement repeating the central thought expressed in the thesis sentence.

### Exercise 4

1. By learning to communicate with our pets we can better understand them; therefore, we will treat them better as "sensitive, intelligent beings."
2. Writers of the long essay like this one will commonly write a conclusion in order to make sure that readers will remember the thesis statement. An emphatic conclusion will help the writer to fulfill his stated purpose. The conclusion is not common in short essays; however, writers who wish to make certain that readers keep the stated purpose in mind will include a conclusion.

I believe that the conclusion was helpful in emphasizing the writer's stated purpose — the thesis sentence.

| Voc. Test 1 | Voc. Test 2 | Voc. Test 3 | Match-Up 1 |
|---|---|---|---|
| 1. a | 1. a | 1. c | 1. d |
| 2. c | 2. c | 2. a | 2. c |
| 3. a | 3. d | 3. b | 3. a |
| 4. d | 4. a | 4. d | 4. e |
| 5. a | 5. a | 5. a | 5. b |
| 6. b | 6. b | 6. c | |
| 7. b | 7. d | 7. b | |
| 8. c | 8. d | 8. d | |
| 9. d | 9. c | 9. b | |
| 10. c | 10. a | 10. a | |
| 11. d | | | |
| 12. b | | | |

# 2 Structuring the Paragraph

Good paragraphs possess four qualities: *unity, completeness, order,* and *coherence.* Let us consider each of these qualities.

## Unity — The Topic Sentence

A main idea, stated or implied by the writer, is the unifying point around which the supporting sentences of a paragraph revolve. A good topic sentence usually expresses a single main idea. It tells the reader what the paragraph is about. It develops a new but related idea of the central thought (thesis) of the whole paper. It may also indicate the kind of development that will follow. What do the following topic sentences, for example, tell you about the central thought of the paper and the kind of development that will follow?

▶ Children cheat in school for many reasons.

Clouds may be divided into four classes.

The quarterback in football and the general of the army are alike in many ways.

To the vexing question of how one can know precisely what the words mean, two contrasting answers are frequently given.

The life of the ocean is divided into distinct realms.

"Desert" is an unfortunate word all around and most of its usual associations are inaccurate as well as unfavorable.

A topic sentence, however, is seldom explicit enough by itself to convey fully the meaning the writer intended. It places too great a burden of understanding upon the reader, since most topic sentences are expressed in the form of an assertion — a generalization that lacks particulars that will make clear exactly what the writer had in mind. This function belongs to the detailed support. As you read the following topic sentence, try to discern exactly what the writer has in mind.

▶ The history of less ancient periods, too, reveals the juvenile character of their chief actors.

This general assertion obviously leaves the reader with too many unanswered questions: What are the ancient periods? In what ways do these periods reveal the juvenile character of their chief actors? Who were the chief actors? It is the remaining sentences of the paragraph supporting the generalization with particulars that give the meaning the writer intended.

▶ The history of less ancient periods, too, reveals the juvenile character of their chief actors. Many observers have remarked on the smallness of the armor which has come down to us from the Middle Ages. Actually, the men who wore this armor were not grown-ups. They were married at thir-

*Support*

teen, were warriors and leaders in their late teens, and senile at thirty-five or forty. Without some familiarity with the juvenile mentality and the aberrations of juvenile delinquency it would be difficult to make sense of the romanticism, trickery, and savagery which characterized the Middle Ages. Nor did things change markedly in the sixteenth century. Montaigne tells us that he hardly ever met a man as old as fifty. In the first half of the sixteenth century, Charles V became Holy Roman Emperor at the age of twenty, Francis I became King of France at twenty-one, and Henry VIII King of England at eighteen.

Eric Hoffer
"A Time for Juveniles"

How does a writer structure a good topic sentence? He must first have a definite purpose or point of view. He must have a strong reason for stressing a particular aspect of his thought about a subject. In thinking about his visit to Hong Kong, a writer recalls many details. One condition, however, left a deep impression on him — the corruption. He wishes his readers to know about such corruption. He phrases a topic sentence stressing this idea: "Hong Kong today is a corrupt city." It is the idea of *corrupt*, not the rest of the sentence, that he will develop fully. He could have expressed a number of other dominant impressions about Hong Kong in much the same way, such as "Hong Kong is a city of intrigue" or "Hong Kong is a sad city." These statements make good topic sentences because they are limited and express an attitude or point of view.

Statements like the following, on the other hand, would probably be weak topic sentences because they are simply statements of fact.

► Shakespeare is an Elizabethan writer.

Boston is the capital of Massachusetts.

Hong Kong is a city in Asia.

Each of these statements is merely factual; it would be very difficult, therefore, to develop them as topics for a paragraph. The statements that follow would probably make poor topic sentences because they are too broad for adequate development in paragraph length.

▶ Literature presents a mirror of life.

The dictionary has an interesting history.

Rome has a glorious and tragic story.

The difference between a poor topic sentence and a good one is that the poor topic sentence does not have a clearly stated main idea that shows the writer's purpose or point of view. A poor topic sentence, as we have already seen, is too limited or too broad and general to be developed into an effective paragraph. A sentence, for example, like "Hong Kong is a city in Asia" is sufficient in itself. A writer would find it difficult to say anything else. And a statement like "Every individual in the U.S. is entitled to free public education," on the other hand, is too broad to treat adequately in a short theme.

In phrasing a topic sentence, a writer must make his main idea unmistakably clear.

▶ New York is a *dangerous* city *at night.*

Integration will *benefit* the *white* citizen.

A college student has the *right* to *protest.*

San Francisco is a *beautiful* city *at dawn.*

Animals use colors chiefly *for protection.*

*In my early school years,* teachers *frightened* me.

Where is the most effective position in a paragraph for the topic sentence? The main idea is commonly expressed in the first sentence of a paragraph. It is emphatic in that position and it can function also as a kind of introduction. A series of paragraphs, all beginning with topic sentences, however, can produce a stultifying mechanical effect. A writer obtains variety and emphasis, therefore, by placing his topic sentence in other positions. In developing a paragraph inductively, a writer ends his discussion with a statement of the main idea so that he can emphasize or summarize the preceding thought. Sometimes a writer will place his topic sentence in the middle of the paragraph so that he can reverse the direction of the developing thought. Occasionally, a writer will place his topic sentence in other positions than the beginning, middle, or end. At times a writer will begin with a statement of the main idea and restate it in slightly different words in the final sentence in order to emphasize the central thought.

Complete the following exercises and the assignment in order to review the discussion of the main idea.

## EXERCISE 1     **Topic Sentence**

Read each statement below. Decide whether or not the statement would be a good topic sentence for a paragraph developing the main idea it states. If you consider any statement to be a good topic sentence, underline the word or group of words that names the topic and underline also the word or group of words that controls the topic.

1. A teacher, like a salesman, must learn the art of selling.

2. The old wharf is an exciting place to be when the fishing fleet returns home.

3. Ice fishing is a cold and dangerous job.

4. Roman emperors were frequently called "Caesar."

5. The Painted Desert is especially beautiful when the sun sets.

6. On Saturday nights Charing Cross Hospital is a bedlam.

7. Lincoln was assassinated while watching a play.

8. The changes in dress during the last decade of this century were extreme.

9. The entertainment industry attracts many colorful characters.

10. I face graduation from high school with mixed emotions.

## EXERCISE 2     **Topic Sentence**

Read each statement below. Decide whether or not the statement would be a good topic sentence for a paragraph developing the main idea it states. If you consider any statement to be a good topic sentence, underline the word or word group that names the topic and underline also the word or word group that controls the topic.

1. Henry Smith is a conservative in his political thinking.

2. The route through the mountain pass was especially hazardous in winter.

3. My first high school dance was a frightening experience.

4. Exemption from the draft for brains was discriminatory.

5. President John F. Kennedy was assassinated in Dallas, Texas.

6. Capital punishment is not a deterrent to murder.

7. London, with its historic sites, is a tremendous tourist attraction.

8. His folks talked like any other Danes in the neighborhood.

9. The potential danger of influenza should never be underestimated.

10. The "Bridge of Sighs" in Venice, Italy, is appropriately named.

## ASSIGNMENT    Writing the Topic Sentence

Write a good topic sentence under any ten of the following topics.

| | |
|---|---|
| 1. college football | 11. friends |
| 2. comics | 12. parents |
| 3. art | 13. civil rights |
| 4. clothes | 14. minority groups |
| 5. sewing | 15. space |
| 6. occupations | 16. weather |
| 7. school politics | 17. gardening |
| 8. dating | 18. cooking |
| 9. music | 19. religion |
| 10. games | 20. social groups |

EXAMPLE:    college basketball
            *College basketball* at State University is big business.

1.


2.


3.


4.


5.


6.


7.

8.

9.

10.

## Completeness — The Support

How long should a piece of writing be? This question troubles many beginning writers. Sadly enough, there is no satisfactory answer. Most teachers of writing feel that a theme of approximately 500 words is a good length for beginning writers. Most modern paragraphs are from 75 to 300 words long (6 to 25 sentences). Many contemporary paragraphs, especially those in newspapers and magazines (such as *Time*), may be only one or two sentences in length; other paragraphs in textbooks, learned journals, and magazines such as *Harper's* and *The Atlantic* may be a page or more. Word or sentence count, therefore, may serve only as a guide for the length of an average paragraph.

Theme or paragraph completeness is a much better way of viewing length. How complete should a piece of writing be? This question can be answered. A good paragraph fulfills its function of developing fully the main idea. A short theme or any piece of writing longer than a paragraph is complete when it fulfills its function of developing a thesis fully. You must, therefore, develop the central thought until you feel that it is sufficiently clear and acceptable, whether it requires a sentence, a paragraph, or four or five pages. With some subjects you will be able to accomplish your purpose with little supporting and explanatory material. With most subjects, you will need much more complete development. Incompleteness, not overdevelopment, is common with beginning writers. The short theme — a piece of writing that develops a single central thought — can usually be developed effectively in about 500 words.

Let us first discuss paragraph completeness, since the whole depends on the separate parts. In your opinion, is the following paragraph complete? Does the writer make the main idea clear and provide adequate support for it?

> ▶ A cat's tail is a good barometer of its intentions. By various movements of its tail a cat will signal many of its wants. Other movements indicate its attitudes. An excited or aggressively aroused cat will whip its entire tail back and forth.

At first glance, it would appear that this paragraph is complete. The writer begins with a concise topic sentence telling us that a cat's tail is a good barometer of its intentions. He adds additional information of a general nature in the following two sentences. Then, he presents a supporting example concerning the aggressively aroused cat. But the paragraph is not explicit; the writer has insufficient supporting material for the opening generalizations. He leaves us with too much information to fill in. What are some other ways that cats communicate their intentions with their tails? How do they communicate specific wishes or desires? Is such communication effective? If he is to answer these questions that come into the reader's mind, he must present more supporting material for his beginning generalizations. The original paragraph that follows begins with a concise topic sentence that is supported with particulars.

> ▶ A cat's tail is a good barometer of its intentions. An excited or aggressively aroused cat will whip its entire tail back and forth. When I talk to Sam, he holds up his end of the conversation by occasionally flicking the tip of his tail. Mother cats move their tails back and forth to invite their kittens to play. A kitten raises its tail perpendicularly to beg for attention; older cats may do so to beg for food. When your cat holds its tail aloft while crisscrossing in front of you, it is trying to say, "Follow me" — usually to the kitchen, or more precisely, to the refrigerator. Unfortunately, many cats have lost their tails in refrigerator doors as a consequence.
>
> Michael Fox
> *"What Is Your Pet Trying To Tell You"*

## Kinds of Support

Let us now strengthen our understanding of paragraph structure by analyzing the structure of our model paragraph, putting to use the information we have assimilated to this point in the discussion. The writer of the model paragraph begins with the highest generalization (the main idea in the topic sentence): "A cat's tail is a good barometer of its intentions." He follows immediately with six major supporting statements and ends with a final sentence to add humor to the writing. If we place this material in outline form, we can see better the recurrent pattern in the flow of thought from general to particular.

*Topic Sentence*
*(Highest generalization)*
    ▶ I. A cat's tail is a good barometer of its intentions.

*Major Support*
    A. An excited or aggressively aroused cat will whip its entire tail back and forth.

*Major Support*
    B. When I talk to Sam, he holds up his end of the conversation by occasionally flicking the tip of his tail.

| | |
|---|---|
| *Major Support* | C. Mother cats move their tails back and forth to invite their kittens to play. |
| *Major Support* | D. A kitten raises its tail perpendicularly to beg for attention; |
| *Major Support* | E. Older cats may do so to beg for food. |
| *Major Support* | F. When your cat holds its tail aloft while crisscrossing in front of you, it is trying to say, "Follow me" — usually to the kitchen, or more precisely, to the refrigerator. |
| *Added for humor* | Unfortunately, many cats have lost their tails in refrigerator doors as a consequence. |

Study the model paragraph that follows. Observe that the writer presents a number of major supporting statements in order to inform his reader fully that "Benjamin Franklin was a recognized scientist."

▶ Benjamin Franklin was a recognized scientist. Franklin invented such useful items as the stove, bifocals, and the lightning rod. He invented the "long arm" to get his books down from high shelves; today, this device is used by clerks in stores all over the world. He built a combination chair and stepladder for the kitchen and a draft for fireplaces. He has also been credited with the invention of the rocking chair. Franklin was first to explain "luminosity" (phosphorescence) in sea water. His comments on animalcules in sea water are considered by many scientists to be the earliest conjectures on the existence and nature of microorganisms.

In outline form the above paragraph would look something like the following:

▶ I. Benjamin Franklin was a recognized scientist.

    A. Franklin invented such useful items as the stove, bifocals, and the lightning rod.

    B. He invented the "long arm" to get his books down from high shelves.

C. He built a combination chair and step-ladder for the kitchen and a draft for fireplaces.

D. He has also been credited with the invention of the rocking chair.

E. Franklin was the first to explain "luminosity" (phosphorescence) in sea water.

F. His comments on animalcules in sea water are considered by many scientists to be the earliest conjectures on the existence and nature of microorganisms.

The writer of the model paragraph that follows found it necessary to explain many of his major supporting statements with minor support in order to fully explain his main idea. Observe the organization into a topic sentence with four major supporting statements; notice that the major supporting statements are followed with minor support.

▶ Benjamin Franklin accomplished many things in his eighty-four years. He was a recognized inventor. Franklin gave to the world the stove, bifocals, and the lightning rod. He invented a draft for fireplaces and a combination chair and step-ladder for the kitchen. He was also a city-planner. Franklin reorganized the British Post Office, established a city police system, and an efficient fire control organization. He was instrumental in providing his city with a public hospital and a subscription library. Franklin was a military strategist. He organized a successful defense of his colony when it was threatened by the French and Indians. He led a force of men into the wilderness near Bethlehem and supervised the building of three important forts in that area. Finally, Franklin was a very active statesman. He was a member of the committee which drew up the Declaration of Independence, a delegate to the Constitutional Convention, and a popular and very valuable ambassador to England and France for over twenty-five years.

An outline of the above paragraph would look something like the following:

▶ I. Benjamin Franklin accomplished many things in his eighty-four years.

A. He was a recognized inventor.

    1. Franklin gave to the world the stove, bifocals, and the lightning rod.

    2. He invented a draft for fireplaces and a combination chair and step-ladder for the kitchen.

B. He was also a city-planner.

    1. Franklin reorganized the British Post Office, established a city police system, and an efficient fire control organization.

    2. He was instrumental in providing his city with a public hospital and a subscription library.

C. Franklin was a military strategist.

    1. He organized a successful defense of his colony when it was threatened by the French and Indians.

    2. He led a force of men into the wilderness near Bethlehem and supervised the building of three important forts in that area.

D. Finally, Franklin was a very active statesman.*

    1. He was a member of the committee which drew up the Declaration of Independence, a delegate to the Constitutional Convention, and a popular and very valuable ambassador to England and France for over twenty-five years.

Major supporting statement D has actually three supporting statements combined in the one statement.

▶ D. Finally, Franklin was a very active statesman.

    1. He was a member of the committee which drew up the Declaration of Independence.

    2. He was a delegate to the Constitutional Convention.

    3. He was a popular and very valuable ambassador to England and France for over twenty-five years.

------

*In an outline each heading should have at least two supporting statements.

What kind of particulars (details) make up the supporting material? On the basis of the intent or purpose of the writer, supporting details may be classified into three kinds: *expository, narrative,* and *descriptive.* We will examine support briefly at this stage of the discussion and consider it in much greater depth in the subsequent chapters of the book.

*Expository details* (the kind we have been studying so far in this analysis of structure) are used by a writer when he is explaining or informing. The primary function of expository details is to make the meaning of a general statement clear and to give proof to the assertion of the main idea. In addition, the writer uses these kinds of details to define a word or term (definition), to show likenesses (comparison) or differences (contrast) between two subjects or among more than two subjects, to explain how to do something or how something happened (process), to establish classes (classification), to identify and show relationships between the parts and the whole (partition), and to show causes and effects (causal analysis).

Study the model paragraph below. Observe how the completeness of the supporting material and its use of particulars serve to support the opening generalization.

▶ But bronc riding is a gentle art compared with the sport of riding bulls, which some say is the world's most dangerous event. Nostrils flared and ears extended like semaphores, your average crossbred Brahma bull is 2500 pounds of muscle and meanness. He'll do whatever he can to throw a cowboy off his back, and likely as not will charge him afterward with an ambition to do real harm. Bucked off in the dirt and choking with dust, the bull rider hasn't got time to nurse his wounded pride; he's up, running, and over the fence before the bull makes him a victim.

Dan McGowan
"The Rodeo Cowboy"

*Narrative details* enable a writer to tell a story, usually in time sequence. These details make clear an action or happening in which human beings are often involved in some kind of conflict. In the model narrative paragraph that follows, an Englishman tells about an American football game.

▶ The game began. I do not pretend to understand even the coarser of the finer points of this American college football, which must have been originally devised during an early revolutionary phase of American life, for, like a revolution, it is an odd mixture of secret plotting, with so many heads motionless and close together in the scrums, and sudden violent action. When either side pressed toward goal, we all stood up. The danger over or the prize lost, we sat down again. The enormous clock ran off seconds when the ball was actually in play. It stopped when the game stopped. And the game was always stopping. Referees threw down little colored flags; linesmen ran on, like half-crazed surveyors, with measuring equipment; trainers and first-aid men trotted up with water, sponges, liniment, perhaps disinfectant, brandy, antibiotics, blood transfusions, oxygen tents, God knows what; players came off, other players went on; three men in white occasionally turned somersaults; the cheerleaders leapt and wildly gesticulated, the obedient fans noisily responded; the two cowboys fired their cannon. Meanwhile, the doomsday voices behind me were announcing the quarter-time and half-time scores of distant games. Nor were these figures regarded as a distraction, taking attention away from the games before our eyes. In the new *Admass* sporting life, these scores, so many figures on paper, are more important than actual games, the mere rough-and-tumble round the ball. A good *Admass* sportsman wants to know what is happening everywhere except in front of his nose. He attends one match to learn quickly what remote teams are scoring in other matches. And now, with the Horned Frogs ahead of the Longhorns, as hundreds of thousands of spectators were hearing elsewhere, the interval came.

J. B. Priestley
"An Englishman's Outrageous View of Texas Football"

*Descriptive details* are used by a writer when he is creating a word picture of some place, something, or somebody. They appeal to the reader's senses of sight, sound, touch, taste, and smell. Since descriptive details emanate from a writer's powers of observation, they are also commonly used in the other forms of discourse.

In the model paragraph that follows, the writer's purpose is to create a word picture of the football stadium in which the game he told about in the previous paragraph was played.

▶ The professor and I carried our cushions to the top of the stand and then found our places among a group of his colleagues, of both sexes, belonging to the department of language and literature. Nodding and smiling a welcome, Middle English, Romance Languages, Modern Novel and Elizabethan Drama pleasantly acknowledged my presence, with that slight archness and hint of the deprecatory which scholars display when discovered attending some unscholarly college function. From this height, the whole stadium was spread below us, all open to our view. The scene had more color than we find in our football grounds. The crowd opposite, mostly students in colored shirts and blouses, looked almost like a vast heap of those tiny sweets known in my childhood as "hundreds and thousands." Two large students' military bands, one in orange uniforms, the other in purple, the colors of their respective teams, could just be distinguished, massed together, on the lower slopes, where the sousaphones gleamed and blared. In the space between the touchline and the stand, there were cheerleaders in white, men and girls, already beginning to signal to and encourage, with enormous rhythmical gestures, their obedient sections of students. One end of the ground, to my right, was dominated by an illuminated electric clock, ready to mark off every second of play. Above the crowd at the other end, lower than we were, I could see ranks of parked cars, extending apparently into far, open country, glittering, glimmering and then fading into the haze, like some plague of gray and green beetles unaccountably stricken with death. Down on the turf a host of players, enough to make a dozen teams, all uniformed, leather-armored, numbered, were throwing passes and punting the balls and loosening up. Other men, mostly in white, not cheerleaders but athletic directors, coaches, referees and linesmen, trainers and first-aid men, were gathering along the touchlines. From somewhere behind us, voices through loud-speakers, harsh and appallingly amplified, made announcements, called doctors to the telephone. The bowl, you might say, was busy.

J. B. Priestley
"An Englishman's Outrageous View of Texas Football"

## Paragraph Unit

Sometimes a writer will need more than one paragraph to fulfill a particular function in a piece of writing. When more than one paragraph functions as an introduction, a conclusion, or a support of a single main idea, this unit is called a paragraph unit. You have studied paragraph units as introductions and conclusions in the Exercises. The paragraph unit below is an example of supporting material found in the body or middle paragraphs of a piece of writing. The writer uses a paragraph unit of three short paragraphs to develop the main idea that "Sometimes a cowboy needs help escaping a bull, and that's where the rodeo clown comes in."

▶ Sometimes a cowboy needs help escaping a bull, and that's where the rodeo clown comes in. This fellow dresses for laughs in baggy pants, polka-dot shirt and cleated baseball shoes. But his aim is dead serious: preventing serious injury or death.

 The clown is a combination gymnast and bullfighter. He will egg the bull on at close range, then run like a rabbit to escape the Brahma brute, sprinting aside just in time to keep from getting hit. Or he may work with a reinforced barrel, using it to distract the bull or climbing inside it for protection when the animal decides to charge.

 Occasionally an unlucky clown will get trampled and hurt by a four-legged pursuer. He goes off to mend but is almost always back again. He seldom, very seldom gives up.

Dan McGowan<br>"The Rodeo Cowboy"

Study the paragraph unit that follows. Notice first that the writer begins the discussion with a statement of the topic sentence of the unit: "Humor is often the best way to keep a small misunderstanding from escalating into a big deal." Next, observe that the writer needs paragraphs 1, 2, and 3 to develop fully the examples he uses to support the opening generalization. Finally, the writer repeats the idea of the topic sentence with a separate paragraph (paragraph 4).

▶ [1]Humor is often the best way to keep a small misunderstanding from escalating into a big deal. Recently a neighbor of mine had a squabble with his wife as she drove him to the airport. Airborne, he felt miserable, and he knew she did, too. Two hours after she returned home, she received a long-distance phone call. "Person-to-person for Mrs. I. A. Pologize," intoned the operator. "That's spelled 'P' as in . . . ." In a twinkling, the whole day changed from grim to lovely at both ends of the wire.

[2]An English hostess with a quick wit was giving a formal dinner for eight distinguished guests whom she hoped to enlist in a major charity drive. Austerity was *de rigueur* in England at the time, and she had drafted her children to serve the meal.

She knew that anything could happen — and it did, just as her son, with the studied concentration of a tightrope walker, brought in a large roast turkey. He successfully elbowed the swinging dining-room door, but the backswing deplattered the bird onto the dining-room floor.

³The boy stood rooted; guests stared at their plates. Moving only her head, the hostess smiled at her son. "No harm, Daniel," she said. "Just pick him up and take him back to the kitchen" — she enunciated clearly so he would think about what she was saying — "and bring in the *other* one."

⁴A wink and a one-liner instantly changed the dinner from a red-faced embarrassment to a conspiracy of fun.

William D. Ellis
"Solve That Problem — With Humor"

As you read the next model paragraph unit, keep the following questions in mind:

1. What is the topic sentence?
2. How many paragraphs does the writer use to develop his main idea?
3. With how many examples does the writer support his opening generalization?
4. How many paragraphs does the writer need to develop fully his first example?
5. How many paragraphs does the writer need to develop his second example?

▶ ¹Occasionally, humor goes beyond saving arguments, saving face or saving jobs; it can save life itself. Viktor E. Frankl was a psychiatrist imprisoned in a German concentration camp during World War II. As the shrinking number of surviving prisoners descended to new depths of hell, Frankl and his closest prisoner friend sought desperately for ways to keep from dying. Piled on top of malnutrition, exhaustion and disease, suicidal despair was the big killer in these citadels of degradation.

²As a psychiatrist, Frankl knew that humor was one of the soul's best survival weapons, since it can create, if only for moments, aloofness from horror. Therefore, Frankl made a rule that once each day he and his friend must invent and tell an amusing anecdote, specifically about something which could happen after their liberation.

[3]Others were caught up in the contagion of defiant laughter. One starving prisoner forecast that in the future he might be at a prestigious formal dinner, and when the soup was being served, he would shatter protocol by imploring the hostess, "Ladle it from the *bottom!*"

[4]Frankl tells of another prisoner, who nodded toward one of the most despised *capos* — favored prisoners who acted as guards and became as arrogant as the SS men. "Imagine!" he quipped. "I knew him when he was only the president of a bank!"

[5]If humor can be used successfully against such odds, what can't you and I do with it in daily life?

William D. Ellis
"Solve That Problem — With Humor"

## VOCABULARY PREVIEW

| | | |
|---|---|---|
| dominant | faddism | eventually |
| passive | encroachment | detonations |
| gape | impunity | prevailed |
| hype | emancipation | diminished |
| trendy | accumulated | apparently |

Complete the three following exercises to review the use of supporting material to reinforce the main idea.

## EXERCISE 3   **Paragraph Analysis**

Read the model paragraph below. Answer the questions that follow.
Answers are at the end of the chapter.

▶ If you have ever watched a meeting between two suspicious
cats, you may have witnessed the full array of facial expressions that indicate a cat's emotions and intentions. The domi-
nant° cat keeps a cool front, showing little or no expression
when facing up to its rival. Its face is a model of passive° indifference with upright ears, straight whiskers, and eyes directed
fearlessly ahead. It may even close its eyes. The fearful cat will
flatten its ears and hiss. Its eyes are open wide and the pupils
are clearly enlarged. If the cat is torn between flight and attack, it will twist its ears sideways and stare almost cross-eyed
with moderately enlarged pupils. In another reaction, a cat
may gape° with its eyes half-closed, as if drugged, when it
has sniffed some strange odor or the urine of another cat.

Michael Fox
"What Is Your Pet Trying To Tell You?"

1. What is the main idea of this paragraph?

2. How does the writer give order (organization) to the supporting
   material?

3. How many major supporting statements are there in the paragraph? How many minor supporting statements?

## EXERCISE 4    **Paragraph Analysis**

Read the model paragraph below. Answer the questions that follow.

> ▶ Working cowboys regard the wave of cowboy hype° with mixed feelings. Some bitterly denounce the trendy° faddism° as an encroachment° on a sacred sanctuary. While others are more philosophical. "I think it's a compliment," says Harvey Howell. "The cowboy is a state of mind to people nowadays. Whenever somebody wants to feel independent and self-reliant, they dress up and act like cowboys."
>
> Marshall Trimble
> "The Working Cowboy"

1. What sentence best expresses the main idea?

2. How many major supporting statements are there in the paragraph?

3. What material may be classified as minor support?

## EXERCISE 5    Paragraph Analysis

Read the model paragraph below. Answer the questions that follow.

▶ All was now bustle and hubbub in the late quiet schoolroom. The scholars were hurried through their lessons, without stopping at trifles; those who were nimble skipped over half with impunity,° and those who were tardy, had a smart application now and then in the rear, to quicken their speed, or help them over a tall word. Books were flung aside without being put away on the shelves, inkstands were overturned, benches thrown down, and the whole school was turned loose an hour before the usual time, bursting forth like a legion of young imps, yelping and racketing about the green, in joy at their early emancipation.°

Washington Irving
"The Legend of Sleepy Hollow"

1. Is the main idea developed chiefly with expository, narrative, or descriptive details?

2. What sentence expresses the main idea?

## Order

Mastering the skills of writing concise and cogent topic sentences will help you achieve paragraph unity, and structuring valid and sufficient major and minor support will give your paragraphs completeness. But you will need also some kind of consistent and logical order or arrangement of your ideas to give your flowing thought coherence and direction. The brief paragraph that follows, for example, begins with a succinctly stated main idea that is supported adequately; nevertheless, the thought is confused.

> ▶ Cape Cod is unique. It was then molded for more than 100 centuries by winds, waves, tides and currents. You can even pick up pebbles brought by glaciers from the Laurentian Mountains in Canada. A peninsula which stands farther out to sea than any other portion of our Atlantic coast, it was created, geologists say, by mile-high glaciers which dropped deposits here in the last Ice Age — about 11,000 years ago. You can see mile after mile of original glacial deposits sliced by the elements into clean-sloping cliffs. Layers, some as distinct as in a cake, show the advances and retreats of the ice.

Something is wrong. The writer expresses several ideas that are in themselves interesting and important. Yet, the relationship of one idea to another and to the central thought of the entire passage is confusing. The paragraph lacks a smooth and logical development; it has no consistent order or pattern of development.

In contrast, the paragraph below illustrates a smooth flow of thought from the opening topic sentence through the support. The writer plans a concise topic sentence and develops the main idea with two orders or patterns that rise naturally from the supporting material and his purpose.

> ▶ Cape Cod is unique. A peninsula which stands farther out to sea than any other portion of our Atlantic coast, it was created, geologists say, by mile-high glaciers which dropped deposits here in the last Ice Age — about 11,000 years ago. It was then molded for more than 100 centuries by winds, waves, tides and currents. You can see mile after mile of original glacial deposits sliced by the elements into clean-sloping cliffs. Layers, some as distinct as in a cake, show the advances and retreats of

the ice. You can even pick up pebbles brought by glaciers from the Laurentian Mountains in Canada.

Don Wharton
"They're Saving America's Priceless Seashore"

The writer makes clear his purpose with the topic sentence "Cape Cod is unique." A glance at his supporting material indicates the two kinds of development that are logical: by time and by cause and effect. He begins, therefore, about 11,000 years ago by discussing the mile-high glaciers (a cause) that formed the Cape (an effect or result). He moves onward through time for more than 100 centuries citing additional causes — the winds, waves, tides, and currents — that have molded the Cape. Finally, he describes the Cape as it looks today — the result of those causes.

Read the following student paragraph. As you read, try to determine the topic sentence and the method of development:

▶ The twentieth century is the age of progress. Without a college education we would be unable to cope with the changing times. It would be impossible to develop skills essential to satisfy the daily needs of the public. How would a doctor perform an operation without a college education? Or a teacher teach his class without being better educated than his students?

Although the first sentence appears at first glance to be the topic sentence, the second sentence states the main idea: a college education enables one to cope with the changing times. It is a poor topic sentence because it is too general. With revision this main idea could be the thesis of a longer piece of writing. In addition, the writer does not support the generalization with material that makes it acceptable. His support consists first of a somewhat confusing generalization about skills essential to satisfy the daily needs of the public; however, he does not mention specific skills or any definite needs. He concludes his paragraph with two questions that he does not answer; the reader, therefore, is again lost as to what he means. The writer, on the other hand, has attempted to write a general to a particular paragraph; the structural pattern is obvious.

Effective development of a main idea, then, is the result of skillfully organizing various methods of structuring thought into some kind of a consistent pattern or patterns. In this chapter some simple methods, involving essentially an arrangement of sentences into logical and emphatic orders of development, will be discussed. In the remainder of the book, some more complex orders of development will be considered.

Structurally, a middle paragraph may be viewed as "an essay in miniature." The thesis of the essay serves the same function as the topic sentence in the paragraph. As a cluster of paragraphs revolve around and develop the thesis, so a number of sentences revolve around and support the topic sentence of a paragraph. Thus, by positioning his topic sentence, a writer can impose upon his flowing thought a certain kind of organizational structure. If he begins the paragraph with a topic sentence, a writer's thought will flow from the *general to the particular*. If he places his topic sentence in the last line of the paragraph, his thought has moved from the *particular to the general*. If he chooses to begin with a topic sentence, move through the support, and restate the topic sentence in slightly different words in the final sentence of the paragraph, a writer structures his thought by moving from *general to particular to general*. Finally, a writer may decide to begin with a question and follow with the answer *(question to answer)*.

In addition to these four imposed orders of development are two natural orders of development — *space and time*. When a writer is describing someone, some place, or something, he finds that the natural order is by moving through space. When he is telling a story, he finds that the natural order is through a time sequence of the happenings.

## General to Particular

*General to particular* is the most common of all orders. It gives a structural order to *deductive* thinking. A writer begins with a generalization, then moves through the support. In the model paragraph that follows, observe the simple organization. The writer begins with his topic sentence and his thought flows from this generalization through the particulars supporting it.

> ▶ Cats also use a rich variety of vocal sounds to communicate their moods, intentions, and desires — the hiss and growl of fear and anger; the meow for attention; the purr for contact and grooming or petting; the "chirp" call, or chattering when eying birds; the loud, deep meow call when in heat; and the howling caterwauling when cats congregate outdoors at night. These sounds vary with age and sex and also with breed and individual temperament. Siamese are quite "talkative," while other

cats rarely make noise. Some cats have a mouselike squeak instead of the customary meow. Why cats purr is still a mystery, but I believe it may be a way of maintaining friendly contact and even "grooming" a companion from a distance.

Michael Fox<br>
"What Is Your Pet Trying To Tell You?"

Study the following model paragraph; note the position of the topic sentence at the beginning and the sentences that revolve around that main idea to develop and support it.

▶ Gardner taught himself to write in the same practical way he had learned law, writing for the pulp market by night after practicing law all day. Suffering a ninety percent rejection rate, he set himself a quota of 60,000 words a month. To maintain this staggering output, he turned to the subject matter he knew best — the West — and stole as much time from the law office as possible to roam the backcountry in search of material. His schedule is reflected in a letter he wrote to an editor who had ordered a story: "A lucky break in the law, and because I knew you were in a rush, has enabled me to put in a straight twenty-four hours with the exception of six for sleeping."

Francis L. and Roberta B. Fugate<br>
"Erle Stanley Gardner"

## Particular to General

Another common order in organizing and developing the expository paragraph is *particular to general*. Sometimes this pattern is called *inductive order*, since the writer leads his reader through various kinds of support to a concluding statement. By presenting the support first, a writer can gain a reader's interest, lead the reader to accept the final conclusion on the strength of the evidence, or emphasize the point he is making by a cogent climactic statement. In the model paragraph that follows, the writer Rupert Furneaux leads his readers through particulars describing conditions just prior to the massive eruption of Krakatoa. He gives meaning to these particulars in the final topic sentence: "The appearance of tranquillity was deceptive; the Crack of Doom was but a step away."

▶ It was now 10 a.m. on that memorable Monday. A pall of ash blanketed the Straits of Sunda. The darkness extended for a hundred miles. According to one estimate the dust cloud rose to an altitude of fifty miles, making a box of inky blackness. Krakatoa's roar died to a murmur. To thousands of exhausted people the sudden silence brought the hope that the volcano was in retreat, its fires extinguished, its eruption exhausted. The appearance of tranquillity was deceptive; the Crack of Doom was but a step away.

Rupert Furneaux
*Krakatoa*

Study the following passage by Dan McGowan who tells us about the role the clown plays in the dangerous sport of bull riding. Note how McGowan places the most important information in the final sentence.

▶ Sometimes a cowboy needs help escaping a bull, and that's where the rodeo clown comes in. This fellow dresses for laughs in baggy pants, polka-dot shirt and cleated baseball shoes. But his aim is dead serious: preventing serious injury or death.

Dan McGowan
"The Rodeo Cowboy"

This brief paragraph is effective communication because the writer organizes his flow of thought from particulars to general.

## General to Particular to General

In the model paragraph that follows, the writer begins with the generalization "Soon after the spraying had ended there were unmistakable signs that all was not well." She then follows with particulars to support that generalization. In the final sentence she states most emphatically the main idea of the topic sentence, but with slightly different words: "But now the stream insects were dead, killed by the DDT, and there was nothing for a young salmon to eat."

▶ Soon after the spraying had ended there were unmistakable signs that all was not well. Within two days dead and dying fish, including many young salmon, were found along the banks of the stream. Brook trout also appeared among the dead fish, and along the roads and in the woods birds were dying. All the life of the stream was stilled. Before the spraying there had been a rich assortment of the water life that forms the food of salmon and trout — caddis fly larvae, living in loosely fitting protective cases of leaves, stems or gravel cemented together with saliva, stonefly nymphs clinging to rocks in the swirling currents, and the wormlike larvae of blackflies edging the stones under riffles or where the stream spills over steeply slanting rocks. But now the stream insects were dead, killed by the DDT, and there was nothing for a young salmon to eat.

Rachel Carson<br>*Silent Spring*

## Question to Answer

In the *question-to-answer* order of development, a writer begins with a question and answers it with sufficient facts and other material until he feels that the answer is acceptable to the reader. This kind of paragraph has no stated topic sentence; however, the question itself reveals the writer's purpose. Study the model paragraph that follows:

▶ *How long have they been here?* There are ancient campsites and homesites, reliably dated by the carbon 14 method, that go back more than 10,000 years. A few scientists have found sites to which they assign ages of 30,000 to 40,000 years, but the dating results are not considered conclusive. Few anthropologists accept the extreme ages, which remain possible nonetheless. The oldest reliably dated campsite is not, by any logical or scientific necessity, the "true oldest" or the "first". If we ever were to find the "first", there would be no way of recognizing it as such. Moreover, the "first" site is now most probably at the bottom of the Bering Sea.

Nicholas Rosa<br>"Ice Age Pioneers"

Complete the following four exercises to review the discussion of paragraph order.

## EXERCISE 6    Paragraph Order

Read the model paragraph below. Answer the questions that follow.
Answers are at the end of the chapter.

▶ Millions of years ago, a volcano built a mountain on the floor
of the Atlantic. In eruption after eruption, it gushed up a great
pile of volcanic rock, until it had accumulated° a mass a hundred miles across at its base, reaching upward toward the surface of the sea. Finally its cone emerged as an island with an
area of about 200 square miles. Thousands of years passed, and
thousands of thousands. Eventually° the waves of the Atlantic
cut down the cone and reduced it to a shoal — all of it, that is,
but a small fragment which remained above water. This fragment we know as Bermuda.

Rachel Carson
*The Sea Around Us*

1. In what sentence is the main idea clearly stated?

2. What is the advantage of moving from the particular to general with
this kind of material?

## EXERCISE 7    Paragraph Order

Read the model paragraph below. Answer the questions that follow.

▶ At half-past four, the reports sounded distant but gradually they became louder, and finally so heavy that the ground trembled under our feet. Everyone was afoot. The poor superstitious natives, thinking that the end of the world had come, flocked together like sheep and made the scene still more dismal by their continuous loud praying. The dull, thundering sounds continued, and far from decreasing in violence, they increased in strength. Sleep was impossible, from detonations° startling people every two or three minutes. The air, charged with sulphurous fumes, was stifling. Thick clouds darkened the sky. A greyish streak was seen on the horizon. Day broke, but the sun was not visible. The rumble had ceased and a death-like calm prevailed° around. Everything, however, looked strange. One hour, two hours passed without the light becoming brighter. At half-past seven, the light even diminished,° and at 8 o'clock it became impossible to read without lamp light. A death-like stillness prevailed, only broken by the dull rumble. In the distance an unsteady light could be distinguished, apparently° coming from the crater of Krakatoa. Thus the dreadful night drew to an end.

Rupert Furneaux
*Krakatoa*

1. In what sentence is the main idea expressed?

2. What kind of details support the writer's main idea: expository, narrative, or descriptive?

3. In what way does chronological or time order play an important role in the structure of this paragraph?

4. Does the writer emphasize his purpose in the last part of this paragraph?

## VOCABULARY TEST FOUR

Four words are lined up below each of fifteen words taken from exercises 3 through 7. Select the one that matches best and write its letter in the blank to the right. Answers are at the end of the chapter.

1. dominant
   (a) ruling or controlling    (b) inferior    (c) aroused
   (d) influencing    *A*

2. passive
   (a) calm, submissive, unresisting    (b) superior
   (c) patient, unstirred    (d) angry    *C*

3. gape
   (a) stand    (b) stop    (c) react    (d) stare    *D*

4. hype
   (a) style    (b) type    (c) inflated publicity    (d) role    *c*

5. trendy
   (a) quaint    (b) fashionable    (c) silly    (d) amusing    *B*

6. faddism
   (a) custom    (b) mannerism    (c) craze    (d) belief    *c*

7. encroachment
   (a) involvement    (b) invasion    (c) suspicion
   (d) sacrilege    *b*

8. impunity
   (a) without punishment    (b) ease    (c) speed
   (d) reward    *a*

9. emancipation
   (a) recess    (b) punishment    (c) dismissal    (d) freedom    *d*

10. accumulated
    (a) exploded    (b) settled    (c) increased, piled up
    (d) manufactured    *C*

11. eventually
    (a) relentlessly    (b) powerfully    (c) gradually
    (d) finally    *d*

12. detonations
    (a) thick gases    (b) violent explosions    (c) noises
    (d) dense ashes    *b*

13. prevailed
    (a) became dominant    (b) appeared    (c) covered
    (d) spread    *a*

14. diminished
    (a) became stronger    (b) paled    (c) lessened, decreased
    (d) flickered

*c*

15. apparently
    (a) certainly    (b) swiftly    (c) doubtfully
    (d) evidently, obviously

*d*

**VOCABULARY PREVIEW**

| | | |
|---|---|---|
| awesome | urgent | oppression |
| export | obvious | capricious |
| per capita | exploitation | spurious |
| distracting | | |

## EXERCISE 8    Paragraph Order

Read the model paragraph below. Answer the questions that follow.

▶ The scale of the Middle East's oil wealth is awesome.° Five
Arab states — Saudi Arabia, Kuwait, Abu Dhabi, Qatar and
Libya — with a total population little more than that of the
single city of Sao Paulo had export° earnings in 1980 of $163
billion, about the same as the whole of France. Kuwait is the
richest country in the world with an annual per capita° income
of more than $19,000. Saudi Arabia's wealth held abroad
jumped from $2.3 billion in 1972 to about $150 billion by the
middle of this year. That alone is enough to buy all of the 50
biggest banks in the world. Yet not one of those 50 banks is
Arab.

Peter Truell
"The Ambitions of the Rich"

1. In what position is the topic sentence?

2. What are the key words that express the assertion (main idea)?

3. What is the function of sentence 2?

4. Explain briefly the direction of the writer's flowing thought (generalization, major support, minor support).

5. Since this paragraph is the introductory paragraph of a short essay on banking in the Arab world, what might be the function of the last two sentences?

## EXERCISE 9    Paragraph Order

Read the model paragraph below. Answer the questions that follow.

▶ The worst thing about the movement [Women's Liberation] is that it is distracting° the attention of thousands of women from more urgent° and important questions. They should get their priorities straight. Instead of yapping about men treating them as "sex objects" (and, personally, I have always *liked* being treated as a sex object), they might better devote themselves to more socially useful protests: against the war in Indochina, against nuclear, chemical and biological weapons, against environmental pollution, to name a few of the more obvious.° Or the exploitation° of migrant workers, the oppression° of the blacks, the American Indians, the Alaskan Eskimos. Or any one of at least several hundred other projects more immediate and more deserving than the issue of whether or not women should do housework and let men whistle at them in the streets. There is only so much time and energy that each person has available to devote to causes. To try to persuade people to concentrate this time and energy on something as capricious° and spurious° as Women's Lib is not only wasteful but truly evil . . . .

Amitai Etzioni
"The Women's Movement — Tokens Vs. Objectives"

1. What is the purpose of the writer?

2. What is the function of the last sentence?

3. Explain the movement of the writer's thought.

**MATCH-UP TWO**

Match the definitions in column 2 with the words in column 1 taken from exercises 8 and 9 by placing the letter of the word in the blank. Answers are at the end of the chapter.

| | | |
|---|---|---|
| a. awesome | 1. pressing | _e_ |
| b. export | 2. use for profit | _g_ |
| c. per capita | 3. evident | _f_ |
| d. distracting | 4. cruel treatment | _h_ |
| e. urgent | 5. for the individual person | _c_ |
| f. obvious | 6. changeable, fickle | _i_ |
| g. exploitation | 7. false | _j_ |
| h. oppression | 8. overwhelming | _a_ |
| i. capricious | 9. turning aside, diverting | _d_ |
| j. spurious | 10. send out of country | _b_ |

## Coherence

Coherence is essentially a technique of connecting ideas smoothly and logically in written communication. In a coherent piece of writing, a writer leads his reader clearly and logically from one idea to another in his developing thought. He weaves his ideas so skillfully together that the reader can see quickly the relationship of one idea to another and to the central thought (thesis) of the whole. Some of the most effective methods achieving coherence are the following.

1. By overall planning
2. By paragraph unity and order
3. By transitional words and expressions
4. By pronoun reference
5. By repetition of key words and ideas
6. By parallel structure
7. By maintaining a consistent point of view

## Overall Planning

By *overall planning*, a writer gains coherence. Introduction, occasional summaries that mark the end of one particular train of thought, transitional sentences and paragraphs that move the reader smoothly onward to another link in the developing chain of thought, and conclusions — all play significant roles in coherence. We have discussed these techniques earlier in this chapter.

## Paragraph Unity and Order

Most important for coherence, however, are paragraph *unity and order.* Making main ideas perfectly clear by placing them in brief, emphatic topic sentences will help the writer guide his reader smoothly onward through his flowing thought. The topic sentence, you now know, highlights the main idea of its own paragraph and serves as a vital link to the thought of the preceding paragraph and to the thesis of the whole piece of writing. A writer also gives direction to his flowing thought by organizing the whole in a *thesis-support* or a *support-thesis* paper; when such papers are properly prepared, the reader can soon grasp the continuity necessary to carry him smoothly and logically from sentence to sentence and paragraph to paragraph.

But other gaps in thought must also be bridged; therefore, experienced writers rely on transitional words and expressions, pronoun references, repetition of key words and ideas, parallel structure, and a consistent point of view to gain this kind of paragraph and sentence coherence.

Read the model paragraph that follows. Then compare it with the original version as the student wrote it. Both paragraphs possess unity, completeness, and order. Yet the second version is a better piece of writing because it has coherence. As you compare the two paragraphs, observe the smoothness that the writer gains in the second paragraph by such transitional words as *therefore, for example,* and *nevertheless,* by using pronouns as substitutes for nouns, and by an earnest attempt at parallel structure concerning the Eastern man and the frontiersman. Perhaps the writing lacks consistency in point of view, but it is a definite improvement over the first model because of its transitional and linking devices.

MODEL ONE

▶ What is masculinity? One dictionary defines it as: manly, virile, robust. Masculinity as a composite of these terms would be: resolute, dignified, honorable, sexually potent, sturdy, healthy, lusty, and most important male. All these qualities are not visible to the naked eye. Social mores play an important part in interpretation. Ancient Grecian society accepted homosexuality as perfectly natural. Our society regards it as illegal and an unhealthy approach to life. Tchambuli tribesmen of New Guinea, reformed headhunters, are artists. They enjoy painting, music, drama. They spend much time ornamenting themselves, conducting neighborhood plays, and gossiping. We do not consider such conduct masculine. In the early days, the Eastern man wore a powdered wig, ruffled shirt, ornamented breeches, and the Eastern man carried a jeweled snuff-box. This man regarded the frontiersman as not far above an animal. The frontiersman looked upon the Eastern man as a soft, unreliable Fop. This country could not have endured without both. Today it is becoming increasingly more difficult to tell which is the male and which is the female. The older generation has firm convictions as to what constitutes masculinity. Shoulder-length hair, ring bedecked fingers, necklaces, and dirty unshod feet do not meet established specifications. The Nehru jacket and the necklace are fast becoming masculine attire.

Role playing is necessary to any society. Man's role should remain one of authority. The role does not possess a fixed image. The role has, is, and will be modified by society. Masculinity is nothing more than a reflection of authority.

MODEL TWO

▶ What is masculinity? One dictionary defines it as: manly; virile; robust; *therefore,* a composite of *these* definitive terms would be: One *who* is resolute, dignified, honorable, sexually potent, sturdy, healthy, lusty, and most important, male. It is immediately obvious that all of *these* qualities are not visible to the naked eye; *moreover,* social mores would play an important part in interpretation. [For example,] ancient Grecian *society* accepted homosexuality as perfectly natural, but *our society* regards it as illegal and certainly an unhealthy approach to life. Tchambuli tribesmen of New Guinea, reformed headhunters, are *artists who* enjoy painting, music, and drama. *They* spend much of *their* time ornamenting *themselves,* conducting neighborhood plays, and gossiping. Certainly not the type of conduct *we* consider *masculine.* During the early expansion of this country, the Eastern man, with *his* powdered wig, ruffled shirt, ornamented breeches, and jeweled snuff-box regarded the frontiersman as

*[margin notes:]*

[Italics mine]

*Transitional words*

*Pronoun reference*

*Repetition of "society"*

*Pronoun reference*

*Use of "masculine"*

not far above an animal; for *his* part, the frontiersman looked upon *his* Eastern counterpart as a
soft, unreliable Fop; *nevertheless,* this country   *Transitional*
could not have endured without *both.* Currently,   *words*
it is becoming increasingly more difficult to tell
*Use of*   which is the *male* and which is the female among
*synonym*   our younger generation. Previously conditioned
*"male"*   by two wars, the older generation has firm convictions as to what constitutes *masculinity.*
Shoulder-length hair, ring bedecked fingers, necklaces, and dirty unshod feet do not meet established specifications. *However,* the Nehru jacket,
named for a man *who* appeared neither sexually
potent, sturdy, healthy, or lusty, and the necklace
are fast becoming *masculine* attire.   *Repetition of*
*Repetition*   *Role* playing is necessary to any *society.* Man's   *"masculine"*
*of "role"*   *role* should remain one of authority. The role does
not possess a fixed image. The role has, is, and
will be modified by *society. Masculinity* is nothing more than a reflection of authority.

## Transitional Words and Expressions

By using *transitional words and expressions,* a writer gains coherence.
Some of the most frequently used words and expressions for coherence
are the following:

*To Indicate Addition:* again, also, and, and then, besides, equally
important, finally, first, further, furthermore, in addition, indeed,
in fact, in the second place, likewise, moreover, next, too, secondly, other

*To Indicate Comparison (Likenesses):* at the same time, in the same
way, in like manner, likewise, similarly

*To Indicate Concession:* although this may be true, at the same
time, after all, certainly, doubtless, granted that, I admit, I con-
cede, naturally, no doubt, surely

*To Indicate Consequences or Result:* all in all, accordingly, after all,
and so, as a consequence, as a result, at last, consequently, finally,
hence, in conclusion, so, therefore, then, thus

*To Indicate Condition:* as if, if, as though, even if

*To Indicate Contrast:* and yet, although true, at the same time, but,
conversely, for all that, however, in contrast, nevertheless, not-
withstanding, on the one hand, on the other hand, rather, still,
whereas, yet

*To Indicate Examples:* especially, for example, for instance, for one thing, frequently, in general, in particular, in this way, namely, occasionally, specifically, that is, to illustrate, thus, usually

*To Indicate Reason:* because, since, for

*To Indicate Repetition:* and so again, as has been said, in fact, indeed, in other words, to recapitulate, to repeat, I repeat

*To Indicate Summary:* in brief, in short, to sum up, to summarize, in conclusion, to conclude

*Relative Pronouns, Demonstrative Adjectives, and Other Pronouns:* this, that, these, those, who, whom, whose, which, what, that, it, they, them, few, many, most, several, he, she, and so forth.

As you read the model paragraph that follows, observe how the italicized words aid the writer's flow of thought.

*[Italics mine]*

▶ *But* precisely how and why this matching of student to college takes place remains unclear. *Certainly* the "image" of a college has a great deal to do with the selective application of the "right" type of student. *But* in no college is the match between student needs and capacities and the institution's provisions and demands perfect.

*Nor* should a perfect match be viewed as the ideal. Education, *after all*, aims at inducing change in students; and some disparity between what the entering freshman is and what the college thinks he should become by graduation is necessary if college is to be more than stagnation or play. *But* no one really knows how to define the optimal disparity. If the gap between what the student wants and expects and what the college provides and asks is too great, then frustration, a sense of failure, or discontent is likely *to result.* *But if* what the student brings with him to college and what the college expects from him are too perfectly matched, the result is likely to be that stagnation which some observers think characteristic of student development at many major American colleges.

*Furthermore,* an ideal match for men students may not be at all ideal for women; *yet* little is known about the educational differences between the sexes. Most studies concentrate on one or the other sex, yet generalize to both. *But* anyone who has taught both sexes can personally document the enormous difference between their educational outlooks, concerns, and motivations. It is not yet clear, *for example,* to what extent student development as described in two classic studies of Bennington and Vassar should be generalized to most students, most liberal-arts students, most female students, or most female liberal-arts students. *Other accounts* of contemporary students seem relevant primarily to men; *thus, for example,* very few of the "activists" in the present generation are drawn from among co-eds. Whether we consider it a result of anatomy or social conditioning, women view their educations and their lives very differently than do men.

Robert S. Morison<br>"The Faces in the Lecture Room"

## Pronoun References

By using *pronouns* as substitutes for their noun antecedent, a writer can carry his reader back to the thought in a previous sentence. Thus, pronouns provide a natural connecting link. Observe, in the model paragraph that follows, the links provided by pronoun reference to its antecedent.

▶ Gardner's firm was employed to defend the Chinese. One of the lawyers who could speak what sounded like Chinese got the first defendant acquitted by convincing a detective who did not know the difference between a Chinese lottery ticket and a laundry bill that there had been a mix-up. Gardner was slated to defend the next case and devised a ploy which would do credit to Perry Mason at his best. He reasoned that Caucasian detectives probably did not know one Chinese from another and identified suspects by the places where they worked. The night before the next arrest was scheduled, Gardner went to Chinatown and switched workers from one business to another; nobody remained in his own place of business.

The following afternoon the district attorney and his minions headed for the establishment of Wong Duck, against whom they thought they had an ironclad case. They hoped that the evidence would be so overwhelming that Wong Duck would plead guilty and pay his fine, as would the other nineteen defendants. But the man they arrested insisted he was not Wong Duck. "Wait a minute," said a local deputy who had made a number of Chinatown arrests. "That's *not* Wong Duck."

While the district attorney was trying to sort out the mess, the Oxnard newspaper got wind of the affair and came up with the headline "Wong Duck May Be Wrong Duck Says Deputy Sheriff." The district attorney decided to drop all the gambling cases, and young Erle Stanley Gardner became *t'ai chong tze* — "the big lawyer" — as far as the Chinese were concerned. Thus, Gardner accumulated a following of loyal friends and clients, who incidentally launched him upon a study of the Chinese people and their language and who one day would provide him with background material for thousands upon thousands of words of fiction.

Francis L. and Roberta B. Fugate
"Erle Stanley Gardner"

## Repetition of Key Words and Phrases

By repeating key words and phrases, a writer can keep the dominant subject in the reader's mind and maintain the kind of continuity necessary for a smooth flow of logical thought. In the model paragraph that follows, the writer keeps the word *adobe* in the reader's mind to assure that the "uninitiated" will become familiar with the term.

▶ To the uninitiated, the term "adobe house" may evoke an image of a small, ill lit mud shack with dirt floors and bugs. That image may have been true in the past and may still be true in many under-developed countries. But modern, western adobe structures can be well designed, airy, well lit, and integrated with solar collector features.

Although adobe is associated with the Southwest, there are few places in the world where some form of adobe has not been used. One of the most easily obtained materials, sun-dried earth blocks have been used for thousands of years. Residential adobe ruins in Egypt predate the Great Pyramid of Giza. The ruins of Tyre and Nineveh are structurally related to the still-occupied pueblos at Taos and Acoma in New Mexico. One of the seven wonders of the ancient world, the Hanging Gardens of Babylon, was probably built of adobe bricks. The arid lands of the world, where sand and clay are found, and where the sunshine is bountiful, have long histories of earth construction. Because of this construction in highly populated areas such as India, Africa, and the Middle East, about eighty percent of all residential structures in the world today are of adobe.

James Maurer
"Adobe: Mud for Castles and Hovels"

## Parallel Structure

Through *parallelism* (parallel structure), a writer can link together similar or logically related ideas that would otherwise be placed in separate statements. In achieving parallel structure, a writer places similar or logically related ideas in the same kinds of grammatical constructions. He joins subjects with subjects, complements (predicates) with complements, modifiers with modifiers. Thus, he joins together words: nouns with nouns, adjectives with adjectives, adverbs with adverbs, and verbs with verbs. He can also join together groups of words with other equal groups of words: prepositional phrase with prepositional phrase, verbal phrase with verbal phrase, main clause with main clause, and subordinate clause with subordinate clause. The most common type of parallelism involves placing items in a series.

▶ Football, basketball, and baseball are his favorite sports.

Football,
basketball,   are his favorite sports.
baseball

The thief rushed out of the bank, across the street, and into the crowd of people milling about in the city park.

                        out of the bank,
The thief rushed   across the street,
                        into the crowd.

When the autumn leaves begin to fall, when the nights grow longer, and when the birds fly south, he longs to return home.

When the autumn leaves
   begin to fall,
when the nights grow longer,   he longs to return home.
when the birds fly south,

The value of truth and sincerity is always stronger than the value of lies and cynicism.

$$\textit{The value} \quad \genfrac{}{}{0pt}{}{\text{of truth}}{\text{of sincerity}} \quad \genfrac{}{}{0pt}{}{\text{is always stronger}}{\text{than \textit{the value}}} \quad \genfrac{}{}{0pt}{}{\text{of lies}}{\text{(of) cynicism.}}$$

In the writing that follows, observe the effective use of *parallel structure*.

▶ This great war effort must be carried through to its victorious conclusion by the indomitable will and determination of the people as one great whole.

It must not be impeded by the faint of heart.

It must not be impeded by those who put their own selfish interests above the interests of the Nation.

It must not be impeded by those who pervert honest criticism into falsification of fact.

It must not be impeded by self-styled experts either in economics or military problems who know neither true figures nor geography itself.

It must not be impeded by a few bogus patriots who use the sacred freedom of the press to echo the sentiments of the propagandists in Tokyo and Berlin.

And, above all, it shall not be imperiled by the handful of noisy traitors — betrayers of America, betrayers of Christianity itself — would-be dictators who in their hearts and souls have yielded to Hitlerism and would have this Republic do likewise.

Franklin Delano Roosevelt
"The Price of Civilization Must Be Paid in
Hard Work and Sorrow and Blood"

## Consistent Point of View

A writer gains coherence *by maintaining a consistent point of view.* Unnecessary, sudden, and illogical shifts in point of view; that is, in subject, person, number, tense, voice, and mood, affect sentence and paragraph relationships, thus obscuring meaning. Avoid shifts in the following:

1. Shifts in subject or voice

    SHIFT:    The store was robbed by the two wanted criminals as we entered it.
*(A shift in subjects from store to we; a shift in voice from passive to active)*

    IMPROVED:    We saw the two wanted criminals robbing the store as we entered it.
*(Both verbs in active voice)*

    SHIFT:    Jane dislikes Paris, but London was enjoyed by her.
*(Shift in subject and voice)*

    IMPROVED:    Jane disliked Paris, but she enjoyed London.
*(One subject only; both verbs in active voice)*

2. Shifts in tense

    SHIFT:    Helen opened the door and rushes into the yard after William.
*(A shift from past tense to present tense)*

    IMPROVED:    Helen opens the door and rushes into the yard after William.
*(Both present tenses)*

    SHIFT:    The curtain opens and the play began.
*(Shift from present tense to past tense)*

    IMPROVED:    The curtain opened and the play began.
*(Both verbs in the past tense)*

3. Shifts in mood

    SHIFT:    Raise the ball onto your fingertips, and then you should lay it gently against the backboard.
*(Shift from the imperative to the indicative mood)*

    IMPROVED:    Raise the ball onto your fingertips and then lay it gently against the backboard.
*(Both verbs in the imperative mood)*

4. Shifts in person

    SHIFT:    When *you* pass the examination, *one* should feel a little proud.
*(A shift from second person to third person)*

    IMPROVED:    When *you* pass that examination, *you* should feel a little proud.
*(Both in the second person)*

    IMPROVED:    When *one* passes that examination, *he* (or one) should feel a little proud.
*(Both in the third person)*

    SHIFT:    A *student* needs to study long hours for Professor White's class. *You* will find the lectures filled with facts and the examinations difficult.
*(A shift from third person to second)*

IMPROVED:  A *student* needs to study long hours for Professor White's class. *He* will find the lectures filled with facts and the examinations difficult.
*(Both in the third person)*

5. Shifts in number

SHIFT:  If a *person* follows those suggestions, *they* will get into difficulty.
*(A shift from singular to plural number)*

IMPROVED:  If a *person* follows those suggestions, *he or she* will get into difficulty.
*(Both third person singular)*

In the student model that follows, notice that frequent shifts in subject and person cause confusion. Observe also the shifts in tense and voice.

▶ Good study habits are necessary for success in college. The art of studying must be learned in order to excel in anything. Two hours for each hour of class time is required but is not enough if you are careless and haphazard in your study habits. He is just putting in time that is of little or no use. A student must have much self-discipline and motivation to learn to the best of their ability.

Study how the paragraph below illustrates a consistent point of view. Observe the ways in which the writer achieves his consistent point of view: a dominant subject, the verbs in the same tense and voice, and correct pronoun reference.

▶ If a student is going to be successful in college, he must acquire good study habits. He should put in two hours work outside of class for every hour in class. He must find a place to study that is free from noise and visitors who will disturb him once he gets going. He must learn the skills and techniques of efficient reading so that he can use his study time effectively. He must take care of his health by eating properly, getting enough exercise, and sleeping sufficiently. Above all, he must have the self-discipline and motivation to keep him at the job for the next four years of his life.

Complete the two exercises that follow to review the discussion on coherence.

**VOCABULARY PREVIEW**

| | | |
|---|---|---|
| avert | litigation | emaciated |
| bias | incomprehensible | subsidized |
| status | significance | exotic |
| peignoir | affluence | adaptability |
| chutney | impervious | regenerates |

## EXERCISE 10     **Coherence**

Study the paragraph unit below. Underline any transitional words or phrases. Circle any repetitions of key words or phrases.
Answers are at the end of the chapter.

▶ Intelligence tests seek to avert° bias,° first by avoiding, so far as possible, test items which favor one group as against another, and secondly by taking care that subjects used in the standardization of these tests shall be representative of the populations to whom the tests will be subsequently administered.

Thus, in getting up a vocabulary list, one would avoid words with which individuals of higher status° group would be more familiar than would a lower status group — "peignoir,"° "chutney"° and "litigation,"° for example. Again, in testing a person for ability to detect missing parts, one would use a picture of a horse rather than a yak, a drum rather than a bass viol. Similarly in planning questions of general comprehension one must take into consideration the customs and attitudes of different places. Thus the questions "Why are shoes made of leather?" and "Why does the state require people to get a marriage license?" would be suitable for Europeans and Americans but might be quite incomprehensible° to persons living where shoes are not worn and where the state is not so particular.

However, there is considerable evidence to show that so-called "race" differences have been greatly overestimated. General intelligence seems to be a very general commodity. It is not so much the significance° of the differences in ability found between groups as the exploitation of these differences which have sometimes given intelligence tests a bad reputation.

David Wechsler
"Measuring the I.Q. Test"

## EXERCISE 11    Coherence

Study the paragraph below. Underline any transitional words or phrases. Circle any repetitions and key words.

▶ American historian Bruce Catton (1899–1978) wrote: "... No American in the 1880s could have surveyed the New York slum section of his day without wondering if he were not seeing the final collapse of the American dream."

Catton later added: "But things did get better. The dream did not die. . . ."

Those words were written in 1955. At that time, getting a good education, a satisfying job, a house in the suburbs, at least one car, the promise of a secure retirement, and the firm hope that the following generation would do even better made up a "dream" that seemed within the grasp of most Americans.

However, that dream depended on the continuing increase of national affluence° (wealth). By now, such economic growth has definitely slowed down. We are faced with soaring energy costs, water shortages, various environmental concerns, and increasing competition from foreign manufacturers. And this has led to high inflation and unemployment. It has recently been estimated by the U.S. Dept. of Commerce that the income of the average American *in 1967 dollars* has actually gone down in the past few years. This has prompted a number of writers to state that "the great age of American affluence" is over.

Michael Cusak
"The American Dream; Past . . . and Future"

## Paragraph to Theme

At this point in your study, you may have discovered that certain topics could not be adequately developed in a paragraph or paragraph unit. This fact should not surprise you, for Chapter 1 explained that these units were part of a longer piece of writing. Your instructor and the author of this book, nevertheless, may ask you to concentrate on the paragraph and paragraph unit throughout the course because, as was mentioned earlier in this chapter, these pieces of writing are essays in miniature. Once you have mastered the skills and techniques of writing these smaller units, you will be better prepared to attack the longer pieces of writing.

Let us now review the structure of the paragraph first; then move onto the paragraph unit and finally to the short theme in order to explain the purpose of this approach to writing.

In the model paragraph below, observe that the topic sentence gives unity to the writer's thought. Notice also that the writer explains fully her main idea by presenting sufficient supporting material. It is not enough to say that "woman's lot was not a happy one"; the writer must make that generalization very clear by offering proof.

|   |   |
|---|---|
| | ▶ What we know for certain of the condition of women in early primitive societies is little. *But it* |
| *Topic Sentence* | *is clear that woman's lot was not a happy one.* As a slave, she was inherited as property and sold when it was to the advantage of her owner. Always bound by the control of others, she was |
| *Support* | given long and exhausting labor and was worn out by constant childbearing. Tribal man's opinion of woman is seen in the statement made by a Chippewayan Indian chief. "Women were made for labor; one of them can carry, or haul, as much as two men can do. They also pitch our tents, make and mend our clothing, keep us warm at night; |
| *Support* | and, in fact, there is no such thing as travelling any considerable distance without their assistance."* Many primitive societies also believed that woman differed from man in not having a soul, thus by nature deserving her low position. |

Anita Wilkes Dore
*The Emerging Woman: Quest for Equality*

---

* Mary Beard, *Woman as a Force in History* (New York: P. F. Collier, Inc., 1946), p. 65.

In the following paragraph unit excerpted from a book review, the writer states his main idea in the first sentence of the first paragraph: "An unfortunate holdover from such politicizing of suffering badly flaws this book." He supports this statement with evidence from the book that its author claims the United States bombed Hiroshima and Nagasaki for experimental and political aims.

He begins paragraph 2 with a concise topic sentence contradicting this view: "This is simply not true." He follows with a supporting view of this generalization in the remaining sentences of that paragraph and the entire third paragraph.

In the final paragraph, the writer repeats his main evidence: "Yet dropping the bomb, insofar as it forced the Japanese surrender, saved many more lives than it took. For the 200,000 who were killed, millions may have been spared."

▶ An unfortunate holdover from such politicizing of suffering badly flaws this book. We are told flatly, for example, that Hiroshima and Nagasaki were bombed not to hasten the end of the war against Japan but "to clearly establish America's postwar international position and strategic supremacy in an anticipated Cold War setting. One tragedy of Hiroshima and Nagasaki is that this historically unprecedented devastation of human society stemmed from essentially experimental and political aims."

This is simply not true. Japan may have been militarily defeated by the time the A-bomb was dropped on Hiroshima, but unfortunately the militarists in control of Japan refused to recognize that fact. The bomb enabled the emerging peace party to arrange a surrender. Two days after the Hiroshima bombing, the emperor told the prime minister that "a new kind of weapon" used there now made surrender inevitable — and prepared to overrule the die-hard militarists who wished to continue fighting.

Had this not happened, a seaborne Allied invasion of Japan would have taken place — preparations for "Operation Olympic" had already been made. Vast numbers of Japanese and American soldiers, as well as Japanese civilians, would have been killed. Wartime fanaticism is sometimes hard for revisionist historians to imagine, writing 35 years after the fact.

Certainly to drop the bomb was a frightening responsibility. This responsibility was all too lightly passed off by Americans in authority at the time, blindly concentrating on winning the war. Yet dropping the bomb, insofar as it forced the Japanese surrender, saved many more lives than it took. For the 200,000 who were killed, millions may have been spared.

Frank Gibney
"The A-Bomb and Its Japanese Victims"

Finally, let us consider a short theme — a combination of paragraphs or paragraph units revolving around and developing a central thought: a statement that reveals the writer's purpose. In the following short piece of writing, "Cows to the Rescue," the writer wishes to tell his readers that the poor in India have been given a scheme that will lift them above the poverty level. He begins his discussion, therefore, with a statement of his central thought in the first sentence: "Mini-miracles are taking place in parts of India which were once impervious to growth." In the remaining sentences of that paragraph, the writer explains fully the meaning of the opening generalization with specifics and details. The reader soon learns that the mini-miracles are actually a "development of a new breed of cow and a new type of fodder, both well suited to arid conditions."

He supports his thesis with three separate paragraphs, each with a stated main idea in the first sentence, and a paragraph unit (paragraphs 5 and 6) developed around an implied main idea: the success of the program. Each topic sentence is adequately supported with examples and explanatory material.

### COWS TO THE RESCUE
**From a Correspondent in India**

▶ [1]*Mini-miracles are taking place in parts of India which were once considered impervious° to growth.* The poor in these places are very very poor and so is the land: skills, capital and water are all too scarce for conventional farming. And the cattle which can survive on the local scrub are too emaciated° to earn their keep. But now this picture is being transformed by the development of a new breed of cow and a new type of fodder, both well suited to arid conditions. The result is the beginnings of a thriving dairy industry which can turn idle land and idle labour profitably productive.

*Thesis*

*Explanation*

*Topic idea*

[2]*This project is the brainchild of a nonprofit voluntary agency, Bharatiya Agro Industries Foundation (BAIF) which is* paid partly by foreign donors, partly by a Bombay foundation but mostly by the service contracts it gets from central and local government. These services include

*Support*

door-to-door deliveries of semen, seeds for the new fodder and how-to-do-it advice on building cheap houses, installing pumps and running simple bio-gas systems. The charges are low enough for small farmers to afford but those who are too poor to pay are subsidized° by the government.

*Topic statement*

[3]*Scientists at the main BAIF campus near Pune made their breakthrough by inseminating nondescript local cows with imported semen of the highest quality.* (Imported cows would be too expensive and could not survive harsh local condi-

*Support*

tions.) They developed a breed that is two thirds exotic,° one third local and combines high milk yields with high adaptability.° Semen for further inseminations is packed in cartridges, floating in cans of liquid nitrogen, and delivered to farmers by trained veterinarians mounted on motorcy-

*Explanation*

cles. The success rate of inseminations is high, the cost very low. From the first calving by artificial insemination, it takes three to four years to establish a self-perpetuating breed.

*Topic idea*

[4]*The fodder for these new cows is completely exotic in origin:* it comes from a tree called

*Explanation*

leucaena leucocaphala which is native to El Salvador and reached India by way of Hawaii. This tree, renamed ku-babul, yields large harvests of protein-rich fodder and quickly regenerates° itself with little water and less care. It even enriches the soil by generously "fixing" nitrogen and humus.

*Paragraph unit*

[5]The cow-tree cycle produces an annual income 20 times the cost of establishing it before the milking life of the first crossbred cow comes to an

*Implied topic idea*

end after 8–10 years. Pilot projects have proved that by using these methods, a poor family can raise enough income from less than a hectare of land to lift itself above India's poverty line. The landless can join the programme too: the foundation gives them one-acre plots of public land on long leases.

⁶So far only about 8,000 villages, in 20-village units, are participating in the dairy scheme, most of them in the barren Deccan plateau and equally barren parts of north central India. But the potential for expansion is enormous. At least 60m hectares of land are lying idle in India today. *At the rate of one hectare per family, this would be enough to rescue all 300m people whom India considers poor.*

*Support*

*Restatement of idea of mini-miracle*

The transition from paragraph or paragraph unit to the short theme or longer piece of writing is not difficult once you become proficient in writing good paragraphs. The structure of expository writing, therefore, is essentially the same regardless of the length of the discussion. The longer piece of writing will have more middle paragraphs of supporting material than the short theme and may include an introductory paragraph or paragraph unit and a concluding paragraph or paragraph unit.

Your purpose and the kind of material will determine the kind of development and the length of that development. One idea may be adequately explained in a paragraph unit; most central thoughts, however, require a short theme or a longer piece of writing for effective communication. Before you have finished this book, you should be able to express your thoughts effectively in each of these units of writing.

## Topic Sentences for Discussion or Written Assignments

1. These sentences may be used for discussion or for written assignments about topic sentences and kinds of development.
   a. Men are maligned by stereotyped portrayals in mass media.
   b. The prevalent image of the happy, fulfilled, and secure housewife is bunk — pure bunk.
   c. His folks talked like other folks in the neighborhood.
   d. Proud of his wonderful achievements, civilized man looks down upon the humbler members of mankind.
   e. The great past of Greece is conspicuously visible on the Acropolis.
   f. New kinds of business are constantly arising to threaten the markets of old businesses.

---

**MATCH-UP THREE**

Match the definitions in column 2 with the words in column 1 taken from the exercises and the essay by placing the letter of the word in the blank. Answers are at the end of the chapter.

| | | | |
|---|---|---|---|
| a. avert | 1. lawsuit, legal action | *f* |
| b. bias | 2. incapable of being affected | *j* |
| c. status | 3. meaning, great importance | *h* |
| d. peignoir | 4. wasted away | *k* |
| e. chutney | 5. abundance, wealth | *i* |
| f. litigation | 6. helped or aided | *l* |
| g. incomprehensible | 7. unreasonable feeling against | *B* |
| h. significance | 8. loose dressing gown | *d* |
| i. affluence | 9. prevent, turn away | *a* |
| j. impervious | 10. foreign | *m* |
| k. emaciated | 11. sweet or sour sauce or relish | *e* |
| l. subsidized | 12. relative position, rank | *c* |
| m. exotic | 13. ability to adjust | *n* |
| n. adaptability | 14. not understandable nor intelligible | *g* |
| o. regenerates | 15. renews itself, produces anew | *o* |

---

g. The wartime service of American women was prodigious.

h. As a matter of fact, we are all of us original in our expression until our wings are clipped.

i. I have come to marvel at the instinct of animals to make use of natural laws for healing themselves.

j. The interpretation of words is a never-ending task for any citizen in modern society.

k. The success of the marginal businessman is almost always greeted with mixed feelings.

2. Select any three of the following statements. Use each of them as the topic sentence of a paragraph or paragraph unit. If you choose, you may rewrite the statement or use the statement to suggest a topic sentence of your own construction. Develop each paragraph or paragraph unit by a different order. Keep in mind as you structure your thought what you have learned about *unity, completeness, order,* and *coherence.*

a. Going to college is serious business.
b. I will never forget my first experience in racial prejudice (cruelty to animals), (man's inhumanity to man), (and so on).
c. I could not shoot the deer.
d. Pollution is a problem on our campus.
e. Women belong in the home.
f. Going to college is expensive.
g. Teen-agers are realists (activists), (romanticists), (idealists), (and so on).
h. At our college there is too much emphasis on meeting the right people (athletics), (grades), (and so on).
i. That date was a disaster.
j. Winning is everything.

## Answers: Chapter 2

### Exercise 3

1. Two suspicious cats exhibit facial expressions to indicate their emotions and intentions (sentence 1).
2. The flow of thought moves from the generalization (topic sentence) through particulars (supporting sentences).
3. There are three major supporting statements and four minor supporting sentences. The following outline of the paragraph will enable you to see its structure more clearly.
   I. If you have ever watched a meeting between two suspicious cats, you may have witnessed a full array of facial expressions that indicate a cat's emotions and intentions.
      A. The dominant cat keeps a cool front, showing little or no expression when facing up to its rival.
         1. Its face is a model of passive indifference with upright ears, straight whiskers, and eyes directed fearlessly ahead.
         2. It may even close its eyes.
      B. The fearful cat will flatten its ears and hiss.
         1. Its eyes are open wide and the pupils are clearly enlarged.
         2. If the cat is torn between flight and attack, it will twist its ears sideways and stare almost cross-eyed with moderately enlarged pupils.
      C. In another reaction, a cat may gape with its eyes half-closed, as if drugged, when it has sniffed some strange odor or urine of another cat.

### Exercise 6

1. The main idea is best expressed in the last sentence.
2. The writer can gain reader interest, lead the reader to accept the final conclusion on the strength of the evidence, and emphasize the point he or she is making by a cogent, climactic statement. In this particular paragraph, Rachel Carson holds back the name of the island until the final sentence; thus, she gains reader interest as well as presenting evidence.

*Exercise 10*

The words that should be underlined appear in *italic* type; the words that should be circled, in **boldface** type:

▶ Intelligence **tests** seek to avert bias, *first* by avoiding, so far as possible, **test** items which favor one **group** as against another, and *secondly* by taking care that subjects used in the standardization of these **tests** shall be representative of the populations to whom the **tests** will be subsequently administered.

*Thus*, in getting up a vocabulary list, one would avoid words with which individuals of a higher **status group** would be more familiar than would a lower **status group** — "peignoir," "chutney" and "litigation," *for example*. *Again*, in **testing** a person for ability to detect missing parts, one would use a picture of a horse rather than a yak, a drum rather than a bass viol. *Similarly* in planning questions of general comprehension one must take into consideration the customs and attitudes of **different** places. *Thus* the questions "Why are shoes made of leather?" and "Why does the state require people to get a marriage license?" would be suitable for Europeans and Americans but might be quite incomprehensible to persons living where shoes are not worn and where the state is not so particular.

*However*, there is considerable evidence to show that so-called "race" **differences** have been greatly overestimated. General intelligence seems to be a very general commodity. It is not so much the significance of the **differences** in ability found between **groups** as the exploitation of these **differences** which have sometimes given **intelligence tests** a bad reputation.

| Voc. Test 4 | | Match-Up 2 | | Match-Up 3 | |
|---|---|---|---|---|---|
| 1. | a | 1. | e | 1. | f |
| 2. | c | 2. | g | 2. | j |
| 3. | d | 3. | f | 3. | h |
| 4. | c | 4. | h | 4. | k |
| 5. | b | 5. | c | 5. | i |
| 6. | c | 6. | i | 6. | l |
| 7. | b | 7. | j | 7. | b |
| 8. | a | 8. | a | 8. | d |
| 9. | d | 9. | d | 9. | a |
| 10. | c | 10. | b | 10. | m |
| 11. | d | | | 11. | e |
| 12. | b | | | 12. | c |
| 13. | a | | | 13. | n |
| 14. | c | | | 14. | g |
| 15. | d | | | 15. | o |

# 3

# Planning the Whole Paper

You probably know now that fundamental to effective writing is skillful organization of thought. If you have reached this conclusion, you are also aware that good organization involves other processes besides giving order to your flowing thought. Especially important to effective organization of the whole paper are certain processes that should be completed before you put your thoughts onto paper. If you do not select a subject that is interesting to you and that you know something about, you are in trouble. If you do not have in mind exactly what you want to say about a subject before you begin writing, you are in trouble. If you do not limit a broad and general subject, you are in trouble. If you do not have in mind some possible ways of organizing the material before you begin to write, you are in trouble.

Planning the whole paper, therefore, before you begin to put your thoughts onto paper is absolutely essential for successful writing. This book suggests that you follow these steps before you write.

1. Select a subject.
2. Limit the subject.
   a. Break down the subject.
   b. Write a title.
3. Determine your purpose.
4. State your purpose.
   a. Statement of thesis
   b. Statement of purpose
5. Gather material.
6. Prepare an outline.

This book suggests three steps in writing the paper.

7. Prepare a first draft.
8. Revise the paper.
9. Write the final copy.

## Select a Subject

What shall I write about? Most beginning writers are constantly asking this question. Most experienced writers, you will find, begin with an interest in and knowledge of some subject and a desire to share a particular point of view about that subject with their readers. Beginning writers, however, find it difficult to get started because they feel that they have nothing important to write about. More often than not, the true problem is that the beginning writer has not used his imagination in selecting an appropriate subject for an audience that should be interested in what he has to say.

In selecting a subject, draw first from your own experiences. Many things that you have done, seen, heard, felt in your lifetime must have left an impression on you. From these experiences, select one that interests you, that is still vivid, or that you have a knowledge of, and that you believe will interest your readers. It might be surfing. It might be fashions or clothes. It might be cheating in classes, student government, a current event, a happening on campus or at home, a personal discovery about yourself, a friend, your parents, or life in general. With some thought you will find a number of suitable subjects for the short theme. Listed below are some broad general subjects, which, *when limited*, become suitable subjects for student themes.

| | | |
|---|---|---|
| Accidents | Customs | Literature |
| Actors | Dance | Love |
| Animals | Dating | Movies |
| Architecture | Death | Music |
| Art | Drama | Nature |
| Athletics | Drugs | People |
| Beauty | Education | Philosophy |
| Birth | Entertainment | Prejudices |
| Brotherhood | Ethics | Radio |
| Camping | Faith | Religion |
| Cars | Family | Schools |
| Censorship | Freedom | Sex |
| Cities | Friends | Social Problems |
| Clothes | Games | Space |
| College | Groups | Sports |
| Comedians | History | Television |
| Comics | Hobbies | Theater |
| Countries | Inventions | Travel |
| Courage | Jobs | War |
| Crime | Language | |

Read this list again. Add any subjects that you have found interesting and that you consider suitable for theme topics.

## Limit the Subject

Broad and general subjects like "Education," "Social Problems," "Television," and "Movies" cannot be treated fully enough in a 500-word or even a 2000-word paper. You must limit broad and general subjects, therefore, for effective development in the time and space requirements of most college written assignments. Suppose you were asked to write a 500-word paper on Rome by your history instructor, or a 500-word paper on "Alcoholism" by your instructor in social science, or a long paper on "Education" by your instructor in first-year writing class. How do you go about limiting the subject so that you can meet the time and space requirements of the assignment? Let us use the broad subject "Education" as our example (the problems of developing the other subjects are the same). In thinking about "Education," you remember vividly your first day on campus. It was memorable because of many things that happened to you. You decide to write on the limited subject "My First Day at State University" because it is a subject that you can write on from your own experiences and that you feel will interest other students who had similar experiences that first day. In addition, you believe that it is certainly a more restricted subject than "Education." With these assurances of a right start in mind, you begin to put your thoughts onto paper. You tell of your experiences on the bus to the campus, meeting new friends and renewing old acquaintances on arriving on campus, finding your way around the large campus; you tell of the events concerned with registration, buying textbooks, paying the high costs of education, and many others. The paper grows and grows; yet you have written only a few sentences about several experiences, or you have written a page or more about only one or two happenings that remained most vividly in your mind, such as the long process of registration or the high cost of college. You are in trouble.

You discover that your first day on campus consisted of a number of experiences, any one of which could be a topic for a paper. How can you avoid this trial-and-error kind of planning that wastes your time and energy and gets you nowhere?

## Break Down the Subject

Before you begin to write, break down the subject into topics and subtopics. Write down the broad and general subject that interests you and that you know something about. Underneath it, list as many topics and subtopics that you can think of. If it is necessary, look up additional information about the subject, as this process will bring other topics to mind. Your breaking down of the subject might look something like the following.

▶ Education
University
First Day
  Riding the Bus
  Eating in the Cafeteria
  Making New Friends
  Renewing Old
    Acquaintances
  Finding My Way around
    Campus
  Choosing the Right
    Courses
  Buying Textbooks
  The High Cost of
    Education
  First Class Meeting
  Registration
  Alone in a Crowd

Travel
Venice
My Visit
  Churches
  Unique Taxicabs
  Streets of Water
  The Piazza of Saint Mark
  The Cathedral of
    Saint Mark
  The Bridge of Sighs
  Grand Canal
  A Dying City
  A City on Water
  "Queen City of the Adriatic"
  A Glimpse of Renaissance
    Glory

## Write a Title

Many of the topics listed under the broad and general subject may serve as titles without change. At this time, however, study each topic or the topic you feel that you wish to develop and decide whether it would serve as a title for your paper. If it will not make a good title, rewrite it. You may wish to change this tentative title later. Remember, a good title is brief, interesting, and informative. Selecting a title at this time is not essential, but you may discover that this thinking about subject will help you arrive at a purpose for writing.

## Determine Your Purpose

As this process of limiting your subject proceeds, you should begin to have an idea of what you want to say about a subject and how you want to say it. If you have reached this stage in your thinking about the subject, you have determined your purpose. In other words, you have answered a question that you must ask yourself if you are to move onward with any kind of success: "What do I intend to do in this paper?" If you intend to tell the story behind the "Bridge of Sighs," your purpose is obvious; you will develop your flowing thought by narration. Your tentative title "The Story of the Bridge of Sighs" may have helped you with determining the purpose, if you had not already decided to tell the story. On the other hand, if you wish to describe the bridge, your purpose is obviously development by description. If your aim is to inform the reader about construction of the bridge or to explain how it got its name, you will develop by exposition.

Your answer to the question, as illustrated in the previous paragraph, will give you a purpose that corresponds to one of the three forms of discourse that were defined earlier in the book. Keep in mind, however, that seldom is a paper developed with a single form of discourse. Most papers are a mixture of the forms, with one form predominant, according to the primary purpose of the paper. Thus, a writer may tell the story of the "Bridge of Sighs" (narration) for the dominant purpose of explaining how the bridge got its name (exposition). In the process of making his meaning clear, he may describe the bridge (description).

## State Your Purpose

Determining your purpose limits your intention to a dominant form of discourse. But this process still does not limit the topic to the kind of specificity necessary for successful development of thought in the time and space requirements of the usual college written assignment, especially the composition or theme. You need to carry the process of limiting your subject one step further by stating your purpose in a sentence. In a paper that develops one central thought, you express your purpose in a *thesis statement.* In papers where the flowing thought does not revolve around a thesis, you express your purpose in a *statement of purpose.* Let us study each of these statements of purpose in detail.

## Statement of Thesis

A *thesis,* you may remember from the earlier discussion, states the central thought or dominant idea of the paper. As a topic sentence unifies a number of sentences in a paragraph, so a thesis statement unifies a number of paragraphs or paragraph units that make up the body of the paper. The thesis, like the topic sentence, is an assertion. It is a generalization that requires further explanation and support to be meaningful; this is the function of the body of the paper. A thesis statement, for example, that reads "President Kennedy was assassinated in Dallas, Texas," is a poor thesis statement because it says all that needs to be said about the topic. Factual statements of this kind may be followed by a sentence or two elaborating on the original idea or repeating it in slightly different words, but they do not need extensive support or explanatory material for meaning. A thesis expressed in the form of a generalization, on the other hand, requires further development if it is to be meaningful. Such is the nature of the generalization; it is not specific enough without particulars that explain and support it. This type of statement may express an opinion or point of view of the writer. It may indicate a judgment that he has reached about the subject. It may express his attitude toward the subject. All such statements must have support if they are to convey the meaning the writer intended. Study the following thesis statements. Are they the kinds of statements that require additional development?

▶ A good hitter has confidence in his ability to hit the ball.

An asset to an aspiring actor is a good voice.

Suspicious teachers encourage students to cheat.

Parental pressure for good grades causes children with average or below-average abilities to cheat in school.

Pollution of the lake in my home town can be eliminated only by a cooperative effort of the citizens, the owners of the industry, and the state government.

Student apathy destroyed our intramural athletic program.

A good thesis is limited. It restricts the discussion to the development of a central thought (dominant idea). This kind of thesis summarizes what the paper is about and indicates clearly which one of several possible topics the writer will develop. A thesis statement that reads "Visiting Venice was a memorable experience" is a poor thesis because it is unrestricted. The writer does not limit his discussion to a single assertion. This kind of thesis cannot unify the supporting material because the flowing thought can go in too many directions. The writer could discuss almost every experience that he had in Venice. "Venice is a dying city," however, is a limited statement of the thesis. It tells the reader that the writer will explain and support this central thought. It indicates also that the writer will explain why Venice is dying. It leads the reader smoothly into the body of the paper. The city is dying because:

1. It is no longer the trade center of the world as it was during the early Renaissance period.
2. It is no longer a great political power.
3. It is no longer a mighty military power.
4. It is no longer a financial giant.
5. It is sinking into the ocean at the rate of three inches a year.

A good thesis indicates development of one restricted topic. It will explain and support one assertion, one opinion, one judgment, or one attitude about the topic. A thesis "Football is a dangerous and exciting game," for example, is unrestricted for the time and space requirements because it expresses two attitudes; each attitude could be developed into a whole paper.

A good thesis is unambiguous. It is an explicit statement of the central thought. It is written in words that reveal to the reader exactly what the writer had in mind. Abstract and general words are poor choices for the thesis. "A bug beats a football team" is a poor thesis because it places the burden of understanding what the writer means on the reader. It leaves too many unanswered questions in his mind. "What kind of a bug?" "What was the football team?" Where? When? This statement might serve as a title for the paper with the thesis: "Infectious hepatitis beat the Holy Cross football team of 1969," but it is far too ambiguous to summarize the support that follows. Concrete and specific words like those used in the model thesis above give the reader the meaning the writer intended. Contrast the three statements that follow. Which statement is the best thesis?

▶ Television creates myths.

Television series about policemen are fabricating a police myth.

"The Thin Blue Line" is fabricating a police myth.

A good thesis will often indicate the direction of the writer's flowing thought. Frequently, a writer will phrase his thesis so that he indicates the direction of his flowing thought. As you read the following thesis statements, observe how each one indicates what the writer intends to do and how he will organize his material.

▶ Ireland and Israel are alike yet different.

Elizabeth C. Winship
"Ireland and Israel — Alike yet Different"

▶ Geologists conceive the earth ball as a series of shells with an inner core.

Edith Raskin
*The Earth Ball*

▶ The two paintings represented two totally different worlds.

Katherine Kuh
*Place, Time, and Painter*

▶ I think that there are six canons of conservative thought.

Russell Kirk
*A Preliminary Delineation: Conservative and Radical*

Do the following assignment to reinforce your understanding of the discussion of thesis statements.

## ASSIGNMENT    Thesis Statement

Explain why or why not you consider each of the statements below a good or poor thesis.

1. My college is an interesting educational institution.

2. Life is a compulsory education.

3. The rock stars Alice Cooper and David Bowie are turning to sensationalism in their performances.

4. Visiting the Mauna Kea Beach Hotel in Hawaii was a memorable experience.

5. Overpopulation of unwanted pets is a serious problem.

6. Our present grading system leads to cheating.

7. Ice hockey is a dangerous and exciting contact sport.

8. Effective prewriting contributes much to a good final paper.

9. Our local government is inefficient in many ways.

10. Venice is a victim of Italian industrialists.

## Statement of Purpose

Not all papers are organized around a thesis. Many papers are organized around a purpose only. In these kinds of papers, a writer organizes his flowing thought around a *statement of purpose*. He may state this purpose in a brief explanatory sentence explaining what he intends to do in the paper. Ulf Hannerez, for example, in "The Rhetoric of Soul: Identification in Negro Society" states his purpose as follows:

▶ In this paper, I will attempt to place this concept of "soul" in its social and cultural matrix, in particular with respect to the tendencies of social change as experienced by ghetto inhabitants.

At this stage in thinking about your subject, you should write down a statement of purpose even though you may omit it from the final copy. It will help you further restrict your topic and may lead to the organization of your thought. If you are describing a person, place, or thing or are telling a story, you obviously do not need a statement of thesis. If you are explaining how to do something (such as repairing a kitchen faucet), or informing the reader how something happened (such as the birth of an island or a volcano), you do not need a statement of thesis. If you are summarizing the causes of alcoholism, you are obviously not developing a dominant idea. But, in all of these papers, you have a clear purpose in mind that can be the unifying point for the paragraph cluster that follows. Statements of purpose are expressed in various forms; some of the most common appear below.

▶ The purpose of this paper is to discuss the complex life at the ocean's edge.

I will suggest two alternatives to our present grading system and discuss the advantages of each.

This paper will give the beginning spectator at a football game a guide to understanding the action on the field.

I will present various definitions of the term "personality" in order to show the difficulty of limiting its meaning to one definition.

My purpose is to describe my feelings as I viewed the "Bridge of Sighs."

I intend to summarize the causes of World War II so the reader will have a better understanding of the true nature of the conflict.

## Gather Material

Material for a paper consists of the kinds of data — facts, opinions, descriptive or narrative details, testimony, examples, causes, effects, likenesses, differences — that you will use to develop your thesis or statement of purpose. Before you can begin to organize the paper, you must have sufficient knowledge of the topic to develop the purpose. Most of the information for writing the paper will come from your own experiences — what you have seen, heard, and felt, and what you have read. How much you remember depends to a great extent upon how deeply you were affected and how strongly you wish to communicate your feelings or opinions about your subject. But memory is also dependent upon your own powers of observation. Too often, as a beginning writer you find yourself with nothing to say about a topic, not because you lack experience but because you can recall only vague and general impressions of what happened or what you read about it or both. You failed to concentrate on the details and specifics that are the kinds of material so necessary to a vivid and effective recall. People actually may not forget as much as they think. Forgetting is more accurately a result of poor learning in the first place. How can you create a word picture of a person if you can only vaguely remember what that individual looked like? How can you support a judgment, explain an attitude, or make an opinion acceptable unless you have evidence rather than half-explanations and vague generalities. Thus, to make full use of your experiences as the source material for papers, you must be a keen observer of experiences, whether real or vicarious.

A procedure for gathering material that has proved successful for countless beginning writers may work for you. Start by taking a mental inventory of your knowledge about a subject when you first begin the limiting process. Decide at that time if you have sufficient information to proceed and if additional material is available in sources close by, especially your school library. When you have selected the topic, jot down on paper as many ideas about it as you are able. As you are limiting the subject, keep adding additional material and eliminating irrelevant material. If necessary, research the subject in various sources, especially those in the library. By this time, you should have a rather substantial list for developing your purpose. To illustrate this procedure, suppose you have recently read about Venice and have decided to write about that city. You begin by jotting down ideas that come into your mind; and, as certain ideas suggest research, you go to the library to read about Venice* — its history, art, pollution, gradual destruction. Your listing of this kind of information might look something like the following:

> ▶ Italian name — Venezia
> on a cluster of mud flats
> original inhabitants flee from mainland
> canals for streets
> many great churches
> Cathedral of Saint Mark
> Piazza of Saint Mark
> city on piles or posts
> great sea power at its peak
> stopping place for Crusaders
> Bridge of Sighs
> 400 bridges
> 26 canals
> S-shaped Grand Canal
> center of a great empire
> end of trade
> memorable art treasures
> flooding of Saint Mark Cathedral
> tides and winds
> water polluted
> six cushions to hold it up
> rivers diverted
> sinks 8 inches in twenty years
> twenty washouts in 1969
> industry on mainland
> tides flooding city
> fall of bell tower
> saving Venice

As you were listing various ideas, several possible limited topics may have come into your mind — many of them revolving around the idea that Venice is a dying city.

---

* Much of the material for the outlines on the pages which follow can be found in George Weller, "Venice's Fight for Survival" in *The World Book: Year Book 1971* (Chicago: Field Enterprises Educational Corporation, 1971), pp. 143–160.

▶ The Cathedral of Saint Mark
Flooding of the Cathedral
The Bridge of Sighs
"The Queen of the Adriatic"
Picturesque Venice
A Sinking City
A Polluted City
Venice Today
Venice in the 1400s
Can Venice Be Saved?

The topic that interests you most, that has considerable source material, and that you feel will interest your reader is "Dying Venice." You express your purpose in the form of a thesis sentence: *Venice is slowly sinking into the sea.* Your test now is to give order to the information that you have already accumulated and to the additional material that you will gather now about the limited topic. To do this step effectively, you must prepare an outline.

## Prepare an Outline

Outlining is a valuable aid in organizing thought. It gives you a tentative plan of development that is flexible because it can be changed or modified as your thinking about the paper proceeds. Three kinds of outlines are recommended in this book: the *informal outline*, the *topic outline*, and the *sentence outline*.

### Informal Outline

To prepare an informal outline, you simply rearrange the items that you jotted down in gathering material into a logical system of grouping, eliminating any irrelevant information. Suppose, for example, you are the student intrigued with Venice. As you make a mental inventory of the knowledge about the city, you become aware of certain obvious relationships — in other words, bits of information are related to other bits of information because they are about the same thing. Thus, the nature of the thinking process leads to a logical grouping of related ideas. Some ideas are vague and general in nature; they need further development to be meaningful. These ideas become major headings in the topic and sentence outlines. Other materials, consisting of facts, details, and specifics, are meaningful because they explain and support the general ideas (major headings). This kind of information becomes minor headings in the topic and sentence outlines. Since you have decided to develop the limited thesis "Venice is sinking slowly into the sea," you begin to gather material now on this limited topic. Take what is pertinent from the general listing and write down these ideas, adding to them as you research the thesis further. Your listing might look something like the following:

▶ **Thesis Statement:** Venice is sinking slowly into the sea.

*unique structure by early builders*
Venice built on piles and posts in a lagoon
hundreds of islands of clay and white sand
227 canals — 28 miles of them
floating city on six cushions replenished by fresh water of two rivers
Brenta and Piave rivers
S-shaped Grand Canal
buildings alongside canals on cushions
city in sheltered lagoon in Adriatic
islands connected by 400 bridges

*death sentence for city in mid-1500s*
city a great trading center
heart of a great empire extending to Crete
rich banking city
discovery of new sea route to India
vast merchant fleet
powerful ships of war
need for a good harbor
loss of empire
diversion of Brenta and Piave rivers
perfect harbor
destruction of natural cushions
city on piles and posts
beginning of the end

*a sinking city*
Byron in 1818
flooded then once every three or four years
motorboats
petroleum channel
UNESCO report of sinking 8 inches every twenty years
condemned buildings
frequent floods
in seventy years partly under water
alarm depth of 39 inches above high water
in 2061 completely under water depth of 39 inches

In rearranging the items in the previous list, you find that three separate divisions of related thought emerge (these major headings were indicated by italics in the list). Underneath these major headings (which would be topic sentences for a paragraph or a paragraph unit), you now begin to group the details and specifics logically — the particulars that support and explain the generalization. Eliminate any information that does not relate to the major headings. Fill in any gaps in information by researching the topic further. Compare the *informal outline* below with the previous list of items of information. Observe the tighter organizational structure because of the elimination of unrelated ideas, the addition of new material, and the rearranging and combining of related items.

▶ **Thesis Statement:** Venice is sinking slowly into the sea.

*unique structure by early builders*
city in a sheltered lagoon
rests on about 120 islands of clay and white sand
Venice built on piles and posts sunk deep into the mud
floats on six cushions — three of fresh water and three of clay
cushions replenished by fresh water of Brenta and Piave rivers

*death sentence for city in mid-1500s*
city a great trading center
vast merchant fleet defended by many warships
need for a good harbor
rivers filling lagoon with silt
diversion of Brenta River southward
diversion of Piave River northward
a siltless lagoon
destruction of the cushions
beginning of the sinking

*a sinking city*
visit of Byron in 1818
in 1818 city flooded once every three or four years
UNESCO report of city sinking 8 inches every twenty years
many buildings under water up to 3 inches
in seventy years city partly under water
alarm depth of 39 inches above high water
in 2061 city completely covered to alarm depth of 39 inches
end of Venice for all practical purposes

## Topic Outline

For many writers the informal outline is sufficient; however, the beginning writer is advised to use both the topic outline and the sentence outline. The advantage of the sentence outline over the topic outline is that the ideas are expressed in complete sentences; thus, the transition to the written paper is easier. However, for many written assignments, expressing the ideas simply with a word or group of words (a topic) is sufficient. Both outlines follow the same structural pattern. Each major heading is numbered with Roman numerals: I, II, III, and so forth. The subheads are capital letters: A, B, C, . . . . Additional subdividing requires arabic numerals: 1, 2, 3, . . . ; then small letters: a, b, c, . . . . If further subdividing is necessary, follow with arabic numerals in parentheses (1), (2), (3), and small letters in parentheses: (a), (b), (c). Periods are used after the figures and letters except for those in parentheses. The headings in any one group are equally important. In longer papers, one might include an *introduction* and a *conclusion.* No single heading should stand alone; that is, a major heading "I" requires a major heading "II," a minor heading "A" requires a minor heading "B," and so forth.

A topic outline for your paper on "Dying Venice" might look something like the one that follows.

▶ **Thesis Statement:** Venice is sinking slowly into the sea.

    I.  Unique structure

        A.  A sheltered lagoon

        B.  120 islands

            1.  City on piles and posts in mud

            2.  Floats on six cushions
               a.  Three of fresh water
               b.  Three of clay

        C.  Cushions replenished by water of Brenta and Piave rivers

    II.  Death sentence for city in mid-1500s

        A.  Great trading center

            1.  Vast merchant fleet defended by many warships

            2.  Necessity of a good harbor

        B.  Lagoon filling with silt

    C. Improving the harbor

        1. Diverting Brenta southward
        2. Diverting Piavc northward

    D. Elimination of fresh water supply to cushion

        1. Destruction of cushion
        2. Begins sinking of city

III. A sinking city

    A. Byron's visit in 1818

        1. City flooded once every three or four years
        2. Byron's vision of a submerged city

    B. UNESCO report

    C. City today

        1. Frequent floods
        2. Alarm depth

    D. City in seventy years

    E. City in the year 2061

        1. Covered to alarm depth
        2. End of city for all practical purposes

## Sentence Outline

The sentence outline expresses clearly the idea hinted by the topic. Thus, it enables the writer to evaluate more fully the effectiveness of his plan of development. What you are looking for in evaluating your outline is relationships. Do the major headings explain and support the thesis statement? Do the subheadings explain and support the major headings? If not, should they be eliminated or restated? A good outline, therefore, should indicate a logical progression of your flowing thought. The outline offers you an opportunity to check your material, to evaluate your projected plan of development, and to establish logical relationships of the parts of the paper to each other and to the thesis. Any errors can be corrected before you actually begin to write the paper. Study the sentence outline that follows. Observe how the sentence outline explains better than a topic outline exactly what the writer has in mind.

▶ DYING VENICE

**Thesis Statement:** Venice is sinking slowly into the sea.

I. Secret of Venice lies in its unique structure by early builders.

    A. Venice consists of 120 islands in a sheltered lagoon in the Adriatic Sea.

        1. The city rests on piles and posts driven deep into the mud.

        2. It floats on six horizontal submarine cushions.
           a. Three of these cushions are of fresh water.
           b. The other three are of clay.

    B. These cushions were constantly replenished by fresh water from the Brenta and Piave rivers.

II. A decision to provide a siltless lagoon for Venetian shipping in the mid-1500s was a death sentence for the city.

    A. In the mid-1500s Venice was the greatest trading center in the world.

        1. It had a vast merchant fleet defended by many warships.

        2. A good harbor was necessary for this large commercial fleet and its warships.

    B. The lagoon was filling with silt brought down by the two rivers.

    C. Venetian leaders decide to improve the harbor.

        1. They divert the Brenta southward.

        2. They divert the Piave northward.

    D. This action takes the natural water supply away from the cushion.

        1. The underwater cushion can no longer support the enormous weight of the city.

        2. Venice begins to sink gradually into the sea.

III. Venice is a sinking city.

    A. Lord Byron visits the city in 1818.

        1. At that time its streets were flooded once every three or four years.

        2. Byron saw Venice as a submerged city in the future.

    B. United Nations Educational, Scientific, and Cultural Organization (UNESCO) reports that Venice will have sunk 8 inches into the sea in twenty years.

    C. Today's alarm depth is any flood that rises 39 inches above high tide.

    D. It has been flooded often — in the years 1966, 1967, 1968, and 1969.

    E. In seventy years the streets, piazzas, buildings, homes, and churches may be under water.

    F. By the year 2061 the situation could become very serious.

        1. Venice could be completely covered to the alarm depth.

        2. If this happened, the city would be for all practical purposes unhabitable.

## Prepare a First Draft

With your outline and notes alongside, you can begin to write your paper. If you have a well-planned outline, you should find this task much easier than in your previous writing experiences. Remember that you have done the really important processes in your prewriting. At this time, you are interested in getting your thoughts onto paper as rapidly as possible. Begin, therefore, at a place in the paper, whether it be in the middle or with the introductory sentences, that will enable you to get moving. Do not be afraid to modify your outline plan if your flowing thought requires changes. Write as carefully as you can, but do not concentrate on correctness in mechanics, spelling, and punctuation. You can attack these kinds of problems in the revision. Leave space between the lines and at the margins for later revisions and additions. When you have finished this process, set the paper aside for a day or two.

## Revise the Paper

When you return to the paper read it aloud. Make corrections or additions between the lines or in the margins in red ink. In revising the paper, use the following suggestions as a guide.

*Title*
1. Is the title interesting?
2. Does the title clue the reader to what the paper is about?

*Introduction*
1. Does the paper require a formal introduction?
2. If the paper does not require a formal introduction, have you indicated clearly what is the limited topic — statement of thesis or statement of purpose?
3. Does the introduction include background material, definitions of terms, and other facts and details if that kind of information is necessary for the reader's better understanding of what is to follow?
4. Does the introduction lead the reader smoothly into the body of the paper?

*Thesis*
1. Does it adequately limit the subject?
2. Does the thesis express clearly the central thought (dominant idea) in your mind?
3. Does the thesis limit the development to one single purpose?

*Middle or Body*
1. Does each paragraph or paragraph unit relate to and develop a particular phase of your developing thought in relation to the thesis or statement of purpose?
2. Is each paragraph or paragraph unit effectively organized according to the requirements of a good paragraph: unity, order, completeness, and coherence?

*Conclusion*
1. Does the paper require a formal conclusion?
2. Have you said everything that needs to be said?
3. Is the conclusion final?

*Check for Correctness*
1. Are your sentences well written?
2. Are there any errors in spelling, mechanics, or punctuation?
3. Are the style and tone consistent with the subject?

## Write the Final Copy

After you have finished the revised copy, write or type the final paper according to the instructions given to you by your instructor. The requirements by most instructors are similar to the following:

1. Write legibly in blue or black ink on lined paper (8½ by 11 inches).
2. Write on one side only.
3. Center the title on the top line of the first page; leave a space between the title and the first line of the text.
4. Do not enclose the title in quotation marks unless it is quoted material.
5. Leave margins — 2 inches at the left and 1¼ inches at the top, right, and bottom. Indicate paragraph indentations by leaving ½ inch.
6. Number the pages after the first page in the upper right-hand corner in arabic numerals: 1, 2, 3, 4, . . . .
7. Hand the paper in flat with a title page on which you include your name, title of the paper, and the date.

For typewritten papers:

1. Type double spaced on unlined paper (8½ by 11 inches).
2. Type on one side of page only.
3. Center the title about 2½ inches from the top of the first page and leave about 1½ inches between it and the first line of the text.
4. Do not enclose the title in quotation marks unless it is quoted material.
5. Leave margins — 2 inches at the left and 1½ inches at the top, right, and bottom. Indent five spaces to indicate a new paragraph.
6. Number the pages after the first page in the upper right-hand corner in arabic numerals: 1, 2, 3, 4, . . . .
7. Hand in the paper flat with a title page that includes your name, title of the paper, and the date.

Instructors like to receive a clean final copy; however, they prefer to receive a paper free of errors. In checking your final copy, you may discover minor errors involving spelling, mechanics, and punctuation. If you can correct errors without spoiling the appearance of the paper, make the necessary changes. If the changes mean major revisions or if the changes will spoil the appearance of the paper, rewrite or retype the page. In making minor corrections, follow these suggestions:

1. Erase cleanly and make corrections in ink as neatly as possible.
2. If you are changing a word, draw a straight line through it and write the correct form directly above.

> received
> ▶ Venice ~~recivd~~ a supply of fresh water from two rivers.

3. If you omitted a word, place a caret (∧) at the place below the line where the omission occurred.

> fresh
> ▶ Venice received a supply of ∧ water from two rivers.

4. If you wish to cancel a paragraph indentation, write the sign "No ¶" in the left margin.
5. If you wish to indicate paragraph indentation, write the sign "¶" in the left margin.
6. If you observed an error in a quotation, do not correct the error. Place *sic (thus it is)* in brackets after the mistake.

> ▶ "Catullus, with a few friends, entered the service of Memmius Gemelus [*sic*] who was the proconsul of Bithynia."

# 4 Moving Through Time — Narration

*Narration* tells a story. Narration may be an account of an incident or a sequence of incidents that joined together make up a complete, interesting, and significant action. Narration answers the question "What happened?" It is the purpose of the writer that frequently distinguishes narration from the other forms of discourse, for narration is seldom a pure form. It usually combines with *description*. Narration is also used to inform and explain *(exposition)*.

Narration has been divided into different types. A very common division is into *fictional* narration and *factual* narration. Fictional narration (fiction) tells a story about people and incidents that are wholly or partially imaginary. Factual narration (nonfiction) tells a story about real people and actual happenings.

Within these two major divisions are many kinds of narration. Narration may be a simple anecdote, a short fable, an allegory, or a fairy tale. It recounts a personal experience, an autobiography, or a biography. It includes a news story, a factual history, or a travel account. It could also be a short story or a novel.

This book considers three types of narration: the *simple narrative,* the *personal experience,* and the *narration with a plot.*

## The Simple Narrative

The *simple narrative* is a factual account of a real event or events usually developed according to the time order of the happenings. It is a kind of informal essay, since the story has the expository purpose of informing and explaining rather than being an end in itself. It is like the *narration with a plot* story that we take up later in this chapter. It is concerned with action. It has a beginning, a middle, and an end. It involves people in some kind of a struggle. But the simple narrative differs from the narration with a plot in that the writer of the simple narrative cannot make things happen; he must report as accurately as possible what happened. He can dramatize the action, but he cannot control the outcome. The writer of the narration with a plot can make things happen; he can create an initial situation, complicate the struggle between opposing forces, bring the struggle to the kind of climax he wishes, and end his story with a resolution he chooses. He can do these things because the narration with a plot is fictional; the simple narrative is factual.

### VOCABULARY PREVIEW

| | | | |
|---|---|---|---|
| utilize | grapples | novices | converging |
| articulating | intruder | impact | turbulence |
| manual | stupor | billowed | precarious |
| pantomime | foils | buffeted | allopathic |
| transfixed | retractable | bleak | degraded |

## The Narrative Incident

The two kinds of simple narrative discussed in this book are the *narrative incident* and the *anecdote.* In structuring the *narrative incident* (an account of a fire, a battle, a discovery, a natural occurrence, a robbery, and so on), a writer with the purpose of informing and explaining will organize his factual account of what happened in time order. He may give a vividness to the events, but he must tell a true story — a record of an actual event or events. In the model simple narrative incident that follows, the writer presents in chronological order the various settlements along the Colorado River.

▶ The Colorado River attracted its first inhabitants nearly 4,000 years ago, but they were primitive hunters and food-gatherers, not skilled enough to utilize° the lifegiving power of the river.

Then the Spanish came.

Hernando de Alarcon, who captained a boat from the river's mouth at the Sea of Cortez to a point nearly 100 miles north, envisioned a possible shipping trade, but since he was actually looking for gold and couldn't find any, he gave up on any future projects. But he liked the river and named it *El Rio de Buena Guia*, the River of Good Guidance. Later in that year of 1540 a group led by Melchoir Diaz renamed it *Rio del Tisori*, River of the Firebrand. In 1604, it got another name when an expedition led by Juan de Onate labelled it *Rio de Buena Esperanza*, River of Good Hope.

Finally, in 1701, Fray Eusebio Francisco Kino explored and drew extensive maps of the region and called the river which sliced through it "Colorado."

The Spanish abandoned the river because there was no gold there, and for the next 200 years it pursued the course it had always pursued.

But at the turn of the Twentieth Century, the river was invaded by a new breed, and it was tougher and more determined. They would tame the Colorado.

They were ranchers, farmers, and land developers who looked upon the Colorado as a natural resource whose lifegiving waters could make the desert flourish. They also sought treasure, but theirs was land, not gold.

Sam Lowe
"The American Nile"

In the next model of narrative incident, the writer, a former slave, organizes events in time order to support the conclusion hinted in the last paragraph of the paragraph unit: religion played no role in the way a slave was treated.

▶ My master had a deeply pious and exemplary slave, an elderly man, who one day had a misunderstanding with the overseer, when the latter attempted to flog him. He fled to the woods; it was noon; at evening he came home orderly. The next morning, my master, taking one of his sons with him, a rope and cowhide in his hand, led the poor old man away into the stable, tied him up, and ordered the son to lay on thirty-nine lashes, which he did, making the keen end of the cowhide lap around and strike him in the tenderest part of his side, till the blood sped out, as if a lance had been used.

While my master's son was thus engaged, the sufferer's little daughter, a child six years of age, stood at the door, weeping in agony for the fate of her father. I heard the old man articulating° in a low tone of voice; I listened at the intervals between the stripes, and lo! he was praying!

When the last lash was laid on, he was let down; and leaving him to put on his clothes, they passed out of the door, and drove the man's weeping child away! I was mending a hinge to one of the barn doors; I saw and heard what I have stated. Six months after, this same man's eldest daughter, a girl fifteen years old, was sold to slave traders, where he never saw her more.

This poor slave and his wife were both Methodists; so was the wife of the young master who flogged him. My old master was an Episcopalian.

James W. C. Pennington
"The Fugitive Blacksmith"

Complete the following two exercises to review the discussion of the simple narrative.

## EXERCISE 1   Simple Narrative

---

Read the model narrative excerpt below. Answer the questions that follow. Answers are at the end of the chapter.

▶ Something very important has happened. Helen has taken the second step in her education. She has learned that *everything has a name, and that the manual° alphabet is the key to everything she wants to know.*

In a previous letter I think I wrote you that "mug" and "milk" had given Helen more trouble than all the rest. She confused the nouns with the verb "drink." She didn't know the word for "drink," but went through the pantomime° of drinking whenever she spelled "mug" or "milk." This morning, while she was washing, she wanted to know the name for "water." When she wants to know the name of anything, she points to it and pats my hand. I spelled "w-a-t-e-r" and thought no more about it until after breakfast. Then it occurred to me that with the help of this new word I might succeed in straightening out the "mug-milk" difficulty. We went out to the pump-house, and I made Helen hold her mug under the spout while I pumped. As the cold water gushed forth, filling the mug, I spelled "w-a-t-e-r" in Helen's free hand. The word coming so close upon the sensation of cold water rushing over her hand seemed to startle her. She dropped the mug and stood as one transfixed.° A new light came into her face. She spelled "water" several times. Then she dropped on the ground and asked for its name and pointed to the pump and the trellis, and suddenly turning round she asked for my name. I spelled "Teacher." Just then the nurse brought Helen's little sister into the pump-house, and Helen spelled "baby" and pointed to the nurse. All the way back to the house she was highly excited, and learned the name of every object she touched, so that in a few hours she had added thirty new words to her vocabulary. Here are some of them: *Door, open, shut, give, go, come,* and a great many more.*

Anne Sullivan<br>"Letter, April 5, 1887"

---

* Helen Adams Keller was a remarkable person who conquered the handicap of blindness. A serious illness destroyed her sight before she was two years old. With the help of her teacher and companion Anne Sullivan, Helen Keller achieved success and fame to become one of the most famous and admired women of her time.

1. In what position in the narrative does Anne Sullivan state the expository purpose?

2. What is the story about?

3. How does the action conclude?

4. Is the struggle or action of this narrative the kind that one usually associates with the dictionary meanings of those words? Explain.

5. What characteristics of this story help one to classify it as a simple narrative?

## EXERCISE 2    Simple Narrative

Read the model narrative selection below. Answer the questions that follow.

▶ At about the same hour and minute of the clock that the President is shot in Ford's Theatre a giant of a young man rides on a big one-eyed bay horse to the door of the Seward house on Lafayette Square, gets off his horse, rings the doorbell, says he is a messenger from the attending physician and has a package of medicine that must be personally delivered to the sickroom of the Secretary of State. The servant at the door tries to stop the young man, who enters and goes up the stairs, suddenly to turn in a furious rush on Fred Seward, beating him on the head with the pistol, tearing the scalp, fracturing the skull, and battering the pistol to pieces.

Young Seward grapples° with the intruder,° and in their scuffling the two of them come to the Secretary's room and fall together through the door. There Fred Seward fades out and for days knows nothing, in a stupor° of unconsciousness. The Secretary's daughter and a soldier-nurse, Sergeant George T. Robinson, spring from their chairs. The murder-bent young giant knocks them right and left, gives Robinson a knife thrust, then rushes to the bed where the Secretary of State has lain nearly two weeks with a steel frame about the head and face. He stabs over and again at the throat of the sick man, delivers three ugly gashes in the cheek and neck. The steel frame foils a death gash. And the quick wit or odd luck of the victim still further foils° him; the Secretary of State rolls off between the bed and the wall.

Now the stranger in the house hurls himself down the stairs, slashes an attendant on the way, is out the front door unhurt, leaps into saddle, and rides out Vermont Avenue toward an eastern suburb. Behind him he has left a quiet home transferred into a battlefield hospital, five persons bleeding from ghastly wounds, failing of death for any of them. Behind him too he has left a bloodstained knife, the battered pistol, and his slouch hat.

Carl Sandburg<br>
Abraham Lincoln: The Prairie Years and the War Years

1. At what point in time does Sandburg begin this factual narration?

2. Where does the action take place?

3. What is the struggle that holds our attention in the narration?

4. How does the writer give order to the story?

5. Why does the writer use the present tense?

6. Is this account a simple journalistic report of actual events? Explain your answer.

Read the factual narrative by Lawrence Elliott, then answer the questions that follow.

▶ TRAPPED IN MID-AIR

**Lawrence Elliott**

At 2:06 P.M. last September 28, a Sunday, a red-and-white Pilatus-Turbo-Porter took off from the small airfield at Yverdon in western Switzerland and climbed into a clearing sky. Aboard were seven first-time parachutists. Each had paid $90 for three hours of instruction and the privilege of stepping out of a plane 2000 feet above the ground.

The Pilatus, equipped with retractable° skis, was in the charge of jumpmaster Jean-Charles Portier, a seasoned instructor who had already taken two planeloads of novices° up that day. "It's safer than skiing," Portier told them, "and certainly easier. All you have to do is go when you're told and 'give' a little when you land." In fact, the local parachute club had supervised some 1500 jumps at Yverdon from the start of the year with only a single casualty, a jumper who stiffened at the moment of impact° and broke a leg.

Most of the novices sat on a bench in the rear of the Pilatus but two were on the floor facing the door. Charles-André Roux was the second of these. He was a cabinetmaker's apprentice, an outgoing, adventuresome young man, and the jump was a 20th-birthday present from his two sisters.

There was hardly any talking as the plane climbed. Once someone called out, "Hey, do I get my money back if this thing doesn't open?" Portier smiled patiently; he had heard the little joke often. At 2000 feet, he slid the door back and the wind's rush filled the plane.

The first jumper got ready to go. His parachute release was already hooked to a long strap permanently fixed to the metal bench leg. This would automatically open the chute, but not until the jumper was well below the plane. Following instructions, the novice slid forward until his legs dangled outside the open doorway. A tap on the shoulder, and he pushed himself off and slid into space. Three seconds later his chute billowed° up. Already far behind the plane, he floated gently toward the earth. Then it was Roux's turn. At Portier's signal, he pushed off.

No one knows why but Roux's parachute came swirling out of its pack too soon. As it whipped straight back in the slipstream, it was caught and held fast by the tail ski. The stunned jumper, buffeted° and deafened by the wind, dangled helplessly at the end of the shroud lines 40 feet away. With a shock like an explosion inside his chest, he knew that he was probably going to die.

**Thumbs Up.** The wind spun him around so he faced backward. The harness straps were digging into his thighs. He tried to jerk the chute clear of the ski, but it didn't work. Determinedly, he pulled the twisted shroud lines around until he was facing the plane again.

Portier, in the plane's open doorway, thrust out his right fist, thumb up. "Are you all right?" he was asking.

Roux stuck up his own thumb. But then he pointed to the emergency chute on his chest and pantomimed pulling the release.

"No! No!" Portier yelled, wagging his forefinger in emphatic warning. The braking action of an open parachute could yank the plane out of control and send it diving to the ground. He pumped both hands, palms out, to say, "Stay calm! We'll find a way out!"

Roux understood. Gulping for breath, pounded by the wind, he let himself be turned around again.

Portier closed the door to reduce drag on the laboring airplane and went forward to talk with pilot Daniel Nebel. Nebel realized what had happened from the abrupt deceleration of the plane. Now he made several sharp turns in an effort to shake the trapped jumper loose — at the same time climbing to give him more time to activate his emergency chute if he fell free.

Portier knelt next to the pilot's seat and the two men went over the obvious ideas. Roux could not be reached from the plane, not even by someone lowered on the parachute release strap. If they tried to land, they would kill him. How much fuel did they have left? "With this drag, less than two hours."

• • •

Back on the ground, Pierre Jomini, a parachute club member, heard an unusual sound overhead — the flap of fabric caught in the wind. Looking up, he saw the Pilatus trailing a snarled parachute and jumper. Overcoming his amazement, Jomini ran to the airfield's control room to see what he could do to help. He called the plane on the radio. Portier reported that Roux seemed uninjured and calm, but the outlook was bleak.°

Suddenly it occurred to the jumpmaster and pilot that while the dangling parachutist couldn't be reached from the plane, maybe someone lowered from a helicopter could cut his tangled shroud lines, allowing him to fall free and release his emergency chute. Portier told Jomini to call for a helicopter with a winch.

***Calling 47 47 47.*** Jomini came back on the radio. The Swiss Air Rescue operations center in Zurich had been contacted. Portier began fleshing out the plan. Suppose someone *could* reach Roux: the jumper might be unconscious by then and have to be lifted to the helicopter by the man on the end of the rescue line. The question was: who would that man be?

"Listen," said Jomini, "I might as well try it myself." He went to get his parachute and helmet, tied a razor-edged knife to his harness, and went back to the control room to wait.

The call to the Air Rescue operations center in Zurich — number 47 47 47 — was logged in at 2:29 P.M. Adolf Rüfenacht was contacted: known for some spectacular mountain rescues, he was considered the best winch operator in the Air Rescue service. Within ten minutes, he was in a helicopter bound for Yverdon.

Experienced helicopter pilot Andreas Haefele, on rescue duty at a field south of Bern, was reached at 2:40. By 2:54 his red Alouette III helicopter was airborne.

By now the Pilatus had been in the air nearly an hour, circling the airfield at 3300 feet and an airspeed of 47 miles an hour, about as slow as it could safely fly. Below, a crowd was converging,° the curious as well as emergency ambulance, fire and police crews.

Roux could see it all. He was cold: his legs felt heavy, dead. Periodically he made himself turn forward in case Portier had something to tell him. There were continuing signals of encouragement, but nothing more.

Then the jumpmaster was in the doorway again, whirling an upraised forefinger over his head. Roux understood: a helicopter was coming. The idea that someone might be lowered from it in mid-air crossed his mind, but he dismissed it as outlandish. All the same he flashed back another thumbs-up sign. Portier closed the door, convinced Roux had the mettle for the rescue attempt: a lesser man might already have doomed them all by releasing the emergency chute in a panic.

•  •  •

Haefele landed his helicopter at the airfield at 3:19. Minutes later, Rüfenacht arrived and the two had a hasty conference with Jomini. The Pilatus was down to perhaps 30 minutes of fuel, Jomini told them, then starkly laid out their task. They would have to lower him on a winch, in the wake of the Pilatus slipstream, and position him in mid-air close enough to reach the snared jumper. He would decide then whether to cut Roux loose or try lifting him up into the helicopter.

*"Lower! Lower!"*     At 3:32 the three clambered into the Alouette and took off. By this time Roux's chest was aching; but physical discomfort still had not dampened his hopes. Then he heard a far-off thunder. It came closer and the big red Alouette, suddenly appearing out of the mist overhead, descended toward them.

Roux's heart surged. He waved at the pilot and began slamming his feet together and tugging on the harness straps, trying to restore circulation to his legs. He wanted to be ready for whatever the rescuers might try.

Jomini was already hooked onto the winch cable, waiting for operator Rüfenacht's signal. From now on everything would depend on the closest co-ordination of the two aircraft. Rüfenacht took over the radio; watching the jumper and the plane through an open doorway, he would transmit precise positioning instructions to his pilot, who could see nothing below him but a red-and-white wingtip to the right.

They were all desperately conscious of time. But the first approach left them too high — the more winch line Rüfenacht had to pay out, the less control he would have over Jomini at the end of it. "Lower," he said crisply into his microphone. "Lower, lower. . . ." When the helicopter was within 50 feet of the plane, he snapped, "Hold!"

On signal, Jomini slipped over the side. Rüfenacht pushed the winch's drop button and Jomini descended smoothly, passing close behind the tail of the plane. At this level he came into the full turbulence° of the slipstream and, turning on the winch hook, swung wildly out of control.

"Lower!" commanded Rüfenacht, and the Alouette sank even closer to the plane, lowering Jomini beneath the worst of the propeller wash. Now the two aircraft were flying together as though directed by a single hand — every rise and fall, in the shifting air currents, instantly duplicated.

*Count of Three.*     Jomini felt his feet brush Roux's shoulders. He held up a hand, signaling the winch operator to halt his descent. Then he pushed himself back from the shroud lines to look down at Roux — who was staring right back at him. Nothing needed to be said: when the man on the winch hook held up the knife, Roux nodded that he understood what was about to happen. Jomini then pointed to the emergency chute. Roux nodded again — he knew he had to allow three seconds before pulling the release, in order to clear the aircraft. Everything had now been covered.

Jomini took all 24 shroud lines into his left hand and began to cut. Roux watched every move. Then, eyes widening, he suddenly dropped away. Jomini began to count off three seconds in his head: *one thousand one, one thousand two, one thousand three.* Then *pop,* on cue, the white canopy blossomed out and began sailing slowly earthward.

Portier called, "His chute is open!" and cheers rang out. The pilot knew Roux was free when he felt the plane lift and shudder slightly. He turned, made straight for the field, and landed with only 15 minutes of fuel in reserve.

Roux made a perfect landing in a potato field about three miles from the airfield — 90 minutes after he had first jumped from the Pilatus. The helicopter followed him down and he climbed aboard, carrying the folds of his parachute; Rüfenacht, grinning broadly, pumped his hand.

After brief hospital treatment for cold and shock, Roux called home. His father answered: "Say, I just heard something on the radio about a spectacular rescue of a parachutist. Did you see any of it?"

"Listen, Dad," said Charles-André Roux, "you'd better sit down. I have something to tell you."

QUESTIONS ON    **Trapped in Mid-Air**

1. What information does the writer present for reader understanding in the introductory paragraphs?

2. In the middle paragraphs, what is the struggle that the principal characters are involved in?

3. Mention a few incidents that develop tension and suspense.

4. How is the struggle resolved?

5. How does the writer give order to the series of events that make up the story?

6. The *Reader's Digest* lists this story as a "Drama in Real Life." Write a brief paragraph using the characteristics of the simple narrative to support this view.

## Suggested Written Assignments

1. Write an account of a happening on campus, in your neighborhood, or at some other place as if it were a news story for a local newspaper.
2. Write a simple narration about a fire, an accident, a riot, a robbery, or some other unusual happening that you witnessed.

## The Anecdote

The *anecdote* is usually a short account of an interesting — frequently an amusing — biographical incident. It is used often in a speech or a piece of writing as part of the introductory material to gain reader interest and lead him smoothly into the main discussion. In writing the anecdote, the writer presents quickly and briefly the situation and complication, following immediately with the resolution — often a kind of surprise ending that provides the humor. The model anecdote that follows illustrates this kind of structure.

▶ I was always told that I was a sickly and precarious° and tiresome and uncertain child, and lived mainly on allopathic° medicines during the first seven years of my life. I asked my mother about this, in her old age — she was in her eighty-eighth year — and said:
"I suppose that during all that time you were uneasy about me?"
"Yes, the whole time."
"Afraid I wouldn't live?"
After a reflective pause — ostensibly to think out the facts — "No — afraid you would."

*Mark Twain's Autobiography*

The next model anecdote illustrates the use of an incident to support a belief that the writer holds, as well as for humorous effect.

▶ The country schoolhouse was three miles from my uncle's farm. It stood in a clearing in the woods and would hold about twenty-five boys and girls. We attended the school with more or less regularity once or twice a week, in summer, walking to it in the cool of the morning by the forest paths, and back in the gloaming at the end of the day. All the pupils brought their dinners in baskets — corn dodger, buttermilk, and other good things — and sat in the shade of the trees at noon and ate them. It is the part of my education which I look back upon with the most satisfaction. My first visit to the school was when I was seven. A strapping girl of fifteen, in the customary sunbonnet and calico dress, asked me if I "used tobacco" — meaning did I chew it. I said no. It roused her scorn. She reported me to all the crowd, and said:

"Here is a boy seven years old who can't chew tobacco."

By the looks and comments which this produced I realized that I was a degraded° object, and was cruelly ashamed of myself. I determined to reform. But I only made myself sick; I was not able to learn to chew tobacco. I learned to smoke fairly well, but that did not conciliate anybody and I remained a poor thing, and characterless. I longed to be respected, but I never was able to rise. Children have but little charity for one another's defects.

*Mark Twain's Autobiography*

---

### VOCABULARY TEST FIVE

Four words are lined up below each of twenty words taken from the essays and paragraphs. Select the one that matches best and write its letter in the blank to the right. Answers are at the end of the chapter.

1. utilize                                   _____
   (a) make use of    (b) understanding    (c) control    (d) dam

2. articulating                           _____
   (a) moaning    (b) complaining    (c) speaking clearly
   (d) begging

3. manual                                _____
   (a) sign    (b) by hand    (c) naming    (d) braille

4. pantomime                          _____
   (a) custom    (b) acting through gestures    (c) ritual
   (d) labor

5. transfixed                          _____
   (a) surprised    (b) amazed, awed    (c) deaf    (d) confused

6. grapples                             _____
   (a) entreats    (b) argues    (c) wrestles    (d) delays

7. intruder    _____
   (a) unwelcome visitor    (b) opponent    (c) murderer    (d) spy

8. stupor    _____
   (a) hospital room    (b) state of emergency
   (c) situation of crisis    (d) state of suspended sensibility

9. foils    _____
   (a) shields    (b) ensures    (c) prevents, frustrates
   (d) delays

10. retractable    _____
    (a) capable of being drawn in    (b) parallel    (c) strong
    (d) remarkable

11. novices    _____
    (a) victims    (b) beginners    (c) students    (d) veterans

12. impact    _____
    (a) exposure    (b) landing    (c) danger
    (d) forceful contact

13. billowed    _____
    (a) surged    (b) blew    (c) moved    (d) tangled

14. buffeted    _____
    (a) dazed    (b) struck repeatedly    (c) blown
    (d) twisted

15. bleak    _____
    (a) dangerous    (b) hopeful    (c) depressing    (d) critical

16. converging    _____
    (a) cheering    (b) tending to meet    (c) moving apart
    (d) rushing madly

17. turbulence    _____
    (a) impact    (b) position    (c) knowledge
    (d) violent disorder or disturbance

18. precarious    _____
    (a) irritable    (b) stubborn    (c) hazardous, dangerous
    (d) precious

19. allopathic    _____
    (a) related to a method of healing a disease    (b) foreign
    (c) questionable    (d) drug free

20. degraded    _____
    (a) precious    (b) downgraded, lower in dignity    (c) lost
    (d) humiliated

## Suggested Written Assignments

1. Write a humorous anecdote that might serve as an introduction to a longer piece of writing.
2. Write an anecdote that supports a belief you feel strongly enough about to communicate its significance to others.

## The Personal Experience

The personal experience paper tells "what happened" to you. It recounts a happening or a series of related happenings that a reader can relive vicariously with you. Your source for this kind of paper is your own experiences. But, to write a personal experience paper that will hold reader interest and be worthwhile reading, you must do more than ramble on and on from one incident to another in time sequence as does the writer of the following brief experience.

▶ MY TRIP TO LONDON

We left Los Angeles International Airport on Sunday evening. Five hours later, we arrived at Buffalo, New York. We cleared customs two hours later. We departed on a charter plane that wasn't too expensive. When we arrived in London, it was raining. We took a bus to London traveling over a historic route. I enjoyed visiting the many historic sites in and around the city. We stayed in a fairly inexpensive hotel near the railroad station. I visited many museums, churches, and art galleries. There were famous men and women buried beneath the floors of some of the churches. We saw several excellent plays and visited some night clubs and pubs where we had a lot of fun. I found London a very exciting place to visit.

This model personal experience illustrates what you should not do in writing narration. First, it is dull reading because it goes nowhere; the writer probably has no reason in mind for telling the story other than completing a written assignment on narration. The reader's reaction is sure to be, "So what! You went to London." Many personal experience papers by high school students and college students in a beginning writing course sound very much like this account of a trip to London. Papers with titles like, "My Trip," "A Summer Vacation," "My First Date," "The Big Game," "My Job," and "Visiting the Big City" end up often as a mere listing of things that happened to the writer, arranged in time sequence.

If you are going to write effective narration — especially the personal experience paper — you must observe life, interpret what happened to you, and convey that meaning to the reader so he can relive with you some kind of meaningful experience. Before you begin to write about a personal experience, ask yourself the question "What did the experience mean to me?" In other words, did you learn something about the place you visited? about the people involved in the experience? about yourself? If the experience was important to you, you will find that your reader may share its meaning. If the experience left you with a deeper understanding — emotional or intellectual — of life, you will find that is worthwhile telling.

If you think about experiences you have had, you will be able to find many reasons for writing the personal experience paper. If you had an exciting experience, you may wish to convey that excitement to your reader by vividly recounting the incident. If you grew up in a ghetto, on a farm, in a foreign country, in a city, by the sea, you might wish to tell your reader what it was like living in such a place. You might wish to explain what it was like growing up without a parent or parents or with parents who never really tried to understand you. You might want to point out some aspect concerning human nature because you are interested in people. An experience taught you something about yourself or other people giving you new insight and better understanding of love, honor, courage, compassion, sacrifice, jealousy, or ambition. You may have learned from an experience how society affects an individual's life. You discovered that it was difficult to find acceptance with certain individuals or groups because of your race, religion, or socioeconomic status. You learned that wearing long hair and a bushy beard made it difficult to compete in the job market.

Write down the meaning of the experience to you or the discovery that you made through the experience in a complete sentence — the central thought or controlling idea around which you can organize the incidents and details that will develop the story. Since the main idea grows out of what happened to you, you may have it already in mind before you begin writing. If you do not have a clear purpose in mind, think about some past experience. Why did some seemingly unimportant happening remain in your mind? "My first date was a humiliating experience" is certainly a better guide to what you will include in your narration than "My First Date," because it focuses on a discovery that you made through that experience. "Camping out is not for an amateur woodsman" will lead to a more unified, meaningful experience than "Camping out." "Visiting the Bowery was a depressing two hours for me" indicates that you have interpreted life and will attempt to convey that meaning to your reader so that he can learn something worthwhile from reading the story. The possibility of significant personal experiences is unlimited because many things have happened to you in your life that are important if you think about them.

Select incidents and details that will explain the meaning of your story. You cannot possibly write down everything that happened to you on your first date or during your visit to New York City. If you did, the narrative would be a disaster — a listing of events without purpose or logical sequence. If your first date was a humiliating experience, details about the car you or your date drove, a description of your girl friend or boy friend, information about the band at the dance you went to, an account of an accident you witnessed on the way home, running out of gas, or a reprimand by your parents for staying out too late are pointless unless each gives meaning to the controlling idea.

Discard, therefore, any incidents and details that do not relate to and contribute something to the emotional or intellectual meaning you are interpreting for the reader. Suppose a young man had by his speech and actions created the impression that he was a very self-confident individual who made few mistakes. Then, when he tells about running out of gas on his first date, he helps to explain his humiliation. A vivid description of his beautiful girl friend might enable the reader to enjoy that beauty vicariously but contributes nothing to the humiliating experience. Thus, unless you can relate material to the controlling idea, you must eliminate it. If this kind of scrutiny of incidents and details leaves you with little to write about, you may be reasonably sure that you had nothing really worthwhile to tell in the beginning.

Finally, use specific details to interpret meaning. Vague generalities and broad statements about your emotional and intellectual reactions to persons, places, and things leave the reader with little or no basis for understanding the experience. "We left Los Angeles International Airport on Sunday evening." Who is "we"? The charter plane wasn't too expensive. How expensive is "not too expensive"? Why was the route to London historic? What churches, museums, art galleries did the writer visit? Who were the famous men and women buried beneath the floors of some churches? Why were the night clubs and pubs fun?

Observe the vague generalities in the sentence that follows. It serves to set the locality of the incidents that follow.

▶ When I was a boy in a small town in mid-America, I had one ambition — to be a steamboatman.

Compare that version with the following rewritten sentence using specific details.

▶ When I was a boy in the small town of Hannibal, Missouri, on the west bank of the Mississippi River, I had one ambition — to be a steamboatman.

As you read the model introductory paragraph of a personal experience by Samuel L. Clemens, observe his use of specific details and his use of examples to make clear the meaning of "transient ambitions." Notice also his statement of the main idea — "That was, to be a steamboatman" — and the repetition of that idea in the final sentence.

▶ When I was a boy, there was but one permanent ambition among my comrades in our village on the west bank of the Mississippi River. That was, to be a steamboatman. We had transient ambitions of other sorts, but they were only transient. When a circus came and went, it left us all burning to become clowns; the first negro minstrel show that ever came to our section left us all suffering to try that kind of life; now and then we had a hope that, if we lived and were good, God would permit us to be pirates. These ambitions faded out, each in its turn, but the ambition to be a steamboatman always remained.

Samuel Langhorne Clemens
*Life on the Mississippi*

## VOCABULARY PREVIEW

| | | |
|---|---|---|
| overwhelming | fugitive | ensuing |
| timidity | profusion | abject |
| confide | admonished | apprehension |
| invariably | contemptible | valiantly |

Read the model personal experience that follows.

▶ Take Thy Breakfast and Get Warm*
**James W. C. Pennington**

I continued my flight on the public road; and a little after the sun rose, I came in sight of a toll gate again. For a moment all the events which followed my passing a toll gate on Wednesday morning came fresh to my recollection, and produced some hesitation; but at all events, said I, I will try again.

On arriving at the gate, I found it attended by an elderly woman, whom I afterwards learned was a widow, and an excellent Christian woman. I asked her if I was in Pennsylvania. On being informed that I was, I asked her if she knew where I could get employ? She said she did not; but advised me to go to W. W., a Quaker, who lived about three miles from her, whom I would find to take an interest in me. She gave me directions which way to take; I thanked her, and bade her good morning, and was very careful to follow her directions.

In about half an hour I stood trembling at the door of W. W. After knocking, the door opened upon a comfortably spread table, the sight of which seemed at once to increase my hunger sevenfold. Not daring to enter, I said I had been sent to him in search of employ. "Well," said he, "come in and take thy breakfast, and get warm, and we will talk about it; thee must be cold without any coat." "*Come in and take thy breakfast, and get warm!*" These words spoken by a stranger, but with such an air of simple sincerity and fatherly kindness, made an overwhelming° impression upon my mind. They made me feel, spite of all my fear and timidity,° that I had, in the providence of God, found a friend and a home. He at once gained my confidence; and I felt that I might confide° to him a fact which I had, as yet, confided to no one.

From that day to this, whenever I discover the least disposition in my heart to disregard the wretched condition of any poor or distressed persons with whom I meet, I call to mind these words — "*Come in and take thy breakfast, and get warm.*" They invariably° remind me of what I was at that time; my condition was as wretched as that of any human being can possibly be, with the exception of the loss of health or reason. I had but four pieces of clothing about my person, having left all the rest in the hands of my captors. I was a starving fugitive,°

___
* Title by the author of the textbook.

without home or friends — a reward offered for my person in the public papers — pursued by cruel manhunters, and no claim upon him to whose door I went. Had he turned me away, I must have perished. Nay, he took me in, and gave me of his food, and shared with me his own garments. Such treatment I had never before received at the hands of any white man.

A few such men in slaveholding America, have stood, and even now stand, like Abrahams and Lots, to stay its forthcoming and well-earned and just judgment.

In this personal experience, the Reverend James W. C. Pennington makes an important discovery from the events that happened to him as he was escaping from slavery in the state of Maryland. He states clearly the controlling thought around which the narrative revolves: "A few such men in slave-holding America, have stood, and even now stand, like Abrahams and Lots, to stay its forthcoming and well-earned and just judgment."

The incident of the woman at the toll gate and especially his treatment by "the Quaker" support the writer's purpose. Reverend Pennington does not waste words in describing his kind reception at the house of W. W.; he sums up the entire episode in one sentence: "Come in and take thy breakfast, and get warm!" He follows with a detailed presentation of the impression that the kindness and humanity of the stranger made "upon his mind."

Read the model personal experience that follows. Be prepared to answer questions on it.

▶ From THE STORY OF MY LIFE
**Helen Keller**

[1]One day, while I was playing with my new doll, Miss Sullivan put my big rag doll into my lap also, spelled "d-o-l-l" and tried to make me understand that "d-o-l-l" applied to both. Earlier in the day we had had a tussle over the words "m-u-g" and "w-a-t-e-r." Miss Sullivan had tried to impress it upon me that "m-u-g" is *mug* and that "w-a-t-e-r" is *water*, but I persisted in confounding the two. In despair she had dropped the subject for the time, only to renew it at the first opportunity. I became impatient at her repeated attempts and, seizing the new doll, I dashed it upon the floor. I was keenly delighted when I felt the fragments of the broken doll at my feet. Neither sorrow nor regret followed my passionate outburst. I had not loved the

doll. In the still, dark world in which I lived there was no strong sentiment of tenderness. I felt my teacher sweep the fragments to one side of the hearth, and I had a sense of satisfaction that the cause of my discomfort was removed. She brought me my hat, and I knew I was going out into the warm sunshine. This thought, if a wordless sensation may be called a thought, made me hop and skip with pleasure.

[2]We walked down the path to the well-house, attracted by the fragrance of the honeysuckle with which it was covered. Some one was drawing water and my teacher placed my hand under the spout. As the cool stream gushed over one hand she spelled into the other the word *water*, first slowly, then rapidly. I stood still, my whole attention fixed upon the motions of her fingers. Suddenly I felt a misty consciousness as of something forgotten — a thrill of returning thought; and somehow the mystery of language was revealed to me. I knew then that "w-a-t-e-r" meant the wonderful cool something that was flowing over my hand. That living word awakened my soul, gave it light, hope, joy, set it free! There were barriers still, it is true, but barriers that could in time be swept away.

## QUESTIONS ON    The Story of My Life

1. What did this experience mean to Helen Keller?

2. What was the purpose of the first paragraph?

3. How does Helen Keller give order to this personal experience?

4. How concentrated are the details leading up to the discovery that Helen made?

5. Write a brief paragraph in which you contrast this personal experience with the more expository narrative written by Anne Sullivan in her letter of April 5, 1887. (See page 137.)

## Suggested Written Assignments

1. Write a personal experience paper stressing something that you learned about a place.
2. Write a personal experience paper concerning a discovery you made about yourself or some other person or group.

## Narration with a Plot

The *narration with a plot* is also a concern of this chapter. The writer's purpose is to tell a story that interests and entertains his reader. This kind of narration (a number of incidents that make a "single, whole, and complete" action) consists of a *character(s)* involved in some kind of struggle *(conflict)*. The struggle starts with an *initial situation* (some happening that sets the action in motion), moves into a complication *(conflict)*, then onward through incidents joined one to another by causal relationships to a *climax* (the high point in the story where the tension and suspense are the greatest), and ends with a *resolution* (the outcome of the conflict). In some narration-with-a-plot stories, the writer may stress a central or dominating idea by organizing his action to make his central idea *(theme)* meaningful. If the *theme* dominates the action as the writer's purpose, the narration is called a *story of theme*.

### Structuring Narration with a Plot

Plot is the subject of narration. If you are going to give unity, completeness, order, and coherence to your story, you must limit the scope of the action to fulfill the requirements of the usual college written assignment. You cannot possibly compress into a few pages all the incidents, events, and thoughts experienced by one or several persons (characters), or the mass of descriptive details that delineate one character or several characters important to the action of the story, or all the details necessary to reproduce the place or places where the story happens. Thus, from the mass of expository, descriptive, and narrative details available, you select those that will best fulfill the demands of plot structure.

To give some kind of order to the imaginary or real picture of life that you are creating, you must be discriminating; therefore, you make one conflict the heart of the plot instead of two or three; you involve one or two people in the struggle instead of a dozen; you tie together five or six incidents to give a meaningful whole action rather than a hundred. You delineate a character to the extent that the reader can understand why that character acts as he does rather than devoting pages to a detailed portrayal of the people in conflict.

In achieving unity in narration, you do not organize your material around a statement of thesis or statement of purpose as in exposition or with a statement of the central controversial issue as in persuasion. You gain unity in narration by linking each element in the chain of plot to the whole action and to one another by causal relationships. One happening causes another or results from a previous incident; all together they give meaning to the whole action.

You gain completeness when you give meaning to a conflict by resolving the struggle — by untying the knot that you tied in the beginning of the action. You achieve coherence when you give order to the sequence of events *(time order)*. You move your reader logically through a series of happenings beginning with an initial situation, onward to a complication (conflict), to other tense and suspenseful events that reach a climax in the struggle, and finally to a resolution of the conflict. To achieve coherence, you must maintain a consistent point of view; that is, the reader must know at all times who is telling the story if he is to understand what is happening and relate each event to the developing plot. Let us first read a narrative with a plot (short story) by William Carlos Williams. We will then see how the writer fulfills the requirements of effective narration by breaking the story down into its parts and explaining his structuring of plot.

### ▶ THE USE OF FORCE
**William Carlos Williams**

They were new patients to me, all I had was the name, Olson. Please come down as soon as you can, my daughter is very sick.

When I arrived I was met by the mother, a big startled-looking woman, very clean and apologetic who merely said, Is this the doctor? and let me in. In the back, she added, You must excuse us, doctor, we have her in the kitchen where it is warm. It is very damp here sometimes.

The child was fully dressed and sitting on her father's lap near the kitchen table. He tried to get up, but I motioned for him not to bother, took off my overcoat and started to look things over. I could see that they were all very nervous, eyeing me up and down distrustfully. As often, in such cases, they weren't telling me more than they had to, it was up to me to tell them; that's why they were spending three dollars on me.

The child was fairly eating me up with her cold, steady eyes, and no expression to her face whatever. She did not move and seemed, inwardly, quiet; an unusually attractive little thing, and as strong as a heifer in appearance. But her face was flushed, she was breathing rapidly, and I realized that she had a high fever. She had magnificent blonde hair, in profusion.° One of those picture children often reproduced in advertising leaflets and the photogravure sections of the Sunday papers.

She's had a fever for three days, began the father and we don't know what it comes from. My wife has given her things, you know, like people do, but it don't do no good. And there's been a lot of sickness around. So we tho't you'd better look her over and tell us what is the matter.

As doctors often do I took a trial shot at it as a point of departure. Has she had a sore throat?

Both parents answered me together, No . . . No, she says her throat don't hurt her.

Does your throat hurt you? added the mother to the child. But the little girl's expression didn't change nor did she move her eyes from my face.

Have you looked?

I tried to, said the mother, but I couldn't see.

As it happens we had been having a number of cases of diphtheria in the school to which this child went during that month and we were all, quite apparently, thinking of that, though no one had as yet spoken of the thing.

Well, I said, suppose we take a look at the throat first. I smiled in my best professional manner and asking for the child's first name I said, come on Mathilda, open your mouth and let's take a look at your throat.

Nothing doing.

Aw, come on, I coaxed, just open your mouth wide and let me take a look. Look, I said opening both hands wide, I haven't anything in my hands. Just open up and let me see.

Such a nice man, put in the mother. Look how kind he is to you. Come on, do what he tells you to do. He won't hurt you.

At that I ground my teeth in disgust. If only they wouldn't use the word "hurt" I might be able to get somewhere. But I did not allow myself to be hurried or disturbed but speaking quietly and slowly I approached the child again.

As I moved my chair a little nearer suddenly with one cat-like movement both her hands clawed instinctively for my eyes and she almost reached them too. In fact she knocked my glasses flying and they fell, though unbroken, several feet away from me on the kitchen floor.

Both the mother and father almost turned themselves inside

out in embarrassment and apology. You bad girl, said the mother, taking her and shaking her by one arm. Look what you've done. The nice man . . .

For heaven's sake, I broke in. Don't call me a nice man to her. I'm here to look at her throat on the chance that she might have diphtheria and possibly die of it. But that's nothing to her. Look here, I said to the child, we're going to look at your throat. You're old enough to understand what I'm saying. Will you open it now by yourself or shall we have to open it for you?

Not a move. Even her expression hadn't changed. Her breaths however were coming faster and faster. Then the battle began. I had to do it. I had to have a throat culture for her own protection. But first I told the parents that it was entirely up to them. I explained the danger but said that I would not insist on a throat examination so long as they would take the responsibility.

If you don't do what the doctor says you'll have to go to the hospital, the mother admonished° her severely.

Oh yeah? I had to smile to myself. After all, I had already fallen in love with the savage brat, the parents were contemptible° to me. In the ensuing° struggle they grew more and more abject,° crushed, exhausted while she surely rose to magnificent heights of insane fury of effort bred of her terror of me.

The father tried his best, and he was a big man but the fact that she was his daughter, his shame at her behavior and his dread of hurting her made him release her just at the critical times when I had almost achieved success, till I wanted to kill him. But his dread also that she might have diphtheria made him tell me to go on, go on though he himself was almost fainting, while the mother moved back and forth behind us raising and lowering her hands in an agony of apprehension.°

Put her in front of you on your lap, I ordered, and hold both her wrists.

But as soon as he did the child let out a scream. Don't, you're hurting me. Let go of my hands. Let them go I tell you. Then she shrieked terrifyingly, hysterically. Stop it! Stop it! You're killing me!

Do you think she can stand it, doctor, said the mother.

You get out, said the husband to the wife. Do you want her to die of diphtheria?

Come on now, hold her, I said.

Then I grasped the child's head with my left hand and tried to get the wooden tongue depressor between her teeth. She fought, with clenched teeth, desperately! But now I also had grown furious — at a child. I tried to hold myself down but I couldn't. I know how to expose a throat for inspection. And I did my best. When finally I got the wooden spatula behind the last teeth and just the point of it into the mouth cavity, she opened up for an instant but before I could see anything she came down again and gripping the wooden blade between her molars she reduced it to splinters before I could get it out again.

Aren't you ashamed, the mother yelled at her. Aren't you ashamed to act like that in front of the doctor?

Get me a smooth-handled spoon of some sort, I told the mother. We're going through with this. The child's mouth was already bleeding. Her tongue was cut and she was screaming in wild hysterical shrieks. Perhaps I should have desisted and come back in an hour or more. No doubt it would have been better. But I have seen at least two children lying dead in bed of neglect in such cases, and feeling that I must get a diagnosis now or never I went at it again. But the worst of it was that I too had got beyond reason. I could have torn the child apart in my own fury and enjoyed it. It was a pleasure to attack her. My face was burning with it.

The damned little brat must be protected against her own idiocy, one says to one's self at such times. Others must be protected against her. It is a social necessity. And all these things are true. But a blind fury, a feeling of adult shame, bred of a longing for muscular release are the operatives. One goes on to the end.

In a final unreasoning assault I overpowered the child's neck and jaws. I forced the heavy silver spoon back of her teeth and down her throat till she gagged. And there it was — both tonsils covered with membrane. She had fought valiantly° to keep me from knowing her secret. She had been hiding that sore throat for three days at least and lying to her parents in order to escape just such an outcome as this.

Now truly she was furious. She had been on the defensive before but now she attacked. Tried to get off her father's lap and fly at me while tears of defeat blinded her eyes.

***The Beginning.*** In writing narration with a plot, you set the action in motion and prepare the reader for understanding the sequence of events in the beginning paragraph or paragraphs. You create an imaginary initial situation that is the start of a sequence of incidents that become meaningful as you join them together to form a unified action. You begin at a certain place and at a certain time. You introduce the character or characters involved in the action. You provide the reader with enough information about the situation and the individuals involved in the story so that he will be able to understand

**MATCH-UP FOUR**

Match the definitions in column 2 with the words in column 1 taken from the model narratives by placing the letter of the word in the blank. Answers are at the end of the chapter.

| | | |
|---|---|---|
| a. overwhelming | 1. constantly | ＿＿＿ |
| b. timidity | 2. boldly courageous | ＿＿＿ |
| c. confide | 3. to warn, caution | ＿＿＿ |
| d. invariably | 4. feeling of disgust | ＿＿＿ |
| e. fugitive | 5. lack of self-assurance | ＿＿＿ |
| f. profusion | 6. following in order | ＿＿＿ |
| g. admonished | 7. utterly hopeless | ＿＿＿ |
| h. contemptible | 8. fear of trouble, worry | ＿＿＿ |
| i. ensuing | 9. overcoming, destroying | ＿＿＿ |
| j. abject | 10. to have trust in one | ＿＿＿ |
| k. apprehension | 11. abundance, great quantity | ＿＿＿ |
| l. valiantly | 12. a person who flees | ＿＿＿ |

what will follow. In structuring the beginning, you have two purposes in mind: (1) to gain his interest so he will want to continue with the story, and (2) to give him the information he needs to understand the action that follows.

Does William Carlos Williams in "The Use of Force" gain your interest? What kinds of information can we consider part of the *exposition* (information necessary to understand the story)? What is the time of the story? Where does the story take place? Do you think that more detailed information concerning the time and place of the action would have helped with your understanding of the action that followed? How fully does he describe the people involved in the action? Would more elaborate descriptions of the mother and father have helped you to understand their part in the action better? Why do you think Williams selected a doctor as the protagonist (the main character in the conflict)?

▶ They were new patients to me, all I had was the name, Olson. Please come down as soon as you can, my daughter is very sick.

When I arrived I was met by the mother, a big startled-looking woman, very clean and apologetic who merely said, Is this the doctor? and let me in. In the back, she added, You must excuse us, doctor, we have her in the kitchen where it is warm. It is very damp here sometimes.

The child was fully dressed and sitting on her father's lap near the kitchen table. He tried to get up, but I motioned for him not to bother, took off my overcoat and started to look things over. I could see that they were all very nervous, eyeing me up and down distrustfully. As often, in such cases, they weren't telling me more than they had to, it was up to me to tell them; that's why they were spending three dollars on me.

In these three paragraphs, the writer presents all the necessary information the reader needs to understand the story. He tells us that the Olsons were new patients; their daughter was sick. He describes very briefly the mother and father. He gives us the place of the action — in the kitchen, but he does not mention a specific time of the action. It was probably winter because it is very cold and the doctor wears an overcoat. But we cannot be sure.

Developing exposition in beginning a narration demands more from you than merely giving the reader the necessary information to understand the story. You must make this information interesting and a logical part of the story. By itself, this kind of information could be a listing of facts, a place, a time, a date. But you gain interest by weaving very selected details of an expository nature into the action so unobtrusively that the reader is unaware of it. In these early paragraphs William Carlos Williams begins to build tension and suspense. He tells us that "they were all very nervous, eyeing me up and down distrustfully." Then he describes the child; she is beautiful and obviously very sick. But, he doesn't elaborate on her beauty. He does, however, point out other characteristics of the child that are important to the story. "The child was fairly eating me up with her cold, steady eyes, and no expression to her face whatever." She was "as strong as a heifer in appearance."

Next, he presents more exposition concerning her fever and the possibility that she could have diphtheria. Then, he moves into the initial situation. He uses gentle persuasion to get the child to open her mouth.

▶ . . . I said, come on, Mathilda, open your mouth and let's take a look at your throat.

Nothing doing.

Aw, come on, I coaxed, just open your mouth wide and let me take a look. Look, I said, opening both hands wide, I haven't anything in my hands. Just open up and let me see.

This second attempt at persuasion narrows the struggle; no longer does the doctor say "let's take a look at your throat." He says "let me take a look." The struggle between the child and the doctor begins. More important to the meaning of the story, the doctor at this time in the action is in complete control of the situation. He says, "But I did not allow myself to be hurried or disturbed but speaking quietly and slowly I approached the child again."

## EXERCISE 3    **Narration**

Answer the following questions concerning the beginning of "The Use of Force."

1. Does the writer give a specific time for the action?

2. Where does the action of the story take place?

3. Who are the main characters?

4. What is the initial situation?

5. How does the writer gain your interest and create tension?

*The Middle.*   The middle consists of a series of paragraphs that present a number of happenings, arising out of the initial situation. The part includes the main action of the story; it results from a *complication* — a struggle between opposing forces. This struggle *(conflict)* gives meaning to the action and provides the elements of interest and suspense so necessary for good narration. As the struggle moves toward a *climax* (the high point of the action), tensions increase, and suspense develops within the reader as to the final outcome.

Some of the common conflicts in which humans are involved are the struggle of (1) man against man, (2) man against nature, (3) man against society, and (4) man against himself. *

Conflicts of man against man are most easily recognized. Man against man in war, in sports, in business, in love are just a few of the unlimited number of areas for this kind of conflict. The struggle of brother American against brother American in the Civil War is a fertile source of man-against-man conflicts. In sports, men compete against men for team victories and individual honors as in the Olympic Games. In business, men compete for power, financial rewards, prestige. The conflicts that arise in love have given us some of the greatest literature.

Man against nature is another common conflict. Man struggles to survive on his farm against the inexorable forces of the wind, rain, and drought that destroy without mercy. Man fights the sea by building dikes and jetties to hold it back from eating away his land. Men in ships fight to survive in typhoons. Men fight against disease.

In "The Use of Force," the conflict appears to be the easily recognized conflict of man against man (doctor against little girl). Certainly this struggle is obvious. But, as you read the following excerpts from the story, study carefully the actions of the doctor and his comments concerning the change that takes place within him. With this evidence and the clue to meaning that the title of the story gives, you might arrive at the conclusion that the real conflict that gives the story its meaning and reveals the writer's purpose — the theme of the story — is man against himself.

> ▶ Look, here, I said to the child, we're going to look at your throat. You're old enough to understand what I'm saying. Will you open it now by yourself or shall we have to open it for you?

With these words, the writer begins the complication. Struggle after

---

* In this discussion of conflicts, the word *woman* can be readily substituted for *man.*

struggle between the doctor and child follows, each one growing in intensity. The child fights back as she is assaulted by the doctor, aided by her parents. But a change is taking place in the doctor; he becomes furious.

> ▶ Then I grasped the child's head with my left hand and tried to get the wooden tongue depressor between her teeth. She fought, with clenched teeth, desperately! But now I also had grown furious — at a child. I tried to hold myself down but I couldn't. I know how to expose a throat for inspection. And I did my best.

Finally, the doctor decides the throat must be opened to protect the child against herself and to protect others from her. "It is a social necessity." But, there is another reason for opening her mouth — a "blind fury, a feeling of adult shame, bred of a longing for muscular release are the operatives. One goes on to the end."

> ▶ Get me a smooth-handled spoon of some sort, I told the mother. We're going through with this. The child's mouth was already bleeding. Her tongue was cut and she was screaming in wild hysterical shrieks. Perhaps I should have desisted and come back in an hour or more. No doubt it would have been better. But I have seen at least two children lying dead in bed of neglect in such cases, and feeling that I must get the diagnosis now or never I went at it again. But the worst of it was that I too had got beyond reason. I could have torn the child apart in my own fury and enjoyed it. It was a pleasure to attack her. My face was burning with it.

Thus, the conflict between the doctor and himself has reached a climax; force takes over; he "had got beyond reason."

## EXERCISE 4    Narration

Answer the following questions concerning the middle of "The Use of Force."

1. What are the two conflicts in "The Use of Force"?

2. Explain the complication in the conflict of doctor against the child.

3. How does the writer explain the struggle of the doctor with himself?

4. Who tells the story?

5. What is the climax of the action?

*The Resolution.*    The end of the narration is called the *resolution* or *denouement*. It consists of the events that follow the climax in the plot structure. In these final paragraphs the writer concludes the action with a final unraveling of the plot. If he posed a question at the beginning, he answers it; if he tied a knot of circumstances at the start, he unties the knot. If he created a mystery, he solves it. Above all, he brings the struggle to a conclusion. He may also add anything he feels necessary to explain the action and give meaning to the plot. William Carlos Williams ends the action in "The Use of Force" quickly; the doctor "in a final unreasoning assault" overpowers the child. She has diphtheria. He concludes the story with the defeat of the child. But, the writer again emphasizes the theme that the climax revealed; the child was overpowered "in a final unreasoning assault." The writer is saying that the use of force — even in a noble cause — does something to the humanity of the person employing it. The use of force exposed the disease in the child, but it also exposed the disease lying in the nature of man that brings him down to the level of the beast.

Writing the narration with a plot story demands that you know what you are doing. Structure is very important, but good narration is more than joining together a series of incidents into a complete, unified, coherent action. It is interesting and significant because it tells of people in some kind of conflict — a struggle that the reader identifies with and becomes involved in as he moves from incident to incident to the climax.

If "The Use of Force" is worthwhile reading, it is because we experience the doctor's struggle with himself and realize that force is destructive. It kills the humanity within us. If mankind uses force to solve its problems, it will be inevitably the loser.

*Point of View.*    You have seen in this analysis of "The Use of Force" how moving the reader through time using a sequence of events or happenings and joining those incidents together also by causal relationships give order and coherence to the narration. *Point of view* is equally important in achieving order and coherence in narration. In narration, point of view means "through whose eyes" the reader sees the action. It answers the questions: "Who tells the story?" and "What part does the *narrator* (the person who tells the story) play in the action?" By selecting a particular point of view, a writer can control what the reader sees and, to a lesser extent, what he feels about what is happening.

There are two common points of view: the "I" point of view (*first-person* narrative) and the "he" point of view (*third-person* narrative). If you decide to tell a story in the first-person narrative, you must decide whether to tell a story through the eyes of the *narrator/main character* or the *narrator/minor character*. If you select the first-person narrator/

main character, you limit yourself to telling about those incidents, thoughts, feelings, reactions that you experienced. Since you are *inside* the story (part of the action), you cannot adopt an all-knowing view of the action. If you are going to achieve a sense of reality, you cannot stand outside the action to comment, interpret, or present knowledge of all the events or feeling and emotions within all the characters, as you can when you adopt the third-person omniscient point of view. Using the first-person narrator/main character, you achieve a closeness to the reader since you are relating an action in which you play a leading part. "The Use of Force" was first-person-narrative/main character.

The excerpt that follows was taken from a story entitled "The Brutal Tale of a Teen-Age Gang Leader." The story was told to Ira Henry Freeman, but he decided to tell it through the eyes of "Frenchie," the teen-age gang leader.

▶ I was not yet 14 years old when Gus Gibbons, president of the Little Bishops, picked me to be president of his new Fifth Division. The Bishops were then one of the largest street clubs in New York City. The five divisions had 150 or 200 members between 13 and 18. They claimed a turf extending for two miles along Fulton Street in Brooklyn and had brother clubs in Harlem and the Bronx.

I was an important sahib for so young a kid. But I was tall for my age, a little smarter than most of the other bops, or gang members, and had the prestige of having already been busted — arrested — twice by the cops.

My first arrest had been for gang fighting. The second was for firing a zip gun at some kids in John Marshall Junior High School. That is the same school that was in the papers recently because a thirteen-year-old girl was raped there. The principal committed suicide in despair. There were rapes and fights when I went there, too, but our principal did not kill himself. He just left.

I had made the zip gun in shop class out of a toy airplane launcher. Afterward I made more of them for other bops in my division. Our zip guns could throw a .22-caliber cartridge twenty-five yards and were as good as any homemades in Brooklyn.

A few months later, however, I stumbled on a load that made them seem like cap pistols. In an empty lot on Sands Street I found a wooden crate containing two dozen brand new .38-caliber service revolvers and four marine signal flare guns. This was probably a shipment for the Brooklyn Navy Yard that had been hijacked off South Brooklyn piers and hidden temporarily.

I nearly broke my back lugging the crate to Lenny's candy store, where my club hung out. Lenny was a right guy who had been a bop in a street club as a kid and who still hated cops. He let us hide the guns in his cellar. We shook down little kids at school for their lunch money until we had collected $50. With that we bought some ammunition from a fence on the docks.

The sudden haul made a spectacular difference in our division's chances. With our new artillery we might rise to be top club in the city.

Overnight I was no longer afraid of Gus Gibbons, although he was seventeen, much bigger and much meaner than I. I had taken two of the flare pistols for myself and test-fired them on a roof with shot-gun shells. When I let go with both of those cannons at once, I got ideas of becoming the Hitler of all the Little People [junior gang members].

Although Hitler and his Nazis had been wiped out years before, we still looked up to them as the meanest bops in history. Even today some bop gang leaders call themselves Hitler or Goering or Fuehrer, and I know one club — Negro at that — named the Gestapos.

Ira Henry Freeman
"The Brutal Tale of a Teen-age Gang Leader"

If you select the first-person narrator/minor character, you can relate those incidents in which the minor character is involved. You can present his thoughts, feelings, reactions. You can give insight into the actions of the main character by this point of view — but you cannot relate the thoughts or feelings of the main character, or present an all-knowing view of the action since you are inside the story, and you are limited by your position as a minor character.

If you decide to tell the story in the *third-person narrative,* you stand *outside* the action (you are not part of the story). You lose the closeness of the first-person narrative, but you gain a freedom of movement that is equally important. You have a choice of telling the story as an *omniscient* (all-knowing) *narrator* or as a *limited narrator.* As the third-person omniscient narrator, you can move freely about, seeing everything that happens, describing the feelings, thoughts, and reactions of all the characters and making comments of your own or explaining and interpreting whenever you wish.

Leo Tolstoy, in his story "The Death of Ivan Ilych," uses the third-person omniscient point of view because he wishes great freedom of

movement. It is important to his purpose to be able to present incidents in which other characters are involved and to make known to the
reader the thoughts and feelings of other people in the story besides
Ivan, who is the main character in the plot. As a matter of fact, the
story begins with the death of Ivan Ilych. The reactions of minor
characters to the death of Ivan are necessary for Tolstoy's purpose of
showing the selfishness and lack of humanity of men. He writes:

▶ "Gentlemen," he said, "Ivan Ilych has died!"

"You don't say so!"

"Here, read it yourself," replied Peter Ivanovich, handing
Fëdor Vasilievich the paper still damp from the press. Sur-
rounded by a black border were the words: "Praskovya
Fëdorovna Golovina, with profound sorrow, informs relatives
and friends of the demise of her beloved husband Ivan Ilych
Golovin, Member of the Court of Justice, which occurred on
February the 4th of this year 1882. The funeral will take place
on Friday at one o'clock in the afternoon."

Ivan Ilych had been a colleague of the gentlemen present
and was liked by them all. He had been ill for some weeks with
an illness said to be incurable. His post had been kept open for
him, but there had been conjectures that in case of his death
Alexeev might receive his appointment, and that either Vinnikov or Shtabel would succeed Alexeev. So on receiving the
news of Ivan Ilych's death the first thought of each of the
gentlemen in that private room was of the changes and promotions it might occasion among themselves or their acquaintances.

"I shall be sure to get Shtabel's place or Vinnikov's," thought
Fëdor Vasilievich. "I was promised that long ago, and the promotion means an extra eight-hundred rubles a year for me
besides the allowance."

"Now I must apply for my brother-in-law's transfer from
Kaluga," thought Peter Ivanovich. "My wife will be very glad,
and then she won't be able to say that I never do anything for
her relations."

"I thought he would never leave his bed again," said Peter
Ivanovich aloud. "It's very sad."

"But what really was the matter with him?"

"The doctors couldn't say — at least they could, but each of
them said something different. When last I saw him I thought
he was getting better."

"And I haven't been to see him since the holidays. I always meant to go."

"Had he any property?"

"I think his wife had a little — but something quite trifling."

"We shall have to go see her, but they live so terribly far away."

"Far away from you, you mean. Everything's far away from your place."

"You see, he never can forgive my living on the other side of the river," said Peter Ivanovich, smiling at Shebek. Then, still talking of the distances between different parts of the city, they returned to the Court.

Besides considerations as to the possible transfers and promotions likely to result from Ivan Ilych's death, the mere fact of the death of a near acquaintance aroused, as usual, in all who heard of it the complacent feeling that, "it is he who is dead and not I."

Each one thought or felt, "Well, he's dead but I'm alive!" But the more intimate of Ivan Ilych's acquaintances, his so-called friends, could not help thinking also that they would now have to fulfill the very tiresome demands of propriety by attending the funeral service and paying a visit of condolence to the widow.

Leo Tolstoy
"The Death of Ivan Ilych"

**VOCABULARY PREVIEW**

| | | |
|---|---|---|
| agitated | indomitable | abandoned |
| penetrating | resolution | stout |
| discord | impenetrable | pumice |
| remote | obscurity | porous |
| frail | allay | intact |

In the next model narrative, Joseph Conrad tells the story of the destruction of the *Nan-Shan* in the third-person but the point of view of Jukes, the mate, is a less omniscient view than in the previous model narrative by Tolstoy. Conrad, as the writer, enters the narrative to tell us at the beginning that "the *Nan-Shan* was being looted by the storm with a senseless, destructive fury . . ." Through this sentence,

Conrad states the central thought of the narrative which he supports in the following sentences with descriptive and narrative details. This sentence sets also the tone or mood of hopelessness and despair that dominates the incident and that is repeated by Conrad in the last two sentences: "An impenetrable obscurity pressed down upon the ghostly glimmers of the sea. A dull conviction seized upon Jukes that there was nothing to be done."

Conrad also enters the narrative in his comments on the captain's voice, writing that it sounded, "as if sent out from some remote spot of peace beyond the black wastes of the gale . . ."

▶ The *Nan-Shan* was being looted by the storm with a senseless, destructive fury: trysails torn out of the extra gaskets, double-lashed awnings blown away, bridge swept clean, weather-cloths burst, rails twisted, light-screens smashed — and two of the boats had gone already. They had gone unheard and un-seen, melting, as it were, in the shock and smother of the wave. It was only later, when upon the white flash of another high sea hurling itself amidships, Jukes had a vision of two pairs of davits leaping black and empty out of the solid blackness, with one overhauled fall flying and an iron-bound block capering in the air, that he became aware of what had happened within about three yards of his back.

He poked his head forward, groping for the ear of his com-mander. His lips touched it — big, fleshy, very wet. He cried in an agitated° tone, "Our boats are going now, sir."

And again he heard that voice, forced and ringing feebly, but with a penetrating° effect of quietness in the enormous dis-cord° of noises, as if sent out from some remote° spot of peace beyond the black wastes of the gale; again he heard a man's voice — the frail° and indomitable° sound that can be made to carry an infinity of thought, resolution° and purpose, that shall be pronouncing confident words on the last day, when heavens fall, and justice is done — again he heard it, and it was crying to him, as if from very, very far — "All right."

He thought he had not managed to make himself under-stood. "Our boats — I say boats — the boats, sir! Two gone!"

The same voice, within a foot of him and yet so remote, yelled sensibly, "Can't be helped."

Captain MacWhirr had never turned his face, but Jukes caught some more words on the wind.

"What can — expect — when hammering through — such — Bound to leave — something behind — stands to reason."

Watchfully Jukes listened for more. No more came. This was all Captain MacWhirr had to say; and Jukes could picture to himself rather than see the broad squat back before him. An impenetrable° obscurity° pressed down upon the ghostly glimmers of the sea. A dull conviction seized upon Jukes that there was nothing to be done.

Joseph Conrad
"Typhoon"

In writing a narration in the *third-person limited narrator,* called also *third-person objective,* you decide to present the action of the story through the eyes of the main character or a minor character, but you remain outside the story as the detached observer. You do not make comments or interpret action. You relate what the main character or minor character sees and experiences, but you do not intrude into the action or the minds of the characters. As a result, you gain realism for the story since the reader draws his own conclusions concerning what is happening and the role the characters play in it.

The narrative below illustrates the third-person limited narrator. Pliny the Younger (A.D. 61 or 62–c.113) tells the story of the death of his uncle (Pliny the Elder) who perished in the eruption of Vesuvius in A.D. 79. Notice that this account is a more objective, factual story than the incidents told in the two previous models of narration in the third-person.

▶ Meanwhile on Mount Vesuvius broad sheets of fire and leaping flames blazed at several points, their bright glare emphasized by the darkness of night. My uncle tried to allay° the fears of his companions by repeatedly declaring that these were nothing but bonfires left by the peasants in their terror, or else empty houses on fire in the districts they had abandoned.° Then he went to rest and certainly slept, for as he was a stout° man his breathing was rather loud and heavy and could be heard by people coming and going outside his door. By this time the courtyard giving access to his room was full of ashes mixed with pumice° stones, so that its level had risen, and if he had stayed in the room any longer he would never have got out. He was wakened and came out and joined Pomponianus and the rest of the household, who had sat up all night. They debated whether to stay indoors or take their chance in the open, for the buildings were now shaking with violent shocks and seemed to be swaying to and fro as if they were torn from their foundations. Outside, on the other hand, there was the danger of falling pumice stones, even though these were light and porous;° however, after comparing the risks they chose the latter. In my uncle's case one reason outweighed the other, but for the others it was a choice of fears. As a protection against falling objects they put pillows on their heads tied down with cloths.

Elsewhere there was daylight by this time, but they were still in darkness, blacker and denser than any ordinary night, which they relieved by lighting torches and various kinds of lamps. My uncle decided to go down to the shores and investigate on the spot the possibility of any escape by sea, but he found the waves still wild and dangerous. A sheet was spread on the ground for him to lie down, and he repeatedly asked for cold water to drink. Then the flames and smell of sulphur that gave warning of the approaching fire drove the others to take flight and roused him to stand up. He stood leaning on two slaves and then suddenly collapsed, I imagine because the dense fumes choked his breathing by blocking his windpipe, which was constitutionally weak and narrow and often inflamed. When daylight returned on the twenty-sixth — two° days after the last day he had seen — his body was found intact° and uninjured, still fully clothed and looking more like sleep than death.

Pliny the Younger
"The Counsel of the Dead"

Occasionally, a writer will use the first-person plural "we" or the third-person plural "they" point of view. Experienced writers will use a mixed point of view for a particular purpose. And finally, the second-person "you" is rarely used except in explaining a process (how to do something).

**MATCH-UP FIVE**

Match the definitions in column 2 with the words in column 1 taken from the model narratives by placing the letter of the word in the blank. Answers are at the end of the chapter.

| | | | | |
|---|---|---|---|---|
| a. | agitated | 1. | to leave or forsake | _____ |
| b. | penetrating | 2. | discerning, passing through | _____ |
| c. | discord | 3. | weak, feeble, fragile | _____ |
| d. | remote | 4. | to calm, quiet | _____ |
| e. | frail | 5. | determination | _____ |
| f. | indomitable | 6. | thick-set, stocky | _____ |
| g. | resolution | 7. | conflict, struggle | _____ |
| h. | impenetrable | 8. | spongy volcanic glass | _____ |
| i. | obscurity | 9. | moved violently, disturbed | _____ |
| j. | allay | 10. | unable to pierce, understand | _____ |
| k. | abandoned | 11. | unknown | _____ |
| l. | stout | 12. | far away, distant | _____ |
| m. | pumice | 13. | complete, not altered | _____ |
| n. | porous | 14. | unconquerable | _____ |
| o. | intact | 15. | full of holes | _____ |

**VOCABULARY PREVIEW**

| | | | |
|---|---|---|---|
| abundant | bristled | mercenary | indignation |
| conveyed | singularity | hussy | humiliate |
| condemned | intolerably | embezzled | scrutinized |
| enigmatical | vile | destitution | impulsively |
| deceived | repulsion | squandered | wailed |

Complete the following exercises to review the discussion point of view in the narrative.

## EXERCISE 5    Point of View

Read the model paragraph below. Answer the questions that follow.

> ▶ It has long been my purpose to follow the example of other retired officers and employ the too abundant° leisure of an old man in setting down, with the aid of my journal and in the fullest possible detail, a narrative of some one of the episodes of my life at sea. The decision was made last night; I shall write of my first ship, the *Bounty*, of the mutiny on board, of my long residence on the island of Tahiti in the South Sea, and of how I was conveyed° home in irons, to be tried by court-martial and condemned° to death. Two natures clashed on the stage of that drama of long ago, two men as strong and enigmatical° as any I have known — Fletcher Christian and William Bligh.
>
> Charles Nordhoff and James Norman Hall
> *Mutiny on the Bounty*

1. Who will tell the story of the *Bounty*?

2. From what point of view will the narrator tell the story?

3. Who will be the main characters in the conflict?

## EXERCISE 6    **Point of View**

Read the paragraphs below. Answer the questions that follow.

▶ As he was about to descend, he heard a voice from a distance, hallooing, "Rip Van Winkle! Rip Van Winkle!" He looked round, but could see nothing but a crow winging its solitary flight across the mountain. He thought his fancy must have deceived° him, and turned again to descend, when he heard the same cry ring through the still evening air: "Rip Van Winkle! Rip Van Winkle!" — at the same time Wolf bristled° up his back, and, giving a loud growl, skulked to his master's side, looking fearfully down into the glen. Rip now felt a vague apprehension stealing over him; he looked anxiously in the same direction, and perceived a strange figure slowly toiling up the rocks, and bending under the weight of something he carried on his back. He was surprised to see any human being in this lonely and unfrequented place; but supposing it to be some one of the neighborhood in need of assistance, he hastened down to yield it.

On nearer approach he was still more surprised at the singularity° of the stranger's appearance. He was a short, square-built old fellow, with thick bushy hair and a grizzled beard. His dress was of the antique Dutch fashion — a cloth jerkin, strapped round the waist — several pair of breeches, the outer one of ample volume, decorated with rows of buttons down the sides, and bunches at the knees. He bore on his shoulder a stout keg . . . .

Washington Irving
"Rip Van Winkle"

1. Who tells the story?

2. What is the point of view?

In his comments on the short story that follows, Sean O'Faolain writes: "What I am saying is that every short story has some bright destination and that every step into the story must imperceptibly lead toward its point of illumination."* Read Anton Chekhov's "The Chorus Girl" the first time to simply enjoy a poignant story of two women and a man in what appears to be a rather commonplace situation. Then read it a second time in order to answer the questions that follow it. Remember that the writer of a short story must compress in a short space of variety of information for reader understanding. Chekhov is a master of this "compressed technique"; note especially the amount of information that he conveys, not details, in the opening paragraph.

▶ THE CHORUS GIRL
**Anton Chekhov**

One day when she was younger and better-looking, and when her voice was stronger, Nikolay Petrovitch Kolpakov, her adorer, was sitting in the outer room of her summer villa. It was intolerably° hot and stifling. Kolpakov, who had just dined and drunk a whole bottle of inferior port, felt ill-humored and out of sorts. Both were bored and waiting for the heat of the day to be over in order to go for a walk.

All at once there was a sudden ring at the door. Kolpakov, who was sitting with his coat off, in his slippers, jumped up and looked inquiringly at Pasha.

"It must be the postman or one of the girls," said the singer.

Kolpakov did not mind being found by the postman or Pasha's lady friends, but by way of precaution gathered up his clothes and went into the next room, while Pasha ran to open the door. To her great surprise in the doorway stood, not the postman and not a girl friend, but an unknown woman, young and beautiful, who was dressed like a lady, and from all outward signs was one.

The stranger was pale and was breathing heavily as though she had been running up a steep flight of stairs.

"What is it?" asked Pasha.

The lady did not at once answer. She took a step forward, slowly looked about the room, and sat down in a way that suggested that from fatigue, or perhaps illness, she could not stand; then for a long time her pale lips quivered as she tried in vain to speak.

---

* "Comments on 'The Chorus Girl' " in Short Stories edited by Sean O'Faolain.

"Is my husband here?" she asked at last, raising to Pasha her big eyes with their red tear-stained lids.

"Husband?" whispered Pasha, and was suddenly so frightened that her hands and feet turned cold.

"What husband?" she repeated, beginning to tremble.

"My husband, . . . Nikolay Petrovitch Kolpakov."

"N . . . no, madam. . . . I . . . I don't know any husband."

A minute passed in silence. The stranger several times passed her handkerchief over her pale lips and held her breath to stop her inward trembling, while Pasha stood before her motionless, like a post, and looked at her with astonishment and terror.

"So you say he is not here?" the lady asked, this time speaking with a firm voice and smiling oddly.

"I . . . I don't know who it is you are asking about."

"You are horrid, mean, vile° . . ." the stranger muttered, scanning Pasha with hatred and repulsion.° "Yes, yes . . . you are horrid. I am very, very glad that at last I can tell you so!"

Pasha felt that on this lady in black with the angry eyes and white slender fingers she produced the impression of something horrid and unseemly, and she felt ashamed of her chubby red cheeks, the pockmark on her nose, and the fringe on her forehead, which never could be combed back. And it seemed to her that if she had been thin, and had had no powder on her face and no fringe on her forehead, then she could have disguised the fact that she was not "respectable," and she would not have felt so frightened and ashamed to stand facing this unknown, mysterious lady.

"Where is my husband?" the lady went on. "Though I don't care whether he is here or not, but I ought to tell you that the money has been missed, and they are looking for Nikolay Petrovitch. . . . They mean to arrest him. That's your doing!"

The lady got up and walked about the room in great excitement. Pasha looked at her and was so frightened that she could not understand.

"He'll be found and arrested today," said the lady, and she gave a sob, and in that sound could be heard her resentment and vexation. "I know who has brought him to this awful position! Low, horrid creature! Loathsome, mercenary° hussy°!" The lady's lips worked and her nose wrinkled up with disgust. "I am helpless, do you hear, you low woman? . . . I am helpless; you are stronger than I am, but there is One to defend me and my children! God sees all! He is just! He will punish you for every tear I have shed, for all my sleepless nights! The time will come; you will think of me! . . ."

Silence followed again. The lady walked about the room and wrung her hands, while Pasha still gazed blankly at her in amazement, not understanding and expecting something terrible.

"I know nothing about it, madam," she said, and suddenly burst into tears.

"You are lying!" cried the lady, and her eyes flashed angrily at her. "I know all about it! I've known about you a long time. I know that for the last month he has been spending every day with you!"

"Yes, What then? What of it? I have a great many visitors, but I don't force anyone to come. He is free to do as he likes."

"I tell you they have discovered that money is missing! He has embezzled° money at the office! For a sake of such a . . . creature as you, for your sake he has actually committed a crime. Listen," said the lady in a resolute voice, stopping short, facing Pasha. "You can have no principles: you live simply to do harm — that's your object; but one can't imagine you have fallen so low that you have no trace of human feeling left! He has a wife, children . . . If he is condemned and sent into exile we shall starve, the children and I. . . . Understand that! And yet there is a chance of saving him and us from destitution° and disgrace. If I take them nine hundred roubles today they will let him alone. Only nine hundred roubles!"

"What nine hundred roubles?" Pasha asked softly. "I . . . I don't know. . . . I haven't taken it."

"I am not asking you for nine hundred roubles. . . . You have no money, and I don't want your money. I ask you for something else. . . . Men usually give expensive things to women like you. Only give me back the things my husband has given you!"

"Madam, he has never made me a present of anything!" Pasha wailed, beginning to understand.

"Where is the money? He has squandered° his own and mine and other people's. . . . What has become of it all? Listen, I beg you! I was carried away by indignation° and have said a lot of nasty things to you, but I apologize. You must hate me, I know, but if you are capable of sympathy, put yourself in my position! I implore you to give me back the things!"

"H'm!" said Pasha, and she shrugged her shoulders. "I would with pleasure, but, God is my witness, he never made me a present of anything. Believe me, on my conscience. However, you are right, though," said the singer in confusion, "he did bring me two little things. Certainly I will give them back, if you wish it."

Pasha pulled out one of the drawers in the toilet-table and took out of it a hollow gold bracelet and a thin ring with a ruby in it. "Here, madam!" she said, handing the visitor these articles.

The lady flushed and her face quivered. She was offended.

"What are you giving me?" she said. "I am not asking for charity, but for what does not belong to you . . . what you have taken advantage of your position to squeeze out of my husband . . . that weak, unhappy man. . . . On Thursday, when I saw you with my husband at the harbor you were wearing expensive brooches and bracelets. So it's no use your playing the innocent lamb to me! I ask you for the last time: will you give me the things, or not?"

"You are a queer one, upon my word," said Pasha, beginning to feel offended. "I assure you that, except the bracelet and this little ring, I've never seen a thing from your Nikolay Petrovitch. He brings me nothing but sweet cakes."

"Sweet cakes!" laughed the stranger. "At home the children have nothing to eat, and here you have sweet cakes. You absolutely refuse to restore the presents?"

Receiving no answer, the lady sat down and stared into space, pondering.

"What's to be done now?" she said. "If I don't get nine hundred roubles, he is ruined, and the children and I are ruined, too. Shall I kill this low woman or go down on my knees to her?"

The lady pressed her handkerchief to her face and broke into sobs.

"I beg you!" Pasha heard through the stranger's sobs. "You see you have plundered and ruined my husband. Save him. . . . You have no feeling for him, but the children . . . the children. . . . What have the children done?"

Pasha imagined little children standing in the street, crying with hunger, and she, too, sobbed.

"What can I do, madam?" she said. "You say that I am a low woman and that I have ruined Nikolay Petrovitch, and I assure you . . . before God Almighty, I have had nothing from him whatever. . . . There is only one girl in our chorus who has a rich admirer; all the rest of us live from hand to mouth on bread and kvass. Nikolay Petrovitch is a highly educated, refined gentleman, so I've made him welcome. We are bound to make gentlemen welcome."

"I ask you for the things! Give me the things! I am crying . . . I am humiliating myself. . . . If you like I will go down on my knees! If you wish it!"

Pasha shrieked with horror and waved her hands. She felt that this pale, beautiful lady who expressed herself so grandly, as though she were on the stage, really might go down on her knees to her, simply from pride, from grandeur, to exalt herself and humiliate° the chorus girl.

"Very well, I will give you things!" said Pasha, wiping her eyes and bustling about. "By all means. Only they are not from Nikolay Petrovitch. . . . I got these from other gentlemen. As you please. . . ."

Pasha pulled out the upper drawer of the chest, took out a diamond brooch, a coral necklace, some rings and bracelets, and gave them all to the lady.

"Take them if you like, only I've never had anything from your husband. Take them and grow rich," Pasha went on, offended at the threat to go down on her knees. "And if you are a lady . . . his lawful wife, you should keep him to yourself. I should think so! I did not ask him to come; he came of himself."

Through her tears the lady scrutinized° the articles given her and said:

"This isn't everything. . . . There won't be five hundred roubles' worth here."

Pasha impulsively° flung out of the chest a gold watch, a cigar-case and studs, and said, flinging up her hands:

"I've nothing else left. . . . You can search!"

The visitor gave a sigh, with trembling hands twisted the things up in her handkerchief, and went out without uttering a word, without even nodding her head.

The door from the next room opened and Kolpakov walked in. He was pale and kept shaking his head nervously, as though he had swallowed something very bitter; tears were glistening in his eyes.

"What presents did you make me?" Pasha asked, pouncing upon him. "When did you, allow me to ask you?"

"Presents . . . that's no matter!" said Kolpakov, and he tossed his head. "My God! She cried before you, she humbled herself . . ."

"I am asking you, what presents did you make me?" Pasha cried.

"My God! She, a lady, so proud, so pure. . . . She was ready to go down on her knees to . . . to this wench! And I've brought her to this! I've allowed it!"

He clutched his head in his hands and moaned.

"No, I shall never forgive myself for this! I shall never forgive myself! Get away from me . . . you low creature!" he cried with repulsion, backing away from Pasha, and thrusting her off with trembling hands. "She would have gone down on her knees, and . . . and to you! Oh, my God!"

Pasha lay down, and began wailing aloud. She was already regretting her things which she had given away so impulsively,° and her feelings were hurt. She remembered how three years ago a merchant had beaten her for no sort of reason, and she wailed° more loudly than ever.

## QUESTIONS ON     **The Chorus Girl**

Answers are at the end of the chapter.

### *Beginning*

1. What is the time and place of the story?

2. Who tells the story?

3. What important information does Chekhov convey to his readers in the opening along with the setting? Answer by explaining the meaning behind the following phrases.
   a. She was younger and better looking . . .

   b. her adorer

   c. her summer villa

d. Kolpakov had drunk a whole bottle of inferior port.

### Middle

4. What happening begins the action of the story?

5. What is the first name of the chorus girl?

6. What does the dialogue between the man's mistress and his wife reveal about the character of each? of the husband?

7. What is the climax?

*Resolution*

8. What is the illumination that the story has so imperceptibly moved toward?

## VOCABULARY TEST SIX

Four words are lined up below each of 20 words taken from the model paragraphs and short story. Select the one that matches best and write its letter in the blank to the right. Answers are at the end of the chapter.

1. abundant _____
   (a) frequent    (b) boring    (c) plentiful
   (d) commonplace

2. conveyed _____
   (a) transferred    (b) brought, carried    (c) sailed
   (d) secreted

3. enigmatical _____
   (a) puzzling    (b) forceful    (c) trustworthy    (d) rude

4. deceived _____
   (a) confused    (b) warned    (c) tricked, misled
   (d) failed

5. bristled _____
   (a) raised    (b) stood patiently    (c) straightened
   (d) made rigid with anger

6. singularity _____
   (a) uniqueness    (b) sinfulness    (c) awkwardness
   (d) state of being unmarried

7. intolerably _____
   (a) unusually    (b) unendurably, unbearably
   (c) oddly    (d) unseasonably

8. vile _____
   (a) foul, loathsome    (b) vicious    (c) dishonest
   (d) grasping

9. repulsion _____
   (a) anger    (b) distrust    (c) aversion, distaste
   (d) pity, shame

10. mercenary _____
    (a) immoral    (b) bold, brazen    (c) practical
    (d) grasping

11. hussy _____
    (a) peasant    (b) actress    (c) immoral or lewd woman
    (d) deceiver

12. embezzled _____
    (a) stolen    (b) borrowed    (c) counterfeited    (d) lost

13. destitution                                              ____
    (a) punishment    (b) utter poverty    (c) disgrace
    (d) pardon

14. squandered                                               ____
    (a) misused    (b) lent    (c) invested
    (d) spent wastefully or foolishly

15. indignation                                              ____
    (a) self-pity    (b) accusation    (c) righteous anger
    (d) grief

16. humiliate                                                ____
    (a) scorn    (b) to embarrass    (c) insult    (d) discredit

17. scrutinized                                              ____
    (a) examined carefully    (b) evaluated    (c) recorded
    (d) held

18. impulsively                                              ____
    (a) unconsciously    (b) immediately    (c) rashly
    (d) uncivilly

19. wailed                                                   ____
    (a) complained    (b) screamed    (c) shouted
    (d) mourned bitterly

20. condemned                                                ____
    (a) recommended    (b) blamed    (c) brought
    (d) sentenced

## Suggested Written Assignment

Writing the short story probably requires more experience than you have at this time. However, if your instructor wishes, you may make an attempt at this kind of narration.

## Answers: Chapter 4

### Exercise 1

1. Anne Sullivan states her purpose in italicized sentence 3.
2. Helen Keller's associating the water that touched her hand with the word *water* was the key to the puzzle. Thus, she discovered a method of learning to communicate with another person.
3. She added thirty new words to her vocabulary that same day.
4. No. Anne Sullivan does not dramatize the incident; she was mainly interested in informing: to tell her friend about the method she used. Compare

this account of that incident with Helen Keller's personal experience presented later in this chapter.

5. The story is organized in time order; it is a factual account of a real happening with a stated expository purpose that is supported by the action of the event. It has a beginning, a middle, and an end.

### The Chorus Girl

This short story is an excellent example of the compressed technique of story telling; Chekhov was a master of that technique through which a writer conveys meaning by the events and action rather than telling the reader the meaning of the events and actions.

1. In the first sentence, Chekhov writes: "One day when she was younger and better looking." Thus, the story takes place sometime in the past.
   They were in the outer room of her summer villa.
2. The chorus girl tells the story.
3. a. The chorus girl is older now than when the story took place.
   b. She is the mistress of Nikolay Petrovitch Kolpakov.
   c. Apparently, her lovers have been or are generous since she lives in her summer villa.
   d. It is not usual to drink an entire bottle of port at that time of the day. The incident shows Petrovitch's self-indulgent nature, his social status, and poor financial position.
4. There is a sudden ring at the door.
5. Pasha is her first name; no last name is given.
6. Pasha is ashamed of her appearance and lack of respectability. Chekhov writes: "And it seemed to her that if she had been thin, and had had no powder on her face and no fringe on her forehead, then she could have disguised the fact that she was not "respectable" and she would not have felt so frightened and ashamed to stand facing this unknown, mysterious lady."
   The wife is a beautiful lady who is angry and humiliated. She is loyal to her husband. Although she is destitute, she is a proud woman who will take nothing that she does not believe her husband gave Pasha.
7. The climax occurs when the husband comes out and attacks Pasha.
8. Pasha and the reader now understand the true character of Nikolay Petrovitch Kolpakov. (As Sean O'Faolain writes: "Kolpakov is revealed as 'stingy, self-indulgent, gross, tasteless, playing the hero at the end, deceiving not only the two women but unmasked as a fraud who lives by deceiving himself.' " P. 70.)

### Voc. Test 5

| | | | |
|---|---|---|---|
| 1. a | 6. c | 11. b | 16. b |
| 2. c | 7. a | 12. d | 17. d |
| 3. b | 8. d | 13. a | 18. c |
| 4. b | 9. c | 14. b | 19. a |
| 5. b | 10. a | 15. c | 20. b |

| *Match-Up 4* | *Match-Up 5* | *Voc. Test 6* |
|---|---|---|
| 1. d | 1. k | 1. c |
| 2. l | 2. b | 2. b |
| 3. g | 3. e | 3. a |
| 4. h | 4. j | 4. c |
| 5. b | 5. g | 5. d |
| 6. i | 6. l | 6. a |
| 7. j | 7. c | 7. b |
| 8. k | 8. m | 8. a |
| 9. a | 9. a | 9. c |
| 10. c | 10. h | 10. d |
| 11. f | 11. i | 11. c |
| 12. e | 12. d | 12. a |
| | 13. o | 13. b |
| | 14. f | 14. d |
| | 15. n | 15. c |
| | | 16. b |
| | | 17. a |
| | | 18. c |
| | | 19. d |
| | | 20. d |

# 5

## Moving Through Space — Description

Description is a form of discourse by which a writer presents a word picture of a person, place, object, or happening. It appeals to the reader's sense of sight, hearing, touch, taste, and smell. Description is seldom a pure form; it is more commonly a subordinate part of another form of discourse, especially narration. There are two kinds of description: *informative description* and *emotional description*.

### Structuring Description

In creating for the reader your mind's image of a person, place, object, or happening, you cannot possibly present every descriptive detail or all of the sensory perceptions evoked in you as you view the original. You select, therefore, from a mass of details (as you did in writing narration) those that will best fulfill your purpose of an informative or emotional description; and you give unity, order, and coherence to the writing as you arrange the details so that they represent the image as you experienced it.

To write good description, you must first become a keen observer of life. You learn to see not only the whole but also the details that are joined together into a logical pattern making up the whole. You gain the ability to make the kind of distinctions necessary for good description by choosing the right words; that is, words that will communicate the objective impression or the emotional impression that you experienced as you viewed the person, place, object, or happening. Finally, you move your reader smoothly and logically onward through the word picture, giving it order by moving through space and achieving coherence by selecting a fixed or moving point of view — a position in space from which you as the observer describe the original.

## Word Choice

To write good descriptions, you must be able to use words discriminatingly. In order to present your reader with a reasonably true picture of what you see, you must be objective, selecting words that are precise and factual. On the other hand, some descriptions demand evocative words to capture impressionistic feelings about a person or thing. They call for words that will arouse the reader's emotions.

To create pictures with words, you must first know something about the power of words. Words in the English language may be classified into words with denotative meanings and connotative meanings. The denotative meaning of a word is its dictionary meaning. *House*, for example, is defined as "a building intended as a dwelling for human beings." The denotation of a word, then, means what the word stands for. It is the precise, literal, factual meaning. *Cat*, defined literally, is "a small, lithe, soft-furred animal, domesticated since ancient times and often kept as a pet or for killing mice." *Hiss* in its literal sense means "to make a sound like that of a prolonged *s*, as of a goose, or snake, or of escaping steam, air, etc." If a writer's purpose is to present exact information, he will use words with denotative meanings.

▶ Those houses were built in the early '50s.

That cat was nearly hit by an automobile yesterday.

The connotative meaning of a word, on the other hand, is what the word suggests. The word *home*, for example, though it means the same as *house*, suggests something more than "a building intended as a dwelling." It means in its connotative sense "a place where an individual's affections are centered." *Cat* has also the connotative meaning of "a spiteful woman." Two words, therefore, may share the same denotative meaning, but they may have connotative meanings quite different. Consider the words in the following list. Observe the shades of meaning around the denotative meaning.

▶ imitate, copy, forge, mirror, counterfeit, reproduce
small, little, stunted, puny, dwarfish, tiny
stout, corpulent, fat, obese, plump, chubby, fleshy
thin, slender, slim, lean, lank, gaunt, emaciated
dog, mongrel, pup, puppy, mutt, canine, whelp
old, ancient, stale, obsolete, antique, elderly, senile
late, tardy, slow, dilatory, belated, overdue

What do the following words or phrases connote to you personally?

| | | | |
|---|---|---|---|
| church | oily | mother | honesty |
| rose | ocean | love | examination |
| snow | eternal | test | youth |

| | | |
|---|---|---|
| censorship | suppression of news | free press |
| citizen | politician | statesman |

| | | |
|---|---|---|
| Zest | Mr. Clean | Tide |
| Filter Tip | Easy Off | Mountain Grown |

Words may be classified also as *abstract* (general) or concrete (specific). An abstract or general word names a group or a class. A concrete word names a particular object, quality, event — a member of a class or group. The word *emotion*, for example, names a class. The words *joy, love, hate, jealousy, sorrow*, on the other hand, name a particular emotion. Study the following sentences.

▶ Those animals are very hungry.

Those lions and tigers are very hungry.

Most students who applied for that position were well educated.

Most of the graduate students who applied for the teaching assistantship were working for their doctorates.

In the yard were some trees and many flowers.

In the back yard were an oak tree, a towering pine, and three chestnut trees. There were also several planters of geraniums and three beds of violets.

Word choice is vitally important to effective writing. Word choice should fit the purpose and the subject. The beginning writer, therefore, should choose his words wisely in order to achieve effective and stimulating communication of his ideas.

The subject of the two descriptive selections that follow is the same: stars. Write a paragraph or two discussing the different treatment, especially the word choice and emotional mood of each.

▶ STAR is a huge ball of glowing gas in the sky. The sun is a star. It is the only star close enough to the earth to look like a ball. The other billions of stars are so far away that they are no more than pinpoints of light — if they can be seen at all.

Stars are the biggest things man knows of. The largest stars would more than fill the space between the earth and the sun. Such stars have a *diameter* (distance through the center) about 1,000 times as large as the sun's. The smallest stars are smaller than the earth.

We can hardly imagine the great distances that separate the stars. The star nearest the sun is more than 25 million million miles away from the sun. But even this great distance is only one-billionth the distance from the sun to the farthest stars known to man.

"Star"
*The World Book Encyclopedia*

▶ A few stars are known which are hardly bigger than the earth, but the majority are so large that hundreds of thousands of earths could be packed inside each and leave room to spare; here and there we come upon a giant star large enough to contain millions of millions of earths. And the total number of stars in the universe is probably something like the total number of grains of sand on all the sea-shores of the world. Such is the littleness of our home in space when measured up against the total substance of the universe.

This vast multitude of stars are wandering about in space. A few form groups which journey in company, but the majority are solitary travellers. And they travel through a universe so spacious that it is an event of almost unimaginable rarity for a star to come anywhere near to another star. For the most part each voyages in splendid isolation, like a ship on an empty ocean. In a scale model in which stars are ships, the average ship will be well over a million miles from its nearest neighbor, whence it is easy to understand why a ship seldom finds another within hailing distance.

Sir James Jeans
*The Mysterious Universe*

## Images and Figurative Language

"The etymologist," says Emerson in his essay "The Poet," "finds the deadest word to have been once a brilliant picture. Language is fossil poetry. As the limestone of the continent consists of infinite masses of the shells of animalcules, so language is made up of images or tropes (figures of speech), which now, in their secondary use, have long ceased to remind us of their poetic origin."*

*Images*, as defined for our purposes, are rhetorical and literary devices that evoke in the reader mental and visual pictures of something not actually present. Images can be effective rhetorical and poetic devices because they evoke emotions, give a freshness and vividness to writing, and meaning to things that otherwise would be difficult for the reader to understand. Observe the series of images in the passages that follow.

▶ The lieutenant of the youth's company was shot in the hand. He began to swear so wondrously that a nervous laugh went along the regimental line. The officer's profanity sounded conventional. It relieved the tightened senses of the new men. It was as if he had hit his fingers with a tack hammer at home.

He held the wounded member carefully away from his side so that the blood would not drip upon his trousers.

The captain of the company, tucking his sword under his arm, produced a handkerchief and began to bind with it the lieutenant's wound. And they disputed as to how the binding should be done.

---

* Ralph Waldo Emerson, "The Poet" in *Essays* (Philadelphia: David McKay Publisher, 1890), p. 27.

The battle flag in the distance jerked about madly. It seemed to be struggling to free itself from an agony. The billowing smoke was filled with horizontal flashes.

Men running swiftly emerged from it. They grew in numbers until it was seen that the whole command was fleeing. The flag suddenly sank down as if dying. Its motion as it fell was a gesture of despair.

Wild yells came from behind the walls of smoke. A sketch in gray and red dissolved into a moblike body of men who galloped like wild horses.

The veteran regiments on the right and left of the 304th immediately began to jeer. With the passionate song of the bullets and the banshee shrieks of shells were mingled loud catcalls and bits of facetious advice concerning places of safety.

But the new regiment was breathless with horror. "Gawd! Saunders's got crushed!" whispered the man at the youth's elbow. They shrank back and crouched as if compelled to await a flood.

Stephen Crane
*The Red Badge of Courage*

Crane creates a series of impressionistic pictures of the battle through skillful and deliberate word choice. He uses literal terms and figurative language to convey his factual and emotional description of the battle. The result is a memorable reading experience.

*Figurative language* (figures of speech), for the most part, is the expression of emotions and ideas by comparing and identifying one thing with something else more familiar to the reader or listener. It is a language conveying meaning beyond the literal meaning of words. It evokes emotions, makes vivid sensory experiences, and elicits images. On many occasions figurative language enables a writer to communicate experiences that he would find very difficult or even impossible to describe in literal terms. It enables a writer also to accomplish in a few words much that he would find impossible to accomplish in many words. When Crane wanted to make clear and vivid the fears of the young soldier as he stood facing an unknown and unseen enemy, he identifies the enemy with a "composite monster"; therefore, he writes, "The composite monster which had caused the other troops to flee had not appeared . . . ." A few pages later he uses the same metaphor and develops the animal imagery more fully.

▶ To the youth it was an onslaught of redoubtable dragons. He became like the man who has lost his legs at the approach of the red and green monster. He waited in a sort of horrified, listening attitude. He seemed to shut his eyes and wait to be gobbled.

When William Wordsworth wished to describe the beauty and solitariness of Lucy, a young girl who is the subject of several of his poems, he expressed those qualities in the following poetic words:

▶ A violet by a mossy stone
Half hidden from the eye!
Fair as a Star, when only one
Is shining in the sky.

William Wordsworth
"She Dwelt Among the Untrodden Ways"

The most common kinds of figurative language (figures of speech) are simile, metaphor, personification, and allusion. A *simile* is a directly stated comparison introduced by the word *like* or *as*. A well-written simile is effective because it is vivid and evocative. It enables a writer to express meaning far beyond literal terms. Crane compares the feelings of the youth to those of a man who has "lost his legs at the approach of the red and green monster." Wordsworth's Lucy is not just beautiful and solitary; she is "fair as a Star, when only one is shining in the sky." Study the following similes; observe the things compared, the evocative effect, the enrichment of meaning.

▶ But my body was like a harp and her words and gestures like fingers running upon wires.

James Joyce
"Araby"

▶ Pepe's wrist flicked like the head of a snake.

John Steinbeck
"Flight"

▶ The lazy geese, like a snow cloud
Dripping their snow on the green grass . . .

John Crowe Ransom
"Bells for John Whiteside's Daughter"

▶ . . . she was aware of the cars screaming by on her left, like juggernauts on a treadmill that had run amuck.

Jon Cleary
*The Green Helmet*

▶ . . . and the huge sleeping crowd had begun to stir again, coming awake like a giant animal thirsting for excitement and, perhaps, hoping for blood.

Jon Cleary
*The Green Helmet*

▶ Weighed down with its heavy load, the plane felt clumsy, like a duck with clipped wings.

Anne Morrow Lindbergh
*North to the Orient*

▶ The squat ferryboats below plowed across our wake, and great flat barges carrying rectangular mounds of different colored earth like spools of gold and tawny silk.

Anne Morrow Lindbergh
*North to the Orient*

▶ The asteroids occur as a single swarm.

Sir James Jeans
*The Universe Around Us*

A *metaphor* is an implied comparison without the introductory word *like* or *as*. Like the simile, the metaphor identifies one object with another and makes meaning clear and vivid by similarities — usually the second partner of the comparison is more familiar and more evocative.

▶ In ten years of studied undercover work they have rolled back the tide of public distaste . . .

Keith Monroe
"They Made the Cigar Respectable"

▶ That time of year thou mayst in me behold
When yellow leaves, or none, or few, do hang
Upon those boughs, which shake against the cold,
Bare ruin'd choirs, where late the sweet birds sang.

William Shakespeare
"Sonnet 73"

▶ Yet the diaphragm is the bellows that blows the fire of life into your speech and adds oomph to your personality.

Stephen Price
"Put Your Best Foot Forward"

▶ The moon was a ghostly galleon tossed upon cloudy seas . . .

Alfred Noyes
"The Highwayman"

▶ No man is an island, entire of itself; every man is a piece of the continent, a part of the main . . .

John Donne
"Meditation XVII"

▶ It [the sea] is a silent jungle . . .

J. Y. Cousteau
*The Silent World*

*Personification* is a figure of speech endowing animals, ideas, abstractions, and inanimate objects with human characteristics. Such common expressions as "the lonely hills," "the tired mountains," "the peaceful ocean," "a restful hamlet" are examples of personification.

▶ And do whate'er thou wilt, swift-footed Time . . .

William Shakespeare
"Sonnet 19"

▶ The forests, somber and dull, stood motionless and silent on each side of the broad stream.

Joseph Conrad
"The Lagoon"

▶ A plaintive murmur rose in the night, a murmur saddening and startling, as if the great solitudes of the surrounding woods had tried to whisper into his ear the wisdom of their immense and lofty indifference.

Joseph Conrad
"The Lagoon"

An *allusion* is a reference to famous people and events in history, literature (including the Bible), and mythology.

▶ We of these later days, living in the narrow temperate zone surrounding our sun and peering into the far future, see an ice age of a different kind threatening us. Just as Tantalus, standing in a lake so deep that he only just escaped drowning, was yet destined to die of thirst, so it is the tragedy of our race that it is probably destined to die of cold, while the greater part of the substance of the universe still remains too hot for life to obtain a footing.

Sir James Jeans
*The Mysterious Universe*

▶ Also Ulysses once — that other war.
   (Is it because we find his scrawl
   Today on every privy door
   That we forget his ancient role?)
Also was there — he did it for wages —
When a Cathay-drunk Genoese set sail.
Whenever "longen folk to goon on pilgrimages,"
Kilroy is there;
   he tells The Miller's Tale.

Peter Viereck
"Kilroy"

Read the figures of speech that follow. How many can you identify?

▶ Then pretty soon Sherburn sort of laughed; not the pleasant kind, but the kind that makes you feel like when you are eating bread that's got sand in it.

Samuel Clemens
*The Adventures of Huckleberry Finn*

▶ The handsome houses on the streets to the college were not fully awake, but they looked very friendly.

Lionel Trilling
"Of This Time, of That Place"

▶ Coolidge-Hoover prosperity was not yet dead, but it was dying. Under the impact of the shock of panic a multitude of ills which hitherto had passed unnoticed or had been offset by stock-market optimism began to beset the body economic, as poisons seep through the human system when a vital organ has ceased to function normally.

Frederick Lewis Allen
*Only Yesterday*

▶ Believe me, Gentlemen, the way still before you is intricate, dark, and full of perplexed and treacherous mazes. Those who think they have the clue may lead us out of this labyrinth.

Edmund Burke
"Letter to the Sheriffs of Bristol"

▶ When eventually he began his back swing, it was with a slowness which reminded those who had travelled in Switzerland of moving glaciers. A cautious pause at the top, and the clubhead would descend to strike the ball squarely and dispatch it fifty yards down the course in a perfectly straight line.

P. G. Wodehouse
*The Crime Wave at Blandings*

▶ Chestnut Street sings a music of its own.

Christopher Morley
*Travels in Philadelphia*

▶ It [the opium den] was a cheerful spot, comfortable, home-like, cosy. It reminded me somewhat of the little intimate beerhouses of Berlin, where the tired working-man could go in the evening and spend a peaceful hour.

W. Somerset Maugham
*On a Chinese Screen*

## Assignment: Connotative and Denotative Words

Discuss the following words or word groups as to their connotative and denotative meaning.

pig                           statesman
rat                           politician
a man                      an atheist
a gentleman          a churchgoer
a bum                      dog
a derelict             German shepherd
intoxicated           typewriter
a problem drinker   electric typewriter
leprosy                   car
Hansen's disease     Cadillac

## Assignment: Abstract and Concrete Words

Discuss the following words or word groups as to their abstract and concrete meaning.

cow                    U.S.S. *Missouri*
pride                  bird
book                  robin
Bible                  flower
building            violet
dessert             food
apple pie         bread
pie                   meat
ship                  steak
battleship        sirloin steak

## Dominant Impression

In structuring description, you do not organize and develop your mass of descriptive details around a statement of thesis or statement of purpose (exposition) and a unified whole action or a theme (narration). You can organize and give unity to descriptive writing by selecting details and arranging them so that they emphasize a single characteristic, aspect, or feature of the person, place, object, or happening you are describing.

With this kind of pattern, you present the *dominant impression*. It might be a person's blue eyes, striking hair, long nose, weather-beaten face or animal-like appearance that left its mark on you. It could be also a mood or feeling that deeply affected you, such as the courage of a condemned man, the senseless fury of a typhoon, the calm and peace of an isolated valley in the shadow of a lofty mountain, the eternal sadness of the ebbing tide, the immenseness of an unlimited universe. Each of these feelings could be the unifying force for a description.

In the model description that follows, the writer focuses on the tremendous force and height of the tidal wave resulting from the eruption of the volcano on the island of Krakatoa. Notice especially his use of strong verbs like *swirled, rearing, rampaged, funnelled, dwarfed,* etc.

▶ From the truncated island swirled a wall of water, rolling outward in an ever widening circle. This huge mass of sea water crossed the Straits in all directions, mounting in height as the sea bed shallowed. Rearing to mountainous size as it approached the shore, it rampaged up breaches, rolled across the countryside and clawed at hills, destroying everything and everyone in its path. It funnelled into a wedge-shaped bore, at least a hundred feet high, at the Strait's narrow eastern entrance. It escaped freely through its wide western end, sweeping across the Indian Ocean, touching at Cape Horn, and rolling up the Atlantic. Two days after it left Krakatoa, it lapped the shores of the English Channel, 11,500 miles away, raising water levels by two inches.

Several of the survivors attempted to describe the great wave. The magnitude of the experience was too great for them. The sight of the grey wall of water appearing from nowhere was an experience which no one could have described adequately. The air was filled with swirling dust and falling pumice. It was blacker than the blackest night. Huge tracts of land were submerged. Towns and houses were in ruins. Corpses lay everywhere. The wave came without warning. It rose higher than the highest palm tree. It was preceded and followed by a tempest of wind. It dwarfed everything. It was a towering wall of solid water. It moved at tremendous speed. People were submerged before they knew what struck them. In an instant they were floundering and struggling in foaming water, jerking, pulling, dragging and shoving them. They were hurled into a maelstrom of tossing, twisting, black chaos. Those who stood on high ground did not wait to watch Nature's wonder; they turned to run in precipitous, gasping, tortured flight.

Rupert Furneaux
*Krakatoa*

In the description that follows, observe how the writers emphasize the darkness in the character of Fletcher Christian, the protagonist of the novel *Mutiny on the Bounty*. Later in the novel, Fletcher Christian leads the seamen in mutiny against the cruelty of Captain Bligh. The authors of the novel, Charles Nordhoff and James Norman Hall, describe Christian with black (darkness) dominating the impression (italics are mine).

▶ Fletcher Christian was at that time in his twenty-fourth year, — a fine figure of a seaman in his plain blue, gold-buttoned frock, — handsomely and strongly built, with thick *dark* brown hair and a complexion naturally *dark*, and burned by the sun to a shade rarely seen among the white race. His mouth and chin expressed resolution of character, and his eyes, *black*, deep-set, and brilliant, had something of hypnotic power in their far-away gaze. He looked more like a *Spaniard* than an Englishman, though his family had been settled since the fifteenth century on the Isle of Man. Christian was what women call a romantic-looking man; his moods of gaiety alternated with fits of *black depression* and he possessed a fiery temper which he controlled by efforts that brought the sweat to his brow. . . .

Charles Nordhoff and James Norman Hall
*Mutiny on the Bounty*

In addition to the dominant impression of darkness of character, the writers in describing Christian also selected details that a leader of a mutiny against the British naval system would have to possess. Fletcher Christian's "mouth and chin expressed resolution of character"; "his eyes, black, deep-set, and brilliant, had something of hypnotic power in their far-away gaze." "His moods of gaiety alternated with fits of black depression and he possessed a fiery temper which he controlled by efforts that brought the sweat to his brow. . . ."

In the model descriptive paragraph that follows, the details emphasize the intense heat that Captain Hornblower experienced as his ship entered the little bay of Coiba.

▶ It was terribly hot in that little bay in the island of Coiba. The lofty mountains all about cut off any wind that might be blowing, and at the same time reflected the heat to a focus in the bay. As the cable rasped out through the hawsehole Hornblower felt the heat descend upon him. He was wet with sweat even while he stood still on the quarterdeck; he longed for a bath and for a little leisure, to rest until the cool of the evening, but he could not allow himself any such luxury. Time was, as ever, of vital importance. He must make himself secure before the Spaniards could discover where he had hidden himself.

C. S. Forester
*Beat To Quarters*

**VOCABULARY PREVIEW**

| | | |
|---|---|---|
| tortuous | vengeful | resonated |
| shelving | infernal | fetched |
| bewitched | prodigious | ambience |
| implacable | gamut | nostalgia |
| inscrutable | perceptible | venerable |

## EXERCISE 1    Dominant Impression

Read the description below. Answer the questions that follow. Answers are at the end of the chapter.

> ▶ Inch by inch His Britannic Majesty's frigate *Lydia* crept into
> the bay. The cutter was out ahead, with Rayner sounding in-
> dustriously, while with a dying breath of air behind her and a
> shred of sail set the *Lydia* felt her way between the two head-
> lands into the tortuous° channel. Those capes, one each side of
> the entrance, were steep rocky cliffs, and the one overlapped
> the other a trifle so that only an eye sharpened by necessity,
> and which had made the most of its recent opportunities of
> learning the typical rock formations of that coast, could have
> guessed at the possibility of an expanse of water behind them.
>     Hornblower took his eye from the ship's course as she
> crawled round the corner to study the bay before him. There
> were mountains all round it, but on the farther side the slope
> down to the water was not nearly so steep, and on the water's
> edge there, at the foot of the dazzling green which clothed the
> banks all round, there was a hint of golden sand which told of
> the sort of bottom which he sought. It would be shelving°
> there, without a doubt, and free from rock.
>
> C. S. Forester<br>*Beat to Quarters*

1. What is the dominant impression?

2. Underline the words or word groups that, in your opinion, contribute to the effectiveness of the dominant impression.

## EXERCISE 2  Dominant Impression

Read the description below. Answer the questions that follow.

▶ "Going up that river was like traveling back to the earliest beginnings of the world, when vegetation rioted on the earth and the big trees were kings. An empty stream, a great silence, an impenetrable forest. The air was warm, thick, heavy, sluggish. There was no joy in the brilliance of sunshine. The long stretches of the waterway ran on, deserted, into the gloom of overshadowed distances. On silvery sandbanks hippos and alligators sunned themselves side by side. The broadening waters flowed through a mob of wooded islands; you lost your way on that river as you would in a desert, and butted all day long against shoals, trying to find the channel, till you thought yourself bewitched° and cut off forever from everything you had known once — somewhere — far away — in another existence perhaps. There were moments when one's past came back to one, as it will sometimes when you have not a moment to spare to yourself; but it came in the shape of an unrestful and noisy dream, remembered with wonder amongst the overwhelming realities of this strange world of plants, and water, and silence. And this stillness of life did not in the least resemble a peace. It was the stillness of an implacable° force brooding over an inscrutable° intention. It looked at you with a vengeful° aspect. I got used to it afterwards; I did not see it anymore; I had no time. I had to keep guessing at the channel; I had to discern, mostly by inspiration, the signs of hidden banks; I watched for sunken stones; I was learning to clap my teeth smartly before my heart flew out, when I shaved by a fluke some infernal° sly old snag that would have ripped the life out of the tin-pot steamboat and drowned all the pilgrims. . . .

Joseph Conrad
*The Heart of Darkness*

1. What is the dominant impression, especially the mood or tone that Joseph Conrad creates?

2. Underline the words or word groups that help the reader grasp the dominant impression.

3. To what senses does the writer appeal? Select some words or word groups that appeal to the senses of hearing and feeling.

## EXERCISE 3   Dominant Impression

Read the description below. Answer the questions that follow. Answers are at the end of the chapter.

▶ The cabin, small though it was, housed a prodigious° stink. The first thing the nostrils noticed was the sooty, stuffy smell of the lamp, but they immediately became aware of a whole gamut° of supplementary odours. There was the flat bilge smell, tolerable, in fact almost unnoticed by Hornblower, who had smelt bilge for twenty years. There was a penetrating smell of cheese, and as if to set that off there was a perceptible° smell of rats. There was a smell of wet clothing, and finally there was a mixture of human odours, the long-confined body odour of unwashed men predominating.

And all this mixture of smells was balanced by a battery of noises. Every timber resonated° the shrieking of the rigging; to be inside the cabin was to be like a mouse inside a violin while it was being played. Overhead the continual footfalls on the quarterdeck and the clatter of ropes being thrown down made it seem — to continue the analogy — as if someone else were tapping the body of the violin at the same time with small mallets. The wooden sheathing of the brig creaked and crackled with the vessel's motion in the water like a giant's knuckles rapping on the exterior; and the shot in the racks rolled just a trifle with each movement, too, thumping solemnly and unexpectedly just at the end of the roll as they fetched° up.

C. S. Forester
*Lord Hornblower*

1. What is the dominant impression?

2. Underline the words or word groups that help create the dominant impression.

3. Write the two similes that enrich the meaning of the descriptive passage.

## Suggested Topics for Discussion and Writing Description

1. A winter evening
2. A street in your home town
3. A place in the country
4. An unusual character
5. A room
6. An old castle on a river bank
7. A desolate area of land
8. A view of the land from the sea
9. Looking down from a mountain
10. A mysterious house

## Point of View

*Point of view* in description is the position in space from which the observer views the person, place, object, or happening. When writing description, you may select a fixed or moving position. You may view the subject, for example, from a fixed physical position in space, such as from the top of a hill, the foothills of a towering mountain range, from a bridge high above a turbulent river, from the dock as a ship departs, from the rear of a spacious banquet hall, or from the shore of a lake out onto the lake. From whatever fixed position you take, you then describe your subject in some kind of natural and logical order. You may decide to move from the most distant point to the nearest point, or from the nearest point to the most distant point, from top to bottom or from bottom to top, from right to left or from left to right, from inside to outside or from outside to inside, from front to back or from back to front. You may wish to focus on a single dominant impression and move to the less important aspects or from the less important aspects to the dominant impression; for example, a snow-capped mountain peak in a rugged mountain range, the large red nose of a melancholy clown, the deep lines in the tired face of a great man, or the loneliness of a solitary figure standing in a large stadium after the big game.

You may wish to describe your subject from a shifting point of view You may be moving through a crowd in order to describe individual reactions to a crime, an accident, a holocaust. You may wish to describe various rooms in a famous building, such as the White House. You may be describing a battlefield, a natural wonder of the world, or a lonely seashore as you fly over it. The possibilities are, of course, almost limitless.

In the model descriptive passage that follows, Lieutenant Ramage is located on a terrace in a magnificent palace that stands high above the Tyrrhenian Sea across from the mainland of Italy.

▶ Ramage recalled with a shock that barely three hours earlier Gianna had burst into the court on board the *Trumpeter*. Now he was a guest in a magnificent palace, sitting in a comfortable cane chair on this terrace, overlooking a garden flanked by myrtle hedges and ablaze with the last of the season's oleander and roses, with small, pointed cypresses scattered about like sentries among the orange trees and arbutus.

From the terrace, looking across the blue Tyrrhenian Sea toward the distant mainland of Italy, he found it hard to believe there could be war in any part of the world, least of all just over the horizon: the line-of-battle ships, frigates and smaller craft at anchor in the Roads at the bottom of the garden, were, in this sharp clear light and against this background and atmosphere, things of grace and beauty, not specifically designed to kill, sink, burn, and destroy.

The far horizon to the eastward was beginning to turn a faint mauve in the late afternoon, while behind him the sun would soon dip behind Mount Pigno and draw a shadow over the town and port of Bastia. To his left the outline of the Island of Capraia, dissolving in the haze, would soon be invisible like Elba directly in front of him and tiny Pianosa to the right. Out of sight over the horizon, British frigates were blockading. . . .

Dudley Pope
*Ramage*

In the next model descriptive paragraph, the view is from a rowboat a safe distance in the ocean from the burning ship. Notice the use of strong adjectives and verbs. Observe also the use of the simile and personification in his description of the death of the ship as the death of a woman.

▶ I looked at the burning ship. Between the darkness of earth and heaven she was burning fiercely upon a disc of purple sea shot by the blood-red play of gleams; upon a disc of water glittering and sinister. A high, clear flame, an immense and lonely flame, ascended from the ocean, and from its summit the black smoke poured continuously at the sky. She burned furiously; mournful and imposing like a funeral pyre kindled in the night, surrounded by the sea, watched over by the stars. A magnificent death had come like a grace, like a gift, like a reward to that old ship at the end of her laborious day. The surrender of her weary ghost to the keeper of stars and sea was stirring like the sight of a glorious triumph. The masts fell just before daybreak, and for a moment there was a burst and turmoil of sparks that seemed to fill with flying fire the night patient and watchful, the vast night lying silent upon the sea. At daylight she was only a charred shell, floating still under a cloud of smoke and bearing a glowing mass of coal within.

Joseph Conrad<br>
Youth

In the description that follows, C. S. Forester describes the land in the distance through the eyes of Hornblower, who views it through a telescope high up in the fore-top gallant mast head of the vessel.

▶ The climb hand over hand up the fore-top gallant shrouds tried him severely; breathing heavily, he reached the fore-top gallant mast head, and settled himself to point the telescope as steadily as his heaving chest and sudden nervousness would allow. Clay was sitting nonchalantly astride the yard-arm fifteen feet away, but Hornblower ignored him. The slight corkscrew roll of the ship was sweeping him in a vast circle, up, forward, sideways, and down; at first he could only fix the distant mountains in snatches, but after a time he was able to keep them under fairly continuous observation. It was a strange landscape, which the telescope revealed to him. There were the sharp peaks of several volcanoes; two very tall ones to larboard, a host of smaller ones both to starboard and to port. As he looked he saw a puff of grey steam emerge from one peak — not from the summit, but from a vent in the side — and ascend lazily to join the strip of white cloud which hung over it. Besides these cones there was a long mountain range of which the peaks appeared to be spurs, but the range itself seemed to be made up of a chain of old volcanoes, truncated and weathered down by the passage of centuries; that strip of coast must have been a hell's kitchen when they were all in eruption together. The upper parts of the peaks and of the mountains were a warm grey — grey with a hint of pink — and lower he could see what looked like green cataracts which must be vegetation stretching up along gullies in the mountain sides. Hornblower noted the relative heights and positions of the volcanoes, and from these data he drew a map in his mind and compared it with the section of the chart which he also carried in his mind's eye. There was no doubting their similarity.

C. S. Forester
*Beat To Quarters*

By describing a subject from a fixed physical position, a writer, of course, limits his view. He can describe only what he sees from that position. Sometimes writers describe a subject from a shifting point of view. A writer may be in a moving airplane, an automobile, a ship. He may be moving in a crowd of people, walking in a park, a museum, an old house. He may be climbing a hill, a mountain, up the stairs from one floor of a house to another. As he moves along he describes what he sees, feels, tastes, hears, and touches. Stephen Crane presents this kind of movement in the selection that follows. Henry Fleming, the youthful hero of *The Red Badge of Courage*, runs away from the fighting in his first battle. Crane creates a series of impressions as he describes the flight of the youth.

▶ He ran like a blind man. Two or three times he fell down. Once he knocked his shoulder so heavily against a tree that he went headlong.

Since he had turned his back upon the fight his fears had been wondrously magnified. Death about to thrust him between the shoulder blades was far more dreadful than death about to smite him between the eyes. When he thought of it later, he conceived the impression that it is better to view the appalling than to be merely within hearing. The noises of the battle were like stones; he believed himself liable to be crushed.

As he ran on he mingled with others. He dimly saw men on his right and on his left, and he heard footsteps behind him. He thought that all the regiment was fleeing, pursued by these ominous crashes.

In his flight the sound of these following footsteps gave him his one meager relief. He felt vaguely that death must make a first choice of the men who were nearest; the initial morsels for the dragons would be then those who were following him. So he displayed the zeal of an insane sprinter in his purpose to keep them in the rear. There was a race.

As he, leading, went across a little field, he found himself in a region of shells. They hurtled over his head with long wild screams. As he listened he imagined them to have rows of cruel teeth, that grinned at him. Once one lit before him and the livid lightning of the explosion effectually barred the way in his chosen direction. He groveled on the ground and then springing up went careering off through some bushes.

He experienced a thrill of amazement when he came within view of a battery in action. The men there seemed to be in conventional moods, altogether unaware of the impending annihilation. The battery was disputing with a distant antagonist and the gunners were wrapped in admiration of their shooting. They were continually bending in coaxing postures over the guns. They seemed to be patting them on the back and encouraging them with words. The guns, *stolid and undaunted*, spoke with dogged valor.

Stephen Crane
*The Red Badge of Courage*

## EXERCISE 4    Point of View

Read the description below. Answer the questions that follow.

▶ Stepping through the front door into the red-carpeted lobby filled with nineteenth century furnishings, one can almost forget the twentieth century, so convincing is the Old South ambience.° Standing on one side of the lobby is a long, narrow glass-top counter containing perhaps the most interesting examples of nostalgia° the Excelsior has to offer. On view are several old guest registers dating from 1877 and signed by venerable° visitors like presidents Rutherford B. Hayes (January 3, 1878), Ulysses S. Grant (1883), and Lyndon B. Johnson (October 26, 1969). Other interesting signatures are those of the poet Oscar Wilde and industrialists W. H. Vanderbilt and Jay Gould. The case also contains newspaper clippings and books about Gould's wheelings and dealings and about the Old South's notorious Diamond Bessie murder trial.

Gracing the dining room is a Chippendale table from the 1860s, seating sixteen. The dining chairs are thought to have belonged to Mrs. Kate Woods who owned the hotel in the late 1800s. Furnished with an original Chickering square piano as well as a 1919 baby grand, the adjoining ballroom is often the setting for wedding receptions and dances.

Like the lobby, the Excelsior's sixteen bedrooms are showplaces of nineteenth-century life. All are furnished with period pieces made more than a hundred years ago of mahogany, walnut, rosewood, and cherry. Most rooms have high ceilings with antique fans, fireplaces, and outdoor balconies reminiscent of French Louisiana architecture. From each room guests enjoy an impressive view of the beautiful Old World Courtyard and garden with a geometrically laid antique brick patio surrounding a central fountain.

Had it not been for the foresight of the garden club members, the Excelsior Hotel and Jefferson itself would have gone the way of the majestic steamboats that once plowed the nearby rivers.

Robert M. McCorkle
*Excelsior Hotel*

1. What is the point of view from which the writer describes the hotel?

2. What is the dominant impression?

3. In what paragraph is the purpose of this description stated?

4. How does the writer support his stated purpose?

## VOCABULARY TEST SEVEN

Four words are lined up below each of fifteen words taken from the model paragraphs in the exercises. Select the one that matches best and write its letter in the blank to the right. Answers are at the end of the chapter.

1. tortuous    *a*
   (a) twisting    (b) narrow    (c) shallow    (d) painful

2. shelving    *c*
   (a) shallow    (b) peaceful    (c) forming sand banks
   (d) sandy

3. bewitched    *b*
   (a) isolated    (b) under a spell    (c) becalmed    (d) stuck    *d*

4. implacable
   (a) sinister    (b) strange    (c) powerful    (d) unbending, relentless    *b*

5. inscrutable
   (a) deliberate    (b) undiscoverable    (c) penetrating    (d) doubtful    *a*

6. vengeful
   (a) harmful, spiteful    (b) kind    (c) cruel    (d) mad    *D* ~~A~~

7. infernal
   (a) heavenly    (b) odd    (c) sterile    (d) hellish    *B* ~~D~~

8. prodigious
   (a) terrible    (b) extraordinary    (c) wide-spread    (d) long lasting    *C* ~~B~~

9. gamut
   (a) history    (b) small cabin    (c) entire range    (d) variety    *A*

10. perceptible
    (a) recognizable    (b) slight    (c) heavy    (d) definite    *D*

11. resonated
    (a) increased    (b) blotted out    (c) deadened    (d) resounded    *C*

12. fetched
    (a) destroyed    (b) drew    (c) returned    (d) ended    *C*

13. ambience
    (a) atmosphere    (b) environment    (c) custom    (d) society

14. nostalgia *a*
    (a) longing for the past      (b) future yearnings
    (c) furnishings      (d) antiques
15. venerable *c*
    (a) proven      (b) ancient      (c) respected      (d) political

## Informative Description

In writing description, your purpose determines whether you will structure informative description or emotional description. If you wish to reproduce the original as it actually appears in life without personal reactions to it or without imaginative suggestion, you write informative description. You concentrate on the literal, objective, factual details and produce a photographic image of the original. In the model description that follows, the writers present an informal description of a copy of Michelangelo's famous statue of *David* that stands on a raised terrace in the Loggia dei Lanzi in Florence, Italy. With a careful selection of factual details, a series of questions that they do not attempt to answer, and a very meaningful simile: "The body is awkward, like that of a tough youth, streetwise and confident," the writers reproduce for the readers a figure that is something much more than a superhuman figure formed out of "intractable" stone.

▶ The *David* is marble, over thirteen feet tall.
    The figure is completely nude; the limbs and torso, now aged by rain and sun, once had a smoothness that remains only on the surface of the face. Never painted or decorated, unlike the statuary of former times, its first impact is of intractable stone formed into a superhuman figure. But what is the boy like? The *Kritios Boy* and *The Spearbearer* are obvious idealizations of the human figure. How is David different from these two? Compare his face with that of Augustus and with a prophet from the doors at Chartres. Is this David an idealization of youth? His face is not symmetrical, the hands are enormous, and the arms and legs are too long. The body is awkward, like that of a tough youth, streetwise and confident. The brooding face is reticent but filled with a fierce courage. The body turns, a knee flexed; does the boy search the horizons for Goliath? The muscles of the neck and torso are tense, standing forth under the skin. The veins in arms, elbows, and hands rise to enliven the surface of the skin. The toes on one foot grasp the ground, while the toes of the other play over the rocky ledge.

Has the stone been thrown, or does it lie in his curved fingers? Does he ready the sling, or does it lie on his shoulder, no longer useful, but used?

Mary Ann Frese Witt, et al.
*The Humanities*

Next, read this description of a Missouri farm. Observe how the writer fulfills his purpose of informing the reader with his objectivity, his precise and concrete word choices, his skilled movement through space. In writing this informative description, Samuel Clemens relies heavily on the concrete and specific to make true his picture of the farm. He does not write that "the farmhouse stood in the yard," "the yard was fenced with rails and palings," "in the front yard were a dozen or more tall trees." Instead, he tells us that "the farmhouse stood in the *middle* of a *very large* yard," "the yard was fenced on *three* sides with *rails* and on the *rear* side with *high palings*," "in a *corner* of the *front* yard were a *dozen lofty hickory* trees and a *dozen black walnuts*."

Samuel Clemens does not jump aimlessly from one salient aspect of the whole scene to another. He moves in a natural order from the farmhouse — the dominant impression — to the less important aspects: the fences, orchard, fields, quarters, trees.

In addition, he does not overload his description with excessive details and specifics. Even the keenest observer cannot hope to perceive a thing as it really exists. A writer of description, therefore, must select skillfully those aspects which will enable the reader to create the images. Samuel Clemens does not generalize; on the other hand, he does not carry his concreteness to extremes; for example, he writes a "very large yard," "high palings," "corner of the front yard," "lofty hickory trees." He does not detail each image by citing feet and inches for yard area or tree height. With this kind of selectivity, he permits the reader to complete the total picture.

▶ The farmhouse stood in the middle of a very large yard, and the yard was fenced on three sides with rails and on the rear side with high palings; against these stood the smoke-house; beyond the palings was the orchard; beyond the orchard were the negro quarters and the tobacco fields. The front yard was entered over a stile made of sawed-off logs of graduated heights; I do not remember any gate. In a corner of the front yard were a dozen lofty hickory trees and a dozen black walnuts, and in the nutting season riches were to be gathered there.

*Mark Twain's Autobiography*

Read the model informative description below. Be prepared to answer questions that follow it.

▶ AT LAST, THE FACE OF VENUS
**Sharon Begley and Mary Lord**

Scientists have finally managed a good look at the face of Venus, and it's a real stunner. Earth's nearest neighbor has mountains taller than Everest, valleys deeper than the Dead Sea rift and highlands bigger than Australia. Venus turns out to be so different from the guesses of astronomers that they will have to rethink many of their ideas about how planets were created.

The new map of Venus, released last week, was constructed from radar measurements taken in the past eighteen months by the orbiting Pioneer Venus spacecraft. Venus looks something like Earth drained of its seas. But it contains sharper contrasts: peaks 35,400 feet high and a valley 9,500 feet deep. About 60 percent of the Venusian surface consists of a gently rolling plain, varying just 3,000 feet from its lowest to its highest point.

*Crust.* Venus possesses two fault-scarred land masses comparable to Earth's highlands. The larger mass, named Terra Aphrodite* after the Greek goddess of love and beauty, runs 6,000 miles around Venus's equator. Geologists think that the sheer walls enclosing its deep valleys formed when two parts of the planet's crust crunched together and then tore apart. The second Venusian highland, called Terra Ishtar after the Babylonian goddess of war and love, contains mountain ranges and the highest peak on Venus: Maxwell Montes (named four years ago when astronomers were naming some features after radio scientists). The peak is scarred by a 60-mile-wide, 3,000-foot-deep crater that may have resulted from a volcanic eruption.

Venus's most intriguing feature is its crust. Unlike Earth, whose crust is broken into six major "plates," the crust of Venus is one thick piece. Thus, Venus will have fewer earthquakes since pieces of crust cannot scrape together as they do on Earth.

*Lava.* The major geologic activity on Venus today appears to exist in two volcanoes. Soaring 13,000 feet, they are sur-

---

* Venus's features were to be named after mythical goddesses. To appease American feminists, some will also be named for famous women.

rounded by rock that looks like solidified lava. If the region is still volcanically active, it would spoil the geologic concept that big planets are active and small ones like Venus are quiet. That wouldn't be the first surprise presented by Pioneer. In 1978, scientists discovered that Venus's atmosphere contains high amounts of argon gas. Since earlier theories predicted that planets near the Sun, such as Venus, would have only tiny amounts of this gas, the discovery sent astronomers back to their calculators. Pioneer will continue to observe Venus for at least three more years, giving scientists further chances to study, and perhaps solve, these planetary puzzles.

## QUESTIONS ON     At Last, The Face of Venus

1. What is the thesis of this informative description?

2. How do the writers gain reader interest?

3. What does 60 per cent of the surface of Venus consist of?

4. Why is the crust of Venus its most intriguing feature?

5. What sent astronomers back to their calculators?

6. Why were you able to answer the three previous questions?

## Emotional Description

In writing emotional description, your purpose is to communicate your feelings about the subject rather than to inform. You aim at presenting a word picture of the original that will create a vivid — even unforgettable — impression in the reader's mind. Thus, you appeal to senses other than the sense of sight. You select the connotative word, and you detail the sound, smell, taste, and touch as well as what you see. You enrich the impression with a figurative language, especially the metaphor, and you evoke in the reader feelings about the person, place, object, or happening that you are viewing or viewed. In the model description that follows, Rachel Carson describes, as did the writer of the first model informative description, the edge of the sea. But Carson's word picture is different from the earlier one. "The edge of the sea is a strange and beautiful place." The tides don't ebb in her creation — they "retreat in their eternal rhythms"; the edge of the sea is not divided into zones — it remains "an elusive and indefinable boundary."

> ▶ The edge of the sea is a strange and beautiful place. All through the long history of Earth it has been an area of unrest where waves have broken heavily against the land, where the tides have pressed forward over the continents, receded, and then returned. For no two successive days is the shore line precisely the same. Not only do the tides advance and retreat in their eternal rhythms, but the level of the sea itself is never at rest. It rises or falls as the glaciers melt or grow, as the floor of the deep ocean basins shifts under its increasing load of sediments, or as the earth's crust along the continental margins warps up or down in adjustment to strain and tension. Today a little more land may belong to the sea, tomorrow a little less. Always the edge of the sea remains an elusive and indefinable boundary.
>
> Rachel Carson
> *The Edge of the Sea*

In *Typhoon*, Joseph Conrad describes a hurricane. Conrad's dominant impression is one of personal, overpowering wrath. Notice the powerful verbs, evocative adjectives, and purposeful similes. The hurricane *explodes, isolates,* and *attacks.* It *fastens* on man's mind and "*seeks* to *rout* his very spirit out of him." It is *formidable, swift, overpowering, disintegrating,* and *furious.* The hurricane is "like the sudden smashing of a vial of wrath." It attacks "like a personal enemy."

▶ It was something formidable and swift, like the sudden smashing of a vial of wrath. It seemed to explode all round the ship with an overpowering concussion and a rush of great waters, as if an immense dam had been blown up to windward. In an instant the men lost touch of each other. This is the disintegrating power of a great wind: it isolates one from one's kind. An earthquake, a landslip, an avalanche, overtake a man incidentally, as it were — without passion. A furious gale attacks him like a personal enemy, tries to grasp his limbs, fastens upon his mind, seeks to rout his very spirit out of him . . . .

> Joseph Conrad
> *Typhoon*

Next, compare Samuel Clemens's recollection of his days in Missouri with the informative description of the Missouri farm. Observe his selection of words rich in feeling and emotion so that the reader will experience the evocative memory of those days.

▶ I can call back the solemn twilight and mystery of the deep woods, the earthy smells, the faint odors of the wild flowers, the sheen of rain-washed foliage, the rattling clatter of drops when the wind shook the trees, the far-off hammering of woodpeckers and the muffled drumming of wood-pheasants in the remoteness of the forest, the snapshot glimpses of disturbed wild creatures scurrying through the grass — I can call it all back and make it as real as it ever was, and as blessed. I can call back the prairie, and its loneliness and peace, and a vast hawk hanging motionless in the sky with his wings spread wide and the blue of the vault showing through the fringe of their end-feathers. I can see the woods in their autumn dress, the oaks purple, the hickories washed with gold, the maples and the sumachs luminous with crimson fires, and I can hear the rustle made by the fallen leaves as we plowed through them. I can see the blue clusters of wild grapes hanging amongst the foliage of the saplings, and I remember the taste of them and the smell. I know how the wild blackberries looked and how they tasted; and the same with the pawpaws, the hazelnuts, and the persimmons; and I can feel the thumping rain upon my head of hickory-nuts and walnuts when we were out in the frosty dawn to scramble for them with the pigs, and the gusts of wind loosed them and sent them down. I know the stain of blackberries and how pretty it is, and I know the stain of walnut hulls, and how little it minds soap and water, also what grudged experience it had of either of them. I know the taste of maple sap and when to gather it, and how to arrange the troughs and the delivery tubes, and how to boil down the juice, and how to hook the sugar after it is made; also how much better hooked sugar tastes than any that is honestly come by, let bigots say what they will.

*Mark Twain's Autobiography*

How different is this subjective description from the objective picture of his Missouri farm in *Mark Twain's Autobiography!* In this description the general, not the specific, the subjective, not the objective, the connotative word and the abstract, not the concrete word and phrase, and his feelings about the subject, not its appearance, dominate. He is not creating a person, place, object, or happening as he viewed it. He is leaving the reader with a mood in order to capture the memory of those "golden days."

**VOCABULARY PREVIEW**

| | | |
|---|---|---|
| pinnacle | illimitable | accentuating |
| campanile | stimulus | benignant |
| array | flagellated | confluence |
| irrelevant | | |

# EXERCISE 5    Description

Read the description below. Answer the questions that follow.

▶ As from a pinnacle,° Presley, from where he now stood, dominated the entire country. The sun had begun to set, everything
in the range of his vision was overlaid with a sheen of gold.

First, close at hand, it was the Seed ranch, carpeting the little
hollow behind the Mission with a spread of greens, some dark,
some vivid, some pale almost to yellowness. Beyond that was
the Mission itself, its venerable campanile,° in whose arches
hung the Spanish King's bells, already glowing ruddy in the
sunset. Farther on, he could make out Annixter's ranch house,
marked by the skeleton-like tower of the artesian well, and, a
little farther to the east, the huddled, tiled roofs of Guadalajara.
Far to the west and north, he saw Bonneville very plain, and
the dome of the courthouse, a purple silhouette against the
glare of the sky. Other points detached themselves, swimming
in a golden mist, projecting blue shadows far before them; the
mammoth live-oak by Hooven's, towering superb and
magnificent; the line of eucalyptus trees, behind which he
knew was the Los Muertos ranch house — his home; the wa-
tering-tank, the great iron-hooped tower of wood that stood at
the joining of the Lower Road and the County Road; the long
wind-break of poplar trees and the white walls of Caraher's
saloon on the County Road.

Frank Norris
*The Octopus*

1. From what point of view does the writer describe the landscape? At
   what time?

2. How do Presley's eyes travel as he views the scene before him?

3. What points detached themselves from the panoramic view?

4. What things does he supply from memory that he cannot see from his point of view?

5. Is this description dominantly informative or emotional?

6. What colors enrich this description?

## EXERCISE 6    **Description**

Read the description below. Answer the questions that follow.

▶ But all this seemed to be only foreground, a mere array° of
accessories — a mass of irrelevant° details. Beyond Annixter's,
beyond Guadalajara, beyond the Lower Road, beyond Broderson Creek, on to the south and west, infinite, illimitable,°
stretching out there under the sheen of the sunset forever and
forever, flat, vast, unbroken, a huge scroll, unrolling between
the horizons, spread the great stretches of the ranch of Los
Muertos, bare of crops, shaved close in the recent harvest. Near
at hand were hills, but on that far southern horizon only the
curve of the great earth itself checked the view. Adjoining Los
Muertos, and widening to the west, opened the Broderson
ranch. The Osterman ranch to the northwest carried on the
great sweep of landscape; ranch after ranch. Then, as the imagination itself expanded under the stimulus° of that measureless
range of vision, even those great ranches resolved themselves
into mere foreground, mere accessories, irrelevant details. Beyond the fine line of the horizons, over the curve of the globe,
the shoulder of the earth, were other ranches, equally vast, and
beyond these, others, and beyond these, still others, the im-
mensities multiplying, lengthening out vaster and vaster. The
whole gigantic sweep of the San Joaquin expanded, Titanic,
before the eye of the mind, flagellated° with heat, quivering
and shimmering under the sun's red eye. At long intervals, a
faint breath of wind out of the south passed slowly over the
levels of the baked and empty earth, accentuating° the silence,
marking off the stillness. It seemed to exhale from the land
itself, a prolonged sigh as of deep fatigue. It was the season after
the harvest, and the great earth, the mother, after its period of
reproduction, its pains of labour, delivered of the fruit of its
loins, slept the sleep of exhaustion, the infinite repose of the
colossus, benignant,° eternal, strong, the nourisher of nations,
the feeder of an entire world.

Frank Norris
*The Octopus*

1. Is this continuation of the description by Presley presented in Exercise 5 essentially an informative or emotional description?

2. Underline several words or word groups that enable the writer to create the tone that he desires.

3. What is the dominant impression the writer creates?

4. What word in particular is repeated to create the dominant impression?

5. To what senses does the writer appeal in this description?

## EXERCISE 7    Description

Read the description below. Answer the questions that follow.

▶ On the summit of one of the heights of the Odenwald, a wild
and romantic tract of Upper Germany, that lies not far from
the confluence° of the Main and the Rhine, there stood, many,
many years since, the Castle of the Baron Von Landshort. It is
now quite fallen to decay, and almost buried among beech-
trees and dark firs; above which, however, its old watch-tower
may still be seen, struggling, like the former possessor I have
mentioned, to carry a high head, and look down upon the
neighboring country.

Washington Irving
"The Spectre Bridegroom"

1. Is this description essentially informative or emotional?

2. What is the position of the observer?

3. What do you consider to be the writer's purpose?

4. What is the figure of speech in the last two lines?

**MATCH-UP SIX**

Match the definitions in column 2 with the words in column 1 taken from the model paragraphs in the exercises by placing the letter of the word in the blank. Answers are at the end of the chapter.

| | | | |
|---|---|---|---|
| a. pinnacle | 1. emphasizes | _h_ | |
| b. campanile | 2. something that motivates | _f_ | |
| c. array | 3. a bell tower | _b_ | |
| d. irrelevant | 4. arrangement | _c_ | |
| e. illimitable | 5. kindly | _i_ | |
| f. stimulus | 6. junction | _j_ | |
| g. flagellated | 7. lofty peak | _a_ | |
| h. accentuating | 8. boundless, vast | _e_ | |
| i. benignant | 9. whipped, lashed | _g_ | |
| j. confluence | 10. not suitable, fitting | _d_ | |

**VOCABULARY PREVIEW**

| | | |
|---|---|---|
| quiescent | exultation | gaunt |
| acquiescent | saunter | attired |
| defiance | quizzical | elusive |
| insidiously | | |

## EXERCISE 8     **Description**

Read the description below. Answer the questions that follow.

▶ The rudder met and counteracted the tendency of the *Porta Coeli* to fall off, and the boom-mainsail caught the wind and forced her forward. In a moment the *Porta Coeli* changed from something quiescent° and acquiescent° into something fierce and desperate. She ceased to yield to wind and sea, ceased to let them hurtle past her; now she met them, she fought against them, battled with them. She was like some tigress previously content to evade the hunters by slinking from cover to cover, but now hurling herself on her tormentors mad with fighting fury. The wind laid her over, the spray burst in sheets across her bows. Her gentle rise and swoop were transformed into an illogical jerky motion as she met the steep waves with immovable resolution; she lurched and she shuddered as she battered her way through the waves. The forces of the world, the old primitive powers that had ruled earth and water since the creation, were being set at defiance° by man, weak, mortal man, who by virtue of the brain inside his fragile skull was able not merely to face the forces of the world but to bend them to his will, compel them to serve him. Nature sent this brisk westerly gale up the Channel; subtly and insidiously° the *Porta Coeli* was making use of it to claw her way westward — a slow, painful, difficult way, but westward all the same. Hornblower, standing by the wheel, felt a surge of exultation° as the *Porta Coeli* thrashed forward. He was like Prometheus stealing fire from the gods; he was the successful rebel against the blind laws of nature; he could take pride in being a mere mortal man.

C. S. Forester
*Lord Hornblower*

1. What is the dominant impression?

2. Underline some words or word groups that help the writer create that dominant impression.

3. What simile expresses the way Hornblower felt as he stood on the deck of the *Porta Coeli*? Write the allusion, another simile, and a metaphor.

4. Give the first four words of the sentence that reveals that C. S. Forester is writing in the omniscient view to express his own thoughts at that point.

5. Is this description essentially informative or emotional?

Read the model description by Carl Sandburg that follows. Then review what you have learned about description so that you will be prepared to write an informative description and an emotional description for class assignments.

▶ ABRAHAM LINCOLN: THE PRAIRIE YEARS AND
THE WAR YEARS
**Carl Sandburg**

Lincoln was 51 years old. With each year since he had become a grown man, his name and ways, and stories about him, had been spreading among plain people and their children. So tall and so bony, with so peculiar a slouch and so easy a saunter°, so sad and so haunted-looking, so quizzical° and comic, as if hiding a lantern that lighted and went out and that he lighted again — he was a Strange Friend and the Friendly Stranger. Like something out of a picture book for children — he was. His form of slumping arches and his face of gaunt° sockets were a shape a Great Artist had scrawled from careless clay.

He looked like an original plan for an extra-long horse or a lean tawny buffalo, that a Changer had suddenly whisked into a man-shape. Or he met the eye as a clumsy, mystical giant that had walked out of a Chinese or Russian fairy story, or a bogy who had stumbled out of an ancient Saxon myth with a handkerchief full of presents he wanted to divide among all the children in the world.

He didn't wear clothes. Rather, clothes hung upon him as if on a rack to dry, or on a loose ladder up a windswept chimney. His clothes, to keep the chill or the sun off, seemed to whisper, "He put us on when he was thinking about something else."

He dressed any which way at times, in broadcloth, a silk hat, a silk choker, and a flaming red silk handkerchief, so that one court clerk said Lincoln was "fashionably dressed, as neatly attired° as any lawyer at court, except Ward Lamon." Or again, people said Lincoln looked like a huge skeleton with skin over the bones, and clothes covering the skin.

The stovepipe hat he wore sort of whistled softly: "I am not a hat at all; I am the little garret roof where he tucks in little thoughts he writes on pieces of paper." The hat, size seven and one-eighth, had a brim one and three-quarters inches wide. The inside band in which the more important letters and notes were tucked, measured two and three-quarters inches. The cylinder of the stovepipe was 22 inches in circumference. The hat was lined with heavy silk and, measured inside, exactly six inches deep. And people tried to guess what was going on under that hat. Written in pencil on the imitation satin paper that formed part of the lining was the signature "A. Lincoln, Springfield, Ill.," so that any forgetful person who might take the hat by mistake would know where to bring it back. Also the hatmaker, "George Hall, Springfield, Ill.," had printed his name in the hat so that Lincoln would know where to get another one just like it.

The umbrella with the name "Abraham Lincoln" stitched in, faded and drab from many rains and regular travels, looked sleepy and murmuring, "Sometime we shall have all the sleep we want; we shall turn the law office over to the spiders and the cobwebs; we shall quit politics for keeps."

There could have been times when children and dreamers looked at Abraham Lincoln and lazily drew their eyelids half shut and let their hearts roam about him — and they half-believed him to be a tall horse chestnut tree or a rangy horse or a big wagon or a log barn full of newmown hay — something else or more than a man, a lawyer, a Republican candidate with principles, a prominent citizen — something spreading, elusive,° and mysterious — the Strange Friend and the Friendly Stranger.

---

**MATCH-UP SEVEN**

Match the definitions in column 2 with the words in column 1 taken from the model paragraphs in the exercises and the Lincoln description by placing the letter of the word in the blank. Answers are at the end of the chapter.

| | | |
|---|---|---|
| a. quiescent | 1. clothed, dressed | _i_ |
| b. acquiescent | 2. queer, odd | _g_ |
| c. defiance | 3. cunningly, craftily | _d_ |
| d. insidiously | 4. hard to grasp | _j_ |
| e. exultation | 5. quiet, inactive | _a_ |
| f. saunter | 6. extremely thin | _h_ |
| g. quizzical | 7. leisurely way of walking | _f_ |
| h. gaunt | 8. bold resistance | _c_ |
| i. attired | 9. submissive, yielding | _b_ |
| j. elusive | 10. triumphant joy | _e_ |

## Suggested Topics for Writing Informative Description

1. A classroom
2. A cabin in the mountains
3. Your bedroom
4. Sounds, smells, sights in a factory, bakery or restaurant
5. A view or something seen from a position high above it; for example, a valley from a ski lift

## Suggested Topics for Writing Emotional Description

1. A cemetery
2. A historic shrine
3. A sunset
4. The last boat to the island
5. Graduation
6. A scenic view
7. An airport
8. A family gathering
9. A mysterious house
10. The ebb tide

## Answers: Chapter 5

### Exercise 1

1. The dominant impression is a picture of a bay closed in on all sides except the sea by high mountains.
2.

> ▶ Inch by inch His Britannic Majesty's frigate *Lydia* crept into the bay. The cutter was out ahead, with Rayner sounding industriously, while with a dying breath of air behind her and a shred of sail set the *Lydia* felt her way <u>between the two headlands</u> into the tortuous channel. Those capes, one each side of the entrance, were <u>steep rocky cliffs,</u> and the one overlapped the other a trifle so that only an eye sharpened by necessity, and which had made the most of its recent opportunities of learning the typical rock formations of that coast, could have guessed at the possibility of an expanse of water behind them.
>
> Hornblower took his eye from the ship's course as she crawled round the corner to study the bay before him. There were <u>mountains all round</u> it, but on the farther side the slope down to the water was not nearly so steep, and on the water's edge there, at the foot of the dazzling green which clothed the banks all round, there was a hint of golden sand which told of the sort of bottom which he sought. It would be shelving there, without a doubt, and free from rock.

### Exercise 3

1. The dominant impression appeals to the senses of smell and hearing — the noise.
2.

▶ The cabin, small though it was, housed a prodigious stink. The first thing the nostrils noticed was the <u>sooty, stuffy smell</u> of the lamp, but they immediately became aware of a whole gamut° of <u>supplementary odours.</u> There was the <u>flat bilge smell,</u> tolerable, in fact almost unnoticed by Hornblower, who had smelt bilge for 20 years. There was a <u>penetrating smell of cheese,</u> and as if to set that off there was a <u>perceptible° smell of rats.</u> There was a <u>smell of wet clothing,</u> and finally there was a mixture of human odours, the long-confined body odour of unwashed men predominating.

And all this mixture of smells was balanced by a <u>battery of noises.</u> Every <u>timber resonated°</u> the <u>shrieking of the rigging;</u> to be inside the cabin was to be like a mouse inside a violin while it was being played. Overhead the <u>continual footfalls</u> on the quarterdeck and the <u>clatter of ropes</u> being thrown down made it seem — to continue the analogy — as if someone else were <u>tapping</u> the body of the violin at the same time with small mallets. The wooden sheathing of the brig <u>creaked</u> and <u>crackled</u> with the vessel's motion in the water like a giant's <u>knuckles rapping</u> on the exterior; and the shot in the racks rolled just a trifle with each movement, too, <u>thumping</u> solemnly and unexpectedly just at the end of the roll as they fetched° up.

3. . . . to be inside the cabin was to be like a mouse inside a violin while it was being played.

The wooden sheathing of the brig creaked and crackled with the vessel's motion in the water like a giant's knuckles rapping on the exterior. . . .

| Voc. Test 7 | | Match-Up 6 | | Match-Up 7 | |
|---|---|---|---|---|---|
| 1. | a | 1. | h | 1. | i |
| 2. | c | 2. | f | 2. | g |
| 3. | b | 3. | b | 3. | d |
| 4. | d | 4. | c | 4. | j |
| 5. | b | 5. | i | 5. | a |
| 6. | a | 6. | j | 6. | h |
| 7. | d | 7. | a | 7. | f |
| 8. | b | 8. | e | 8. | c |
| 9. | c | 9. | g | 9. | b |
| 10. | a | 10. | d | 10. | e |
| 11. | d | | | | |
| 12. | c | | | | |
| 13. | b | | | | |
| 14. | a | | | | |
| 15. | c | | | | |

# 6

## Explaining and Informing — Comparison, Contrast, and Analogy

*Exposition* is a form of discourse that a writer uses to explain and inform his reader about the subject. Exposition appeals to the reader's intellect and his understanding. It is the most common of the three forms of discourse discussed in this book; narration and description are frequently used in combination with it. The writer of exposition attempts to answer a number of questions. Who is it? What does it mean? What is it like or unlike? How did it happen? How does it work? What are its parts? How does it function? Into what classes may it be divided? What are its causes? What are the effects?

## Methods of Exposition

In organizing and developing thought by exposition, you have a variety of methods from which to choose. Your choice of method or combination of methods will depend largely upon your purpose for writing and the kind of material with which you are working. If you wish to explain and inform by showing likenesses between two or among three or more subjects, you organize and develop by *comparison*. If you wish to explain and inform by showing differences, you write a *contrast* paper. If you wish to make an unknown subject familiar to the reader by comparing it to a known subject, you write *analogy*. You may wish to fulfill your purpose by placing persons, places, things, or ideas into classes (*classification*) or break down a subject into its parts (*analysis by structure*). You may wish to show how the parts work as the whole functions (*analysis by function*) or how to do something or how something is done (*analysis by process*). You may want to explain why a subject exists by concentrating on its causes or discuss its effects (*analysis by causes [effects]*). You may give the meaning of a word or term (*definition*). More often than not, these various methods of organizing and developing thought are used in combination (*combining*) with one method dominating according to the writer's purpose for explaining and informing. Exposition is discussed in this book in the following sequence:

| | |
|---|---|
| *Chapter 6* | *Chapter 8* |
| 1. Comparison | 1. Analysis |
| 2. Contrast |    a. By causes |
| 3. Analogy |    b. By effects |
| *Chapter 7* | *Chapter 9* |
| 1. Analysis | 1. Classification |
|    a. By structure | 2. Definition |
|    b. By function | 3. Combining |
|    c. By process | |

The thought in most expository paragraphs moves from the general to the particular; that is, the main idea is expressed in the first sentence and is followed by sentences of explanation or support. Since the essay is organized in much the same way as the paragraph, you are safe in assuming that most expository essays will open with a statement of the thesis or a statement of purpose (controlling idea) in the first sentence or some other sentence in the first paragraph. This controlling idea will be explained and supported by a number of paragraphs. A writer structuring his thought by moving from the thesis or statement of purpose through the support writes a *thesis-support* paper.

But a writer has other choices. He may wish to present the controlling idea as a conclusion based on the earlier supporting material; therefore, he moves from the particulars to general, structuring a *support-thesis* paper. With a different subject, a writer may begin with a statement of the controlling idea and repeat that idea in slightly different words in the final sentence or final paragraph of the essay; therefore, he writes a *thesis-support-thesis* paper. Finally, he may begin with a question and follow with the answer; he organizes his thought in a *question-to-answer* paper. As we discuss the various methods of developing thought for written expression in the subsequent pages of this book, we shall show how thought is developed by a variety of methods within these four frames or patterns. Let us begin with developing thought by comparison and contrast. As we discuss the various methods of structuring exposition, we shall show how a writer develops his material within the four basic frames that we discussed in an earlier chapter. These basic frames are as follows: general to particular, particular to general, general to particular to general, and question to answer.

In writing comparison and contrast, you clarify and explain your subject by showing likenesses and unlikenesses between two or more persons, places, things, ideas, or situations. You use comparisons and contrasts every day since they are the most natural methods of organizing thought. You may compare two vacuum cleaners, two electric razors, toothpastes, automobiles, or lawn mowers as to price, performance, and durability before buying one. You may wish to point out to a friend how two or more leaders, teams, colleges, courses, and newspapers are alike; therefore you compare them in order to stress similarities. You may, on the other hand, wish to show that socialism differs from capitalism and communism, high school from college, water skiing from snow skiing, an American from an Indian, or ancient Greece from ancient Rome; therefore, you compare the two or more subjects stressing differences (contrast). Beginning writers, however, are cautioned to master the techniques of comparing or contrasting two subjects before moving on to three or more subjects — a more difficult process.

## Comparison

Comparison is a method of organizing and developing thought to show similarities between persons, places, things, ideas, or situations. Contrast is a method of organizing and developing thought to show differences between persons, places, things, ideas, situations. In writing comparison and contrast, some of the methods of structuring ideas are essentially the same.

*First*, define clearly your purpose. You may want simply to show the likenesses or differences between two subjects, for example, a schoolteacher and a salesman, New York and Los Angeles, the Chinese and the Hindu. With this kind of purpose, you create interest usually by selecting subjects with which your reader is not familiar or which your reader would not logically expect to possess like or unlike characteristics. Thus, you are able to hold his interest and, at the same time, to fulfill your purpose of presenting information about the two subjects. You may, on the other hand, compare or contrast two subjects in order to inform your reader about something the two subjects themselves explain, clarify, or establish. You might compare two religions, for instance, to show that they are basically alike or ancient Greece with ancient Rome to emphasize the importance of the "Greek way."

*Second,* list as many points of comparison or contrast as possible.

*Third,* incorporate these points into a preliminary plan much like the one suggested below. Suppose, for example, you were interested in showing that women and blacks in the job market are treated very much alike.

## Preliminary Plan

*Purpose*: To show that in the job market women and blacks face the same kind of handicaps.

▶ 1. Firing
2. Hiring
3. Pay
4. Type of job
5. *Retirement benefits*
6. *Promotions*
7. Transportation
8. Quitting the job

*Fourth,* eliminate any irrelevant or less important points of comparison. In the example preliminary plan, the italicized entries were eliminated.

Read the paragraph below; it served as the source for the listing of points and the preliminary plan above. Observe that the writer states her purpose in the first sentence. Notice also that she develops that purpose with a number of striking similarities between women and blacks in the job market.

*Statement of Purpose*

*Points of Similarity*

▶ Comparison between women and blacks sheds new light on the handicaps they both face in the job market. Both are fired before white men and hired after them. Both are arbitrarily limited to

*Explanation
of Some Points*

the lower-paying, least productive, less-skilled jobs and sometimes the same ones. For many years, for instance, Southern textile mills reserved for white women those jobs that were filled in the North by black men. It is not surprising to learn from the Bureau of Labor Statistics that women average 2.4 years less than men on the jobs they hold, while the black men average two years less than white men. The gap between the races in job tenure is similar to the gap between the sexes. The similarity is worth noting because it suggests reasons why neither blacks nor women gravitate to steady work. *Both* are fired before white men, of course, but both are also more apt to quit because they move away or can't get transportation to the job. Women and blacks often do not have as much control over where they live as white men.

*Points of Similarity*

*Guide Word* Both

Caroline Bird, with Sara Welles Briller
*Born Female*

Study the model comparison below:

*Main point*

*Likenesses*

*Guide words* both, each

▶ It is in these more amiable qualities of her sex, that Isabella's superiority becomes most apparent over her illustrious namesake, Elizabeth of England, *whose history presents some features parallel to her own. Both* were disciplined in early life by the teachings of that stern nurse of wisdom, adversity. *Both* were made to experience the deepest humiliation at the hands of their nearest relative, who should have cherished and protected them. *Both* succeeded in establishing themselves on the throne after the most precarious vicissitudes. *Each* conducted her kingdom, through a long and triumphant reign, to a height of glory which it had never before reached. *Both* lived to see the vanity of all earthly grandeur, and to fall the victims of an inconsolable melancholy; and *both* left behind an illustrious name, unrivalled in the subsequent annals of their country.

W. H. Prescott
*History of the Reign of Ferdinand and Isabella*

In this paragraph, Prescott announces his comparison in the first sentence. He presents six points of similarity making effective use of the guide word *both* and also the word *each*. Thus, the reader can see clearly the likenesses between Elizabeth I, queen of England, and Isabella, queen of Spain — two dominant women of the sixteenth century.

An outline of this model comparison will enable you to see better its structural organization and development.

I. It is in these more amiable qualities of her sex, that Isabella's superiority becomes most apparent over her illustrious namesake, Elizabeth of England, whose history presents some features parallel to her own.

A. Both were disciplined in early life by the teachings of that stern nurse of wisdom, adversity.

B. Both were made to experience the deepest humiliation at the hands of their nearest relative, who should have cherished and protected them.

C. Both succeeded in establishing themselves on the throne after the most precarious vicissitudes.

D. Each conducted her kingdom, through a long and triumphant reign, to a height of glory which it had never before reached.

E. Both lived to see the vanity of all earthly grandeur, and to fall the victims of an inconsolable melancholy;

F. And both left behind an illustrious name, unrivalled in the subsequent annals of their country.

Finally, study the model paragraph developed by comparison in which the writer compares the famous Mexican comedian Cantinflas to the extraordinary Charlie Chaplin. Note that the writer presents his statement of comparison in the first sentence: "Like Charlie Chaplin, Cantinflas is a pantomimist," and then merely describes the similar characteristics.

▶ There is much Chaplin pathos in the comedy of Cantinflas. Like Charlie Chaplin, Cantinflas is a pantomimist. He uses his hands, eyes, and legs with the same exquisite timing. He gestures apathetically with his hands, which invariably carry a long-ashed cigarette. He walks with a deliberate curvature of the spine in a pompous swagger that contrasts sharply with his ragged clothes and downtrodden personality. The walk is further accentuated by busy, mobile hips that conflict with the rigidity of the rest of his body. He seems to be going in two directions at once.

Ron Butler
"Cantinflas: Mexico's Prince of Comedy"

To review what you have learned about comparison, complete the three exercises that follow.

**VOCABULARY PREVIEW**

| | | | |
|---|---|---|---|
| perceive | catalogued | lecherous | antipathy |
| exquisitely | heritage | improvident | sinewy |
| inaudible | unique | veritable | pervaded |
| profound | vituperation | penchant | precarious |
| duplication | blasphemous | inclination | innovation |

## EXERCISE 1     **Comparison**

Read the model paragraph unit below. Answer the questions that follow it. Answers are at the end of the chapter.

▶ To understand the psychology and behavior of animals, we need to know how they perceive° the world around them. Both dogs and cats have specialized sensory organs. Their whiskers are highly sensitive touch organs attached to nerves in the skin that transmit signals to the brain. The whiskers help them negotiate their way through narrow spaces, protect their eyes, and tell them the direction that the wind is blowing.

Neither cats nor dogs see as well as human beings. Both animals are thought to be color-blind, though cats are somewhat sensitive to red and green. Their eyes are more acutely sensitive to movement than to brightness or shape. Perhaps to compensate for poor color sensitivity, both animals have exquisitely° sensitive hearing that can pick up high-frequency sounds inaudible° to humans.

Both cats and dogs have a keen sense of smell aided by a second scent organ that is located behind their upper front teeth. This organ is connected to the parts of the brain that regulate sexual, aggressive, and territorial behavior — the animal's instinctive need to protect its turf. It may be responsible for the profound° effect that certain odors, such as catnip or musk, can have on our pets' behavior.

Michael Fox
"What Is Your Pet Trying to Tell You?"

1. In what sentence does the writer indicate clearly the method of development?

2. How many points of similarity does the writer establish between the two subjects?

3. Mention the guide words that helped you distinguish the major support — the separate points of comparison.

4. Write a brief paragraph or paragraph unit explaining the structure and development plan of this paragraph unit, emphasizing the role of the minor support in gaining completeness.

## EXERCISE 2     Comparison

Read the model comparison. Answer the questions that follow.

> ▶ "Denmark or Eire? Visit both? Surely this would be wasteful duplication° of experiences in a crowded itinerary through Europe. I really cannot see how there can be any significant difference between these two little countries. Both of them are northerly and rainy. They lie in the same latitude. Both raise a notable surplus of dairy products for export. Both are unaggressive. Both are Christian. Why waste my time on visiting more than one of the two? Why not toss up?" This imaginary rejoinder of an inadequately informed Tibetan tourist to his Japanese travel agent indicates how gravely mistaken a Western traveller would be if he decided to toss up between Thailand and Burma. Luckily, I did not make this easy but elementary mistake. I found time — though all too short a time — for getting a glimpse of both. In consequence, I can duly register their points of likeness. Both are Buddhist countries of Theravadin school. Both are unaggressive. Both have a relatively low population density for Eastern Asian countries. Both are exporters of rice. Both lie in the tropics. But, when one has catalogued° these common traits one will despair of enumerating all the differences and contrasts.
>
> Arnold Toynbee
> *East to West*

1. In what sentence does the writer state the first comparison?

2. With what words does Toynbee introduce the second comparison?

3. What is the function of the first comparison in addition to showing likenesses between Denmark and Eire?

4. How many points of comparison are in comparison 1? How many in comparison 2?

5. What does the last sentence of the paragraph tell the reader about the writer's purpose for comparing?

## EXERCISE 3     **Comparison**

Read the model paragraph below. Answer the questions that follow it.

▶ Gauchos and cowboys shared a common Iberian heritage° and developed in similar natural and economic environments. Both owed much to distant Moorish and Spanish influences brought to the Western Hemisphere during the sixteenth century. The Gaucho adapted Spanish equipment and methods, blended them with new techniques learned from pampean Indians, and developed a unique° "civilization of leather." Spanish roots sometimes disappeared entirely as the Gaucho borrowed the Indian *chiripa*, a baggy, diaperlike cloth tucked between the legs, the *boleadora*, or bola, three stones attached to connected leather thongs, which was hurled to entangle and down animals, and maté, a favored caffeine-rich tea. The U.S. cowboy would have been more recognizable to the medieval Spanish rider because of the equipment and vocabulary passed to him through Mexico. The Spaniard would have recognized the cowboy's chaps (*chaparreros*), lariat (*la reata*), string of mounts (*remuda*), and other direct or transformed borrowings.

Richard W. Slatta<br>Cowboys and Gauchos

1. Does the writer announce his comparison in the first sentence?

2. What are the two subjects being compared?

3. What is the basis for the comparison?

4. How many points of comparison does the writer present to establish his purpose?

5. How much does the minor support contribute to paragraph completeness?

▶ From COWBOYS AND GAUCHOS
**Richard W. Slatta**

[1]Horsemen have excited awe, admiration, fear, and vitupera-
tion° in plains regions around the world. The man on horseback — whether cowboy or Cossack, Gaucho or *llanero, vaquero* or *boiadeiro* — has elicited wide comment and inspired
a lively body of folklore and literature. Equestrian subcultures
that developed in grasslands, particularly in North and South
America, appear to share many common traits and values;
there are also frequently overlooked but fundamental differences. The Gauchos of the Argentine pampa and the cowboys
of the U.S. West offer a fascinating comparison and contrast.*

[2]Edward Larocque Tinker, an avid admirer and student of
horses and horsemen of many nations, stressed the commonalities among riders who conquered, defended, and labored
on the plains, pampas, llanos, and other grasslands of the
Americas:

*No group could be more alike than the horsemen of the New
World. The* huasos *of Chile, the* gauchos *of Argentina and
Brazil, the* vaqueros *of Mexico . . . , the* llaneros *of Venezuela
and Colombia, and the cowboys of the United States are
brothers under the skin.*

[3]Gauchos and cowboys shared a common Iberian heritage,
and developed in similar natural and economic environments.
Both owed much to distant Moorish and Spanish influences
brought to the Western Hemisphere during the sixteenth century. The Gaucho adapted Spanish equipment and methods,
blended them with new techniques learned from pampean Indians, and developed a unique "civilization of leather." Spanish roots sometimes disappeared entirely as the Gaucho borrowed the Indian *chiripa,* a baggy, diaperlike cloth tucked
between the legs, the *boleadora,* or bola, three stones attached
to connected leather thongs, which was hurled to entangle and
down animals, and maté, a favored caffeine-rich tea. The U.S.
cowboy would have been more recognizable to the medieval
Spanish rider because of the equipment and vocabulary passed
to him through Mexico. The Spaniard would have recognized
the cowboy's chaps (*chaparreros*), lariat (*la reata*), string of
mounts (*remuda*), and other direct or transformed borrowings.

[4]Nineteenth century observers described cowboys and

---

* The words *and contrast* are added by the author of the textbook, since this book uses
separate names for each development.

Gauchos in equivalent, usually unflattering terms. The *Cheyenne Daily Leader* of October 3, 1882, painted a negative portrait of the western horsemen:

*Morally, as a class, they are foulmouthed, blasphemous,° drunken, lecherous,° utterly corrupt. Usually harmless on the plains when sober, they are dreaded in towns, for the liquor has the ascendency over them. They are also as improvident° as the veriest 'Jack' of the sea . . . . They never own any interest in the stock they tend.*

[5]European travelers found the Gaucho of the nineteenth century pampa equally short on morals and long on violent, drunken action. Thomas Joseph Hutchinson, British consul at Rosario, found little to commend Gauchos of the 1860's:

*Gambling is the moving spirit of existence and enjoyment in the real Gaucho. Indeed the veritable° camp Gaucho is a sort of loafer, hanging about pulperias, looking out for Gaucho-flats to fleece of whatever they have about them, drinking* caña *and gin, now and then ripping up somebody with his knife after a dispute of the most insignificant nature.*

[6]The plainsmen's penchant° for violent drinking and gambling particularly disturbed many moralists from urban civilization. Cowboys, or range riders as they were also called, greatly enjoyed cardplaying, especially poker; indeed, the manager of one cattle company termed cardplaying the "most objectionable habit" practiced in cow camps. The Texas Ranchers' Association went so far as to prohibit gambling during roundup. Gauchos enjoyed many activities, from cards (*truco* was the favorite) to *taba* (throwing the knucklebone of a cow and betting on the result), and wagering money on the outcome of horseraces. Both Gauchos and Southwestern cowboys competed in the ring race (*la sortija*) wherein riders tried to lance a small golden ring suspended on a thin thread, using a foot-long stick. The winner rode off with the golden ring as a prize, or presented it to his favorite *china*, or girlfriend.

[7]Cowboys and Gauchos also earned a sometimes justified reputation for rustling livestock. The Cheyenne *Democratic Leader* reported in August 1884 on the problem of rustling in Montana Territory to the north: "There never was a period in the history of this or any other Territory when so much horse thieving was going on." Police reports, rural journals, and complaints by the Argentine Rural Society of large ranchers attest to problems of livestock thefts on the pampa as well.

[8]If the commentators found cowboy and Gaucho character

and morals wanting, the horsemen held their own peculiar set of values concerning outsiders. As Emerson Hough observed in his 1898 classic, *The Story of the Cowboy*, "he is a horseman and nothing more, and has little inclination° for any work that cannot be done with the saddle." The cowboy exhibits a "mild contempt for all walking and driving men." Likewise the Gaucho could not conceive of life without his *tropilla*, or herd of sturdy *pingos*. Emeric Essex Vidal, who published a series of written sketches and paintings about the River Plate in 1820, asserted that Gauchos

*have a great antipathy° to all occupations which they cannot follow on horseback. They scarcely know how to walk, and will not if they can help it, though it were only across the street. When they meet at the* pulpería, *or anywhere else, they remain on horseback, though the conversation may last hours. It is on horseback also that they go a fishing, riding into the water to throw and draw the net. To raise water from a well, they fasten the rope to their horse and make him draw it up, without setting their own feet on the ground.*

As Sir Francis Bond Head correctly noted in 1826, "the print of the human foot on the ground is in his mind the symbol of uncivilization."

[9]Gauchos and cowboys dressed differently, but their distinctive garb elicited detailed descriptions by fascinated onlookers. Theodore Roosevelt, ex-President and historian of the West, described the cowboy attire in *The Outlook* magazine of May 24, 1913. "Lean, sinewy° fellows, accustomed to riding half-broken horses at any speed over any country by day or by night . . . , they wore flannel shirts, with loose handkerchiefs knotted round their necks, broad hats, high heeled boots with jingling spurs, and sometimes leather chaps."

[10]On his visit to the pampas in the late 1840's the English sketcher Robert Elwes captured the central elements of the Gaucho costume:

*They wear very wide white linen drawers called "calzoncillas," handsomely ornamented from the knee downwards with open work, and sometimes having a fringe of silk falling over the feet. A "chiripa," a poncho of some bright colour, is fastened round the waist, and drawn up loosely between the legs, forming a sort of large baggy trousers; and a short jacket, and a broad leathern belt with pockets in it, complete the costume. The belt, which is called a "tirador," is fastened behind with four or more pillared dollars, and in this is stuck a long knife, often sheathed and hafted with silver. Their boots, which are open at the toe, are white, and made with great care from the skin of a horse's hind leg . . . The hat is a narrow-brimmed Panama straw, encircled by a red ribbon, and they wear large silver or iron spurs.*

[11]When fortunate enough to be employed, cowboys and Gauchos performed much the same kind of work. A small group of year-round employees took care of day-to-day herding, maintenance, and other chores. Trail drives, roundup, branding, and castration required additional hands and special skills. Riders hired by the day or by the task swelled the ranch labor force during the busy seasons. Danger of injury or death pervaded° ranch work. *Field and Farm* of February 16, 1895, recorded the tragic tale told by a survivor of one stampede in Colorado:

*The whole herd tumbled and pitched and tossed over us. Foster was literally mangled to sausage meat. His horse was little better, and mine was crushed into a bloody mass. I found that I could not get up, for my leg was broken just below the thigh. I was soon cared for, however, and in six weeks was all right and on the range again. We found 341 dead cattle, two dead horses, one dead cowboy, and two more with broken legs after the herd had passed.*

[12]Both Gauchos and cowboys faced vicious blizzards sweeping out of the western mountains that froze livestock and any horsemen caught in them. Expert horsemen, Gauchos sometimes suffered serious accidents when their mounts fell into one of the myriad animal burrows that honeycombed the pampa. Marion Mulhall, wife of a well-known Irish publisher in Buenos Aires, opined in 1881 that "pampa life is attended with so much danger and hardship that it is said no one has ever seen a grey-haired Gaucho." Both Gauchos and cowboys suffered long layoffs during slack seasons; indeed, unemployment and underemployment partially account for animal rustling for food and profit. Unemployed cowboys rode from ranch to ranch during the winter and Gauchos from *estancia* to *estancia* — a practice known in the U.S. West as "sun downing." The rider arrived at a ranch shortly before sundown or mealtime, asked to rest awhile, and shared meals with the regular hands for a few days. Ranchers preferred feeding drifters to having them kill livestock for food on the range. Yet "slow elk," as illegally killed yearling beef was called by cowboys, also fed many hungry, unemployed riders on the plains.

[13]Vital to the cattle industry, cowboys and Gauchos nevertheless suffered a precarious° existence. Modern technological change foredoomed both in the latter decades of the nineteenth century. Wire fencing, windmills, railroads, farming, and more refined animal breeding spelled an end to the open range of bygone days. The migratory, independent riders of the past gave way to subdued, obedient, dependent peons and ranch hands. The *Denver Sun* recorded the cowboy's epitaph in its issue of November 12, 1892:

*The cowboy, like the buffalo, the prairie wolf, the painted redskin, and the highway robber of the plains, is rapidly becoming extinct in the West. Civilization is as hard on cowboys as it is on the other animals enumerated above.*

Modernity also banished the Gaucho, Eliza Jane McCartney Clements, a missionary to the River Plate region during the 1880's, noted the impact of change on the Gaucho:

*His is a wild, unconventional life, not without its charms, but it is doomed to vanish before the innovation° of the restraints which those using them call civilization.*

## QUESTIONS ON   **Cowboys and Gauchos**

Answers are at the end of the chapter.

1. In what paragraph does the writer announce his development by similarities?

2. In paragraph 3, what guide words help establish the comparison?

3. What is the topic sentence of the paragraph unit beginning with paragraph 4? What paragraphs make up this unit?

4. What is the structural function of the words by Sir Francis Bond Head that serve as the closing statement in paragraph 8? How does the writer's thought flow: general to particular, particular to general, general to particular to general?

5. In paragraphs 9 and 10, what similarity does the writer develop?

6. What two points of likenesses are discussed in paragraph 12? What guide words help the reader recognize the points?

7. What is the function of the final paragraphs?

## VOCABULARY TEST EIGHT

Four words are lined up below each of twenty words taken from the exercises and the essay. Select the one that matches best and write its letter in the blank to the right. Answers are at the end of the chapter.

1. perceive    *A*
   (a) understand, see    (b) feel    (c) confront
   (d) adjust to

2. exquisitely    *C*
   (a) delicate    (b) balanced    (c) highly refined or perfected
   (d) perfectly shaped

3. inaudible    *D*
   (a) not understandable    (b) insensitive    (c) not harmful
   (d) not capable of being heard

4. profound    *C*
   (a) immediate    (b) slight    (c) deep, thorough
   (d) slack

5. duplication    *B*
   (a) history    (b) same as the original    (c) result
   (d) report

6. catalogued    *D*
   (a) enumerated    (b) evaluated    (c) compared
   (d) listed, placed in order

7. heritage    *C*
   (a) that which is passed on    (b) rightful owners
   (c) family history    (d) background, culture

8. unique    *C*
   (a) similar    (b) lasting    (c) matchless, unequaled
   (d) different

9. vituperation    *B*
   (a) controversy    (b) censure, abuse    (c) envy    (d) hate

10. blasphemous    *C*
    (a) evil    (b) filthy    (c) profane, impious    (d) foul

11. lecherous    *D*
    (a) untrustworthy    (b) shifty    (c) wasteful
    (d) lustful, lewd

12. improvident    *A*
    (a) thriftless, lacking foresight    (b) reliable
    (c) unreliable    (d) careless

13. veritable — *B*
    (a) popular    (b) true, genuine    (c) common
    (d) frequent — *C*

14. penchant
    (a) habit    (b) love    (c) a strong taste or liking for
    (d) art

15. inclination — *D*
    (a) patience    (b) expertise    (c) use
    (d) leaning, tendency for — *B*

16. antipathy
    (a) feeling for    (b) dislike, feeling against    (c) hate
    (d) concern for — *C*

17. sinewy
    (a) thin    (b) flexible    (c) strong, tough    (d) weak — *D*

18. pervaded
    (a) accompanied    (b) hindered    (c) prevented
    (d) spread throughout — *B*

19. precarious
    (a) fleeting    (b) dangerous    (c) temporary
    (d) exciting — *C*

20. innovation
    (a) discovery    (b) omen    (c) change, newness    (d) sign

## Suggested Topics for Writing Comparison

1. Luxury and necessity
2. Family: today and yesterday
3. College and high school: teachers (courses, facilities, sports, and so on)
4. Dating and going steady
5. Two famous men or women
6. Two generations of college students
7. Two American automobiles
8. Two magazines (newspapers)
9. Two places
10. Two motion pictures or television shows

## Contrast

In writing contrast, you structure thought differently from comparison since you must consider contrasting points. A preliminary plan and outline, therefore, are even more essential in order to determine true and relevant points of contrast and to present them effectively. Suppose, for example, you were given the assignment to contrast Mussolini and Hitler. Your first step would be to list as many points as possible, making sure that for every point under Subject A, Mussolini, you have a comparable contrasting point under Subject B, Hitler. Your preliminary plan might look something like this one:

### Preliminary Plan

*Purpose:* To show the differences between Mussolini and Hitler.

▶ SUBJECT A (MUSSOLINI)

1. A short fat man with a round face and bald head
2. Moderate and progressive thinker
3. Constantly changed views according to political climate
4. Never regarded Fascist doctrine as a permanent thing
5. Followed a temperate course regarding war
6. Killed by his own people
7. No strong racial feelings
8. Strutted and talked a great deal but didn't mean everything he said

SUBJECT B (HITLER)

1. A short thin man with piercing eyes and a strange hair cut
2. Believed in a weird, irrational ideology
3. Held firm to his beliefs to the end
4. Held to a narrow, rigid doctrine and policy
5. Prepared for and welcomed war
6. Killed himself
7. Persecuted the Jews
8. A fanatic who believed everything he said

Eliminate any irrelevant or less important points of contrast.

Next, decide on a pattern of organization and development that will best fulfill your purpose and suit your material. If you wish to keep each subject in its entirety before the reader, organize and develop by "wholes" — *a subject-at-a-time contrast.* If you wish to emphasize the points of the contrast, develop and organize point by point (alternating pattern).

In the subject-at-a-time pattern, you can begin your contrast with a topic sentence, clarifying your purpose and announcing your contrast. For example, "The two top Fascists, Hitler and Mussolini, were eventually lumped together as twin Fascist dictators, but it is important to understand that there was a great deal of difference between the two men and the two regimes." You then present a complete picture of Subject A in the remainder of the same paragraph or in only the first part of that paragraph. In the second paragraph or in the second part of the first paragraph, you present a complete picture of Subject B, discussing comparable contrasting points. You may find it necessary to clarify, explain, or elaborate on each point in making clear the contrasts. Thus, in this kind of development, you obtain completeness by adequately supporting the contrast between the two or more subjects.

You can modify this pattern slightly by beginning at once with the points of contrast and concluding with a statement of the main idea (particular to general order). In organizing and developing contrast, you must keep both sides before the reader by firmly establishing true points of contrast and maintaining them in logical order throughout the development. A skillfully prepared preliminary plan will help you establish true points of contrast. In addition, a well-structured outline will aid you in organizing the material before you begin to write. Study the sentence outline for the contrast between Mussolini and Hitler.

## MUSSOLINI AND HITLER

*Purpose:* To show the differences between the two top Fascists, Mussolini and Hitler.

▶ I. There were many differences between Mussolini and Hitler.
   A. Mussolini was a pragmatic and moderate Fascist.
   B. There was no racial doctrine in Italian Fascist ideology.
   C. Mussolini changed views constantly.
   D. He followed a temperate course regarding war.
  II. Hitler was very different.

   A. He was an irrational and fanatical Fascist leader.
   B. He slaughtered over five million Jews.
   C. He followed an unswerving and weird ideology.
   D. He welcomed war.

Read now the model paragraphs used for discussion purposes.

▶ Hitler and Mussolini have often been thought of as twin dictators, but there was considerable difference between the two men and their regimes. Until he fell under the influence of Hitler, Mussolini had tended to be pragmatic and often moderate. Though Italian fascism coined the concept of "totalitarianism," it allowed some nonfascist elements to enjoy partial liberty and never achieved a true totalitarian state. Similarly, there was for many years no racial doctrine in Italian fascist ideology. Mussolini himself had few fixed doctrines and increasingly accommodated himself to circumstances. Though he talked of a militaristic policy, he followed a more temperate course in practice and kept the peace for thirteen years, knowing that Italy could not gain from a major war.

Hitler was quite different. He carved out a series of weird, nihilistic goals near the beginning of his career and held to them unswervingly. Though he often showed a fine sense of tactics and timing, he was not so pragmatic and adjustable as Mussolini, but was bent on fixed, narrow ends. He was sexually perverted and his mind betrayed the marks of severe compulsive neurosis and emotional instability, conceiving irrational hatreds and enthusiasms of a thoroughly demonic nature which he was determined to see through to the end. Mussolini merely talked, and strutted, but Hitler meant every bit of his bellicosity, and was willing to wage the most frightful war of all time. To resolve the "Jewish problem," he eventually slaughtered at least five million people. Italian fascism was comparatively restrained and conservative until the Nazi example spurred it to new activity; the radical and dynamic pace of Hitler hardly flagged from January 1933 to April 1945. In the process, anti-Semitism, concentration camps, and total war produced a febrile and sadistic nightmare without any parallel in the Italian experience.

S. E. Clough et al.
*European History in a World Perspective*

The subject-at-a-time pattern works best in short papers since the reader can keep the points of contrast related to each subject more easily in mind than in a rather long paper.

If you wish to stress individual points of contrast instead of the "wholes" or if you are writing a rather long paper containing many points of contrast and clarifying material with each point, you organize and develop the contrast *point by point* or in *alternating pattern*. In structuring this pattern, you may announce the contrast and the main idea in an opening topic sentence or conclude with the main idea. Then you present first one point concerning Subject A, and follow immediately with a comparable and contrasting point concerning Subject B. You continue onward in the same way until you have exhausted all the points. You should, of course, structure a preliminary plan and an outline to assist you in organizing this pattern. Study the following model of point-by-point contrast.

▶ Yet there are differences too. The Hindu is an extreme mystic, the Chinese an intensely practical thinker. The Hindu's caste system has long supported the aristocratic principle in Indian society, whereas the democratic tradition has always been strong in China, even through centuries of monarchy. Of all peoples the Hindus are most lacking in a sense of time, so that even the major events in Indian history are sometimes difficult to date. The Chinese, on the other hand, have a meticulous interest in chronology and consider history the most honorable form of literature. The greatest Indian poetry is narrative, especially epic; the Chinese poets have best expressed themselves in lyrics.

Robert Warnock and George Anderson
*The World in Literature*

Consider now a preliminary plan for the above paragraph.

## Preliminary Plan

*Purpose:* To show the differences between the Hindu and the Chinese.

| ▶ HINDU | CHINESE |
|---|---|
| 1. Hindu — a mystic | 1. Chinese — a practical thinker |
| 2. caste system | 2. democratic system |
| 3. no sense of time | 3. meticulous concerning time |
| 4. narrative poetry | 4. lyrical poetry |

A sentence outline for the same model might look something like the following:

CONTRAST BETWEEN THE HINDU AND THE CHINESE

*Purpose:* To show the differences between the Hindu and the Chinese.

▶ I. There are also differences between the Hindu and the Chinese.
   A. The Hindu is an extreme mystic.
   B. The Chinese is a practical thinker.
   C. The caste system has been an important part of Indian society.
   D. The democratic system has been very strong in China.

E. The Hindu is lacking in a sense of time.

F. The Chinese is very concerned with time.

G. Indian poetry is narrative.

H. Chinese poetry is lyrical.

The model paragraph that follows is the same paragraph rewritten as subject-at-a-time development in the same paragraph.

▶ A contrast of India and China can be found in their religion, social order, sense of historical time, and the dominant form of their poetry. The Hindu is a mystic who, until this century, was governed by the strict codes of the famous social system of caste. His histories show a curious lack of precise dating for even the most important events of his country, and his poetry is predominantly epic or narrative. The Chinese, on the other hand, usually adheres to the practical rules of Confucianism and shows a keen sense of historical chronology. Even though China has existed under centuries of monarchy, its social system is democratic. Its poetry is lyric.

The model paragraphs that follow illustrate a development of the same material in a subject-at-a-time pattern by separate paragraphs. Observe the topic sentence announcing the contrast, the development of each point in the first paragraph, and the corresponding development of the same points of contrast in the second paragraph. Note also the topic sentence of paragraph 2 announcing the differences.

▶ The Hindu and the Chinese differ in their religion, social order, sense of historical time, and the dominant form of their poetry. The Hindu is an extreme mystic in terms of his outlook on life. The religious doctrines of Vedanta even reinforce the famous social system of caste, in which a person is born into a particular level of society. Until recently, he was never able to change his status during his life. He could not attempt a vocation above his station or marry into a higher caste. He was destined to remain fixed at that level and conform to the prescribed actions assigned to his status. The mystic idea of *Dharma*, however, offered hope. If the Hindu lived the "right way," he might hope to be, after death, reborn into a higher and more honorable caste. This culture, unchanged for over two thousand years, has produced a curious lack of a sense of time for even the most important events in Hindu history, but the Indian past is well recounted in its most popular literary form — narrative or epic poetry.

The Chinese are different. The Chinese are intensely practical thinkers. Although the mystical philosophy of Taoism has had its followers, the majority of Chinese have, through the ages, adhered to the utilitarian ideas of Confucianism. Instead of pondering things infinite and eternal, the Confucianist concentrates on everyday realities in an attempt to achieve a moral, well-regulated social order *here* and *now*. Since, in the resulting society, all men are equal, the democratic tradition is strong even through centuries of monarchy. Interest in this democratic heritage has made the Chinese careful accountants of the milestones in their history books — a major genre of their literature. Since these histories provide adequate narratives for the readers, the poets can turn to the simple but exquisite form of lyric poetry in which to express their wonderment at the greatness and beauty of the world.*

To better understand the structure of contrast, complete the exercises that follow.

**VOCABULARY PREVIEW**

| | | |
|---|---|---|
| virtually | fortitude | bigotry |
| haughty | munificent | disparagement |
| arrogant | foibles | edifice |
| irascible | coquetry | despondency |
| dissimulation | levity | sullen |
| magnanimity | sagacious | acute |
| affront | despotic | lamentations |
| condescension | sanguinary | |
| mitigate | countenanced | |

---

* This paragraph unit is a rewritten version of the original paragraph. Keep in mind that the writer is explaining the differences between these two countries and peoples in the centuries before the modern era of Chinese communism and Indian reforms in religion and government.

## EXERCISE 4    Contrast

Read the model paragraph below. Answer the questions that follow.
Answers are at the end of the chapter.

▶ It would be hard to imagine two persons more widely separated
in their backgrounds and careers than Thomas Robert Malthus
and David Ricardo. Malthus, as we know, was the son of an
eccentric member of the English upper middle class; Ricardo
was the son of a Jewish merchant-banker who had immigrated
from Holland. Malthus was tenderly tutored for a university
under the guidance of a philosophically minded father (one of
his tutors went to jail for expressing the wish that the French
revolutionaries would invade and conquer England); Ricardo
went to work for his father at the age of fourteen. Malthus
spent his life in academic research; he was the first professional economist, teaching at the college founded in Haileybury by the East India Company to train its young adminis-
trators; Ricardo set up in business for himself at the age of
twenty-two. Malthus was never well-to-do; by the time he was
twenty-six, Ricardo — who had started with a capital of eight
hundred pounds — was financially independent, and in 1814,
at the age of forty-two, he retired with a fortune variously
estimated to be worth between £500,000 and £1,600,000.

Robert L. Heilbroner
*The Worldly Philosophers*

1. What words indicate that the writer will develop by contrast?

2. Is the development point by point or subject-at-a-time?

3. How many points of contrast does the writer establish?

## EXERCISE 5    Contrast

Read the paragraphs below. Answer the questions that follow.

▶ The Pueblo Indians are pictured as a peaceable, cooperative society, in which no one wishes to be thought a great man and everyone wishes to be thought a good fellow. Sexual relations are taken with little jealousy or other violent response; infidelity is not severely punished. Death, too, is taken in stride, with little violent emotion; indeed, emotion is, in general, subdued. While there are considerable variations in economic status, there is little display of economic power and even less of political power; there is a spirit of cooperation with family and community.

The Dobu, by contrast, are portrayed as virtually° a society of paranoids in which each man's hand is against his neighbor's in sorcery, theft, and abuse; in which husband and wife alternate as captives of the spouse's kin; and in which infidelity is deeply resented. Dobuan economic life is built on sharp practice in interisland trading, on an intense feeling for property rights, and on a hope of getting something for nothing through theft, magic, and fraud. Except for nearby Alor, few pictures as grim as this are to be found in anthropological literature.

David Riesman<br>The Lonely Crowd

1. Does the writer announce clearly the development by contrast in a topic sentence?

2. What guide words establish the contrast?

3. Mention the points that are the basis for the contrast.

4. Does the writer develop the contrast point by point or by subject-at-a-time?

▶ ISABELLA AND ELIZABETH*
**W. H. Prescott**

*Thesis: statement of contrast*

*Point by point*

*Guide phrase:* on the other hand

*Likenesses*

*Change in direction with* but

*Points of contrast* on the other hand

*Likenesses*

*Point by point*
*Guide word* but

[1]But with these few circumstances of their history the resemblance ceases. Their characters afford scarcely a point of contact. Elizabeth, inheriting a large share of the bold and bluff King Harry's temperament, was haughty,° arrogant,° coarse, and irascible;° while with these fiercer qualities she mingled deep dissimulation° and strange irresolution. Isabella, *on the other hand*, tempered the dignity of royal station with the most bland and courteous manners. Once resolved, she was constant in her purposes, and her conduct in public and private life was characterized by candor and integrity. Both may be said to have shown that magnanimity° which is implied by the accomplishment of great objects in the face of great obstacles. *But* Elizabeth was desperately selfish; she was incapable of forgiving, not merely a real injury, but the slightest affront° to her vanity; and she was merciless in exacting retribution. Isabella, *on the other hand*, lived only for others, — was ready at all times to sacrifice self to considerations of public duty, and, far from personal resentments, showed the greatest condescension° and kindness to those who had most sensibly injured her; while her benevolent heart sought every means to mitigate° the authorized severities of the law, even towards the guilty.

[2]Both possessed rare fortitude.° Isabella, indeed, was placed in situations which demanded more frequent and higher displays of it than her rival; but no one will doubt a full measure of this quality in the daughter of Henry the Eighth. Elizabeth was better educated, and every way more highly accomplished, than Isabella. *But* the latter knew enough to maintain her station with dignity; and she encouraged learning by a munificent° patronage. The masculine powers and passions of Elizabeth seemed to divorce her in a great measure from the peculiar attributes of her sex; at

---

*The title is by the author of this textbook.

least from those which constitute its peculiar charm; for she had abundance of its foibles,° — a coquetry° and love of admiration which age could not chill; a levity,° most careless, if not criminal; and a fondness for dress and tawdry magnificence of ornament, which was ridiculous, or disgusting, according to the different periods of life in which it was indulged. Isabella, *on the other hand*, distinguished through life for decorum of manners, and purity beyond the breath of calumny, was content with the legitimate affection which she could inspire within the range of her domestic circle. Far from a frivolous affectation of ornament or dress, she was most simple in her own attire, and seemed to set no value on her jewels but as they could serve the necessities of the state, when they could be no longer useful in this way, she gave them away, as we have seen, to her friends.

*Guide phrase*

*Contrast*

*Comparison*

[3]Both were uncommonly sagacious° in the selection of their ministers; though Elizabeth was drawn into some errors in this particular by her levity,[72] as was Isabella by religious feeling. It was this, combined with her excessive humility, which led to the only grave errors in the administration of the latter. Her rival fell into no such errors; and she was a stranger to the amiable qualities which led to them. Her conduct was certainly not controlled by religious principle; and, though the bulwark of the Protestant faith, it might be difficult to say whether she were at heart most a Protestant or a Catholic. She viewed religion in its connection with the state, — in other words, with herself; and she took measures for enforcing conformity to her own views, not a whit less despotic,° and scarcely less sanguinary,° than those countenanced° for conscience' sake by her more bigoted rival.

*Contrast*

*Contrast in the explanation of Isabella's bigotry*

[4]This feature of bigotry,° which has thrown a shade over Isabella's otherwise beautiful character, might lead to a disparagement° of her intellectual power compared with that of the English queen. To estimate this aright, we must contemplate the results of their respective reigns. Elizabeth found all the materials of prosperity at

hand, and availed herself of them most ably to build up a solid fabric of national grandeur. Isabella created these materials. She saw the faculties of her people locked up in a deathlike lethargy, and she breathed into them the breath of life for those great and heroic enterprises which terminated in such glorious consequences to the monarchy. It is when viewed from the depressed position of her early days that the achievements of her reign seem scarcely less than miraculous. The masculine genius of the English queen stands out relieved beyond its natural dimensions by its separation from the softer qualities of her sex; while her rival's, like some vast but symmetrical edifice,° loses in appearance somewhat of its actual grandeur from the perfect harmony of its proportions.

*Contrast in their deaths*

*Comparison*

*Contrast*

[5]The circumstances of their deaths, which were somewhat similar, displayed the great dissimilarity of their characters. Both pined amidst their royal state, a prey to incurable despondency,° rather than any marked bodily distemper. In Elizabeth it sprung from wounded vanity, a sullen° conviction that she had outlived the admiration on which she had so long fed, — and even the solace of friendship and the attachment of her subjects. Nor did she seek consolation where alone it was to be found, in that sad hour. Isabella, on the other hand, sank under a too acute° sensibility to the sufferings of others. But, amidst the gloom which gathered around her, she looked with the eye of faith to the brighter prospects which unfolded of the future; and, when she resigned her last breath, it was amidst the tears and universal lamentations° of her people.

## VOCABULARY TEST NINE

Four words are lined up below each of twenty-five words taken from the exercises and the essay. Select the one that matches best and write its letter in the blank to the right. Answers are at the end of the chapter.

1. virtually                                                                    *A*

   (a) almost wholly, for the most part     (b) hopelessly
   (c) actually     (d) deliberately
                                                                               *D*
2. haughty

   (a) bold     (b) determined     (c) regular, hereditary
   (d) contemptuously proud
                                                                               *C*
3. arrogant

   (a) courageous     (b) suspicious     (c) scorn for inferiors
   (d) questionable
                                                                               *C*
4. irascible

   (a) not responsible     (b) irritating     (c) apt to anger
   (d) rash
                                                                               *B*
5. dissimulation

   (a) similarity     (b) false appearance     (c) kindness
   (d) consideration
                                                                               *B*
6. magnanimity

   (a) largeness     (b) high-mindedness, nobleness
   (c) quality     (d) open nature
                                                                               *D*
7. affront

   (a) compliment     (b) reference     (c) criticism
   (d) insult
                                                                               *B*
8. condescension

   (a) acting quickly     (b) acting with an air of superiority
   (c) with carefulness     (d) bending one's will
                                                                               *C*
9. mitigate

   (a) increase     (b) destroy     (c) lessen, relieve
   (d) mention
                                                                               *B*
10. fortitude

    (a) character     (b) courage, resoluteness     (c) virtues
    (d) feeling
                                                                               *A*
11. munificent

    (a) liberal, very generous     (b) kind     (c) compelling
    (d) gracious
                                                                               *D*
12. foibles

    (a) charms     (b) strengths     (c) hopes
    (d) faults, weaknesses

13. coquetry *B*
    (a) game at court   (b) flirtation, play at courtship
    (c) coat of arms   (d) French sword
    *A*

14. levity
    (a) fickle, lightness of mind   (b) gravity
    (c) act of magic   (d) type of joke
    *A*

15. sagacious
    (a) shrewd, penetrating, wise   (b) careful   (c) powerful
    (d) unfortunate
    *D*

16. despotic
    (a) demanding   (b) shrewd   (c) cautious
    (d) tyrannical
    *B*

17. sanguinary
    (a) anxious   (b) bloodthirsty   (c) fanciful
    (d) gloomy
    *C*

18. countenanced
    (a) argued   (b) countersigned   (c) favored
    (d) vetoed
    *A*

19. bigotry
    (a) religious intolerance   (b) egotism   (c) insanity
    (d) self-pity
    *A*

20. disparagement
    (a) belittling, lowering another's dignity
    (b) weakening one's case   (c) questioning
    (d) qualification
    *B*

21. edifice
    (a) arch   (b) cathedral   (c) bridge
    (d) building, structure
    *B*

22. despondency
    (a) insecurity   (b) deadly disease   (c) optimism
    (d) hopelessness, dejection
    *D*

23. sullen
    (a) firm   (b) gloomy silence, sad   (c) mistaken
    (d) soft, flexible
    *B*

24. acute
    (a) heavy   (b) false   (c) constant
    (d) keen, quick to perceive
    *A*

25. lamentations
    (a) praises   (b) weeping, wailing   (c) complaints
    (d) riots

**VOCABULARY PREVIEW**

| | | |
|---|---|---|
| reviled | composure | enlightened |
| benevolent | hyperbole | misconceptions |
| dour | vitality | isokinetic |
| infinitely | mysticism | |

## EXERCISE 6    Contrast

Read the model paragraph below. Answer the questions that follow.
Answers are at the end of the chapter.

▶ It would be hard to imagine two persons more widely separated
in their backgrounds and careers than Thomas Robert Malthus
and David Ricardo. Malthus was the son of an eccentric member of the English upper middle class. He attended the university and spent his life in academic research. He was the first
professional economist, teaching at the college founded in
Haileybury by the East India Company to train its young ad-
ministrators. He was never well-to-do. Yet Malthus, a man of
moderate means, defended the wealthy landowners. He was
interested in facts, not theories. Still, he was one of the most
abused men of his day. His theory that the basic trouble with
the world was that there were too many people in it was bit-
terly reviled.° As a result, Malthus' contributions to economics
— aside from his essay on population — were largely looked on
with a kind of benevolent° tolerance, or ignored.

David Ricardo, on the other hand, was the son of a Jewish
merchant-banker who had immigrated from Holland. He went
to work for his father at the age of fourteen. Ricardo set up in
business for himself at the age of twenty-two. In 1814, at the
age of forty-two, he retired with a fortune variously estimated
to be worth between £500,000 and £1,600,000. Ricardo, a man
of considerable wealth, fought against the landlords. He was a
theoretician, caring only for invisible "laws." Yet he was ac-
claimed by all. He became known as the man who educated
the Commons. Ricardo, the economist, walked like a god. His
ideas were avidly discussed.*

Robert L. Heilbroner
*The Worldly Philosophers*

---

*This paragraph unit is a rewritten version of the original paragraph used in Exercise 4.

1. In what sentence does the writer announce the contrast?

2. What is the basis of the contrast?

3. Is the development by the point by point or subject-at-a-time pattern?

Read the model comparison and contrast paragraph unit below. Answer the questions that follow.

▶ Father and son could scarcely have been more different. The "very few" members of the National Association of Manufacturers who supported his election, the President smilingly remarked to their 1961 convention, must have been "under the impression that I was my father's son." Both had a natural charm — but the father, though very emotional underneath, was often dour° and gruff while his son kept outwardly calm. Both had a winning Irish smile — but the father was capable of more angry outbursts than his infinitely° patient son. Both had a tough inner core, capable of making hard decisions and sticking to them — but the father had a more aggressive exterior compared to his son's consistently gentle composure.° The father's normal conversation was often filled with hyperbole° — his son's speech, in private as in public, was more often characterized by quiet understatement.

Both had a hatred of war, but the father leaned more to the concept of a Fortress America while his son felt our concern must be global. On domestic matters, while preferring the simpler machinery and lower taxes of an earlier era, the father emphasized personalities as much as issues. "Do you realize," his son said to me in 1953, "that his first choice for the Presidency last year was Senator [Robert A.] Taft and his second was Justice [William O.] Douglas?"

Father and son also had much in common: a delightful sense of humor, a fierce family loyalty, a concern for the state of the nation, endless vitality° and a constant air of confidence no matter how great the odds or the pressures. ("I still don't know how I did," the candidate said after getting the usual cheery word by telephone from his father after the second Nixon–Kennedy debate. "If I had slipped and fallen flat on the floor, he would have said, 'The graceful way you picked yourself up was terrific.' ")

Theodore C. Sorensen
*Kennedy*

1. What is the purpose of the first sentence?

2. What is the function of sentence 2?

3. What is interesting about this organizational pattern?

4. How many points of similarity does the writer establish? List them.

5. How many points of difference does the writer establish? List them.

Read the model essay that follows. Be prepared to answer questions concerning its structure and development.

▶ HOLMES ON THE RANGE
**Gary Smith**

Tonight is far more than Ali vs Holmes. It is mysticism° vs modern medicine, dark ages vs the 1980s. It is army boots vs adidas, medicine balls vs isokinetics.

The two bodies in the ring will represent violently different schools of training thought. Larry Holmes is one of the few boxers in the world who has been introduced to modern training methods. Muhammad Ali does things that would make a freshman physical education major cringe.

He clomps the Pennsylvania hills in Army boots, with no shock absorbers for his knees or ankles. He does situps on a creaking black table, using techniques that would distress a part-time instructor at Jack LaLanne's.

For skin tone, he has an old Cuban rub him down with lotions from the jungles of Jamaica. After fights, he lets his body go to hell. You couldn't get him to jog to the corner grocery store on a bet, unless there was a fresh delivery of ice cream waiting. He has gained and lost so many pounds so often that the dial on his bathroom scale is seasick.

No other athlete in any other sport would dare treat his body the way Ali does. There are bullfighters more disciplined and more enlightened.°

In Larry Holmes' corner, on the other hand, is a 37-year-old man who believes that all of Ali's medieval misconceptions° *will take their toll by the middle rounds tonight.*

This man is a physical therapist from Las Vegas named Keith Klevin, who has already worked on some of the great brittle pieces of anatomy of our times — Lydell Mitchell's knees, Frank Tanana's shoulder, and Juliet Prowse's legs.

He is the man who worked a magic known as friction massage on Holmes' right bicep just before Larry won the world championship against Ken Norton two years ago, an injury that probably should have canceled the bout.

Klevin has Holmes running in the same kind of shoes as Jim Fixx, not Douglas MacArthur, and puts the champion through a daily isokinetic° exercise program known as proprioceptive neuromuscular facilitation. That's PNF to you.

"It's a method of working the muscles manually," he explains. "Rather than move them up and down, we work them in a diagonal pattern. We also do isometrics, with Larry pushing against me.

"Larry is doing things most fighters wouldn't. They refuse to break away from the old, primitive training methods, and boxing itself rarely encourages anything wholesome or progressive. That's why you see so few young therapists and athletic trainers going into it.

"Last year I saw one of the top contenders in the welterweight division go into a room before a fight and start punching himself in the head to get ready. I see boxers working out in poor shoes, bad cups, poor socks. I see them increasing their sparring instead of reducing it as they get closer to a fight.

"Ali uses a medicine ball that tears down tissue instead of building it up. There are still contenders who think they can drop 20 or 30 pounds for a fight. That takes a long time for the body to adjust to." (Ed note: Ali had to learn this the hard way that night.)

If Holmes loses to an ancient, ill-informed Ali, it will set back modern training techniques two decades.

## QUESTIONS ON     Holmes on the Range

1. What is the function of the first paragraph?

2. Write the sentence that tells the reader how the material will be developed.

3. Is the development of this contrast point by point or subject-at-a-time?

4. Write the guide words that move the reader smoothly into the discussion of Larry Holmes and the contrast.

5. What conclusion does the writer reach?

## MATCH-UP EIGHT

Match the definitions in column 2 with the words in column 1 taken from the exercises and essay by placing the letter of the word in the blank. Answers are at the end of the chapter.

| | | | |
|---|---|---|---|
| a. reviled | 1. calmness, peace of mind | *e* | |
| b. benevolent | 2. incorrect interpretations, mistaken notions | *j* | |
| c. dour | 3. informed, full of knowledge | *i* | |
| d. infinitely | 4. muscular exercises of motion | *k* | |
| e. composure | 5. sullen, unyielding, stern | *c* | |
| f. hyperbole | 6. religious insight or intuition | *h* | |
| g. vitality | 7. countlessly, endlessly | *d* | |
| h. mysticism | 8. kind, charitable | *b* | |
| i. enlightened | 9. great strength and mental vigor | *g* | |
| j. misconceptions | 10. abused with speech, verbal attack | *a* | |
| k. isokinetic | 11. extravagant exaggeration | *f* | |

NOTE: Although no vocabulary study is arranged for the second part of the next essay (the contrast section), you might be interested in looking up the meanings of the following words in the final pages of the complete essay "Cowboys and Gauchos."

| | | |
|---|---|---|
| divergences | inexorably | sophisticated |
| voraciously | docile | rehabilitated |
| provincial | sedentary | variance |
| stereotypical | virtually | probing |
| vagrancy | notoriety | disparate |

▶ COWBOYS AND GAUCHOS
**Richard W. Slatta**

Horsemen have excited awe, admiration, fear, and vituperation in plains regions around the world. The man on horseback — whether cowboy or Cossack, Gaucho or *llanero*, *vaquero* or *boiadeiro* — has elicited wide comment and inspired a lively body of folklore and literature. Equestrian subcultures that developed in grasslands, particularly in North and South America, appear to share many common traits and values;

there are also frequently overlooked but fundamental differences. The Gauchos of the Argentine pampa and the cowboys of the U.S. West offer a fascinating comparison.

Edward Larocque Tinker, an avid admirer and student of horses and horsemen of many nations, stressed the commonalities among riders who conquered, defended, and labored on the plains, pampas, llanos, and other grasslands of the Americas:

*No group could be more alike than the horsemen of the New World. The* huasos *of Chile, the* gauchos *of Argentina and Brazil, the* vaqueros *of Mexico . . . , the* llaneros *of Venezuela and Colombia, and the cowboys of the United States are brothers under the skin.*

Gauchos and cowboys shared a common Iberian heritage, and developed in similar natural and economic environments. Both owed much to distant Moorish and Spanish influences brought to the Western Hemisphere during the sixteenth century. The Gaucho adapted Spanish equipment and methods, blended them with new techniques learned from pampean Indians, and developed a unique "civilization of leather." Spanish roots sometimes disappeared entirely as the Gaucho borrowed the Indian *chiripá,* a baggy, diaperlike cloth tucked between the legs, the *boleadora,* or bola, three stones attached to connected leather thongs, which was hurled to entangle and down animals, and maté, a favored caffeine-rich tea. The U.S. cowboy would have been more recognizable to the medieval Spanish rider because of the equipment and vocabulary passed to him through Mexico. The Spaniard would have recognized the cowboy's chaps (*chaparreros*), lariat (*la reata*), string of mounts (*remuda*), and other direct or transformed borrowings.

Nineteenth century observers described cowboys and Gauchos in equivalent, usually unflattering terms. The *Cheyenne Daily Leader* of October 3, 1882, painted a negative portrait of the western horsemen:

*Morally, as a class, they are foulmouthed, blasphemous, drunken, lecherous, utterly corrupt. Usually harmless on the plains when sober, they are dreaded in towns, for the liquor has the ascendency over them. They are also as improvident as the veriest 'Jack' of the sea . . . . They never own any interest in the stock they tend.*

European travelers found the Gaucho of the nineteenth century pampa equally short on morals and long on violent, drunken action. Thomas Joseph Hutchinson, British consul at Rosario, found little to commend Gauchos of the 1860's:

*Gambling is the moving spirit of existence and enjoyment in the real Gaucho. Indeed the veritable camp Gaucho is a sort of loafer, hanging about* pulperías, *looking out for Gaucho-flats to fleece of whatever they have about them, drinking* caña *and gin, now and then ripping up somebody with his knife after a dispute of the most insignificant nature.*

The plainsmen's penchant for violent drinking and gambling particularly disturbed many moralists from urban civilization. Cowboys, or range riders as they were also called, greatly enjoyed cardplaying, especially poker; indeed, the manager of one cattle company termed cardplaying the "most objectionable habit" practiced in cow camps. The Texas Ranchers' Association went so far as to prohibit gambling during roundup. Gauchos enjoyed many activities, from cards (*truco* was the favorite) to *taba* (throwing the knucklebone of a cow and betting on the result), and wagering money on the outcome of horseraces. Both Gauchos and Southwestern cowboys competed in the ring race (*la sortija*) wherein riders tried to lance a small golden ring suspended on a thin thread, using a foot-long stick. The winner rode off with the golden ring as a prize, or presented it to his favorite *china*, or girlfriend.

Cowboys and Gauchos also earned a sometimes justified reputation for rustling livestock. The Cheyenne *Democratic Leader* reported in August 1884 on the problem of rustling in Montana Territory to the north: "There never was a period in the history of this or any other Territory when so much horse thieving was going on." Police reports, rural journals, and complaints by the Argentine Rural Society of large ranchers attest to problems of livestock thefts on the pampa as well.

If the commentators found cowboy and Gaucho character and morals wanting, the horsemen held their own peculiar set of values concerning outsiders. As Emerson Hough observed in his 1898 classic, *The Story of the Cowboy*, "he is a horseman and nothing more, and has little inclination for any work that cannot be done with the saddle." The cowboy exhibits a "mild contempt for all walking and driving men." Likewise the Gaucho could not conceive of life without his *tropilla*, or herd of sturdy *pingos*. Emeric Essex Vidal, who published a series of written sketches and paintings about the River Plate in 1820, asserted that Gauchos

*have a great antipathy to all occupations which they cannot follow on horseback. They scarcely know how to walk, and will not if they can help it, though it were only across the street. When they meet at the* pulpería, *or anywhere else, they remain on horseback, though the conversation may last hours. It is on horseback also that they go a fishing, riding into the water to throw and draw the net. To raise water from a well, they fasten the rope to their horse and make him draw it up, without setting their own feet on the ground.*

As Sir Francis Bond Head correctly noted in 1826, "the print of the human foot on the ground is in his mind the symbol of uncivilization."

Gauchos and cowboys dressed differently, but their distinctive garb elicited detailed descriptions by fascinated onlookers. Theodore Roosevelt, ex-President and historian of the West, described the cowboy attire in *The Outlook* magazine of May 24, 1913. "Lean, sinewy fellows, accustomed to riding half-broken horses at any speed over any country by day or by night . . . , they wore flannel shirts, with loose handkerchiefs knotted round their necks, broad hats, high heeled boots with jingling spurs, and sometimes leather chaps."

On his visit to the pampas in the late 1840's the English sketcher Robert Elwes captured the central elements of the Gaucho costume:

*They wear very wide white linen drawers called "calzonci-llas," handsomely ornamented from the knee downwards with open work, and sometimes having a fringe of silk falling over the feet. A "chiripa," a poncho of some bright colour, is fastened round the waist, and drawn up loosely between the legs, forming a sort of large baggy trousers; and a short jacket, and a broad leathern belt with pockets in it, complete the costume. The belt, which is called a "tirador," is fastened behind with four or more pillared dollars, and in this is stuck a long knife, often sheathed and hafted with silver. Their boots, which are open at the toe, are white, and made with great care from the skin of a horse's hind leg . . . The hat is a narrow-brimmed Panama straw, encircled by a red ribbon, and they wear large silver or iron spurs.*

When fortunate enough to be employed, cowboys and Gauchos performed much the same kind of work. A small group of year-round employees took care of day-to-day herding, maintenance, and other chores. Trail drives, roundup, branding, and castration required additional hands and special skills. Riders hired by the day or by the task swelled the ranch labor force during the busy seasons. Danger of injury or death pervaded ranch work. *Field and Farm* of February 16, 1895, recorded the tragic tale told by a survivor of one stampede in Colorado:

*The whole herd tumbled and pitched and tossed over us. Foster was literally mangled to sausage meat. His horse was little better, and mine was crushed into a bloody mass. I found that I could not get up, for my leg was broken just below the thigh. I was soon cared for, however, and in six weeks was all right and on the range again. We found 341 dead cattle, two dead horses, one dead cowboy, and two more with broken legs after the herd had passed.*

Both Gauchos and cowboys faced vicious blizzards sweeping out of the western mountains that froze livestock and any horsemen caught in them. Expert horsemen, Gauchos sometimes suffered serious accidents when their mounts fell into one of the myriad animal burrows that honeycombed the pampa. Marion Mulhall, wife of a well-known Irish publisher in Buenos Aires, opined in 1881 that "pampa life is attended with so much danger and hardship that it is said no one has ever seen a grey-haired Gaucho." Both Gauchos and cowboys suffered long layoffs during slack seasons; indeed, umemployment and underemployment partially account for animal rustling for food and profit. Unemployed cowboys rode from ranch to ranch during the winter and Gauchos from *estancia* to *estancia* — a practice known in the U.S. West as "sun downing." The rider arrived at a ranch shortly before sundown or mealtime, asked to rest awhile, and shared meals with the regular hands for a few days. Ranchers preferred feeding drifters to having them kill livestock for food on the range. Yet "slow elk," as illegally killed yearling beef was called by cowboys, also fed many hungry, unemployed riders on the plains.

Vital to the cattle industry, cowboys and Gauchos nevertheless suffered a precarious existence. Modern technological change foredoomed both in the latter decades of the nineteenth century. Wire fencing, windmills, railroads, farming, and more refined animal breeding spelled an end to the open range of bygone days. The migratory, independent riders of the past gave way to subdued, obedient, dependent peons and ranch hands. The *Denver Sun* recorded the cowboy's epitaph in its issue of November 12, 1892:

*The cowboy, like the buffalo, the prairie wolf, the painted redskin, and the highway robber of the plains, is rapidly becoming extinct in the West. Civilization is as hard on cowboys as it is on the other animals enumerated above.*

Modernity also banished the Gaucho. Eliza Jane McCartney Clements, a missionary to the River Plate region during the 1880's, noted the impact of change on the Gaucho:

*His is a wild, free, unconventional life, not without its charms, but it is doomed to vanish before the innovation of the restraints which those using them call civilization.*

The correspondence in values, work, and historical development between the Gaucho and the cowboy should not blind us to significant divergences.° While the cowboy created his own subculture, he did not reject and isolate himself totally from urban life and values to the same extent as did the Gaucho. Most cowboys were literate and read voraciously;° occasional scraps of old newspaper and even labels on food tins of lard, beans, and other items received intense scrutiny. Some left written records of their range experiences in the form of memoirs, yarns, and fictionalized stories that convey the flavor and texture of ranch life. No Gaucho autobiographies exist. Gauchos were illiterate and seldom sought or had contact with urban civilization. News might be read from a provincial° newspaper at the country store and tavern, but singing, gambling, and drinking were more common.

The cowboy's openness to some elements of modernity is also evident in his weapon of choice — the six-shooter. Cowboys carried pistols to defend themselves against wild predators, rattlesnakes, marauding Indians, rustlers, and one another. While gunslingers were few and the stereotypical° duel on Main Street at high noon an infrequent occurrence, cowboys considered the six-shooter necessary equipment. Gauchos, in contrast, continued to favor the traditional *facón*, a long swordlike knife, even after the military introduced firearms to the pampa. Ezequiel Martínez Estrada, one of Argentina's foremost interpreters, explained the centrality of the Gaucho's knife in his memorable *X-Ray of the Pampa*, published in 1933:

*It makes possible food whenever needed, shelter from sun and rain, tranquility during sleep, faithfulness in love, assurance along dangerous roads, and confidence in oneself.*

*It carries the weight of authority because in the hands of a laborer it may symbolize a livelihood without ceasing to be the instrument of liberty and justice. With a knife a man may, in Alberdi's words, "carry the government with him."*

The Gaucho suffered a disadvantaged legal position relative to the cowboy. Western ranchers never had labor shortages, as did *estancieros* on the pampa, and they enjoyed a surplus of young, albeit inexperienced, men eager to ride the range for low wages. Pampean ranchers pushed successfully for restrictive legislation because of persistent labor shortages at critical roundup and branding times. Responsive national and provincial governments passed vagrancy° laws, required work contracts and passports for travel between countries, and wielded the potent threat of military conscription to force Gauchos inexorably° toward lives as outlaws on the harrowing Indian frontier, or as docile,° sedentary° peons for large landowners.

Cowboys enjoyed greater opportunity for upward economic mobility. Large operations such as the sprawling King Ranch in south Texas and the XIT spread in the Texas Panhandle covered vast areas, but small ranchers stood a chance for survival in many regions. *Estancieros* monopolized land control and ownership on the pampa and virtually° eliminated the possibility of the small herder acquiring land.

Finally, the relative culture and ideological impact of the Gaucho and cowboy varied considerably. Cowboys enjoyed only an ephemeral heyday, from about the close of the Civil War to the catastrophic winter of 1885–1886. Overgrazing and overproduction doomed the large operations on the open range to extinction. During that brief ride across the Western historical stage the cowboy became identified with the Great Plains from Texas north to Montana and achieved notoriety° as a regional character. The Gaucho, on the other hand, developed over approximately a century and a half, beginning as a wild cattle hunter in the *vaquerías* of the eighteenth century, working on primitive *estancias* by midcentury, and accompanying the rise of extensive, more sophisticated° ranching during the nineteenth century. The Gaucho spanned a far longer period than did the cowboy, and thus developed a deeper set of traditions.

The Gaucho also became a national symbol in Argentina rather than a regional one like the cowboy of the U.S. West. Leopoldo Lugones, Manuel Gálvez, Ricardo Rojas, and other early twentieth century nationalists, frightened by the flood tide of Italian and other European immigrants, turned to the much maligned, recently extinct Gaucho as a symbol for Argentine national values and character. Traditionalist and folklore groups as well as politicians resurrected and rehabilitated° the forms of Gaucho subculture and expressed nationalistic pride and confidence through them. Argentines elevated the Gaucho to a new pinnacle of prominence, and enshrined him in a rich mythology often at variance° with the stark, squalid, oppressed reality of his existence. *Martín Fierro*, a two-part poem of the Gaucho's persecuted life penned by José Hernández during the 1870's, became the Argentine national literary epic.

The broad outlines of cowboy and Gaucho life and culture parallel one another, but deeper probing° reveals major divergences in their development. These differences merit attention because they illuminate the larger forces, movements, and social interaction that shaped Argentina and the western United States during the nineteenth century. Fascinating in his own right, the dashing "half man, half horse" of the Argentine pampa and the U.S. plains also provides a lens to focus the disparate° historical paths of their respective nations.

## Analysis of *Cowboys and Gauchos*

Writers will frequently compare and contrast two subjects as did Sorenson in showing the likenesses and differences between John Kennedy and his father. In the model essay "Cowboys and Gauchos" (from which the comparison model was excerpted), Richard W. Slatta first shows the likenesses between the cowboy and the gaucho and then follows with a discussion of the differences. The essay, like the model for the longer paper in Chapter 1, "Big Money in Pro Sports," has an introduction, a middle, and a conclusion.

In addition to gaining reader interest, Slatta uses his introductory paragraphs to announce his comparison and contrast development, using the term *comparison* in the last sentence of the first paragraph to mean both methods; he writes: *The Gauchos of the Argentine pampa and the cowboys of the U.S. West offer a fascinating comparison.* In the quoted material in paragraph 2, Mr. Slatta announces clearly the subsequent development by comparison (likenesses): *No group could be more alike than the horsemen of the New World,* and the final word group, *are brothers under the skin.*

The middle paragraphs present the likenesses and the differences. He concludes his discussion of the likenesses with a conclusion by McCartney: "*It* [Gauchos' life] *is doomed to vanish before the innovation of the restraints which those using them call civilization.*" He leads his readers smoothly into a discussion of the differences with the following statement: *The correspondence in values, work, and historical development between the Gaucho and cowboy should not blind us to significant divergences.* The remaining middle paragraphs of the essay present the differences between the two horsemen.

The final paragraph give the reader the purpose of the comparison and contrast. Richard Slatta shows that the differences "provides a lens to focus the disparate historical paths of their respective nations" — the central thought (thesis) of the entire essay.

## Suggested Topics for Writing Contrast

1. Two famous persons (authors, generals, actors, actresses, and so on)
2. A foreign compact car and an American compact car
3. Two sports (football, rugby)
4. Two philosophies, religions, or ideologies
5. College and high school
6. Snow skiing and water skiing
7. London and Paris (any two cities)
8. Living at college and living at home
9. Small college and large college
10. Fraternities: high school and college
11. Two dates
12. Weapons: today and yesterday
13. Christmas: yesterday and today
14. Two customs
15. Two movies, television shows, commercials, and so on

## Points to Remember When Writing Comparison or Contrast

1. Define clearly your purpose.
2. List as many points of comparison or contrast as possible
3. Eliminate any irrelevant or less important points.
4. Review in your mind the kind of organization and development that the material suggests.
5. Use transitional words and expressions to indicate comparisons and contrasts and aid in the flow of thought.

## Analogy

Analogy is a method of organizing and developing thought by comparison. In structuring thought by analogy, a writer explains or clarifies an unfamiliar subject by likening it to a familiar subject. Writers use analogy to make the new, different, complex, difficult more understandable for the reader. Analogy, therefore, explains, clarifies, illustrates, simplifies; it does not prove anything.

In the model analogy below, Emerson compares society to a wave. Most analogies like this model are part of a larger piece of writing.

> ▶ Society is a wave. The wave moves onward, but the water of which it is composed does not. The same particle does not rise from the valley to the ridge. Its unity is only phenomenal. The persons who make up a nation to-day, next year die, and their experience dies with them.
>
> Ralph Waldo Emerson<br>"Self-Reliance"

Writers will usually announce the analogy and then develop it. In addition, analogies, as a rule, rise spontaneously from the material as the writer's thoughts flow onward. Study the following model. Notice that the writer announces the comparison in the first sentence. To make the meaning clear, he compares the atmosphere of the earth to any window.

> ▶ The atmosphere of Earth acts like any window in serving two very important functions. It lets light in and it permits us to look out. It also serves as a shield to keep out dangerous or uncomfortable things. A normal glazed window lets us keep our houses warm by keeping out cold air, and it prevents rain, dirt, and unwelcome insects and animals from coming in. As we have already seen, Earth's atmospheric window also helps to keep our planet at a comfortable temperature by holding back radiated heat and protecting us from dangerous levels of ultraviolet light.
>
> Lately, we have discovered that space is full of a great many very dangerous things against which our atmosphere guards us. It is not a perfect shield, and sometimes one of these dangerous objects does get through. There is even some evidence that a few of these messengers from space contain life, though this has by no means been proved yet.
>
> Lester del Rey<br>*The Mysterious Sky*

In the model analogy that follows, decide which subject is the familiar and which subject is the unfamiliar one. Observe also that again the writer announces his analogy.

▶ We can perhaps form some sort of a picture of the nature of these spontaneous disintegrations or jumps, by comparing the atom to a party of four card-players who agree to break up as soon as a hand is dealt in which each player receives just one complete suit. A room containing millions of such parties may be taken to represent a mass of radio-active substance. Then it can be shown that the number of card-parties will decrease according to the exact law of radioactive decay on one condition — *that the cards are well shuffled between each deal.* If there is adequate shuffling of the cards, the passage of time and the past will mean nothing to the card-players, for the situation is born afresh each time the cards are shuffled. Thus the death-rate per thousand will be constant, as with atoms of radium. But if the cards are merely taken up after each deal, without shuffling, each deal follows inevitably from the preceding, and we have the analogue of the old law of causation. Here the rate of diminution in the number of players would be different from that actually observed in radio-active disintegration. We can only reproduce this by supposing the cards to be continually shuffled, and the shuffler is he whom we have called fate.

Sir James Jeans
*The Mysterious Universe*

**VOCABULARY PREVIEW**

| partial | tendencies | interposes |
|---------|------------|------------|
| apparent | formidable | innumerable |
| irrespective | impinge | constituents |
| categorically | | |

## EXERCISE 8    Analogy

Read the model analogy below. Answer the questions that follow. Answers are at the end of the chapter.

▶ You know the difference between a heap of bricks, on the one hand, and the single house they constitute, on the other. You know the difference between one house and a collection of houses. A book is like a single house. It is a mansion of many rooms, rooms on different levels, of different sizes and shapes, with different outlooks, rooms with different functions to perform. These rooms are independent, in part. Each has its own structure and interior decoration. But they are not absolutely independent and separate. They are connected by doors and arches, by corridors and stairways. Because they are connected, the partial° function which each performs contributes its share to the usefulness of the whole house. Otherwise the house would not be genuinely livable.

The architectural analogy is almost perfect. A good book, like a good house, is an orderly arrangement of parts. Each major part has a certain amount of independence. As we shall see, it may have an interior structure of its own. But it must also be connected with the other parts — that is, related to them functionally — for otherwise it could not contribute its share to the intelligibility of the whole.

As houses are more or less livable, so books are more or less readable. The most readable book is an architectural achievement on the part of the author. The best books are those that have the most intelligible structure and, I might add, the most apparent.°

Mortimer J. Adler
*How to Read a Book*

1. What sentence explains the analogy?

2. What does the writer discuss in paragraph 1? For what purpose?

3. How does the writer structure and develop paragraphs 2 and 3?

4. Mention some word groups that keep the analogy in the mind of the readers.

## EXERCISE 9    Analogy

Read the model analogy below. Answer the questions that follow.

▶ Teaching may be compared to selling commodities. No one
can sell unless someone buys. We should ridicule a merchant
who said that he had sold a great many goods although no one
bought any. But perhaps there are teachers who think that they
have done a good day's teaching irrespective° of what pupils
have learned. There is the same exact equation between teaching and learning that there is between selling and buying. The
only way to increase the learning of pupils is to augment the
quantity and quality of real teaching. Since learning is something that the pupil has to do himself and for himself, the
initiative lies with the learner. The teacher is a guide and director; he steers the boat, but the energy that propels it must
come from those who are learning. The more a teacher is aware
of the past experiences of students, of their hopes, desires, chief
interests, the better will he understand the forces at work that
need to be directed and utilized for the formation of reflective
habits. The number and quality of these factors vary from person to person. They cannot therefore be categorically° enumerated in a book. But there are some tendencies° and forces
that operate in every normal individual, forces that must be
appealed to and utilized if the best methods for the development of good habits of thought are to be employed.

John Dewey
*How We Think*

1. What is the purpose of the first sentence?

2. What particular point does the writer stress in this analogy?

3. Does the writer present the points related to the known subject in this analogy?

4. Explain the points of the analogy as they relate to the known subject (the merchant).

As you read the longer analogy that follows, notice that the writer discusses the known subject in the first part of the essay; then, he moves the reader into the unknown subject with the sentence: "We have been watching a sort of working model of the way in which sunlight struggles through the earth's atmosphere," and the first sentence of paragraph 3, which reads, "The waves of the sea represent the sunlight." Observe also the structure of the brief essay. The flow of the writer's thought is from the particulars of the analogy to the final statement of the central thought in the last sentence: *And that is why the sky looks blue.*

### ▶ WHY THE SKY LOOKS BLUE

**Sir James Jeans**

[1]Imagine that we stand on an ordinary seaside pier, and watch the waves rolling in and striking against the iron columns of the pier. Large waves pay very little attention to the columns — they divide right and left and reunite after passing each column, much as a regiment of soldiers would if a tree stood in their road; it is almost as though the columns had not been there. But the short waves and ripples find the columns of the pier a much more formidable° obstacle. When the short waves impinge° on the columns, they are reflected back and spread as new ripples in all directions. To use the technical term, they are "scattered." The obstacle provided by the iron columns hardly affects the long waves at all, but scatters the short ripples.

[2]We have been watching a sort of working model of the way in which sunlight struggles through the earth's atmosphere. Between us on earth and outer space the atmosphere interposes° innumerable° obstacles in the form of molecules of air, tiny droplets of water, and small particles of dust. These are represented by the columns of the pier.

[3]The waves of the sea represent the sunlight. We know that sunlight is a blend of many colors — as we can prove for ourselves by passing it through a prism, or even through a jug of water, or as nature demonstrates to us when she passes it through the raindrops of a summer shower and produces a rainbow. We also know that light consists of waves, and that the different colors of light are produced by waves of different lengths, red light by long waves and blue light by short waves. The mixture of waves which constitutes sunlight has to struggle past the columns of the pier. And these obstacles treat the light waves much as the columns of the pier treat the sea waves. The long waves which constitute red light are hardly

affected but the short waves which constitute blue light are scattered in all directions.

⁴Thus the different constituents° of sunlight are treated in different ways as they struggle through the earth's atmosphere. A wave of blue light may be scattered by a dust particle, and turned out of its course. After a time a second dust particle again turns it out of its course, and so on, until finally it enters our eyes by a path as zigzag as that of a flash of lightning. Consequently the blue waves of the sunlight enter our eyes from all directions. And that is why the sky looks blue.

---

**MATCH-UP NINE**

Match the definitions in column 2 with the words in column 1 taken from the exercises and essay by placing the letter of the word in the blank. Answers are at the end of the chapter.

| a. partial | 1. difficult, threatening | _g_ |
| b. apparent | 2. countless, numberless | _j_ |
| c. irrespective | 3. have close contact with, encroach | _h_ |
| d. categorically | 4. intrudes, places between | _i_ |
| e. tendencies | 5. elements, separate parts | _d_ |
| f. formidable | 6. without regard to, ignoring | _c_ |
| g. impinge | 7. evident, obvious | _b_ |
| h. interposes | 8. unconditionally, positively | _e_ |
| i. innumerable | 9. trends, leanings | _f_ |
| j. constituents | 10. part of the whole | _a_ |

---

## Answers: Chapter 6

### Exercise 1

1. The writer states his main idea — the announcement of the comparison — in the second sentence.
2. The writer establishes four major points of likenesses.
   a. Their whiskers are highly sensitive touch organs.
   b. Neither cats nor dogs see as well as human beings.
   c. Both animals have exquisitely sensitive hearing.
   d. Both cats and dogs have a keen sense of smell.
3. The writer relies mainly on *both* and *but*; however, he also makes effective use of pronouns referring back to nouns, such as *them, their, it.*
4. No answer

### Cowboys and Gauchos

1. He announces development by similarities in paragraph 2.
2. The guide words and phrases are the following: *both, shared a common Iberian heritage, in similar natural and economic environments.*
3. Topic sentence: Nineteenth-century observers described cowboys and Gauchos in equivalent, usually unflattering terms.

   Paragraphs 4, 5, and 6 comprise the paragraph unit.

4. The closing words by Sir Francis Bond repeat in different words the main idea of the topic sentence of paragraph 8: "the horsemen held their own peculiar set of values concerning outsiders." The writer's thought, therefore, flows from general to particular to general.
5. Gauchos and cowboys dressed differently.
6. a. Both Gauchos and cowboys faced many dangers and hardships.
   b. Both Gauchos and cowboys suffered long layoffs during slack seasons.
7. The writer states that civilization has doomed the way of life of the Gaucho and the cowboy.

### Exercise 4

1. It would be hard to imagine two persons more widely separated in their backgrounds and careers than Thomas Malthus and David Ricardo.
2. The writer develops four points by alternating pattern (point by point).
3. The four points are the following:
   a. Position in society
   b. Education or lack of it
   c. Work or profession
   d. Wealth or success

### Exercise 6

1. The writer announces the contrast in the first sentence of paragraph 1. He leads the reader into the contrast with the guide words *on the other hand* in the first sentence of paragraph 2.
2. The backgrounds and careers of the two men serve as a basis for the contrast.
3. The development is subject-at-a-time.

### Exercise 8

1. The architectural analogy is almost perfect (paragraph 2).
2. The writer discusses the construction of a house; he writes: "A book is like a single house."
3. He develops the comparison between a good book and a good house.
4. He uses the words *difference, like, each, but, so* to keep the analogy in the reader's mind.

### Voc. Test 8

| | | | |
|---|---|---|---|
| 1. a | 6. d | 11. d | 16. b |
| 2. c | 7. c | 12. a | 17. c |
| 3. d | 8. a | 13. b | 18. d |
| 4. c | 9. b | 14. c | 19. b |
| 5. b | 10. c | 15. d | 20. c |

| **Voc. Test 9** | | **Match-Up 8** | **Match-Up 9** |
|---|---|---|---|
| 1. a | 14. a | 1. e | 1. g |
| 2. d | 15. a | 2. j | 2. j |
| 3. c | 16. d | 3. i | 3. h |
| 4. c | 17. b | 4. k | 4. i |
| 5. b | 18. c | 5. c | 5. d |
| 6. b | 19. a | 6. h | 6. c |
| 7. d | 20. a | 7. d | 7. b |
| 8. b | 21. d | 8. b | 8. e |
| 9. c | 22. b | 9. g | 9. f |
| 10. b | 23. d | 10. a | 10. a |
| 11. a | 24. b | 11. f | |
| 12. d | 25. a | | |
| 13. b | | | |

# 7

## Explaining and Informing — Analysis by Structure, Function, Process

Analysis is a method of explaining and informing by which a writer breaks down (divides) his subject into its component parts. In organizing and developing thought by analysis, a writer gives order to his flowing thought by treating each part separately, showing its own importance and its relationship to the whole. Structuring thought by analysis can be used to explain anything, whether it be an object, an organization, a happening, or an idea, that has parts.

### Analysis by Structure

A writer's purpose will determine the kind of analysis he will write. If he is interested in explaining the nature of something — that is, the inherent character or basic structure of a person, place, thing, or idea — he will write an *analysis by structure*. A writer, for example, may be interested in explaining the complex structure of the human heart, eye, or ear. Another writer may wish to explain the nature of a corporation, a poem, a football team, or a political party. Still another writer may wish to explain the qualities of a safe city street, the opportunities a war offered a country, or the nature of theory for preventing pollution in a rural area. Writers with this kind of purpose will concentrate on the structure of the subject, explaining the nature of each part and showing its relationship to the whole.

In developing thought with analysis by structure, a writer will often reveal his purpose and indicate clearly the division of the subject into component parts at the beginning of the writing; for example: "A typical leaf may be divided into three main parts: (1) the blade, (2) the petiole, and (3) the stipules." He will discuss each part, moving frequently through space, showing how each part contributes to the structure of the whole as it suits his purpose. Frequently, he will make clear his parts by using guide words like *first, second, third*, and so on, or figures (1), (2), (3), . . . .

In organizing thought with analysis by structure, you are answering the question: "What is the nature of the subject?" In other words, what are the properties, qualities, characteristics, items, or entities that taken together make the whole thing. You focus your attention, therefore, on the parts as they relate to the whole structure. You are interested in the parts of a leaf to show that it is a tiny miracle in structure. You are not interested in how the leaf works as a food-making factory for the plant (*analysis by function*); or how to do something, such as gathering leaves for a collection (*analysis by process*); or why something happened, such as why a leaf turns color (*analysis by causes*). These other methods of developing thought by analysis will be discussed in the pages of this chapter following the present consideration of analysis by parts.

Suppose, for example, your purpose is to explain that a leaf is a tiny miracle in its structure. You would divide the leaf into its three main parts: (1) the *blade*, (2) the *petiole*, and (3) the *stipules*. You would discuss each part in turn, subdividing to the extent necessary to fulfill your purpose. The *blade*, for instance, could be broken down into three separate layers: (1) an upper layer, (2) a middle layer, and (3) a lower layer — the undersurface of the leaf. In the upper layer are two kinds of cells — the *palisade cells* and the *spongy cells*. In the middle layer is a remarkable "low roofed room" which is a food-making factory for the plant. In the lower layer are thousands of pores (openings) called *stomata*, which let air into the leaf. In the lower layer is also a main vein, a midrib that runs the length of the rib. This *main vein* divides into smaller and smaller branches that become so tiny they can no longer be seen. This system of veins and subveins serves as the leaf's water system.

The *petiole* is the stemlike part of the leaf that holds the blade. It consists chiefly of tubes held together tightly. The base of the petiole is wider than the rest. It is connected firmly to the stem of the plant on which it grows.

Some plants have *stipules;* these parts are shaped like tiny leaves and keep the plant from being blown about by the wind.

In the following model paragraph, the writer divides the whole process of listening to music into "three separate planes" to present, as he writes, "the clearer view to be had of the way in which we listen."

> ▶ We all listen to music according to our separate capacities. But, for the sake of analysis, the whole listening process may become clearer if we break it up into its component parts, so to speak. In a certain sense we all listen to music on three separate planes. For lack of a better terminology, one might name these: (1) the sensuous plane, (2) the expressive plane, (3) the sheerly musical plane.The only advantage to be gained from mechanically splitting up the listening process into these hypothetical planes is the clearer view to be had of the way in which we listen.
>
> Aaron Copland
> *What to Listen for in Music*

Mr. Copland, then, breaks the whole into three component parts: (1) the sensuous plane, (2) the expressive plane, and (3) the sheerly musical plane.

In this type of analysis, a writer asks the question: "What is this a part of?" or "What are parts of this?" The writer then answers the question by structuring his material so that he breaks the whole into its parts by arbitrarily imposing on his subject some basis for division that will accomplish his or her purpose.

In the model paragraph that follows, the writer states her purpose clearly in the first sentence: "Before constructing an imaginary life history of a typical wave, we need to become familiar with some of its physical characteristics." She then breaks the whole (the wave) into its characteristics (the parts) so that the reader will understand better the nature of a typical wave.

▶ Before constructing an imaginary life history of a typical wave, we need to become familiar with some of its physical characteristics. A wave has height, from trough to crest. It has length, the distance from its crest to that of the following wave. The period of the wave refers to the time required for succeeding crests to pass a fixed point. None of these dimensions is static; all change, but bear definite relations to the wind, the depth of the water, and many other matters. Furthermore, the water that composes a wave does not advance with it across the sea; each water particle describes a circular or elliptical orbit with the passage of the wave form, but returns very nearly to its original position. And it is fortunate that this is so, for if the huge masses of water that comprise a wave actually moved across the sea, navigation would be impossible. Those who deal professionally in the lore of waves make frequent use of a picturesque expression — the 'length of fetch.' The 'fetch' is the distance that the waves have run, under the drive of a wind blowing in a constant direction, without obstruction. The greater the fetch, the higher the waves. Really large waves cannot be generated within the confined space of a bay or a small sea. A fetch of perhaps 600 to 800 miles, with winds of gale velocity, is required to get up the largest ocean waves.

Rachel L. Carson
*The Sea Around Us*

In analyzing structure in subjects like a geographical area, a wave, an ear, or a tree, the parts are obvious — they are inherent within the object or thing. In analyzing concepts or ideas, however, a writer must impose on a subject the parts he or she will discuss to make the whole meaningful and fulfill the purpose. In the model structural analysis that follows, the writer treats this kind of a subject — a safe street.

▶ Everyone knows that a well-used city street is apt to be safe. A deserted one is apt to be unsafe. But how does this work, really? And what makes a city street well used or shunned? Why is the inner sidewalk mall in Washington Houses — which is supposed to be an attraction — shunned when the sidewalks of the old city just to its west are not? What about streets that are busy part of the time and then empty abruptly? A city street equipped to make a safety asset out of the presence of strangers, as successful city neighborhoods always do, must have three main qualities:

First, there must be a clear demarcation between public and private spaces. They cannot ooze into each other as they do typically in housing projects where streets, walks, and play areas may seem at first glance to be open to the public but in effect are special preserves. (The fate of Washington Houses' large Christmas tree is a classic example of what happens when the distinction between public and private space is blurred, and the area which should be under public surveillance has no clear practicable limits.)

Second, there must be *eyes* upon the street, eyes belonging to what we might call its natural proprietors. To insure the safety of both residents and strangers, the buildings on a street must be oriented to it. They cannot turn their backs or blank sides on it and leave it blind.

And third, the sidewalk must have users on it fairly continuously, both to add more effective eyes and to induce plenty of people in buildings along the street to watch the sidewalks. Nobody enjoys sitting on a stoop or looking out a window at an empty street. But large numbers of people entertain themselves, off and on, by watching street activity.

Jane Jacobs
*The Death and Life of Great American Cities*

Complete the exercises that follow to review and test yourself on what you have learned about analysis by structure. Keep in mind these points.

1. The writer has a purpose for his division.
2. The writer maintains that purpose throughout the development.
3. The writer will often reveal, in the first sentence, his purpose, the subject of the analysis, and the parts of the whole.
4. The writer will divide and subdivide his subject until he has fulfilled his purpose.
5. Analysis by structure is frequently organized by movement through space (spatial development).

**VOCABULARY PREVIEW**

| | | |
|---|---|---|
| spectacular | innate | scapegoat |
| panoramic | variations | attribute |
| impressive | pigment | deficient |
| stabilized | subtle | vigilance |
| distinct | facet | intolerance |

---

## EXERCISE 1   Analysis

Read the model paragraphs below. Answer the questions that follow. Answers are at the end of the chapter.

▶ The national seashore does have two spectacular° features. One is the magnificent wall of cliffs, 60 to 70 feet high, where the Cape's tablelands meet the Atlantic. The first panoramic° glimpse of the great outer beach from these cliffs — as from Truro Lighthouse — has been called "one of the most memorable experiences in America." People tell tall tales about the winds here blowing back pieces of wood cast over the bank, and Thoreau once recorded that boys and men "amuse themselves by running and trying to jump off the bank with their jackets spread, and being blown back."

North of these impressive° cliffs are eight square miles of some of the most spectacular dunes on our Atlantic coast. The building material came from the highlands to the south — gnawed out of the cliffs by wind and wave, carried for miles by ocean currents, then picked up, shaped, shifted and reshaped by centuries of winds. People who have braved this wilderness during the winter, when the northwest winds blow, report that you can see dunes change shape in an hour. Some are free-moving, other stabilized° with beach grass and low-growing dwarf-like trees.

Don Wharton
*"They're Saving America's Priceless Seashore"*

1. What is the function of the first sentence of paragraph 1?

2. Is the organization of the material spatial or chronological?

3. Into what two parts does the writer divide his subject?

## EXERCISE 2    Analysis

Read the model paragraph below. Answer the questions that follow it.

▶ The life of the ocean is divided into distinct° realms, each with its own group of creatures that feed upon each other and depend on each other in different ways. There is, first of all, the tidal zone, where land and sea meet. Then comes the realm of the shallow seas around the continents, which goes down to about 500 feet. It is in these two zones that the vast majority of marine life occurs. The deep ocean adds two regions, the zone of light and the zone of perpetual darkness. In the clear waters of the western Pacific, light could still be seen at a depth of 1,000 feet through the portholes of the *Trieste* on its seven-mile dive. But for practical purposes the zone of light ends at about 600 feet. Below that level there is too little light to support the growth of the "grass" of the sea — the tiny, single-celled green plants whose ability to form sugar and starch with the aid of sunlight makes them the base of the great food pyramid of the ocean.*

Leonard Engel et al.
*The Sea*

1. Does the first sentence clearly indicate the analysis by structure?

2. What is the "whole" that the writer will break into parts?

---

* Reprinted from *The Sea* by Leonard Engel and the Editors of Time–Life Books.© 1961, 1972. Time Inc.

3. Is the organization of the material spatial or chronological?

4. Into how many parts (distinct realms) does the writer divide "the life of the ocean"? Does he subdivide any major divisions?

5. List some guide words that help the reader follow the writer's flowing thought.

Read the essay that follows, analyzing the ways people learn prejudice. An analysis follows the essay.

▶ HOW CHILDREN LEARN PREJUDICE*
**Ian Stevenson, M.D.**

[1]The first important point about how children learn prejudice
is that they do. They aren't born that way, though some people
think prejudice is innate° and like to quote the old saying,
"You can't change human nature." But you can change it. We
now know that very small children are free of prejudice. Studies of school children have shown that prejudice is slight or
absent among children in the first and second grades. It increases thereafter, building to a peak usually among children in
the fourth and fifth grades. After this, it may fall off again in
adolescence. Other studies have shown that, on the average,
young adults are much freer of prejudice than older ones.

[2]In the early stages of picking up prejudice, children mix it
with ignorance which, as I've said, should be distinguished
from prejudice. A child, as he begins to study the world around
him, tries to organize his experiences. Doing this, he begins to
classify things and people and begins to form connections — or
what psychologists call associations. He needs to do this because he saves time and effort by putting things and people
into categories. But unless he classifies correctly, his categories
will mislead rather than guide him. For example, if a child
learns that "all fires are hot and dangerous," fires have been
put firmly into the category of things to be watched carefully
— and thus he can save himself from harm. But if he learns a
category like "Negroes are lazy" or "foreigners are fools," he's
learned generalizations that mislead because they're unreliable. The thing is that, when we use categories, we need to
remember the exceptions and differences, the individual varia-
tions° that qualify the usefulness of all generalizations. Some
fires, for example, are hotter and more dangerous than others.
If people had avoided all fires as dangerous, we would never
have had central heating.

[3]More importantly, we can ill afford to treat people of any
given group as generally alike — even when it's possible to
make some accurate generalizations about them. So when a
child first begins to group things together, it's advisable that he
learn differences as well as similarities. For example, basic

---

* From "People Aren't Born Prejudiced" by Ian Stevenson, M.D.

among the distinctions he draws is the division into "good" and "bad" — which he makes largely on the grounds of what his parents do and say about things and people. Thus, he may learn that dirt is "bad" because his mother washes him every time he gets dirty. By extension, seeing a Negro child, he might point to him and say, "Bad child," for the Negro child's face is brown, hence unwashed and dirty, and so, "bad." We call this prelogical thinking, and all of us go through this phase before we learn to think more effectively.

[4]But some people remain at this stage and never learn that things that seem alike, such as dirt and brown pigment° are really quite different. Whether a child graduates from this stage to correct thinking or to prejudicial thinking, depends to a great extent on his experiences with his parents and teachers.

***Parents Play Role.***   [5]Generally speaking, a child learns from his parents in two main ways. Each of these may contribute to his development either as a prejudiced personality or a tolerant one. First, a child learns a good deal by direct imitation of his parent. If parents reveal prejudiced attitudes, children will tend to imitate those attitudes. If a mother or father, for example, tells a child, "I don't want you playing with any colored children," they foster in their child's growing mind the connection between "colored" and "bad" — and thus promote the growth of prejudice. If instead of saying "colored children," a mother says "nigger" in a derogatory tone of voice, this makes another harmful connection in a child's mind. Even before he clearly knows to what the words Negro or "nigger" refer, he would know that these words mean something "bad" and hence indicate people for him to avoid. It may be that some colored children, like some white children, are unsuitable playmates. But the prohibition should be made on the grounds of the particular reasons for this unsuitability, not on the basis of skin pigment.

[6]How parents actually behave towards members of other groups in the presence of their children influences children as much or more than what parents say about such people. Still, parents can and do communicate prejudices in subtle° ways, by subtle remarks. For example some parents take pride in belonging to a special group, lay stress on the child's membership in that group, and consequently lead him to believe that other people are inferior because they're outside this group. Sometimes parents are unaware that the pride they take in such membership in a special group can be an insidious form of prejudice against other groups. This isn't always so, because

often pride in belonging can be related to the genuine accomplishments of a group. But just as often, pride stems simply from thinking of the group as special and superior because of its selectivity, not because of its accomplishments. However, this kind of direct transmission of prejudice from parents to children is the conforming type, and so can usually be modified by later experience if the child comes into contact with other unprejudiced people or if he has the opportunity to get to know members of the group toward which he has had prejudiced attitudes. For example, during the Second World War and the Korean War, many white soldiers of both North and South fought with Negro troops; knowing Negroes as people, they lost their old prejudices.

[7]Unfortunately, however, parents tend to restrict their children's experiences with different kinds of people, for fear that the children might be harmfully influenced. This naturally prevents the children from unlearning prejudices. Unfortunately these children who most need broadening and correcting experiences are often deprived of them.

[8]Parents promote prejudice in a second, more subtle and harmful way by their own treatment of their children. Studies of markedly prejudiced persons show that they usually come from families in which they were treated harshly, authoritatively, and unfairly — in other words, they were themselves the objects of prejudice. This parental behavior promotes prejudice in the children — apart from their imitation of it — in two ways. First, if parents treat a child harshly and punish him unfairly, they are relating to the child in terms of power instead of love. Treated as if he were always bad, the child will respond to his parents as if they were always dangerous. Growing skilled in the quick detection of threats or possible injury, he becomes sensitive to danger not only from parents but from other people as well. He makes quick judgments in order not to be caught unaware. Quick judgments are a facet° of prejudiced thinking. An insecure and easily frightened person makes sweeping judgments about whole groups, finding it safer to treat the whole group as if it might be harmful to him. He thinks, often unconsciously and always incorrectly, that then he can never be hurt.

[9]Secondly, when parents relate to a child in terms of power, when they punish him, say, with equal severity for accidentally knocking over a dish or for biting his baby brother, he not only thinks of his parents as dangerous people but he thinks of himself as dangerous, too. He must be bad, otherwise why would he be punished so often? Given this low opinion of

himself, he will often try to raise it by putting the blame on others — using the old unconscious scapegoat° mechanism. Here again, psychological studies have shown that people who are able to blame themselves when they're responsible for things going wrong tend to be much less prejudiced than people who blame others when things go wrong. But a child can only learn to accept blame fairly if his parents attribute° blame fairly to him. If he is blamed for everything, he may — in his own defense — grow up unable to accept the blame for anything. If he cannot blame himself he has to blame others — he has to see them as more deficient° and blameworthy than they are — which means making prejudiced judgments about them.

*School Plays a Role.* [10]School can help undo the damage. Actual personal experience with children of other groups can show a child directly, immediately, and concretely that not all members of a group are blameworthy, stupid, dirty, or dishonest. In addition, unprejudiced teachers can instruct children in the ways of clear thinking that underlie tolerance. There is definite evidence that education reduces prejudices. It's been found, for example, that college graduates are less prejudiced on the whole than people with less education. Direct instruction about different groups and cultures, another study shows, reduced prejudice in those who were taught.

[11]Fortunately, we seem today to be making progress in the direction of less prejudiced belief and behavior. Today, parents treat children with greater respect for them as individuals — in short, with less prejudice. This will continue to exert a healthy influence on the next generation. In fact, one survey has shown that it already has! College students of our generation, it demonstrates, are less prejudiced than college students of the last generation.

[12]But since prejudice against members of a minority group or the peoples of other countries is a luxury we can increasingly ill afford — no parent should relax his vigilance° in guarding against sowing the seeds of intolerance.°

## Analysis of *How Children Learn Prejudice*

In his essay's first paragraph Ian Stevenson introduces the subject by stating the thesis and telling the reader about the nature of prejudice. Prejudice is learned, but it can be changed. He begins this introductory paragraph with a statement of the central thought: "The important point about *how children learn prejudice* is that they do" (italics mine).

Paragraphs 2 and 3 form a paragraph unit that develops the first way children learn prejudice; they mix it with ignorance as they try to organize their experiences.

Paragraph 4 is a transitional paragraph leading the reader into the subsequent discussion concerning whether a child will learn correct thinking or prejudical thinking through his experiences with his parents and his teachers.

In a paragraph unit consisting of paragraphs 5, 6, 7, 8, and 9, Dr. Stevenson develops the second way children learn prejudice. He states the main idea in sentence 1 of paragraph 5; it reads: "Generally speaking, a child learns from his parents in two main ways." He aids the reader in following this analysis into parts with the guide words "First" (paragraph 5, sentence 3) and "second" (paragraph 8, sentence 1).

In discussing the second way — the parents' treatment of their own children — the writer begins paragraph 8 with a statement of the main idea: "Parents promote prejudice in a second, more subtle and harmful way by their own treatment of their children." To fulfill his purpose of explaining this generalization fully, Dr. Stevenson further breaks down his subject and indicates this method of analysis with a sentence reading: "This parental behavior promotes prejudice in the children — apart from their imitation of it — in two ways" (paragraph 8, sentence 3). He uses the guide words "First" (paragraph 8, sentence 4) and "Secondly" (paragraph 9, sentence 1) to help the reader identify each way.

Paragraphs 10 and 11 revolve around a topic sentence that leads the reader into the other aspect of the discussion concerning prejudice — learning correct thinking. Sentence 1 of paragraph 10 reads: "School can help undo the damage."

Paragraph 12 concludes the essay by telling us that "no parent should relax his vigilance in guarding against sowing the seeds of intolerance."

## Suggested Topics for Writing Analysis by Structure

1. A flower, a tree
2. A structure like a bridge, a cottage, a swing set, a tree house
3. An army regiment, a Roman legion
4. An organization like a family, a political party, a club
5. A geographical area
6. A machine

7. A poem
8. An athletic team
9. A work of art, music, painting, sculpture
10. An institution
11. An organ in the human body

---

**MATCH-UP TEN**

Match the definitions in column 2 with the words in column 1 taken from the exercises and essay by placing the letter of the word in the blank. Answers are at the end of the chapter.

| | | | |
|---|---|---|---|
| a. | spectacular | 1. not adequate | _M_ |
| b. | panoramic | 2. clearly different, well-defined | _E_ |
| c. | impressive | 3. crafty, wily, clever | _I_ |
| d. | stabilized | 4. color, substance giving color | _H_ |
| e. | distinct | 5. grand, very showy | _A_ |
| f. | innate | 6. viewing in all directions | _B_ |
| g. | variations | 7. person or group bearing blame for others | _K_ |
| h. | pigment | 8. assign | _L_ |
| i. | subtle | 9. unwillingness to accept other beliefs, races | _O_ |
| j. | facet | 10. alertness, being aware, watchfulness | _N_ |
| k. | scapegoat | 11. phase, one side, one view | _J_ |
| l. | attribute | 12. kept steady, held firm | _D_ |
| m. | deficient | 13. admirable, moving, awesome | _C_ |
| n. | vigilance | 14. differences, changes | _G_ |
| o. | intolerance | 15. possessing from birth | _F_ |

---

## Analysis by Function

If a writer's purpose is to explain how something works, he will write an *analysis-by-function paper*. As he did in the analysis-by-structure paper, he will break down his subject into its component parts. His purpose, however, determines that he will treat his parts differently than in the analysis by structure. He will explain how each of the parts functions in relationship to the operation of the whole thing. In analysis by function, the parts of the ear are important as they operate in the operation of hearing; the parts of the eye to seeing; and the parts of the heart to pumping the blood throughout the body.

Suppose, for example, that you wished to explain how a leaf makes food for a plant. You begin by breaking down the leaf into its main parts: (1) the *blade*, (2) the *petiole*, and (3) the *stipules*. You explain the nature of the *blade*, stressing that it consists of main veins, secondary veins, and small netted veins that serve as a water system. You then explain the function of the thousands of pores (openings) called *stomata* that lie in the lower layer of the leaf. These openings control the flow of air into the leaf. They open in the day when the food making takes place and close at night. You move next to an explanation of the function of the upper layer of the leaf, which lets in the sunlight providing energy for the food-making operation. You follow with a discussion of the two kinds of cells in the middle layer of the leaf. The *palisade cells* and the *spongy cells* work chiefly to use light energy in splitting water molecules into hydrogen and oxygen. This hydrogen is then used to convert carbon dioxide into sugars in a process called *photosynthesis*. A leaf makes food by building sugars from water and carbon dioxide when light and a green substance called *chlorophyll* are present.

Having explained the very important function of the blade, you turn to the *petiole*. In addition to holding the leaf to the plant, the petiole, you point out, brings water into the leaf and carries food made in the "food factory" of the leaf to all parts of the plant. Finally you explain that many plants have *stipules*, which add to the food-making power of the blade. Study the analysis by function that follows.

▶ **Photosynthesis** occurs inside the leaf blade in two kinds of food-making cells — *palisade cells* and *spongy cells*. The tall, slender palisade cells are the chief food producers. They form one to three layers beneath the upper epidermis. The broad, irregularly shaped spongy cells lie between the palisade cells and the lower epidermis. Floating within both kinds of cells are numerous small green bodies known as *chloroplasts*. Each chloroplast contains many molecules of the green pigment chlorophyll.

Water enters the food-making cells from the tiny veins of the blade. Partly surrounding each palisade and spongy cell is an air space filled with carbon dioxide and other gases. The cells absorb carbon dioxide from this air space. When light strikes the chloroplasts, photosynthesis begins. The chlorophyll absorbs energy from the light. This energy splits the water molecules into molecules of hydrogen and oxygen. The hydrogen then combines with carbon dioxide, which results in a

simple sugar. This process is extremely complicated and involves many steps. The oxygen that is left over from the splitting of the water molecules enters the air through the stomata.

The sugar produced by photosynthesis is carried through the
petiole to the stem and all other parts of the plant. In the plant
cells, the sugar may be burned and thus release energy for
growth or other activities. Or the sugar may be chemically
altered and form fats and starches. In addition, the sugar may
be combined with various minerals, and so produce proteins,
vitamins, and other vital substances. The minerals enter the
plant dissolved in the water absorbed by the roots.

"Photosynthesis"
*The World Book Encyclopedia*

In the model analysis-by-function paragraph that follows, the writer
breaks down the way his dog moves through a variety of positions to
indicate his emotional reactions: (1) to another dog moving into his
territory, (2) if he is afraid of the dog, (3) if he feels extremely
threatened, (4) to other dogs acting like young puppies.

▶ I have seen Benji move from his characteristically alert pos-
ture, with tail and ears erect, through a variety of positions as
his emotional reactions change. When another dog moves into
Benji's territory, he may respond with a stiff wag of the tail, a
direct stare, and an aggressive snarl. If he is afraid of the dog,
however, Benji shifts his body weight backward and lowers his
tail in what we have come to recognize as a fearful or defensive
type of aggression. If Benji feels extremely threatened, he
might even curl up with his ears flattened against his head and
remain still or cowed in a display of complete submission. I
have seen other dogs roll over and urinate submissively, very
much like young puppies. Dogs use this same vocabulary of
displays to communicate aggressive or submissive feelings to
people. Dog owners who do not understand that such urination
is a sign of deference frequently make the mistake of disciplin-
ing their dogs for it.

Michael Fox
"What Is Your Pet Trying to Tell You?"

In the next model paragraph unit, Robert F. Weaver explains how
cancer cells work by discussing certain characteristics: lack of control
over growth, tendency to invade, and ability of cancer cells to pass the

malignant properties onto their offspring through cell division. Observe the function of the last paragraph: it states clearly the divisions that the writer has broken his subject into.

▶ Why can we prevent polio with relatively simple vaccines, cure pneumonia with antibiotics, and yet make only modest inroads against cancer? One reason is that cancer is not one disease, but many. The human body contains more than a hundred different types of cells, and each of these can go awry in its own distinctive way. The cancer puzzle is a whole series of puzzles.

On the other hand, we recognize certain characteristics common to most cancer cells. The most obvious trait of these savage cells is that they run amok. They go out of control. Consider, for example, what happens when you cut a finger accidentally. Very quickly the cells around the incision receive a signal to divide more rapidly and heal the wound. Then, as soon as they accomplish the job, another signal tells them to slow down. Normal cells always obey this slow-down sign, preserving an exquisite balance between old cells dying and new cells appearing.

But renegade cancer cells no longer obey. They continue to divide without control until their voracious appetites overwhelm their host.

Cancer cells show a distressing ability to invade the tissues around them, disrupting them and robbing them of food. Worse, they metastasize, or spread. For instance, cancer cells may break off from a bone tumor, migrate through the bloodstream, and establish new tumors in the lungs. Once a tumor has metastasized, the cancer is much harder to treat. This points to the importance of frequent physical examinations and prompt attention to the seven warning signals publicized by the American Cancer Society.

These two characteristics of cancer cells — lack of control over growth and tendency to invade — imply a third quality: the ability of cancer cells to pass the malignant properties on to their progeny, cell division after cell division.

Robert F. Weaver
"The Cancer Puzzle"

In the next model analysis-by-function paragraph, the writers explain the formation of a town or colony of bumblebees by breaking the operation down into two divisions: (1) the role of the queen bee in beginning the colony, and (2) the role of the worker bees in the building and maintenance of the colony.

▶ Higher on the social scale are the bumblebees. The female that survives the winter is a large individual known as a queen. Emerging in the spring, it does not make a burrow of its own but rather seeks out a deserted rodent nest. A large quantity of wax starts to exude from the segments of the queen's abdomen. With this wax the bee constructs a honeypot and fills it with as much as a thimbleful of nectar for use during the night or during bad weather. Then the queen makes a cell and places a pollen ball in it, on which the eggs are deposited. The queen sits on the eggs, and later on the larvae, like a brooding hen, protecting them from the cold to which they are very susceptible. Brooding, like the queen's other behavior, stems from unreasoning instinct. When stimulated to brood, the bumblebee broods. If an experimenter removes the eggs, the queen will utilize any nearby object, even a pebble, as a substitute.

The first bumblebee brood develops into a handful of diminutive worker bees, which the queen assists in cutting their way out of their cocoons. Once on the scene, these workers free the queen from all duties except egg-laying. As the workers take over building and maintenance, the nest's brood cells increase in number and soon form a comb. These cells are not used for brooding a second time: instead, the workers rim them with wax, converting them into storage tanks for nectar and pollen. Bumblebee towns never become as populous as honeybee cities: a thriving bumblebee colony may number 1,000 or 2,000 individuals by summer's end, but most contain only a few hundred.

Peter Farb, et al.
"The Insects"

In the final model analysis-by-function paragraph, the writers explain how three great forces: (1) imperialism, (2) the growing reliance upon science and technology, and (3) the continuous struggle for power on the part of the common man determined the course of events of the hundred years from 1850 to 1950. Such forces acted and reacted together in a complex way to produce mighty conflicts as the world tried to adapt itself to those great forces.

▶ The historian of the twenty-first century, looking back on the hundred years since 1850, may decide that there were three great forces which determined the course of events during those years — imperialism, the growing reliance upon science and technology, and the continuous struggle for power on the part of the common man. Each one of these three brought in its train an incalculable number of lesser forces, some acting for it and some against it. Each of the three was full of vast implications working toward both good and evil; and each one was of inestimable influence upon human thought and expression. Moreover, the three acted and reacted together in the most complex way, so that at times it seems almost as if the true history of the age could never be written, certainly not by anyone in the twentieth century, for he would be much too near the mighty conflicts engendered while the world was trying to adapt itself to the presence of these three great forces.

George K. Anderson and Robert Warnock
"The World in Literature," *Vol. IV*

**VOCABULARY PREVIEW**

| | |
|---|---|
| erosion | comparable |
| depletion | terminal |
| alleviate | alternatives |
| accelerated | reservoir |
| paramount | triadic |

## EXERCISE 3     **Analysis**

Read the model paragraph below. Answer the questions that follow.

▶ When we speak of inflation as a problem, what do we mean?
There are at least two characteristics of inflation which are
undesirable. One characteristic of inflation is that it redistrib-
utes real income. Individuals or business firms whose money
incomes fail to keep pace with price increases suffer a reduc-
tion in real income. This is particularly true of people on an-
nuities and those with other relatively fixed income such as
teachers. On the other hand, those persons whose incomes
increase more rapidly than do prices are able to command a
larger share of the available goods and services. Generally
those who hold property or who are members of strong interest
groups tend to gain at the expense of other individuals or business firms. For this latter group, inflation usually causes an
erosion° of individual savings and a depletion° of the financial
capital of businesses. A second characteristic of inflation is its
effect on resource use. With rapidly rising prices it is in the
interest of some individuals to hold commodity inventories in
the hope of higher profits. This represents a poor use of resources which could be better used to increase output and to
alleviate° shortages. Thus inflation usually results in definite
costs to society.

Howard S. Dye, et al.
*Economics: Principles, Problems, Perspectives*

1. What is the function of sentence 2?


2. Into what parts (characteristics) does the writer break down his
   subject — inflation?

3. What is the function of the last sentence?

4. Write a brief discussion of the structural organization and development of this paragraph.

Read the longer piece of writing that follows. Observe the clear statement of the writer's purpose and the divisions into which he will divide his subject. Observe also his treatment of the function of each division to make clear the function of the community college.

▶ HOW A COMMUNITY COLLEGE FUNCTIONS
**Sigurd Rislov**

[1]Since the turn of the century, a new educational institution has appeared in America. During the past twenty years, it has grown at an accelerated° pace and there are reasons for believing that it will become standard equipment in the nation's public school program.

[2]This institution is the public two-year college, sometimes called a junior college, a community college, or just plain college. The typical community college is a local organization, either district or county. Nine tenths of its students live within a 35-mile radius. There are no fraternities or sororities and usually no dormitories. It boasts small classes, emphasis on teaching, a comprehensive advisory and counseling program for its students, and a personal student–teacher relationship. It undertakes three major functions.

[3]First and paramount° is its program of lower-division, freshman-sophomore, courses paralleling the state university and other senior institutions. Students planning to specialize in any of the regular or academic professional areas, such as law, medicine, dentistry, engineering, teaching, business, psychology, physics, chemistry, botany, can begin college in their own community and transfer with comparable° advanced standing to senior institutions for completion of their training without loss of time or credits. About 35 per cent of the full-time students in community colleges complete advanced work at a senior institution.

[4]Second, it provides terminal° training for students who are not going to be baccalaureate candidates but who want and need more education than high school provides. For these there are such alternatives° as trade courses in airframe and aircraft engine mechanics, auto mechanics, radio and television servicing, metal shop, machine shop, or courses for the semiprofessional technician in the various branches of engineering or in laboratories. Some terminal students take business courses, secretarial training, or agriculture. Others take regular lower-division college courses in order to be more knowledgeable persons with broader intellectual and emotional horizons, whatever their occupations.

[5]Besides these two services for the college-age population, the community college attempts to be an educational and cultural reservoir° for the adult population of the area. This is its third function and it does this in several ways. One is by providing evening courses for people already employed or in business. The content of such courses is determined by the nature of the group for which they are operated and by interests and wants of the population. There may be classes in modern world problems, history, psychology, philosophy, economics, or whatever interest and facilities warrant. Many of the adults in these classes are college graduates who either want to take those courses which their degree requirements excluded, or want to retake some they once had in order to renew acquaintance with an area of worth to them. Others are without academic degrees, but wish to drink deeper at the Pierian spring.

[6]Another primarily adult service of the community college is to act as a focal point for cultural activities. Do those with musical ability wish to cultivate their talents? The college organizes a chorus, an orchestra, or produces an opera with a local cast. Are there people willing to put forth a concerted effort to make better sense out of current affairs? A college-community forum is organized and leading figures in contemporary problems are brought in to present their views and discuss possible solutions. Comparable assistance can be given to amateur thespians, writers, artists, both in performance and appreciation.

[7]This triadic° obligation — to the university-bound student, to the terminal student, and to the adult — is, of course, not assumed by every two-year college. Some have a highly specialized objective to which all else is legitimately subordinate. What has been described is what appears to be the emerging pattern for the typical public two-year college.

## QUESTIONS ON    How a Community College Functions

Answers are at the end of the chapter.

1. What is the function of the first two paragraphs?

2. In what paragraph does the writer state clearly that the development will be with analysis by function?

3. What are the three divisions in his analysis?

**MATCH-UP ELEVEN**

Match the definitions in column 2 with the words in column 1 taken from the exercise and essay by placing the letter of the word in the blank. Answers are at the end of the chapter.

| a. erosion | 1. choice, choice of two | H |
| b. depletion | 2. final | G |
| c. alleviate | 3. groups of three | J |
| d. accelerated | 4. extra supply | I |
| e. paramount | 5. reduction in quantity | B |
| f. comparable | 6. wearing away | A |
| g. terminal | 7. similar, equal | F |
| h. alternatives | 8. quickened, caused to move faster | D |
| i. reservoir | 9. superior to all others, all-important | E |
| j. triadic | 10. lighten or lessen | C |

Read the following analysis of the popularity and success of Cantinflas, Mexico's Prince of Comedy. An analysis follows the essay.

▶ CANTINFLAS: MEXICO'S PRINCE OF COMEDY
**Ron Butler**

[1]Dining with friends recently at an elegant New York restaurant Mexican film star Mario Moreno, who was in town to receive a humanitarian award from Mayor Edward Koch, caused hardly a stir among his fellow patrons. But out in the kitchen there was pandemonium as the largely Hispanic staff jostled for a glimpse of the man known to millions as Cantinflas, the best known, best loved comic actor in the Spanish-speaking world.

Before leaving the restaurant Moreno (alias Cantinflas), aware of the commotion he was causing, went into the kitchen and did a full thirty minutes of pratfalls, smelling, tasting, dropping pot lids, burning fingers, and crying over onions.

[2]His films outgross all others in Latin America, both domestic and foreign. Most U.S. filmgoers know him only as David Niven's ingenious manservant in *Around the World in 80 Days*, or the impish lead in *Pepe*. But in Latin America no actor is more revered. In Mexico's last national election he polled over two thousand write-in votes. Children at play imitate his

slouching gait and quizzical shoulders while their parents, in smart hotels and small *cantinas* alike, laugh and repeat his latest lampoon of high political figures.

[3]In Mexico City a half-block-long mural by Diego Rivera honors heroes of Mexican history. There Cantinflas is again, the central figure. On holidays bootblacks along the city's main thoroughfares often dress and grimace like him in order to drum up business. When he makes a public appearance the government closes all pawn shops in the area, lest the poor hock their meager possessions in order to see him perform.

[4]What makes him so popular? In films, Cantinflas is a sad, bedraggled little street bum whose pants, held up by a piece of rope, are forever on the verge of falling down. He wears a battered felt hat, a faded, long-sleeved undershirt that itches, and a tattered, moth-eaten vest that he treats with the utmost care and respect. It is a costume vaguely modeled after that of a Mexican *cargador*, or porter, whose backbreaking work is poorly paid. His small, wistful brown face is painted dead white around the mouth, his eyes are emphasized. A tiny moustache at each end of his upper lip, seemingly daubed on with shoe polish, is as much a trademark as the famous costume, which hasn't changed in nearly forty years. ("Of course, I send it out to be cleaned now and then," he says.)

[5]When he talks, his words are often a madcap gibberish, a hash of ad libs, doubletalk, innuendos, and words that don't exist or are mercilessly mispronounced. In Spanish, the verb *cantinflear*, inspired by him, means to talk too much but say too little; the noun form means a lovable clown.

"And for your headache," he advises a sick friend, "put this salve on your forehead and rub it very hard."

"Will it stop it from hurting?" the friend asks.

"No, but it will make it smooth."

[6]Cantinflas always plays the good guy, the schnook, says a friend. He is forever trying to help someone else when what he needs most is for someone to help him. But he never asks for help.

[7]A typical Cantinflas gag is to break suddenly into a scene of overwhelming chaos in which monumental disaster is about to occur and cheerfully inquire, "¿Qué tal?" That's roughly the Spanish equivalent of "What's cooking?" It barrel-rolls the typical Mexican audience into the aisles for a full five minutes.

[8]In *Romeo and Juliet*, as he waxes poetic to his lady love on her balcony from the street below, a scrawny dog comes along and wets his leg.

[9]In his guise of a hardworking porter, most Mexicans see

themselves or people they know. Because his problems are so tremendous, theirs seem small by comparison. Humor has strange antecedents — sorrow, misery, hostility, fear. Through a simple and sympathetic portrayal Cantinflas is able to transmute these emotions, turn them around, and make people weep with laughter.

[10]There is much Chaplin pathos in the comedy of Cantinflas. Like Charlie Chaplin, Cantinflas is a pantomimist. He uses his hands, eyes, and legs with the same exquisite timing. He gestures apathetically with his hands, which invariably carry a long-ashed cigarette. He walks with a deliberate curvature of the spine in a pompous swagger that contrasts sharply with his ragged clothes and downtrodden personality. The walk is further accentuated by busy, mobile hips that conflict with the rigidity of the rest of his body. He seems to be going in two directions at once.

[11]But where Chaplin was an actor of frustration, Cantinflas is an actor of triumph. Somehow, despite multiple mistakes, he manages to overcome his devastating predicaments. In one sketch he is a well-meaning but fumbling waiter who spills soup down the neck of a cabinet minister, puts his thumb into a society matron's mashed potatoes, and drops her steak on the floor, only to retrieve it with grimy hands. His restaurant prospers nonetheless.

[12]Cantinflas continually satirizes what Mexicans love most — bullfighting. It was his second major film, *Ni Sangre, Ni Arena* (Neither Blood nor Sand), a brilliant spoof on the Spanish matador Manolete, that catapulted him to international stardom. In it he played dual roles — that of a pretentious, arrogant matador and that of a humble, devoted fan. Through a classic mix-up of identities, the lowly fan is mistaken for the vain bullfighter and the fun begins.

[13]Cantinflas successfully carried the role of the comic-mimic bullfighter offscreen as well, and today is perhaps the only "matador" who can unfailingly fill Mexico City's fifty-thousand-seat Plaza de Toros, the world's largest bullring, time and time again. He is all over the ring, jumping up and down, or dancing a mambo or a cha-cha. The bull, following his movements, seems to stare in amazement. From the moment of his strutting, pigeon-toed entrance through the final minutes of the *corrida*, the crowd belongs to Cantinflas. When the bull paws the ground, Cantinflas paws the ground. He reads a newspaper, undaunted, as the bull rushes by. He hugs the animal or holds its tail, and around in circles they go. He takes a mouthful of water, which is traditionally spit on the ground, and

squirts it in his assistant's face. He tumbles into the charging bull's path and somehow escapes unharmed. His pants fall off, revealing pink, ruffled underwear, and he scampers red faced to the nearest refuge for repairs.

[14]The death and drama of the bullring is not the easiest subject to satirize, yet Cantinflas does it in a way that avoids poor taste. The bull never loses its dignity. Nor its life. For Cantinflas the moment of truth is plunging a mock sword over the bull's horns. On contact, it bursts into a brilliant bouquet of flowers, and the crowd goes wild.

[15]A onetime shoeshine boy who had become a millionaire by forty, Mario Moreno, the son of José and María Guizar Moreno, was born on August 12, 1911, in a respectable but poor section of Mexico City that has since fallen on even harder times. The sixth child in a family of twelve sons and three daughters, he completed high school but received his most valuable education, singing and dancing, in the streets. As he grew, the confines of a well-meaning but domineering father, poverty, and a large family seemed narrow bounds to a youth of his imagination. He was kept at home by the deep love he felt for his mother. At fifteen he was sent to the agricultural school at Chapingo, where he stayed for nine months before running away to the State of Jalapa. He joined the *carpa,* or tent show, and there met his wife, a Russian dancer.

[16]Since 1936, when first seen in a two-reel movie advertisement for trucks, the character of Cantinflas has remained unchanged. "The audience knows him and is very comfortable with him," says Moreno. "A new suit or even a new pair of shoes would change him completely." Indeed, Cantinflas and his antics are so well known that audiences anticipate his reactions to almost every situation. The laughter starts when his name appears on the screen.

[17]Not surprisingly, his portrayal of the pauper has made Moreno one of the world's wealthiest men. He has two film companies, extensive real estate holdings, office buildings, houses in Mexico City and Acapulco, a two-thousand-acre bull-breeding ranch in Toluca, and an annual income counted in millions of dollars.

[18]The bread-and-butter character of Cantinflas feeds well on the filet mignon and caviar diet of Mario Moreno. It is said that Moreno, one of the biggest philanthropists in show business, gives more than half of his earnings to charity (causing more than one anguished exhibitor to throw up his hands and sigh, "The more money he gives to the poor, the higher he raises his fees"). In 1952 Moreno launched a social improvement pro-

gram in Mexico, pledging to raise twenty million pesos a year for the construction of housing units, hospitals, and clinics. The highly successful project, called Madelana Michuca, now has more than a hundred buildings and is still growing.

[19]Moreno receives more than six thousand requests a year to do benefits, but since a heart attack in 1970 he accepts but ten or so — and only those benefiting children. His wife of many years died of cancer in 1966 at the age of fifty.

[20]When the director yells "Cut!" Cantinflas, the grimy, lovable little fool who just wandered in off the streets, becomes Mario Moreno, sophisticated man of the world who reads Shakespeare and Cervantes and pilots his own plane. An elegant silk dressing gown covers his tattered costume. He sips a glass of champagne and leafs casually through an art catalogue. He is a quiet, introspective man, who speaks perfect albeit hesitant English in a low, well-modulated voice. His home, nestled fifteen hundred feet above Mexico City in the Lomas de Chapultepec suburb, is very much his castle: picture windows fifty feet long, jai alai court, fully equipped motion picture theater seating two hundred, large swimming pool with hand-laid tiles, an exquisite collection of pre-Columbian art (including a prized Aztec calendar stone), lavish furnishings — all the expected trim and veneer of a phenomenally successful man, plus that sense of privacy and loneliness that always accompanies fame.

## Analysis of *Cantinflas: Mexico's Prince of Comedy*

The essay you have just read is a well organized and fully developed analysis of the popularity and success of Cantinflas: Mexico's Prince of Comedy. The writer, Ron Butler, presents his thesis in the form of a question in the first sentence of paragraph 4, "What makes him so popular?" Mr. Butler, however, must do more than answer this question if the reader is to fully understand his analysis. To fulfill his purpose, Mr. Butler organizes his material skillfully, for he is aware that many of his readers, especially those who are not familiar with the comic's films in Spanish, may not have heard of or seen him on the screen. In addition to explaining his popularity and success, Butler then must give his readers information about the comic and evidence of his success.

In the first three introductory paragraphs, Butler establishes the fact that Cantinflas is "the best known, best loved comic actor in the Spanish-speaking world." In paragraphs 15 through 20, Butler presents material showing that the comic's "portrayal of the pauper has made

Moreno (Cantinflas) one of the world's wealthiest men"; the one time shoeshine boy became a millionaire by the age of forty.

In analyzing his popularity, Butler first describes the Cantinflas character seen in films and personal appearances. Like Charlie Chaplin, he is a pantomimist, "a sad, bedraggled little street bum," a pathetic Mexican porter who talks in "a madcap gibberish, a hash of ad libs, doubletalk, innuendos," and with "words that don't exist or are mercilessly mispronounced."

In explaining the popularity of this comic portrayal, Butler tells us that, unlike Charlie Chaplin, Cantinflas is "an actor of triumph," not frustration. In spite of his mistakes, bumbling, and disasters, Cantinflas always "manages to overcome his devastating predicaments." The character that Mario Moreno has created has something universal that appeals to all people; Butler writes:

▶ In his guise of a hardworking porter, most Mexicans see themselves or people they know. Because his problems are so tremendous, theirs seem small by comparison. Humor has strange antecedents — sorrow, misery, hostility, fear. Through a simple and sympathetic portrayal Cantinflas is able to transmute these emotions, turn them around, and make people weep with laughter.

## Suggested Topics for Writing Analysis by Function

1. An organ in the human body
2. A machine
3. A city administration, a governmental agency, a school board
4. An institution
5. A newspaper
6. An offensive team in football
7. A weapon
8. A jury
9. A musical instrument
10. A camera

If a writer's purpose is to explain *how to do something* or *how something is done*, he will write an analysis-by-process paper. In organizing and developing thought with analysis by process, a writer will break down his subject into parts (steps in the process), explaining how to perform each step so that the reader can duplicate the process. In writing the analysis-by-process paper, a writer answers the questions: How do you do it? Or how was it done? The following model, "How to Collect Leaves," is an analysis by process. The writer is interested in explaining the process of collecting leaves, not in explaining the structure or the function of a leaf, as was explained in the earlier models.

▶ Collecting leaves or leaf rubbings and prints can be an enjoyable hobby. You can find plants with interesting leaves in fields, forests, and gardens and even along city streets. But before you remove any leaves from a plant, be sure to obtain permission from the owner of the land. In many parks and other public lands, it is illegal to take leaves.

When you collect large leaves, remove only a few. Always pick a complete leaf, including the petiole. In most leaves, the petiole will separate easily from the stem. If you are collecting compound leaves, remember to keep all the leaflets attached to the long petiole. When you collect small leaves, you may need to cut off part of a twig. Keep the leaves attached to the twig, and treat the cutting as if it were a single leaf. Always collect the small needle leaves of firs, pines, and spruces this way.

"How to Collect Leaves"
*The World Book Encyclopedia*

The process of making steel is one process; the steps in giving a speech are another. The procedure for impeaching the President is still another, and the method of scientific investigation is also a process. A process may be as simple as giving directions for assembling a child's bicycle or submitting a paper to an instructor and as complex as explaining how life began, building a space ship, or making a television set.

## Process Analysis: How to Do Something

In writing effective how-to-do-it processes, you break down the operation into a series of related steps — usually in chronological order. You present each step or stage — a series of related steps — by explaining each step or stage in enough detail so that the reader can understand and follow your directions. You define terms, suggest the necessary tools, and expand explanations and instructions whenever ncessary. You will be more effective if you tell the reader why certain procedures are necessary and also emphasize negative orders — things not to do. Keep the language simple and repeat key directions. In the analysis-by-process model that follows, the writer explains how to walk on skis. He presents a series of simple, orderly, and logical steps. He groups the steps into two separate stages: (1) getting started and (2) moving on the skis. He emphasizes negative directions in the admonition "Never lift the skis from the ground, and *keep sliding.*"

▶ Assuming that you have the proper outfit, you now are ready to learn walking or sliding on level ground. Here we go! Lunge forward on one foot, keeping the weight well on the front ski. Before the skis stop, lunge forward again and slide on the other ski, transferring your weight. The chief points to remember are: Never lift the skis from the ground, and *keep sliding.*

Propel your skis with easy, dipping motions of the legs and manage your weight with corresponding balancing motions of the arms. The action somewhat resembles skating, except that the feet are not turned sideways to make a forward push, but are kept in a straight line.

Strand Mikkelsen
"How to Ski"

In writing process analysis, clarity is most important. If you fail to make clear the directions at any given step, the reader will become confused, and the whole process will be a failure. Select a subject therefore, with which you are very familiar — preferably one that you have done yourself many times. Keep the steps in exact order; group related steps into meaningful stages or divisions wherever possible, and use illustrations to establish clearness with complicated operations. If certain materials are needed before beginning the operation, specify them. Make sure that the reader is familiar with new terms and techniques as you proceed with your explanations. Always keep in mind that you are the expert and that you are writing for someone who does not know how to do what you have done many times.

Read the model process paragraph unit that follows. The writer, Norman Lewis, presents information on "How to Read a Book," especially a textbook. Notice the separate divisions. The first paragraph presents steps the reader should take to develop "mood-inducing activities" — a kind of warm-up session before you actually begin reading. In the second paragraph Lewis gives you steps in the reading of the book. Observe how he keeps his steps in exact order with transitional words and expressions: *First, Then turn to, Next,* and *Now.* Notice also the simplicity of language, and in paragraph 2, the parallel structure. Each sentence is an imperative, with "you" as the understood subject.

▶ Start the book at a time when you will be able to lose yourself in it daily for a period of about two weeks. First read the front pages — the dedication, the table of contents, the list of illustrations, the foreword, and the prologue — in order to get into the mood, to get a motivating taste of the flavor of the book. Then turn to the end pages and read the suggestions under the caption "On How to Use This Book." Next, riffle through the pages and examine the multitude of delightful black-and-white and water-color drawings and read the scintillating captions under each. These mood-inducing activities — which, incidentally, should be your habitual way of preparing to read any books as long, as deep, and as inclusive as this one — will prepare you for the actual reading of the text.

Now divide the book into as many approximately equal parts as the number of days you expect to devote to it. To get the most enjoyment and value out of a book of this nature, plan on ten to twenty consecutive days' reading. Develop the discipline of returning religiously to the book every day, or nearly every day, until you have finished it. After the first few days, this will not be a hard discipline to enforce.

Norman Lewis
*How to Read Better and Faster*

## Steps in the How-to-Do-It Process

1. Select a subject with which you are familiar.
2. Specify the materials that are necessary for the operation.
3. Define terms or technical words.
4. Decide on a pattern of development — time order is very common.
5. Use illustrations to aid your explanations of complicated directions.
6. Group steps into meaningful stages whenever possible.
7. Keep the language simple and explanations as brief as possible.
8. Explain reasons for the procedures whenever you believe such explanations will help.
9. Stress things the reader should not do.

**VOCABULARY PREVIEW**

| | | |
|---|---|---|
| encounter | polarize | strenuous |
| poise | accessories | incorporated |
| deliberation | suffocation | metronome |
| conversely | monitor | cadence |
| apprehensive | phenomenon | frustration |

## EXERCISE 4    **Analysis**

Read the model paragraph unit below. Answer questions that follow it. Answers are at the end of the chapter.

▶ Many students encounter° difficulty in getting started. Unfortunately, your listeners form impressions of you during the first few minutes more than they do later in the speech. Getting off to a good start also affects your poise° and self-confidence. If you feel an audience respond early in your speech, you tend to lose your feelings of apprehensions as you gain interest in your subject. Consider the following suggestions:

*Use deliberation° in beginning.* Upon being introduced, rise slowly and walk to the speaker's stand with a firm step, an erect body, a pleasant expression, and a direct and assuring look at your audience. If you slouch up to the speaker's stand, you may give the impression that your speech will be as listless as your walk. If you look away from your audience, you announce that you are sure of neither yourself, your material, nor your desire at the moment. Conversely,° do not leap from your chair and charge to the stand like a warrior to battle. Your audience will be likely to conclude that you are apprehensive.° Either extreme in approaching the speaker's stand calls attention to itself and causes unfavorable impressions.

Upon taking your position at the speaker's stand, pause momentarily before beginning your speech. Arrange your notes on the lectern, adjust the microphone, or put your watch on the table. A brief pause causes your audience to turn their attention from their thoughts of the moment and to polarize° their attention on you. Sometimes speakers start talking before an audience is ready to listen. This condition is likely to happen if you start speaking as you walk to the speaker's stand. Show deliberation in beginning your speech.

Glenn R. Capp<br>
How to Communicate Orally

1. What is the function of paragraph 1?

2. Into what stages does the writer break down the process?

3. What proper procedures does the writer explain in some detail?

4. What things does the writer tell the reader not to do?

## EXERCISE 5    Analysis

Read the model paragraphs below. Answer the questions that follow.

▶ If you're caught: get moving! Ski or snowshoe as fast as you possibly can to the edge of the avalanche. Get rid of all of your accessories,° or as many as you can, and do it at once — ski poles, pack, snowshoes, whatever you have. When the avalanche overtakes you, swim! This sounds ridiculous, but it's the best thing you can do to avoid being sucked under. Swim for your life, lying on your back if possible and with your feet downhill. Of course, you may have no choice, and the avalanche may tumble you whither it wishes, but do what you can to stay on the surface. Cover your mouth and nose — suffocation° is easy in dry-snow avalanches. If you do get pulled under, make a supreme effort to widen a little airspace around you just as you come to a stop, and do it instantly! The snow may harden, pack and freeze almost at once. Then pray for help, and remember that the great magician Houdini made a living proving how long man could survive in tight and nearly airless spaces if he remained calm and confident and didn't panic. How to avoid panic in an avalanche is your problem.

Ann and Myron Sutton<br>
Nature on the Rampage

1. What is the first step in escaping from an avalanche?

2. Into what two divisions do the writers break down the process?

3. What problem does he leave up to the skier?

Read the following essay. Be prepared to answer questions on its organization and development.

▶ CONSERVING ENERGY AS YOU SKI
**Carl Wilgus**

[1]One day a few years ago, as I rode one of the chairs at Sun Valley, it occurred to me that there were quite a number of people standing still on the slope below. Throughout the rest of that season I continued to monitor° this phenomenon,° and the results were almost always the same — lots of people standing. I could think of only four possible reasons that skiers would stop so often: 1) their equipment or clothing needed attention; 2) the view was too good to pass up; 3) they were waiting for other skiers, to regroup; or 4) they were tired and needed a rest.

[2]Watching what skiers did when they stopped led me to believe that the last reason was the most common one. But how could so many people be so badly out of shape? After all, skiing as practiced by the average intermediate skier is not all that strenuous.° I couldn't figure it out.

[3]Later that season, a possible answer came when I was giving a lesson to a high school athlete. His name was Phil, and he stood about 6'1" and weighed about 170 pounds. He told me that he played on both the varsity football and basketball teams and that he was in good shape, but that when it came to skiing, he could only make a few turns before he ran out of gas. On closer inspection, his problem was obvious. He would start out nicely, but with each turn his stance would get lower and lower until, after a half-dozen turns, he would be squatting over his skis. This unnatural position would cause his thighs to burn, and he'd have to stop frequently to give himself a rest.

[4]After this experience, I started looking around, and it became clear that most skiers work much harder on the slopes than they need to. Whether they burn up too much energy physically or mentally, the result is the same — a loss of ski time because they have to stop and rest so frequently. What was needed were ways to help conserve energy.

[5]For Phil, the way to conserve energy was to learn to *let go* between turns. I had him make some turns as if he were the Tin Man from *The Wizard of Oz* — stiff and unbending. Then I had him pretend he was the Scarecrow — loose and floppy. Phil discovered for himself through this process that being totally stiff resulted in early fatigue while being as loose as a goose resulted in sloppy turns. The next step was to combine the elements of tension and relaxation, to learn to vary them and to

find a middle ground. Once Phil got the idea of a brief moment of relaxation between turns, he found that he could cover longer distances on the mountain without stopping.

[6]Another useful exercise for conserving energy while skiing is to exhale as you make a turn and to inhale between turns. This can be helpful for several reasons. Some skiers hold their breath when they ski, and, as a result, they not only run out of oxygen but end up tightening their muscles, putting even more strain on the system. Another advantage of this exercise is that good timing and rhythm are incorporated° in your skiing as breathing and turning become coordinated. This natural, easy, consistent tempo can create a metronome° effect that is energy-conserving. It can be especially valuable toward the end of the day when you are tired and your major concern is to get off the hill safely.

[7]If coordinating your breathing with your turning doesn't appeal to you, try humming or singing. These will also develop a cadence° that will improve timing and conserve energy.

[8]Psychologically, what these exercises do is divert attention from self-defeating behavior to refocus on timing and rhythm — two very important parts of relaxed, natural skiing. They also help reduce anxiety, tension, and frustration,° all of which add to fatigue.

[9]Tuning in to the sound of your skis is another tool you can use to conserve energy. Allow your attention to focus on the intensity and duration of the sound you hear as the edges bite the snow. In general, the harsher the sound, the more effort is being expended. See if you can produce moments of almost total silence between turns. This will indicate that you are not only releasing the edges of your skis but also releasing the tension in your body, allowing yourself a moment of relaxation. This will help you ski longer distances without stopping.

[10]Many novice skiers work much harder than necessary because they keep their attention too close to the body. This is like driving a car while staring at the hood ornament. Stress and anxiety, as well as the need for physical effort, will diminish if you'll focus your attention on some fixed point down the slope. Then ski toward that point while maintaining easy — not strained — eye contact with it.

[11]As we have been made all too aware lately in this country, the more energy we conserve now, the more we'll have for the future. The same holds true for skiing. So take the Soft Path of energy conservation as you ski. You'll not only be able to make longer non-stop runs, but you'll have more energy to burn on the dance floor.

QUESTIONS ON    **Conserving Energy As You Ski**

1. What is the function of the first four paragraphs?

2. In what paragraph does the writer state his thesis?

3. What two steps in conserving energy are discussed in paragraph 5?

4. What is the function of the paragraph unit consisting of paragraphs 6, 7, and 8?

5. How can you ski longer distances without stopping?

6. What should you not do in skiing because it makes you work harder than necessary? How can you correct this defect?

7. What is the function of the last paragraph?

8. Write a paragraph or paragraph unit explaining why this process is effective communication.

## VOCABULARY TEST TEN

Four words are lined up below each of fifteen words taken from the exercises and the essay. Select the one that matches best and write its letter in the blank to the right. Answers are at the end of the chapter.

1. encounter      *B*
   (a) discover     (b) meet, face     (c) fear, dread     (d) avoid

2. poise      *C*
   (a) delivery     (b) position     (c) self-possession, composure
   (d) diction, pronunciation

3. deliberation      *A*
   (a) careful consideration or thought     (b) careful word choice
   (c) tact or diplomacy     (d) confidence

4. conversely      *C*
   (a) seriously     (b) wisely     (c) on the contrary, opposite
   (d) conveniently

5. apprehensive      *D*
   (a) finished     (b) aggressive     (c) frustrated
   (d) fearful, worried

6. polarize      *A*
   (a) fix, direct to     (b) turn about     (c) lavish     (d) stare

7. accessories      *B*
   (a) clothes     (b) auxiliary equipment     (c) fears
   (d) heavy items

8. suffocation      *C*
   (a) freezing     (b) pneumonia     (c) smothering
   (d) being buried

9. monitor      *D*
   (a) research     (b) tabulate     (c) photograph
   (d) check, oversee

10. phenomenon      *C*
    (a) magnificent scene     (b) habitual action
    (c) unusual happening or occurrence     (d) catastrophe

11. strenuous      *A*
    (a) exhausting, arduous     (b) difficult     (c) common
    (d) unusual

12. incorporated      *B*
    (a) organized into     (b) blended, united     (c) embraced
    (d) gradually repelled

13. metronome                                                    $\underline{D}$
    (a) sliding   (b) mechanical   (c) soothing
    (d) instrument for exact timing
                                                                  $\underline{C}$
14. cadence
    (a) balance   (b) breathing habit   (c) rhythmical motion
    (d) fluid motion
                                                                  $\underline{B}$
15. frustration
    (a) fear   (b) defeat   (c) heavy breathing   (d) pain

## Process Analysis: How Something Is Done

Another instance in which you write an analysis-by-process paper is when you wish to explain *how something is done* or *how something happened.* You might wish to explain how Wellington won the Battle of Waterloo, how tobacco is grown, how the ocean got its water, or how Hilary scaled Mount Everest. This kind of analysis-by-process paper is narration to a large extent. It is narration, however, with a purpose. The writer tells his story to fulfill his purpose: to tell how something is done or how something happened. In the model analysis-by-process paragraph that follows, Rachel Carson states the subject in the first sentence — the birth of a volcanic island. She explains also that the event (process) is marked "by prolonged and violent travail."

▶ The birth of a volcanic island is an event marked by prolonged and violent travail: the forces of the earth striving to create, and all the forces of the sea opposing. The sea floor, where an island begins, is probably nowhere more than about fifty miles thick — a thin covering over the vast bulk of the earth. In it are deep cracks and fissures, the results of unequal cooling and shrinkage in past ages. Along such lines of weakness the molten lava from the earth's interior presses up and finally bursts forth into the sea. But a submarine volcano is different from a terrestrial eruption, where lava, molten rocks, gases, and other ejecta are hurled into the air through an open crater. Here on the bottom of the ocean the volcano has resisting it all the weight of the ocean water above it. Despite the immense pressure of, it may be, two or three miles of sea water, the new volcanic cone builds upward toward the surface in flow after flow of lava. Once within reach of the waves, its soft ash and tuff are violently attacked, and for a long period the potential island may remain a shoal, unable to emerge. But, eventually, in new eruptions, the cone is pushed up into the air and a rampart against the attacks of the waves is built of hardened lava.

Rachel Carson
*The Sea Around Us*

Complete the exercises that follow in order to review and test yourself on what you have learned about this kind of process.

## VOCABULARY PREVIEW

| | | |
|---|---|---|
| primeval | expiration | cataclysm |
| dissipated | clyster | disintegrated |
| deluge | rendezvous | asunder |
| fumaroles | relentless | pulverized |
| aromatics | awesome | myriads |

## EXERCISE 6   Analysis

Read the model paragraph unit below. Answer the questions that follow it. Answers are at the end of the chapter.

▶ There was yet no sea. The primeval° ocean was created when the temperature of the earth's surface fell below boiling point of water. Water was present on earth from the beginning, but pent-up in the interior rock, and was released by processes occurring in the infant earth. Water vapor rose in great cloud masses that enveloped and darkened the earth. For a time the new planet's surface may have been so hot that no moisture could fall without immediately being converted to steam. Yet even this "rain" helped carry away heat from the hot rocks, and sped the cooling of the planet by transferring heat from the earth to the upper layers of the atmosphere, where it could be dissipated° into space.

For perhaps thousands of years the great overhanging cloud masses prevented the sun's rays from reaching the face of the earth. It took that long for the crust to cool from the freezing point of rocks (1,000 to 2,000 degrees Fahrenheit) to the boiling point of water (212 degrees Fahrenheit). Finally the day came when the falling raindrops did not hiss away in steam, but stayed to start filling the crevices and corners of the naked planet. Then it rained and the accumulation of the seas began. The accumulation did not take place (in the opinion of modern geologists) through "the greatest deluge° of all time" that has so often been described. So far as anyone can tell, it may merely have rained as it rains today. Nature has plenty of time. It probably took a billion years to fill the oceans. William Rubey, of the United States Geological Survey, thinks that the low valleys and shallow depressions that formed the early seas contained only 5 to 10 per cent of the volume of water in the sea today. But as the eons have passed, water vapor has kept coming up through volcanoes and fumaroles,° adding to the moisture of the atmosphere and thus to the bulk of the seas.

All this may help explain how the ocean got its water . . . .*

Leonard Engel et al.<br>*The Sea*

_____
*Reprinted from *The Sea* by Leonard Engel and the Editors of Time–Life Books. © 1961, 1972. Time Inc.

1. In what sentence does the writer state his purpose?

2. Into what three stages does the writer divide his process?

3. Does the writer order his flowing thought by spatial or chronological development?

4. What is the function of the first sentence?

## EXERCISE 7    Analysis

Read the model paragraph below. Answer the questions that follow it.

▶ Millions of years ago, a volcano built a mountain on the floor of the Atlantic. In eruption after eruption, it gushed up a great pile of volcanic rock, until it had accumulated a mass a hundred miles across at its base, reaching upward toward the surface of the sea. Finally its cone emerged as an island with an area of about 200 square miles. Thousands of years passed, and thousands of thousands. Eventually the waves of the Atlantic cut down the cone and reduced it to a shoal — all of it, that is, but a small fragment which remained above water. This fragment we know as Bermuda.

Rachel Carson
*The Sea Around Us*

1. What is the purpose of the writer?

2. Into what stages does the writer break down the subject?

3. Is the material organized chronologically or spatially?

4. What is the function of the last sentence?

Read the modern process essay that follows. Be prepared to answer questions on its organization and development.

▶ THE ART OF EMBALMING
**Herodotus**

[1]There are a set of men in Egypt who practice the art of embalming, and make it their proper business. These persons, when a body is brought to them, show the bearers various models of corpses, made in wood, and painted so as to resemble nature. The most perfect is said to be after the manner of him whom I do not think it religious to name in connection with such a matter;* the second sort is inferior to the first, and less costly; the third is the cheapest of all. All this the embalmers explain, and then ask in which way it is wished that the corpse should be prepared. The bearers tell them, and having concluded their bargain, take their departure, while the embalmers, left to themselves, proceed to their task.

[2]The mode of embalming, according to the most perfect process, is the following: . . . The skull is cleared by rinsing with drugs; next they make a cut along the flank with a sharp Ethiopian stone, and take out the whole contents of the abdomen, which they then cleanse, washing it thoroughly with palm wine, and again frequently with an infusion of pounded aromatics.° After this they fill the cavity with the purest bruised myrrh, with cassia, and every other sort of spicery except frankincense, and sew up the opening. Then the body is placed in natrum† for seventy days, and covered entirely over.

[3]After the expiration° of that space of time, which must not be exceeded, the body is washed, and wrapped round, from head to foot, with bandages of fine linen cloth, smeared over with gum, which is used generally by the Egyptians in the place of glue, and in this state it is given back to the relations, who enclose it in a wooden case which they have had made for the purpose, shaped into the figure of a man. Then fastening the case, they place it in a sepulchral chamber, upright against the wall. Such is the most costly way of embalming the dead.

[4]If persons wish to avoid expense, and choose the second process, the following is the method pursued: — Syringes are filled with oil made from the cedar-tree, which is then injected

---

* The names of certain gods were not mentioned by Herodotus out of religious respect.
† Natrum, or natron, an alkaline salt found in lakes in North Africa, particularly Egypt. Used as a preservative.

into the abdomen . . . and the body laid in natrum the prescribed number of days. At the end of the time the cedar-oil is
allowed to make its escape; and such is its power that it brings
with it the whole stomach and intestines in a liquid state. The
natrum meanwhile has dissolved the flesh, and so nothing is
left of the dead body but the skin and the bones. It is returned
in this condition to the relatives, without any further trouble
being bestowed upon it.

[5]The third method of embalming, which is practiced in the
case of the poorer classes, is to clear out the intestines with
a clyster,° and let the body lie in natrum the seventy days,
after which it is at once given to those who come to fetch it
away. . . .

[6]Whensoever anyone, Egyptian or foreigner, has lost his life
by falling a prey to a crocodile, or by drowning in the river, the
law compels the inhabitants of the city near which the body is
cast up to bury it in one of the sacred repositories with all
possible magnificence. No one may touch the corpse, not even
any of the friends or relatives but only the priests of the Nile,
who prepare it for burial with their own hands — regarding it
as something more than the mere body of a man — and themselves lay it in the tomb.

## QUESTIONS ON   **The Art of Embalming**

1. What process is explained in this short essay?

2. How many processes does the writer describe?

3. To what process does the writer give the most space? Why?

4. What determines which process will be used? How does this choice help the writer organize and develop his material?

5. What is the function of paragraph 1?

Read the following essay on the mysteries of the moon. An analysis follows the essay.

▶ HAVE WE SOLVED THE MYSTERIES OF THE MOON?
**Kenneth F. Weaver**

No man knows how big that celestial traveler was. A dozen miles across, at least; perhaps twenty, even fifty. It rushed toward its rendezvous° with the moon at relentless° speed — an estimated ten to twenty miles a second — yet soundlessly, without flash or fire.

Then, in one awesome° instant, cataclysm° wrenched the moon. In that moment, as the shock wave penetrated the surface, the monstrous missile disintegrated° and vaporized. The frightful energy of its headlong flight — equal to that of billions of hydrogen bombs — was perhaps almost enough to split the moon asunder.° Part of the energy turned into a vast, searing fireball that momentarily rivaled the light and heat of the sun itself.

Torn loose by the blast, thousands of cubic miles of rock shot outward — some vaporized, some molten, the remainder pulverized° and broken. As the hard-flung fragments arced back into the surface, they gouged myriads° of craters and excavated additional rock.

The swift chain reaction reached at least 1,000 miles in every direction. It laid a carpet of ejecta as much as a mile thick, tapering off to a score of feet or less at the outer edges. Some of the displaced moon stuff reached a velocity that overcame lunar gravity and escaped into space.

On the lunar surface a sea of molten rock and newly created rings of mountains marked the scar of the shattering blast. Earlier collisions had left their heavy marks, but none so vast as this. About 650 miles across, it was the largest (and almost the last) of the huge ringed basins to be formed by impacts on the face of the moon.

It was Imbrium, whose lava-filled bowl we see today — some four billion years later — as the right eye of the man in the moon.

## Analysis of *Have We Solved the Mysteries of the Moon?*

In the previous how-something-is-done model process analysis the writer, Kenneth F. Weaver, explains how the Imbrium basin, "the largest scar on the ravaged" surface of the moon was formed. This basin served as a landing place for Apollo 14, and many of the rocks from it were brought back to earth. In describing this process, Mr. Weaver creates for his readers a sense of awe as the exploding meteorite slammed into the moon with the power of "billions of hydrogen bombs."

In the introductory paragraph, Weaver gains reader interest in the gigantic celestial traveler and maintains that interest by telling a fast-moving story of the powerful force that struck the moon and "split it asunder." Its impact was devastating beyond belief, for it created a basin about 650 miles across. His flow of thought is from particulars to general since it is only in the last brief paragraph that the reader learns that the process created Imbrium, "whose lava-filled bowl we see today — some four billion years later — as the right eye of the man in the moon."

---

## VOCABULARY TEST ELEVEN

Four words are lined up below each of fifteen words taken from the exercises and the essay. Select the one that matches best and write its letter in the blank to the right.

1. primeval        *A*
   (a) primitive, first stage    (b) vaporous    (c) glacial
   (d) volcanic, molten        *D*

2. dissipated
   (a) turned into gases    (b) compressed    (c) evaporated   *B*
   (d) scattered, spread out

3. deluge
   (a) hurricane    (b) flood    (c) eruption    (d) catastrophe

4. fumaroles        *B*
   (a) craters    (b) small holes    (c) hot springs
   (d) geysers

5. aromatics        *C*
   (a) special nuts    (b) sawdust    (c) fragrant spices
   (d) ashes        *A*

6. expiration
   (a) end of something, passing    (b) utilization
   (c) evaluation    (d) discussion        *D*

7. clyster
   (a) tube    (b) operation    (c) preparation of salt
   (d) enema (washing out)        *B*

8. rendezvous
   (a) destination    (b) appointed meeting    (c) destruction
   (d) destiny

9. relentless
   (a) fantastic    (b) frightening    (c) merciless
   (d) destructive

   *C*

10. awesome
    (a) fearful, inspiring terror    (b) sudden, unexpected
    (c) hapless    (d) inspirational

    *A*

11. cataclysm
    (a) explosion    (b) disaster    (c) happening
    (d) period of time

    *B*

12. disintegrated
    (a) struck    (b) penetrated    (c) broke up
    (d) condensed

    *C*

13. asunder
    (a) in halves    (b) into pieces    (c) instantly
    (d) forever

    *B*

14. pulverized
    (a) without minerals    (b) split    (c) in liquid form
    (d) smashed, crushed into powder

    *D*

15. myriads
    (a) indefinite number    (b) formed    (c) different kinds
    (d) a series

    *A*

## Suggested Topics for Writing Analysis by Process

1. How to make something
2. How to plant corn, tobacco, and so on
3. How to use a dictionary
4. How to take notes
5. How to win in a sport
6. How some natural phenomenon happened: an earthquake, hurricane, glacier, thunderstorm, and so on
7. How a President was elected
8. How to fix a flat tire
9. How they lost the battle, game, and so on
10. How to study efficiently
11. How to put something together, a swing set, a bicycle, and so on
12. How to collect rocks, coins, and so on

## Answers: Chapter 7

### Exercise 1

1. The first sentence reveals the writer's purpose and tells the reader that the writer is breaking down his subject into two parts.
2. The organization is spatial (through space).
3. The writer divides his subject (national seashore) into two spectacular features: (1) the magnificent wall of cliffs, and (2) spectacular dunes.

### How a Community College Functions

1. To introduce the subject. He gains reader interest and explains the nature of the community college so that the reader will understand the discussion that follows.
2. In paragraph 2. He states: "It (the community college) undertakes three major functions."
3. The program of lower-division courses paralleling the state university and other senior institutions; terminal training for students who are not going to be baccalaureate candidates but who want and need more education than high school provides; an educational and cultural reservoir for the adult population of the area.

### Exercise 4

1. To introduce the subject by stating the process he is discussing — getting started in giving a speech.
2. He breaks the process into two stages: things to do before reaching the speaker's stand and steps to take once you arrive at the speaker's stand.
3. He details the way a speaker should approach the stand. He also develops the necessity of taking a pause before beginning to speak.
4. Don't slouch. Don't look away from your audience. Don't leap from your chair and charge to the stand. Don't start talking before the audience is ready to listen.

### Exercise 6

1. The writer states his purpose in the last sentence.
2. He divides the process into three stages: (1) processes occurring in the infant earth, especially the cooling of the earth; (2) rain filling up crevices and corners of the naked planet; (3) additional rain that finally filled the oceans.
3. Chronological — the writer moves through time.
4. To gain reader interest and to establish a definite time for beginning the narration with a purpose.

### Match-Up 10

| | | |
|---|---|---|
| 1. m | 6. b | 11. j |
| 2. e | 7. k | 12. d |
| 3. i | 8. l | 13. c |
| 4. h | 9. o | 14. g |
| 5. a | 10. n | 15. f |

| *Match-Up 11* | *Voc. Test 10* | *Voc. Test 11* |
|---|---|---|
| 1. h | 1. b | 1. a |
| 2. g | 2. c | 2. d |
| 3. j | 3. a | 3. b |
| 4. i | 4. c | 4. b |
| 5. b | 5. d | 5. c |
| 6. a | 6. a | 6. a |
| 7. f | 7. b | 7. d |
| 8. d | 8. c | 8. b |
| 9. e | 9. d | 9. c |
| 10. c | 10. c | 10. a |
| | 11. a | 11. b |
| | 12. b | 12. c |
| | 13. d | 13. b |
| | 14. c | 14. d |
| | 15. b | 15. a |

# 8

## Explaining and Informing — Analysis by Causes and by Effects

## Analysis by Causes and by Effects

If a writer wishes to explain the causes or effects of some event, happening, or result, he will write an *analysis by causes or by effects.* Cause-and-effect relationships are common in our daily lives. Helen refuses to go to the dance with Bob. At once Bob begins to seek the reasons for her refusal. The basketball team loses six games in a row after winning the first ten games. Everyone, especially the coach, is asking: "What are the reasons for the defeats?" Bill, the president of the student council, points out to his colleagues on the council what he believes will be some of the effects of the recent tuition raise. Jane, another council member, speaks of some possible results of the new dress code. Jim explains the results of the recent changes in the constitution. What are the causes of increased crime? alcoholism? increased divorces? drug addiction? juvenile delinquency? What effects?

What are the causes and effects of the Civil War, World War I, World War II? Why are there so many accidents? people unemployed? school dropouts? earthquakes? suicides? What effects do these happenings have? Events such as these can be understood and solved only if the causes are found. Cause-and-effect relationships, then, are a very important as well as a common aspect of everyday living.

## Analysis by Causes

In writing analysis by causes, a writer answers the question "What conditions or circumstances cause this?" A writer who wishes to explain, for example, why a leaf turns color would write a paragraph developed by causes.

> ▶ **The Leaf Changes Color**   The leaf is green because it contains a green *pigment* (coloring matter) called *chlorophyll*. This pigment plays a major role in photosynthesis. The leaf also has other colors, but they are hidden by the chlorophyll. As autumn approaches, however, the shorter days and cooler nights cause the chlorophyll in deciduous broad leaves to break down.
>
> The hidden colors of the deciduous broad leaf appear as the chlorophyll breaks down. The leaf may then show the yellow color of the pigment *xanthophyll* or the orange-red tones of the *carotene* pigments. In addition, a group of red and purple pigments called *anthocyanins* forms in the dying leaf. The color of the autumn leaf depends on which of the three pigments is most plentiful in the leaf.
>
> "Why A Leaf Changes Color"
> *The World Book Encyclopedia*

Another writer becomes interested in the Grand Canyon and begins thinking about how it happened and why it is such a rare sight. He gathers information and presents it in a paragraph unit explaining that "a set of very special conditions was necessary" to produce such a rare phenomenon.

> ▶ . . . But most laymen do not ask the next questions: Why is Grand Canyon unique, or why are such canyons, even on a smaller scale, rare? And the answer to those questions is that a set of very special conditions was necessary.
>
> First there must be a thick series of rock strata slowly rising as a considerable river flows over it. Second, that considerable river must carry an unusual amount of hard sand or stone

fragments in suspension so that it will be able to cut downward at least as rapidly as the rock over which it flows is rising. Third, that considerable river must be flowing through very arid country. Otherwise rain, washing over the edges of the cut, will widen it at the top as the cut goes deeper. That is why broad valleys are characteristic of regions with normal rainfall; canyons, large and small, of arid country.

Joseph Wood Krutch
*The Voice of the Desert*

In the first paragraph Joseph Wood Krutch asks questions which most laymen do not ask: "Why is the Grand Canyon unique? Why are such canyons rare?" He answers these questions in the same paragraph: "a set of very special conditions." In paragraph 2 Krutch explains the nature of the conditions that were necessary.

The structure of the next model paragraph is relatively simple; the writer states in the first sentence that "The causes of depression among women are numerous and varied." She supports her opening generalization by listing them: (1) common grief, (2) problems with a spouse or boyfriend, (3) being overlooked for a promotion or raise, (4) disappointment in a child, (5) a dreary, overcast day, (6) lack of a steady boyfriend or a date for the weekend.

▶ The causes of depression among women are numerous and varied. They range from common grief to problems with a spouse or boyfriend, to being overlooked for a promotion or raise, to disappointment in a child. A dreary, overcast day often sparks depression, and many women get "the blues" when they don't have a steady boyfriend or a date for the weekend. Depression may last a few days, a few months or even for years.

Lynn Normant
"Why Women Get Depressed"

Complete the exercises that follow.

**VOCABULARY PREVIEW**

| | | | |
|---|---|---|---|
| transformation | grievances | mutations | susceptibility |
| dominant | redress | malignant | manifest |
| demographic | unscrupulous | predisposition | congenital |
| epitomizes | reluctant | depression | deficiencies |
| catalyst | incidence | schizophrenic | detached |

## EXERCISE 1    Analysis

Read the model paragraphs below. Answer the questions that follow.
Answers are at the end of the chapter.

▶ [4]A prime force behind this transformation° is the postwar baby
boom, an explosion of births lasting roughly from 1947 to
1957. About 43 million children were born then — a fifth of
the present population. They crowded the schools in the 1950s
and 1960s, then flooded the job market in the 1970s. By the
1980s and 1990s they will be a middle-aged bulge in the population, swelling the 35- to 44-year-old age group by 80 per cent
— from 23 million people today to 41 million by 2000. And
early in the next century they will reach retirement, still the
dominant° segment of the total population. "It's like a goat
passing through a boa constrictor," says Hauser.

[5]The baby boom was followed by an equally important de-
mographic° event: the baby bust. The total fertility rate fell
from a postwar high of 3.8 children per woman in 1957 to 1.8
last year — in part because of better contraception methods,
changes in life-style, an increase in abortion and the growth of
the women's movement. There were so few births that the
number of children 13 and under has dropped by 7.6 million
since 1970. No sooner were the schools built to educate the
baby-boom kids (on the average, California opened one school
every week in the 1950s) then many of them were forced to
close and teachers were laid off. In all, the boom-bust cycle has
combined to push up the median age for years to come.

*Newsweek*
"The Graying of America"

1. What does the first sentence tell you about the organization of the
   paragraph unit?

2. What is the first cause of the transformation (the graying of America — a rising number of people over 65 years of age)?

3. What is the function of paragraph 2?

4. Of what kind of material does the support for the statements of the causal relationships consist?

## EXERCISE 2    **Analysis**

Read the model paragraph unit below. Answer the questions that follow it.

▶ ¹Dr. Berry says that age 30–40 is the stage in a woman's life when she is most likely to suffer serious bouts of depression. It is the time when she assesses her life and perhaps tries to figure out why things aren't going as she had planned. She may decide that she has devoted too much time to her husband and children and too little time to her own personal development. Or she may decide that she has devoted too much time to a career when she should have accepted that "last" marriage proposal five years ago.
²The menopausal woman in her 40s epitomizes° female depression. Many women — and much of society as well — tend to view the loss of reproductive capacity as a loss of sexuality. Many women during this stage feel "unattractive" and "useless." Those whose husbands have not deserted them for younger women sometimes feel as though they're being treated as maids. Children are often the catalyst° for depression among women, especially those in their 40s. When children leave the nest for college or marriage, women sometimes feel a personal loss. Disappointment caused by children who quit or flunk out of college, those who resort to drugs and those who marry persons perceived as undesirable mates may cause mothers to be depressed. This is especially true of women who have devoted their lives to making their children happy. Experts say that single women are more likely to suffer offspring-related depression.
³As an example, Dr. Berry tells of a 32-year-old former welfare recipient who is the mother of three children, the eldest of whom is 15 and pregnant. The mother just lost her job, her boyfriend abandoned her and she discovered that she herself was pregnant. "The woman was suffering from severe depression," says Dr. Berry. "Things were going so well for her and then suddenly almost everything went wrong." Dr. Berry also says she has counseled many upper-income women who are just as depressed as this particular woman, but who are perplexed by their depression. "I have all of this, so why am I so unhappy?" is their plea.

Lynn Normant
"Why Women Get Depressed"

**399**

1. What is the organization structure of this paragraph unit?

2. What are the causes the writer discusses in paragraph 1?

3. What causes are given for female depression in paragraph 2?

4. What is the function of paragraph 3?

## EXERCISE 3  Analysis

Read the model paragraph below. Answer the questions that follow.

▶ What caused the second World War? There can be many answers: German grievances° against the peace settlement of
1919 and the failure to redress° them; failure to agree on a
system of general controlled disarmament; failure to accept
the principles of collective security and to operate them; fear of
communism and, on the Soviet side, of capitalism, cutting
across ordinary calculations of international policy; German
strength, which destroyed the balance of power in Europe, and
the resentment of German generals at their previous defeat;
American aloofness from European affairs; Hitler's inordinate
and unscrupulous° ambition — a blanket explanation favoured
by some historians; at the end, perhaps only mutual bluff. The
question of its immediate outbreak is easier to answer. The
house of commons forced war on a reluctant° British government, and the government dragged an even more reluctant
French government in their train. The British people accepted
the decision of parliament and government without complaint.
It is impossible to tell whether they welcomed it or whether
they would have preferred some other outcome. Argument was
almost stilled once the war had started, and, if doubts existed,
they were kept in the shadows.

A. J. P. Taylor
*English History: 1914–1945*

1. What is the function of the first sentence?

2. What three causes have a common base?

3. What fears become causes?

4. Explain the organization of the material of the paragraph.

5. What were the immediate causes?

Study the analysis of the model paragraph unit below.

▶ THE CANCER PUZZLE

**Robert F. Weaver, Ph.D.**

*Thesis Statement: Establishes causal relationship*

*Transitional expression:* First of all,

*First cause: environmental agents*

*What triggers a perfectly normal cell to lose control and become a runaway? First of all, there are environmental agents — substances in the air we breathe, the water we drink, or the food we eat.* The World Health Organization estimates that these agents may be associated with 60 to 90 percent of all human cancer.

*Support*

Sir Percival Pott first drew a connection between chemicals and cancer more than two hundred years ago when he discovered the high incidence° of scrotum cancer in chimney sweeps. The constant exposure of these unwashed boys to carcinogens (cancer producers) in soot inevitably took its toll.

These carcinogens are predominantly hydrocarbons, similar to those found in cigarette tar. Scientific data released by the Surgeon General of the United States support unequivocally the link between cigarette smoking and cancer; 90 percent of all lung-cancer patients are smokers.

*Another environmental factor: radiation*

*Another environmental factor is radiation.* The sun's ultraviolet light, for example, can cause genetic mutations° in exposed skin cells, sometimes leading to cancer. In fact, extensive, long-term exposure to sunlight, especially among light-skinned people, makes skin cancer one of the most common types.

*Support*

*Support*

Emissions from radioactive materials can also make cells go wild, as illustrated by the tragic case of the watch-dial painters of the early 20th century. These women used a luminous paint containing the radioactive element radium. To keep a fine tip on their paintbrushes, they twirled them between their lips. The radium they absorbed in this way led to a high rate of bone disease, including cancer.

*Statement of second cause: viruses*

*Viruses are a second cause of cancer, at least in some animals.* These agents are tiny packages of genes without life of their own that are capable of infecting cells and converting them to virus-reproducing machines.

*Support*

Peyton Rous of the Rockefeller Institute performed the classic tumor-virus experiment in 1911 when he showed that he could produce a malignant° tumor called a sarcoma in a chicken by injecting it with a filtered extract of a tumor from another chicken. The filter removed all animal cells and bacteria, leaving only viruses as possible seeds of cancer.

*Support*

Using similar techniques, virologists have linked tumor viruses with cancer in many species of birds and mammals, including primates. Because no one would ever intentionally perform these experiments on people, we do not have absolute proof that viruses cause any human cancer. But studies suggest such a relationship, and it would be odd indeed if viruses caused cancer in lower mammals but not in humans.

Read the essay that follows. Be prepared to answer questions on its organization and development.

### ▶ WHAT CAUSES MENTAL ILLNESS?*
**Judith Ramsey**

[1]Far more is known about the symptoms of mental illness and how to treat them than about the causes. But it is known that these problems often don't have a single cause.

[2]Some types of mental illness, or at least a predisposition° toward them, can be inherited. For example, depression° is

---

* From "Guide to Recognizing and Handling Mental Illness."

more likely to occur in a person with a family history of depression. Similarly, a child with a schizophrenic° parent may be more likely to develop schizophrenia than a child with non-schizophrenic parents.

[3]But though there may be inherited differences in susceptibility° to mental illness, some triggering factors, perhaps environmental stress or a particular set of circumstances, must be present for mental illness to manifest° itself. For example, one study showed that each of 40 depressed patients had suffered several personal problems in the year preceding breakdown. These included a threat to sexual identity, moving to another community, physical illness and death of a loved one.

[4]Chemical changes in the body also have to do with how the mind functions. Exactly what these changes are and how they work isn't fully understood. Some mental disorders (known as organic psychoses) are caused by physical problems. Among the possible causes of organic psychoses are congenital° defects, prenatal injury, hardening of the arteries in the brain, brain tumors and infections and severe alcoholism. Glandular disturbances and certain nutritional deficiencies° can also produce psychotic symptoms.

[5]Emotional disturbances are also related to how the individual feels about himself and the world around him. For example, someone who is constantly criticized can develop an exaggerated feeling of guilt. He comes to expect everyone will find fault with him and even punish him. Or, if as a youngster he was repeatedly neglected and reprimanded, he may have grown up expecting trouble and rejection. He may have developed a protective reaction of verbally attacking another before the other criticized him. Or perhaps he remained detached° and aloof from other people so as not to give them a chance to reject him. For some people these painful feelings are successfully buried till they run into a crisis situation — for example, the loss of a job or the breakup of a marriage — when the feelings surface again.

## QUESTIONS ON     What Causes Mental Illness?

1. What is the function of the first brief paragraph?

2. What is the topic sentence of paragraph 2?

3. With what kind of material does the writer support the main idea of paragraph 2?

4. What is the cause explained in paragraph 3?

5. What is the function of the guide words "But though" in paragraph 3?

6. What are some causes of organic psychoses?

7. What other things can produce psychotic symptoms?

8. What is the purpose of paragraph 5?

## VOCABULARY TEST TWELVE

Four words are lined up below each of twenty words taken from the exercises and the essays. Select the one that matches best and write its letter in the blank to the right. Answers are at the end of the chapter.

1. transformation                                                    *B*
   (a) miracle    (b) change    (c) trend    (d) result

2. dominant                                                          *C*
   (a) wealthiest    (b) oldest    (c) superior, uppermost
   (d) most critical

3. demographic                                                       *A*
   (a) pertaining to vital and social statistics
   (b) related to demons    (c) political    (d) economic

4. epitomizes                                                        *A*
   (a) summarizes    (b) lessens    (c) indicates    (d) causes

5. catalyst                                                          *C*
   (a) reason    (b) cause    (c) speeding-up agent
   (d) excuse

6. grievances                                                        *D*
   (a) demands    (b) arguments    (c) claims
   (d) resentments, complaints

7. redress                                                           *B*
   (a) removal    (b) satisfy, compensate    (c) consider
   (d) control

8. unscrupulous                                                      *A*
   (a) without conscience    (b) fanatical    (c) evil
   (d) lofty

9. reluctant                                                         *C*
   (a) relative    (b) warlike    (c) unwilling    (d) surprised

10. incidence                                                        *B*
    (a) mortality rate    (b) rate of occurrence    (c) resistance
    (d) danger

11. mutations                                                        *A*
    (a) sudden departures from parent type    (b) occurrences
    (c) mutes    (d) disturbances

12. malignant                                                        *D*
    (a) very large    (b) not deadly    (c) with malice
    (d) causing death, very harmful

13. predisposition                                                   *B*
    (a) reaching    (b) aptness, bent    (c) forewarning
    (d) understanding

14. depression                                                   D

    (a) mental exhaustion    (b) paralysis
    (c) failure to respond to a stimulus
    (d) prolonged dejection, sadness

15. schizophrenic                                                C

    (a) inclination to    (b) uneducated
    (c) losing contact with reality
    (d) seeking new paths of knowledge            D

16. susceptibility

    (a) resistance    (b) immunity    (c) suspicion
    (d) inability to resist or withstand something    A

17. manifest

    (a) show, make itself obvious    (b) to destroy itself
    (c) depress    (d) accelerate                   B

18. congenital

    (a) friendly    (b) existing before birth    (c) after birth
    (d) form of brain damage                        C

19. deficiencies

    (a) vitamins    (b) defects
    (c) lacking some essentials, inadequate    (d) traits      A

20. detached

    (a) separated from others, alone in thought    (b) worried
    (c) depressed    (d) disconnected in sequence

## Analysis by Effects

In writing analysis by effects, a writer answers this question: "Given a set of conditions or circumstances, what will be the effect?" Like analysis-by-cause papers, analysis-by-effect papers are simply organized. Many begin with a question and follow with an answer that states the effects and explains their nature. Rachel Carson in her famous book *Silent Spring* begins a paragraph unit explaining the killing of robins in this pattern:

> ▶ [1]"The campus is serving as a graveyard for most of the robins that attempt to take up residence in the spring," said Dr. Wallace. But why? At first he suspected some disease of the nervous system, but soon it became evident that "in spite of the assurances of the insecticide people that their sprays were

'harmless to birds' the robins were really dying of insecticidal poisoning; they exhibited the well-known symptoms of loss of balance, followed by tremors, convulsions, and death."

[2]Several facts suggested that the robins were being poisoned, not so much by direct contact with the insecticides as indirectly, by eating earthworms. Campus earthworms had been fed inadvertently to crayfish in a research project and all the crayfish had promptly died. A snake kept in a laboratory had gone into violent tremors after being fed such worms. And earthworms are the principal food of robins in the spring.

Rachel Carson
*Silent Spring*

Equally common is the structure that begins with a statement of the relationship: "There is one institutional experience, however, that does have a marked effect on political attitudes, and that is college." Study the following model:

▶ There is one institutional experience, however, that does have a marked effect on political attitudes, and that is college. Studies going back over half a century seem to show that attending college makes a difference, usually in a liberal direction. College students are more liberal than the population generally, and students at the most prestigious or selective colleges are the most liberal of all. Students studying the social sciences tend to be more liberal — and to become even more liberal as time goes on — than those studying engineering or the physical sciences. Students become more liberal the longer they remain in college, with seniors more liberal than freshmen and graduate students more liberal than seniors.

James Q. Wilson
*American Government*

In the first sentence, Professor Wilson announces the causal relationship and follows with particulars supporting that generalization.

Another common structure of the effect relationship is support of the topic sentence that announces the causal relationship with a number of effects — some of which may be developed in greater detail in subsequent paragraphs or paragraph units of the essay. In the following model paragraph unit, excerpted from the essay "The Graying of America" in *Newsweek*, the writer(s) begin with an introduction; paragraphs 2 and 3 of that introductory material present a number of effects that will result when one out of every six Americans will be over 65 years of age. Many of these effects are discussed in detail in later paragraphs of the essay.

▶ [1]Americans have always liked to think of themselves as youthful — and for most of their history they have been. When the first census was taken in 1790, half the people in the country were 16 years old or younger, and as recently as 1970 the median age was under 28. But as the nation moves into its third century, its people, too, are getting older. The median age will pass 30 in 1981, reach 35 by the year 2000 and approach 40 by 2030. Over the same span, the number of people over 65 will more than double to 52 million — one out of every six Americans.

[2]Inevitably, the graying of America will bring sweeping changes — some of them already perceptible. Politicians will feel increasing pressure from their elderly constituents for new social programs, as is now happening in Florida. The economy will have to carry a much bigger burden in pension and social-security benefits. Business will alter the products it makes and the way it sells them. Gerber Products, for example, now sells life insurance as well as baby food; while nobody was looking, the models representing the Pepsi generation have broken out in wrinkles and eyeglasses. Some of the changes will obviously be for the good — a drop in the crime rate and teenage unemployment, for example. And some may be bad — perhaps including a decline in innovation and vitality, leading to what French demographer Alfred Sauvy has called a "population of old people ruminating over old ideas in old houses."

[3]Good or bad, large or small, the adjustments will come slowly because demographic change is by nature an evolutionary process. But they will inevitably bring on yet another new era for a nation long inured to major changes — and this one could prove to be as sweeping a transformation as the opening of the frontier, the industrial revolution or the tide of European immigration after the Civil War. "We are faced with the prospect of very drastic social, economic and political change over the next quarter century," says Philip Hauser, director of the Population Research Center at the University of Chicago.

Newsweek
"The Graying of America"

Study the next model effects example; it represents a short effects paper that is skillfully organized and developed to explain the impact of the automobile on American life.

▶ THE ADVENT OF THE GASOLINE AGE*

**Thomas A. Bailey and David M. Kennedy**

*Thesis: announces the effect structure*

*Topic sentence of paragraph: statement of economic effect*

*The impact of the self-propelled carriage on various aspects of American life was tremendous. A gigantic new industry emerged, dependent on steel, but displacing steel from its kingpin role.* Employing directly or indirectly about 6 million people by 1930, it was a major prop of the nation's prosperity. Thousands of new jobs, moreover, were created by supporting industries. The lengthening list would include rubber, glass, and fabrics, to say nothing of thousands of service stations and garages. America's standard of living, responding to this infectious prosperity, rose to an enviable level.

*Support of main idea*

*Topic sentence: additional economic effects*

*New industries boomed lustily; older ones grew sickly.* The petroleum business experienced a phenomenal development. Hundreds of oil derricks shot up in California, Texas, and Oklahoma, as these states expanded wondrously and the new frontier became an industrial frontier. The once-feared railroad octopus, on the other hand, was hard hit by the competition of passenger cars, buses, and trucks. *An age-old story was repeated: one industry's gains were another industry's pains.*

*Support*

*Repetition of main idea*

*Topic sentence: other effects*

*Other effects were widely felt.* Speedy marketing of perishable foodstuffs, such as fresh fruits, was accelerated. A new prosperity enriched outlying farms, as city dwellers were provided with produce at attractive prices. Countless new roads ribboned out to meet the demand of the American motorist for smoother and faster highways, often paid for by taxes

*Support*

---

* This material was excerpted from *The American Pageant* by Thomas A. Bailey and David M. Kennedy.

on gasoline. The Era of Mud ended as the nation made haste to construct the finest network of hard-surfaced roadways in the world. Lured by new seductiveness in advertising, and encouraged by the perfecting of installment plan buying, countless Americans with short purses acquired the habit of riding as they paid.

*Statement sentence: the social effects*

*Zooming motorcars were agents of social change.* At first a luxury, they rapidly became a necessity. Essentially devices for needed transportation, they soon developed into a badge of freedom and equality — a necessary prop for self-respect. To some, ostentation seemed more important than transportation. Leisure hours could now be spent more pleasurably, as tens of thousands of cooped-up souls responded to the call of the open road on joyriding vacations. Women were further freed from clinging-vine dependence on males. Isolation among the sections was broken down, while the less attractive states lost population at an alarming rate. *America was becoming a nation of nomads.*

*Support*

*Topic sentence of paragraph*

*Topic sentence: other social by-products*

*Other social by-products of the automobile were visible.* Autobuses made possible the consolidation of schools, and to some extent of churches. The trend toward hivelike urbanization was partially slowed. City workers could now live in the suburbs ("suburbia") and commute by motorcar or bus to railroad stations, there to catch the 7:52 for work.

*Support*

*Topic sentence: change of direction to the bad effects of the automobile*

*The demon machine, on the other hand, exacted a terrible toll by catering to the American mania for speed.* Citizens were becoming statistics. Not counting the hundreds of thousands of injured and crippled, the one millionth American had died in a motor accident by 1951 — more than all those killed on the battlefields of all the nation's wars to that date. "The public be rammed" seemed to be the motto of the new age.

*Support*

*Topic sentence: announces additional bad effects*

*Virtuous home life partially broke down as joyriders of all ages forsook the ancestral hearth for the wide open spaces.* The morals of flaming youth sagged correspondingly — at least in the judgment of their elders. Even the disgraceful crime waves of the 1920s and 1930s were partly stimulated by the motorcar, for gangsters could now make quick getaways.

*Support*

*Conclusion*

*Yet no sane American would plead for a return of the old horse and buggy, complete with fly-breeding manure.* Life might be cut short on the highways, and smog might poison the air, but the automobile brought its satisfactions and telescoped more convenience, pleasure, and excitement into a shorter period than ever before.

Most writing by cause or effect is simply organized. Within the general-to-particular framework (deduction) or particular-to-general framework (induction), a writer will develop by time, by climax, by citing conditions or circumstances. To make each cause or effect distinct, writer will use transitional words and phrases. Among the most common transitional expressions are the following:

EFFECT: result     consequence   outcome   outgrowth
         effect

CAUSE:  because    due to        factors   reasons
        bring about basis        sources   give rise to

*Induction* (movement from causes to effect) and *deduction* (movement from effect through causes) are natural orders for developing causal relationships.

Complete the exercises that follow.

**VOCABULARY PREVIEW**

| | | | |
|---|---|---|---|
| pigment | disrupted | stabilized | anticipation |
| mortality | veritable | recede | appreciably |
| impact | pulverized | recipients | agronomists |
| devastating | netherworld | substantially | vulnerable |
| inflicted | inexorable | definitive | acute |

## EXERCISE 4   Analysis

Read the model paragraph below. Answer the questions that follow it. Answers are at the end of the chapter.

▶ An arsenic-contaminated environment affects not only man but animals as well. A report of great interest came from Germany in 1936. In the area about Freiberg, Saxony, smelters for silver and lead poured arsenic fumes into the air, to drift out over the surrounding countryside and settle down upon the vegetation. According to Dr. Hueper, horses, cows, goats, and pigs, which of course fed on this vegetation, showed loss of hair and thickening of the skin. Deer inhabiting nearby forests sometimes had abnormal pigment° spots and precancerous warts. One had a definitely cancerous lesion. Both domestic and wild animals were affected by "arsenical enteritis, gastric ulcers, and cirrhosis of the liver." Sheep kept near the smelters developed cancers of the nasal sinus; at their death arsenic was found in the brain, liver, and tumors. In the area there was also "an extraordinary mortality° among insects, especially bees. After rainfalls which washed the arsenical dust from the leaves and carried it along into the water of brooks and pools, a great many fish died."

Rachel Carson
*Silent Spring*

1. What does the first sentence tell the reader about the flow of the writer's thought?

2. What was the cause of the arsenic-contaminated environment?

3. What was the cause of the death of the fish?

## EXERCISE 5   Analysis

Read the model paragraph below. Answer the questions that follow.

▶ The impact° of the devastating° eruption of Mount St. Helens in Washington will be felt for months — and perhaps years — to come. The cost of repairing damage inflicted° by the volcanic fury may exceed one billion dollars. The wheat and apple crops have been badly damaged and later growth will probably suffer. Weather on earth, but especially in the Northern Hemisphere, will certainly be affected. Water supplies, electrical power, and transportation routes in many communities of the Northwest have been disrupted° or damaged so seriously that extensive and costly repairs are necessary for recovery. Fish in nearby streams were killed by the millions, and shortages of some species appear likely in future years. Finally, it is highly possible that long-term, but yet undetermined health problems have been created by the eruption.

"Exploding Volcano: Full Impact Yet to Come"*

*U.S. News & World Report*

1. What information does the first sentence give the reader about the kind of development?

2. What is the cause of the effects?

---

* This is a rewritten version of paragraph 1 on page 433.

3. What three effects were discussed in a single sentence?

4. Write some other effects of this eruption that the writer does not mention.

## EXERCISE 6    Analysis

Read the model paragraph below. Answer the questions that follow it.

▶ The Berkeley team thinks the murder weapon was an asteroid, a big rock about the size of Manhattan Island. Their scenario for the end of the dinosaur dynasty goes something like this: without warning a large asteroid entered the atmosphere at about 50,000 miles an hour. In seconds, an awesome sonic boom, a veritable° crack of doom, swept across the surface of the earth, killing many animals immediately. Intense heat and firestorms followed and added to the destruction. The asteroid's impact made the entire planet shudder and dug a crater the size of Connecticut. Dust and pulverized° rock from both the ground and the asteroid were ejected high into the stratosphere, blocking the sun's light. Almost overnight the tropical paradise became a gloomy netherworld.° Photosynthesis stopped, and phytoplankton, the tiny marine organisms at the very base of the food chain, were the first to die. The earth's ecosystem collapsed, bringing down with it the dinosaurs as well as many other forms of life.

Wallace Tucker
"Dinosaur Who Dunit?"

1. In what sentence is the meaning of the paragraph given?

2. What was the cause of the extinction of the dinosaurs?

3. Write a paragraph explaining the chain of cause and effect relationships discussed in the paragraph.

## Points to Remember in Writing Analysis by Cause and Effect

As with many of the other patterns of organization and development of thought, you should plan carefully before writing. In planning, follow these suggestions:

1. Have your purpose clearly in mind.
2. Be sure that you have sufficient knowledge of the subject to develop it.
3. Distinguish clearly between causes and effects. A preliminary listing of causes and effects can be helpful in this step.
4. Distinguish between remote causes and immediate causes. Select those causes and effects that best develop your main idea.
5. Don't forget that a writer's special interest in a happening can play a significant part in his selection of conditions; for example: A juvenile drug addict is arrested for stealing drugs. The causes of the crime and his addiction might be different when viewed through the eyes of (1) the drug addict, (2) his parents, (3) the arresting officer, (4) the judge, (5) the family doctor, (6) the defense attorney, (7) the attorney for the prosecution, (8) the parole officer, (9) the store owner who was brutally beaten, (10) the family of the store owner.
6. A complex situation or happening usually consists of several conditions or circumstances; some of these conditions are important and relevant, some unimportant, and some incidental.
7. Do not consider something to be a cause that is not truly a cause; for instance: John received a brain concussion in the final game of the season. In the next few months his grades went steadily down. At the end of the semester, he left school. Many students assumed that the injury was the cause of his poor grades and his leaving school. When he returned in the fall, they learned that the real reasons were his worry over his father's prolonged illness and the financial condition of the family. He left school to help the family until his father could return to work.
8. Avoid making the *post hoc* fallacy. The words *post hoc, ergo propter hoc* mean "after this, therefore because of this." Many people assume that because event B follows event A closely in time that event A caused event B. This fallacy is the source of many superstitions: a black cat crossing our path, spilling salt, breaking a mirror, souring of milk by a clap of thunder, thirteen at a table, and opening an umbrella in the house — to mention only a few. Remember that an event following another event can be a clue to a causal relationship, but it does not definitely establish one.

9. Keep in mind the possibility of chain causes and effects. One cause can be an effect leading to another result. Think of the chain of causes and effects set in motion by the assassination of President Kennedy.

To review and emphasize what you have been learning about causal analysis, read again "What Causes Mental Illness?" Before reading the longer models of an effects paper, read the short essay below, which is organized and developed by cause and effect. Observe the very simple but very well-organized structure. Thomas A. Bailey begins with a statement of the condition — the railways — that affected "intimately countless phases of American life." In this first brief paragraph he states his thesis and presents the first effect: "a sprawling nation became united in a physical sense" (effect 1).

He follows with a series of short paragraphs, each beginning with a topic sentence that states an effect of the coming of the railways: effect 2 was industrialization; effect 3 was the stimulation of mining and agriculture; effect 4 was the great city movement; effect 5 was immigration; and, finally, effect 6 was the making of millionaires.

### ▶ REVOLUTION BY RAILWAYS*
**Thomas A. Bailey**

*Effect 1*    [1]*Metallic fingers of the railroads touched intimately countless phases of American life.* For the first time a sprawling nation became united in a physical sense, bound together with ribs of iron and steel.

*Effect 2*    [2]*More than any other single agency, the railroad network spurred the amazing industrialization of the post-Civil War years.* Puffing locomotives opened fresh markets for manufactured goods, and sped raw materials to the factory. The forging of the rails themselves provided the largest single backlog for the adolescent steel industry.    *Support*

*Effect 3*    [3]*The screeching Iron Horse likewise stimulated mining and agriculture, especially in the West.* It took the farmer out to his land, carried the fruits of his toil to market, and brought him    *Support*

---

* From *The American Pageant.*

his manufactured necessities. Clusters of farm settlements paralleled the railroads, just as they earlier had the rivers.

*Effect 4*    [4]*Railways boomed the cities, and played a leading role in the great cityward movement of the last decades of the century.* The iron monsters could feed enormous concentrations of people, and at the same time insure them a livelihood by providing raw materials and markets.    *Support*

*Effect 5*    [5]*Railroad companies also stimulated the mighty stream of immigration.* Seeking settlers to whom their land grants might be sold at a profit, they advertised seductively in Europe, and sometimes offered to transport the newcomers free to their farms.    *Support*

*Effect 6*    [6]*Finally, the railroad, more than any other single factor, was the maker of millionaires.* A raw new aristocracy, consisting of "lords of the rail," replaced the old Southern "lords of the lash." The multiwebbed lines became the playthings of Wall Street; and colossal wealth was amassed by stock speculators and railroad wreckers like "Jubilee Jim" Fisk and the pious rascal "Uncle Daniel" Drew. As the Benéts have said,    *Support*

> *He toiled not, neither did he spin,*
> *But how he raked the dollars in!*

Mightier millions were made less sensationally by the Vanderbilts, the Hills, and other empire builders.    *Support*

Frequently, writers will combine cause and effect analysis in the same paper. The next model passage is an excerpt from "The Graying of America" — the essay from which the earlier model paragraph unit illustrating the topic sentence that announces effects, many of which may be developed in subsequent paragraphs. Notice also the chain of cause-and-effect relationships where a cause produces an effect and this effect then becomes the cause of a following effect.

▶ From THE GRAYING OF AMERICA
**Newsweek**

[1]Alongside the baby boom, another long-term trend has begun: the number of people over 65 is already rising steadily. There are now about 23 million Americans over what is convention-

ally regarded as retirement age — 3 million more than there were just seven years ago. By the turn of the century, nearly 31 million people will be 65 or older. And in the three decades after that, their number will swell to almost 52 million — more than twice the current total.

[2]Unless there is a new baby boom, the demographic trends are inexorable,° built into the raw data of the births already recorded. The current low level of fertility would produce zero population growth by about 2040, and it would also result in what demographers call a stabilized° age structure — in which all generations and age groups are about the same size and the demographic profile has changed from the traditional triangle to a rectangle. The number of 55-year-olds, for example, would eventually be roughly equal to the number of 5-year-olds or 30-year-olds. At that point, the median age would level off at about 40 — and the notion of a "youth culture" would recede° into the mists of history.

*"One Hell of a Burden."*   [3]Perhaps the most clear-cut question posed by this demographic sea change is an economic one: How will the nation bear the cost of caring for so many old people? In a sense, the number of people each productive worker has to support won't have changed much, since the number of children is destined to shrink as the aged population grows. But the old are considerably more expensive to maintain, living mainly in households of their own and needing more services. Medical costs alone for the over-65 population averaged $1,360 in 1975, almost twice the bill for people under 65.

[4]Pension costs are already soaring. At General Motors Corp., for example, the bill for pensions has doubled in the last decade and will double again over the next ten to fifteen years. In 1967, General Motors had ten workers on its domestic payroll for each retiree drawing a pension. Today, the ratio of General Motors workers to pensioners — what demographers call the dependency ratio — is just 4 to 1. By the early 1990s, it may be close to 1 to 1. "We're building one hell of a burden for our future workers," warns Victor M. Zink, the company's director of employee benefits and services.

[5]This burden is already creating problems for the social-security system. In 1945, the ratio of wage earners to recipients° was a comfortable 35 to 1. Today, with 33 million Americans receiving social-security payments, the dependency ratio has fallen to 3.2 to 1 and by the year 2035 it will be less than 2 to 1. The system already pays more in benefits than it receives

in income at present withholding rates, forcing it to dip into its reserve fund. If rates aren't substantially° raised, the reserves — now totaling $36 billion — will be exhausted within a matter of four years.

*"We've had it."*   [6]To keep the system afloat, working Americans will simply have to give up an ever-higher chunk of their paycheck to the social-security system, which currently takes $965 a year from a person earning $16,500 or more. The only alternative is to use general Federal revenues to help finance the growing deficit. Either way, as the social-security and pension burden mounts, younger workers who must foot the bill may grow increasingly resentful — to the point, some worry, where something approaching intergenerational warfare could break out. "There is a danger," says economist Conrad Jamison, a vice president at California's Security Pacific National Bank, "that in the future workers will just say, 'We've had it. We will no longer support all these old people, these leeches'."

[7]Perhaps more likely, the system itself could be changed to allow the elderly to prolong their working lives and thus share the pension cost. "The real challenge is to find a way to make older people more productive," says management consultant Alonzo McDonald, a partner in McKinsey & Co. "We are not yet sufficiently rich as a society to say that we will carry a major proportion of healthy, wise, experienced individuals without their contributing something."

[8]An increasing number of the elderly themselves would be delighted to cooperate. With people staying healthy longer, fewer are ready to be put out to pasture at 65. "The average age of persons entering nursing homes is now 80, as compared with 70 just a few years ago," says Dr. Robert N. Butler, a gerontologist who heads the National Institute on Aging. Indeed, a 1974 Harris poll found that nearly a third of the nation's over-65 retirees said if they could they still would be working.

[9]For many who feel this way, the answer is likely to be a second career. "We are already seeing a definitive° movement toward this," reports McDonald. "With the anticipation° of many productive years left, more and more people are embarking on new careers in the early 50s — often something totally different — with different motivation — from what they've done before." One result is that the nation's colleges are enrolling more adult students, partially offsetting the decline of traditional students.

[10]As the ranks of the over-65s swell, the second-career movement is bound to gain strength. Already, a number of major

firms have modified their retirement policies to allow workers to stay on the job past their 65th birthdays if they wish. U.S. Steel, for example, has no mandatory retirement age for more than 153,000 nonoffice employees; they can keep working as long as they can do their jobs and pass annual medical exams. And Florida Rep. Claude Pepper, chairman of a House subcommittee on aging, has introduced legislation that would overturn the government's policy of forcing Federal workers to retire at 70.

[11]Any such changes will be slow in coming. Both the social-security system and most private pension funds are actuarially based on a retirement age of 65. The rules of pension programs and union seniority often effectively bar hiring of the elderly even when companies want to; ways might have to be found, for example, to permit a second-career worker to waive rights to a second pension. But if history is a guide, there's nothing impractical about keeping the old at work. In 1900, fully 70 per cent of American men over 65 were employed. By 1960, the figure had dropped to 35 per cent — and since has tumbled further, to 20 per cent. "Before we forget that older people have always worked," says vice-president Merrell Clark of The Edna McConnell Clark Foundation, "we should get them back into the labor force."

[12]In the near term, there simply may not be enough jobs if a lot of senior citizens choose work over retirement. "How will we distribute work among the generations in an increasingly job-short economy?" Clark asks. Although there are no easy answers, the demographic problem may contain the seeds of its own solution. "As we get an older, larger population," says Butler, "we are going to need more people to provide it with services." As the baby boom matures, fewer youths will be entering the labor market — and thus, he concludes, "there may not be as much of a shortage of work as people think." In addition, an increasing reliance on part-time workers could create more jobs. "Before long, a good part of the population may shift from the standard workweek as we know it to a partial workweek," suggests management consultant McDonald. "Perhaps a two- or three-day week, or five days of four hours a day." Eventually, he adds, "we may see a major shift where, after the age of 55, people can move toward a gradually lower level of involvement, with real retirement — total leisure — only after the age of 75."

## QUESTIONS ON     The Graying of America

Answers are at the end of the chapter.

1. Keeping in mind that this excerpt is part of the essay "The Graying of America," what is the function of paragraph 1?

2. What is the cause of the effects discussed in paragraph 2?

3. What kind of an effect does this demographic change (cause) pose? (paragraph 3)

4. The paragraph unit made up of paragraphs 3, 4, and 5 revolves around what key sentence? What effects are considered in this analysis?

5. In the last sentence of paragraph 5, a final effect is stated. What are the causes of that condition?

6. What must Americans do to keep the system — pensions and social security — "afloat"? What may be a final effect on the burden that future Americans have to carry (paragraph 6)?

7. What main idea gives unity to paragraphs 7, 8, 9, 10, and 11?

8. In paragraph 12 the discussion is related to the effects "if a lot of senior citizens choose work over retirement." What are some of these effects?

Study the complete essay that follows. Notice the interesting organizational pattern. The writer(s) state the thesis — a cause and effect relationship — in the first sentence: "The impact of the devastating eruption of Mount St. Helens in Washington will be felt for months — and perhaps years — to come." Then, to gain reader interest, the writer(s) list the effects. The remainder of the essay treats each of these effects separately, discussing the nature of each one in some detail.

▶ EXPLODING VOLCANO: FULL IMPACT YET TO COME

**U.S. News & World Report**

The impact of the devastating eruption of Mount St. Helens in Washington will be felt for months — and perhaps years — to come.

■ Crops such as wheat and apples have been badly damaged by the volcanic fury, and later growth also may suffer.

■ The timber industry in the Northwest could require years to recover.

■ Weather will be affected over much of the earth, especially in the Northern Hemisphere.

■ Water supplies in some Northwestern communities have become so clogged that a major cleanup effort is necessary.

■ Fish in nearby streams were killed by the millions, and shortages of some species appear likely in future years.

■ Electrical power in parts of the Northwest may face disruptions.

■ Transportation routes — from river shipping to highways — will require extensive repairs.

■ Long-term — but as yet undetermined — health problems may have been created.

Many of these problems could be aggravated considerably if Mount St. Helens continues to erupt periodically, as it has in the past. Agricultural experts are particularly worried that the spread of more ash could kill much of the Northwest's wheat crop.

Even without further emissions of ash, the cost of repairing damage inflicted by the eruption may exceed 1 billion dollars — with much of that to be paid for by local, state and federal taxpayers. President Carter, who flew to Washington on May 21 to assess the damage, declared the state a major disaster area, thus making residents eligible for low-interest loans.

***Bomblike blast.***    The devastation began on May 18, when an explosion, estimated at 500 times the force of the atomic bomb that destroyed Hiroshima, ripped off the top 1,200 feet of the 9,700-foot volcano near Vancouver, Wash. In less than seven days, a cloud of volcanic gas containing some toxic chemicals and minute particles of radioactive substances spread over most of North America.

Scientists say that within several months the cloud — invisible to the naked eye in most regions — will cover the Northern Hemisphere in the stratosphere above 55,000 feet. It is expected to last about two years before completing its fall to earth.

The environmental effects are considerable, although they tend to decrease as distances from the volcano increase. The greatest economic impact is expected to be to the agriculture and timber industries in Washington and Idaho.

The logging industry in central Washington suffered the greatest initial economic damage — estimated at 500 million dollars or more. Officials say that some small logging companies may never recover from the loss of equipment — and enough trees were lost to build 200,000 single-family homes, roughly a fifth of the number of housing units to be started this year throughout the U.S.

Forest companies have not completed surveys of the damage, but many experts believe the destruction will not appreciably° affect the price of lumber to consumers in the long run. At present, the lumber industry is working at far less than capacity because so little new housing is being built. The impact of the destruction of timber may be felt, however, when home building revives.

Another consequence of the explosion is a possible shortage of some crops. Researchers at Washington State University are concerned that the state's 460-million-dollar wheat crop will not survive if the ash cover becomes greater than 2 inches — thus choking the plants. In a few places, deposits measured more than a foot, burying uncut alfalfa and hay, but officials say that most affected farmlands are covered by an inch or so.

Over a longer period of time, agronomists° say there is a possibility of damage to crops in a wide area resulting from acid rain from the ash cloud. Scientists fear that toxic materials emitted by the volcano, such as sulfur oxides, hydrogen sulfides and nitrogen oxides, will fall to the ground in precipitation as the volcanic cloud disperses over North America.

Still undetermined is the status of fruit crops important to the region. Robert Mickelson, chief of the Washington State Agriculture Department, says Yakima County, where apples, cherries and peaches are economic mainstays, is among the hardest-hit areas. He is most worried about the cherries because that crop, valued at nearly 50 million dollars, was near harvest and at a vulnerable° stage. About a third of the nation's supply of sweet cherries is grown in Washington.

Also victimized by the blast is the fishing industry, another mainstay of the economies of Washington and Oregon. Fishermen could suffer for many seasons because millions of young salmon and other fish may not survive the high temperatures created by the blast. The resulting scarcity could drive up the price of salmon.

Effects of the eruption on weather also are a matter of widespread concern. Some authorities are convinced that volcanic explosions in the past have been responsible for substantial cooling trends. New England, for example, for a short time was subjected to unseasonably cold winters and summers after an immense eruption in Indonesia in 1815.

*Changes in temperature.*   Scientists say there will probably be no drastic changes resulting from the Mount St. Helens blast — assuming there are no more eruptions. Still, a temporary lowering of temperature — less than 1 degree — can be expected across much of the Northern Hemisphere. Reason for the drop: Dust particles in the atmosphere deflect a bit of the sun's warming rays. Meteorologists say the lowering could make the difference between rain and snow in some regions.

Observes Lester Machta, director of the federal government's Air Resources Laboratories: "These microscopic particles can remain in the stratosphere for months or years."

Officials of the National Oceanic and Atmospheric Administration say a more noticeable effect will be spectacular sunsets and sunrises during the next year or two. These will be caused as solar rays strike microscopic particles of silicon, turning the light into brilliant rose-colored hues.

Of greater concern is the possible disruption of mountain snowpacks, vital sources of water throughout the West. NOAA scientists say volcanic ash falling on high-altitude snowfields — particularly in the Rocky Mountains — could cause an earlier-than-normal melt-off, leaving little stored water for late summer and early fall.

The ash also is worrying doctors studying the effects of fallout on people within a few hundred miles of the volcano. Medical researchers don't believe there is an immediate health threat, but say long-term problems could occur from the ash.

Says Idaho health officer Russell Schaff: "It can be respired deep into the lungs. There may be no acute° symptoms now, but problems could occur years later."

Widespread effects also have been felt by operators of machinery — ranging from air-conditioning units to gas pumps.

The powderlike fallout clogged machines in Washington, Idaho and Oregon, and covered farm animals and crops over a wide area. In some sections of western Idaho, ash drifts of 1 foot or more were reported.

Other damage resulted from mud slides and floods caused by material dislodged by the mountain. Many homes, bridges and highways were devastated, and shipping channels were clogged by silt.

More than two dozen vessels were trapped in the harbors in or near the Columbia River — the major port of Portland, Oreg., in particular. Officials said it could take a year or more to clean up Portland's shipping channel. Damage to water routes was estimated at 15 million dollars.

The explosion also took its toll of roads and communication lines, which were disrupted over wide areas of Washington and Idaho, leaving thousands of persons stranded.

Still another worry: Blowing and shifting ash will clog electrical generators or transformers, disrupting electrical supplies in large portions of the Northwest.

Geologists have redoubled their studies of the mountain to try to determine whether any more big eruptions are imminent. They hope instruments will reveal considerably more about origins of the spectacular explosion of Mount St. Helens that occurred 8 minutes after a moderate earthquake.

*Blowing its top.*  Some scientists think the tremor may have triggered the eruption. Geologists say the peak exploded following the buildup of pressure from gas and magma — molten rock — inside the mountain, which had lain dormant for 123 years.

The blast emitted thousands of tons of volcanic ash into the atmosphere, and its aftereffects were responsible for at least 30 deaths. Another hundred or so residents and campers who had decided to remain near the mountain despite previous upheavals were still missing in late May.

The most immediate damage from the blast, which created a mile-long crater on the north side of the mountain, occurred as a glowing avalanche of hot ash and gases raced 17 miles down the Toutle River Valley. Huge trees were blown down like matchsticks, and dozens of bridges and homes were wiped out. The initial blast also destroyed hundreds of deer, elk and other wildlife.

Some geologists believe the emissions of ash from the volcano may continue for as long as 20 years. Says Sam Frear, a

Forest Service official in Washington: "We're entirely at the mercy of the mountain."

---

**MATCH-UP TWELVE**

Match the definitions in column 2 with the words in column 1 taken from the exercises and the essay by placing the letter in the blank. Answers are at the end of the chapter.

| | | | |
|---|---|---|---|
| a. pigment | 1. genuine, true, real | _g_ |
| b. mortality | 2. world of the dead | _i_ |
| c. impact | 3. crushed, reduced to powder | _h_ |
| d. devastating | 4. death rate | _b_ |
| e. inflicted | 5. not to be moved, unyielding | _j_ |
| f. disrupted | 6. coloring matter | _a_ |
| g. veritable | 7. forceful contact | _c_ |
| h. pulverized | 8. imposed, laid on | _e_ |
| i. netherworld | 9. destroying | _d_ |
| j. inexorable | 10. interrupted, disordered | _f_ |

---

**MATCH-UP THIRTEEN**

Match the definitions in column 2 with the words in column 1 taken from the exercises and the essay by placing the letter in the blank. Answers are at the end of the chapter.

| | | | |
|---|---|---|---|
| a. stabilized | 1. managers of land or crops | _h_ |
| b. recede | 2. actually, noticeably | _g_ |
| c. recipients | 3. severe | _j_ |
| d. substantially | 4. open to attack | _i_ |
| e. definitive | 5. held steady or firm | _a_ |
| f. anticipation | 6. precise, conclusive | _e_ |
| g. appreciably | 7. considerably | _d_ |
| h. agronomists | 8. receivers | _c_ |
| i. vulnerable | 9. expectation, foreseeing | _f_ |
| j. acute | 10. withdraw, go back | _b_ |

## Suggested Topics for an Analysis by Cause or by Effect

1. An economic depression
2. A defeat in a battle, game, political campaign
3. Why you failed a test, course, and so on
4. The effects of a disease, fire, battle, defeat, and so on
5. The causes of war, poverty, divorce, crime, and so on
6. Why you had an accident
7. Why we need a change in policy, administration, values, and so on
8. The effects of alcoholism, drug addiction, gambling, and so on
9. Why people are leaving the city, California, East Germany, and so on
10. Why a child leaves his home.

## Answers: Chapter 8

### Exercise 1

1. The first sentence announces development by causes: "a prime force is the baby boom."
2. The first cause is the baby boom.
3. It presents the second cause and gives evidence to support the generalization.
4. The supporting material consists mainly of statistics.

### Exercise 4

1. The first sentence indicates development with analysis by effects.
2. The cause was smelters for silver and lead that poured arsenic fumes into the air.
3. The rain washed arsenical dust from leaves and carried it into the water of brooks and pools.

### The Graying of America

1. The paragraph leads the student into a discussion of another long-term trend: the number of people over 65 is already rising steadily.
2. The cause is the low level of fertility.
3. The effect is an economic one.
4. The sentence reads: "Perhaps the most clear-cut question posed by this demographic sea change is an economic one."

Old people are more expensive to maintain for these reasons:

a. They live in households of their own.
b. They require many more services than young people.
   (1) Medical costs for old people are almost twice the bill for young people.
   (2) Pension costs are soaring so that in the future we may not be able to support a pension plan system.
   (3) We already have a problem with the social-security system.

5. The effect stated in the last sentence of paragraph 5 is that within four years, if social security rates are not raised, the reserves will be exhausted. The cause is that the system is paying out more in benefits (more older people around) than it receives in income at the present withholding rates.
6. "To keep the system afloat, working Americans will simply have to give up an ever-higher chunk of their paycheck to the social-security system. . . ."

   Americans may no longer be able to "support all these old people." They may refuse to do so.

7. The main idea stated in sentence 1, paragraph 7, unifies this unit; it reads: "Perhaps more likely, the system itself could be changed to allow the elderly to prolong their working lives and thus share the pension cost."
8. The main effect is that there may not be enough jobs. However, the demographic problem may contain its own solution:

   a. More services for the older people
   b. More part-time workers
   c. Shift to partial weekend
   d. A two- or three-day week or five days of four hours a day
   e. Total retirement only after 75 years old

| *Voc. Test 12* | | *Match-Up 12* | *Match-Up 13* |
|---|---|---|---|
| 1. b | 11. a | 1. g | 1. h |
| 2. c | 12. d | 2. i | 2. g |
| 3. a | 13. b | 3. h | 3. j |
| 4. a | 14. d | 4. b | 4. i |
| 5. c | 15. c | 5. j | 5. a |
| 6. d | 16. d | 6. a | 6. e |
| 7. b | 17. a | 7. c | 7. d |
| 8. a | 18. b | 8. e | 8. c |
| 9. c | 19. c | 9. d | 9. f |
| 10. b | 20. a | 10. f | 10. b |

# Explaining and Informing — Classifying, Defining, and Combining

To explain by *classification*, you place persons, places, things, ideas into groups or classes to give order and meaning to them. With a clearly defined purpose in mind, you group or classify on the basis of distinctive characteristics, traits, or qualities. You might wish, for example, to inform the people in your town that you are attending a college that rates high in academic circles. You write an article for the hometown newspaper that includes sections developed by classification: the college faculty may be grouped according to degrees to stress the large number of doctorates on the staff; the student body may be grouped on the basis of grades and high scholarship. Or, as a member of student government, you might find it necessary to place students into groups on the basis of age, marital status, political, religious, or social affiliations; or into groups who are employed full-time, part-time, or not at all while going to school.

## Classification

Many classifications are already part of your experience. You may have given order to piles of books, rocks, coins, Indian arrows, or stamps by placing them readily into identifiable groups. You have probably become aware of classification in your schooling: kinds of plants and animals, races of men, types of clouds, volcanoes, glaciers, and storms. Whatever the classification, the purpose is clear: to give order and meaning to a seemingly disorganized mass of persons, places, things, happenings, or ideas. To show their function, leaves have been placed into the following classes or groups: (1) leaves that protect the plant, (2) leaves that keep the plant warm, (3) leaves that prick and scratch, and (4) leaves that trap animals. With a different purpose in mind, writers have placed leaves into classes such as (1) leaves of broad-leafed trees, (2) leaves of grass, and (3) needle leaves.

This discussion about leaves tells us something about classifying. First, a writer must have a purpose for classification, and his purpose will determine the basis for the classifying. Frequently, the writer will state clearly his purpose in the first sentence — for example, *On the basis of their function in a plant, leaves may be placed into four classes:* (1) leaves that protect the plant, (2) leaves that keep the plant warm, (3) leaves that prick and scratch, and (4) leaves that trap animals. Second, a writer must firmly establish each class on that basis by presenting enough characteristics for the reader to clearly identify the class and to distinguish it from the other classes.

In the model below, the writer clearly establishes each type of glacier by presenting sufficient information about each. He devotes a separate paragraph to presenting characteristics by which the reader may identify each glacier.

▶ There are two principal types of glaciers: the continental and the valley. The continental glaciers are great sheets of ice, called ice caps, that cover parts of continents. The earth has two continental glaciers at present: one spreads over most of Greenland and one over all of Antarctica save for a small window of rock and the peaks of several ranges. The Greenland ice sheet is over 10,000 ft. thick in the central part and covers an area of about 650,000 sq. miles. The Antarctic sheet has been sounded, in one place at least, to a depth of 14,000 ft., and it spreads over an area of 5,500,000 sq. miles. This is larger than conterminous United States in the proportion of 5½ : 3. It is calculated to store 7 million cu. miles of ice, which if melted would raise the ocean level 250 ft.

Valley glaciers are ice streams that originate in the high

snow fields of mountain ranges and flow down valleys to warmer climates, where they melt. Some break up into icebergs and eventually melt in the ocean. In certain places the valley glaciers flow down the mountain valleys to adjacent plains and there spread out as lobate feet. These are called *expanded-foot glaciers.* Generally the sprawling feet of several valley glaciers coalesce to form one major sheet, and this is called a *piedmont glacier.*

A. J. Eardley
*General College Geology*

In classifying, you are answering two questions: What is this a sort of? What are sorts of this? By comparing and contrasting, you place persons, places, things, happenings, or ideas into classes on the basis of significant characteristics. Let us review this process by studying two model classifications. In the first model paragraph, the writer announces the classification in the first sentence and then firmly establishes the two kinds of meteorites by presenting enough characteristics to identify each kind.

▶ Most of these meteorites are of two kinds. One is stony in nature, like a piece of rock from the sky. The largest of these that we have yet found is at Norton, Kansas, and it is estimated to weigh 1 ton. The other kind is composed of an alloy of nickel and iron, similar to what is believed to make up the interior of the Earth. The largest known nickel-iron meteorite is in Grootfontein, in Africa. Its weight is probably more than 60 tons.

Lester del Rey
*The Mysterious Sky*

Study the model paragraph that follows. Notice that the writer announces the classes of ants in the first sentence and then describes the characteristics of each group.

▶ Here too we find three different castes: the queens, which are fully developed females; the workers, females with underdeveloped ovaries, taking care of the brood, foraging, and defending the nest; and at times there are also males. The males and the virgin queens have wings. On a warm summer day they leave their nest in swarms for their wedding flight up to the bright warm sunlight. The males perish soon afterward; the fertilized queens lose their wings and try to start a new nest, or return and find room in the old one. In this case the "Majesties" get on very well together; in fact, many dozen of queens may be found in one colony, all peacefully occupied with their one task, the laying of eggs. The workers are wingless. Thus ants are much more bound to the soil and have a way of life quite different from bees.

Karl von Frisch
*Man and the Living World*

To fulfill your purpose by classifying, you may find it necessary to establish main classes and subclasses. A very familiar example of this more involved method of classifying is the classification of parts of speech on the basis of the way a word is used in a sentence. The plan that follows shows this system of classes and subclasses. It can also serve as a plan for establishing your classification before you begin writing.

BASIS FOR CLASSIFICATION: THE WAY A WORD IS USED IN A SENTENCE

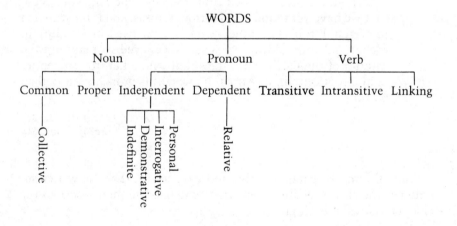

Study the model classification paragraph unit below. Observe the statement of classification in the first sentence: "There are different kinds of prejudice, and *two of these deserve separate considerations.*" He identifies his first type — conforming prejudice — by discussing its nature in two paragraphs. The second type of prejudice — one rooted in a deep sense of personal insecurity — is explained fully in paragraph 3.

▶ There are different kinds of prejudice, and two of these deserve separate consideration. First there is that loosely spoken, loosely held opinion that can be called conforming prejudice: people make prejudiced remarks about other races, nations, religions, or groups because they want to conform to what they think are the conventions of their own group. Attacking or deriding members of another group who "don't belong" gives them a sense of solidarity with their own group. It's rather sad but also fortunate that most prejudice is probably this conforming kind. Fortunate, because this type of prejudice is easily given up when a new situation demands it.

A number of studies have shown that while people may protest about some social change, when the change actually takes place most will fall silently and willingly into line. It's the rare examples of change being resisted with violence that unfortunately receive most publicity. A psychologist interested in this phenomenon once made an amusing study of the differences between what people say they'll do and what they really do in a particular situation that evokes prejudice. Traveling across the country with a Chinese couple, he found that the three of them were received in 250 hotels and restaurants with great hospitality — and only once were refused service. When the trip was over, he wrote to each of the hotels and restaurants and asked if they would serve Chinese people. Ninety-two per cent of those who had actually served them said they would not do so!

The second kind of prejudice is less easily relinquished than the conforming type, for this second kind stems from a more deep-rooted sense of personal insecurity. A prejudiced person of this kind usually has a feeling of failure or guilt about his own accomplishments and to avoid the pain of blaming himself, he turns the blame on others. Just as the Jews once symbolically piled all their guilt on a goat and drove it into the wilderness, so these prejudiced people make scapegoats out of Negroes, Southerners, Jews, Russians, or whoever else fits their need. Moreover, insecure people like these are anxious, too, and anxious people can't discriminate among the small but important differences between people who seem alike. So, on the one hand they often can't think clearly about other people; and on the other, they need to blame scapegoats in order to feel more comfortable. Both these mechanisms promote faulty generalizations; these people respond to others not as individuals but as Negroes, Russians, women, doctors — as if these groups were all alike.

Ian Stevenson, M.D.
"People Aren't Born Prejudiced"

## EXERCISE 1    Classification

Read the model paragraph below. Answer the questions that follow it.
Answers are at the end of the chapter.

> ▶ In every hive lives the mother of the family, the queen bee,
> with her 40,000 to 80,000 children. The total number of her
> progeny is several times larger. But most of them die after a few
> weeks or months, while the queen lives on and is fertile for
> four to five years. She is not weighed down by affairs of state.
> Her most important duty is to lay eggs. This is a full-time job,
> because an active queen daily produces 1,000 eggs; this means
> that day and night she lays an average of one egg per minute.
> The other bees are not involved in this. The so-called worker is
> a sterile female with nonfunctioning ovaries and never lays
> eggs under normal conditions. But the workers excel in all
> other female virtues — domestic tidiness, care for the larder,
> and the tending of the brood. In spring big-headed drones turn
> up in the colonies of bees. These are male bees and their viril-
> ity is their only function. In summer when they become
> useless, the workers begin to resent the presence of the drones
> as if they were parasites in the hive. This leads to the dramatic
> battle of the drones, when the males are mauled and stung and
> chased out of the hive to die an inglorious death. They are
> defenseless against assaults of the workers, since they have no
> sting and do not show much fighting spirit. They do not know
> how to find food and are doomed to starve at the very entrance
> of the hive.

Karl von Frisch
*Man and the Living World*

1. What is the subject of the classification?

2. Into what classes does the writer break down the subject?

3. What characteristics will place a bee in the worker class?

## EXERCISE 2    Classification

Read the model paragraph below. Answer the questions that follow it.

▶ Though at times there was considerable social mobility, medieval society conventionally consisted of three classes; the nobles, the peasants, and the clergy. Each of these groups had its own task to perform. Since the vassals usually gave military service to their lord in return for their fiefs, the nobles were primarily fighters, belonging to an honored society distinct from the peasant people — freemen, villeins, and serfs. In an age of physical violence, society obviously would accord first place to the man with the sword rather than to the man with the hoe. The peasants were the workers; attached to the manors, they produced the crops and did all the menial labor. The Church drew on both the noble and the peasant classes for the clergy. Although the higher churchmen held land as vassals under the feudal system, the clergy formed a class which was considered separate from the nobility and peasantry.

T. Walter Wallbank et al.
*Civilization: Past and Present*

1. Into what classes does the writer break down the subject?

2. How does the writer distinguish the classes?

3. Why was it necessary to discuss more fully the clergy as it related to the other two classes?

4. Does he present the tasks of the clergy? Why do you think he omitted these characteristics?

In the essay that follows, note the statement of the classification and the characteristics of each class.

## ▶ RICH WHITES AND POOR WHITES
**Thomas A. Bailey and David M. Kennedy**

*Background information*

[1]Only a handful of Southern aristocrats lived in Grecian-pillared mansions. Below the 1,733 families in 1850 who owned 100 or more slaves were the less wealthy slaveowners. They totaled in 1850 some 345,000 families, representing about 1,725,000 white persons. Over two-thirds of these families — 255,268 in all — owned fewer than ten slaves each.

[2]Beneath the slaveowners was the great body of non-slaveowning whites who, by 1860, has swelled their numbers to 6,120,825. These rank-and-file citizens, comprising about three-fourths of the free population of the South, had no direct stake in slavery. *They fell roughly into three groups:* (1) the lowland whites, who were by far the most numerous; (2) the poor whites, who were generally disease-ridden; and (3) the semi-isolated mountain whites, who were the most independent-minded.

*Statement of the classification: three groups*

[3]The hundreds of thousands of energetic *lowland whites included such folks as mechanics, lesser tradesmen, and above all, small cotton farmers.* Though owning no slaves themselves, they were among the stoutest defenders of the slave system. The carrot-on-the-stick ever dangling before their noses was the hope of buying a slave or two, and of parlaying their holdings into riches — all in accord with the "American dream." They also took fierce pride in their presumed racial superiority, which would be watered down if the slaves were freed. Many of the poorer lowland whites were hardly better off economically than the Afro-American; some, indeed, were not

*Class one: the lowland whites*

*Characteristics of this group*

so well off. But they clung desperately to their one visible badge of presumed superiority.

*Class two: the poor whites*

[4]*Conspicuous among the millions of non-slaveholders was a considerable sprinkling of poor whites,* whom even the slaves despised as the "poor white trash."

*Characteristics of this group*

Known also as "hillbillies," "crackers," or "clay eaters," they were often listless, pallid, shiftless, and misshapen. Later investigations have revealed that many of them were not so much lazy as sickly, suffering from malnutrition and disease, including hookworm.

*Paragraph unit consisting of paragraphs 5–7*

*Class three: mountain whites*

[5]*Mountain whites of the South are not to be confused with the poor whites of the lowland cotton belt.* They were more or less marooned in the valleys of the Appalachian range, stretching from western Virginia to northern Georgia and Alabama. Civilization had largely passed

*Characteristics of this group*

them by. They were a kind of living ancestry, for some of them retained Elizabethan speech forms and habits that had long since died out in England.

[6]As independent small farmers, the mountain whites had little in common with the aristocracy of the broad cotton lands. Many of them, including the future President Andrew Johnson of Tennessee,

*Characteristics of this group*

hated both the lordly planter and his gangs of blacks. They looked upon the impending strife between North and South as "a rich man's war but a poor man's fight."

[7]The tough-fibered mountain whites constituted a vitally important peninsula of unionism jutting down into the secessionist Southern sea. They ultimately played a significant role in crippling the Confederacy. Their attachment to the

*Characteristics of this group*

Union party of Abraham Lincoln was such that, for generations after the Civil War, the only concentrated Republican strength in the Solid South was to be found in the Southern highlands.

Read the classification essay that follows. Be prepared to answer questions on its organization and development.

▶ CRITICS OF AMERICAN VIETNAM POLICY*
**James Q. Wilson**

[1]To divide the public into supporters and opponents of foreign policy, especially of military interventions, suggests the existence of a simple split between "hawks" and "doves." Though these are favorite journalistic labels, they are quite misleading. There are several different kinds of support, and motives for support, of a military action. One can support it because one trusts and follows the president, especially the president of one's own party; one can support it because one believes it is beneficial to the narrow national interests of the United States; or one can support it because one believes that international well-being or the interests of the allies requires it. Opponents can have one or the other of a parallel set of motives. And given these different motives, one can have a complex mix of opinions about war. For example, "I think it was a grave mistake ever to get involved in Vietnam, but as long as we are fighting there I support our president and the armed forces." Or, "It may have been all right to intervene in the first place, but things haven't gone as we hoped and we ought to pull out now." Or, "The whole war from beginning to end was immoral, unwise, and impolitic." Or, "We should not be fighting there, but since we are, we should go all-out to win." Classifying these and other attitudes as simply "hawk" or "dove" is not very illuminating.

[2]Opinion polls suggest that there were at least three kinds of critics of our participation in Vietnam. The first group consisted disproportionately of older citizens and persons with little schooling. From the beginning they were skeptical about the war, and their skepticism increased somewhat as the war continued. Moreover, they were not much more likely to favor escalation than were college-educated professional persons. However, they saw the war in terms of national interest and the obligation to support men in combat and would have nothing to do with protesters who wanted to use militant tactics to obtain an immediate withdrawal. Ironically, the fact that some opponents of the war engaged in campus riots and public demonstrations may well have prolonged the war, for such tactics deeply offended most citizens including those opposed to the

---

* Title is supplied by the author of this textbook.

war but disinclined to abandon the president or the armed forces. For example, when the Chicago police roughed up antiwar demonstrators at the 1968 Democratic convention, popular reaction was overwhelming on the side of the police, even among people opposed to the war.

[3]The second kind of opponent consisted of those who initially supported the war, or were indifferent to it, but gradually came to oppose it because it seemed pointless or endless. Included in this group were some college students and upper status college graduates. Contrary to popular impression at the time, support for the war was greatest among younger persons and college graduates, at least until near the very end. Though we recall the protests on college campuses against the war, these opponents were not representative of most young persons or even of most college-educated persons.

[4]The third kind of opponent were those persons, small in number, who always opposed the war, not on grounds of national self-interest as did many citizens, but because it violated their political ideology (pacifism, Marxism, or whatever).

## QUESTIONS ON   **Critics of American Vietnam Policy**

Answers are at the end of the chapter.

1. What is the function of the first paragraph?

2. Into what three divisions does the writer place the critics of American participation in Vietnam?

3. On what basis does he make the classification?

4. Until the end of the war, among what group of American society was support for the war the greatest?

5. What was the effect of campus riots and public demonstrations by militant protestors?

6. Into what group would you place the following? (NOTE: Some may belong in no group.)
   a. They saw the war in terms of national interest.

   b. The war violated their political ideology.

   c. They opposed it because it seemed pointless and endless.

   d. They sided with the police in the antiwar demonstration at the 1968 Democratic Convention.

   e. The militant protestors on the campuses.

## Suggested Topics for Writing Classification

| | | | |
|---|---|---|---|
| 1. Intelligence | 5. Governments | 9. Marriages | 12. Teachers |
| 2. Drives | 6. Religions | 10. Weapons | 13. Students |
| 3. Rulers | 7. Friends | 11. Penal | 14. Races |
| 4. Dates | 8. Families | Institutions | 15. Customers |

## Definition

*Definition* is a method of identifying and making clear the meaning of a word or term. By defining, a writer answers the question "What is the meaning of this?" In addition, he puts limits on the word or term in the form of characteristics that distinguish it from other entities. In the example definition sentence that follows, the writer defines the word *incursion*.

▶ The German *incursion*, a sudden hostile invasion into Polish territory, was the beginning of World War II.

In addition to defining the word *incursion*, the writer places limits on its use by characterizing it as a movement that is sudden and hostile. An incursion, therefore, is a certain kind of movement into another's territory; it differs from a visit, from a migration to settle land, or from an invasion that is not sudden and, in some cases, not hostile.

### Simple Definition

Most definitions, like the one in the example sentence above, are short, usually a word synonym, a phrase, or a sentence. Some definitions, however, are a paragraph or an entire essay running on for several pages. The short definition is called a *simple definition;* the longer ones are known as *extended definitions.* You have probably had many occasions in speaking and writing to use the simple definition. You are aware, therefore, of its problems. It must be worked smoothly and unobtrusively into the flowing thought that develops the main idea. Most dictionary entries, like the example that follows, are too mechanical for this purpose. Yet, from studying a dictionary entry at this time, you can learn some things that will help in defining. Study the entry for the italicized word in the sentence:

▶ That kind of cactus is *indigenous* to the Mohave Desert.

**in·dig·e·nous** \in-'dij-ə-nəs\ *adj* [LL *indigenus,* fr. L. *indigena,* n., native, fr. OL *indu, endo* in, within (akin to L *in* and L *de* down) + L *gignere* to beget] 1 :

produced, growing, or living naturally in a particular region or environment 2 :
INBORN, INNATE **syn** see NATIVE — **in·dig·e·nous·ly** *adv* — **in·dig·e·
nous·ness** *n.*

*Webster's Seventh New Collegiate Dictionary*

Answer the following questions:

1. How many meanings are given for the word?
2. What are some possible synonyms (words with nearly the same
   meaning)?
3. Which meaning will fit best in the context of the example sentence?
4. What does the sign "**syn** see NATIVE" mean?

Your answer should be an indication of the problems of working
with a dictionary entry. This kind of definition is obviously too mechanical for smooth incorporation into writing. In addition, a dictionary entry presents multiple meanings of a word; some of these meanings are more general than the original; some are more confusing.
Moreover, the entry points out the difficulty of working with word
synonyms. The word *native* fits very well. Are *inborn* and *innate* as
satisfactory?

When you follow the directions given by the sign "**syn** see NA-
TIVE," under the entry **native,** you will find the following information:

¹**native** \'nāt·iv\ *adj* [ME *natif*, fr. MF, fr. L *nativus*, fr. *natus*, pp. of *nasci* to be
born — more at NATION] 1 : INBORN, INNATE 2 : belonging to a particular
place by birth 3 *archaic* : closely related 4 : belonging to or associated with one
by birth 5 : NATURAL, NORMAL 6 a : grown, produced, or originating in a
particular place or in the vicinity : LOCAL b : INDIGENOUS 7 : SIMPLE,
UNAFFECTED 8 a : constituting the original substance or source b : found
in nature esp. in an unadulterated form 9 *chiefly Austral* : having a usu.
superficial resemblance to a specified English plant or animal — **na·tive·ly** *adv*
— **na·tive·ness** *n.*
   **syn** NATIVE, INDIGENOUS, ENDEMIC, ABORIGINAL meaning belonging to a locality. NATIVE implies birth or origin in a place or region and may
suggest compatibility with it; INDIGENOUS applies to species or races and
adds to NATIVE the implication of not having been introduced from elsewhere; ENDEMIC implies being peculiar to a region; ABORIGINAL implies
having no known race preceding in occupancy of the region.

*Webster's Seventh New Collegiate Dictionary*

In the synonyms at the close of the entry, did you observe the various shades of meaning, especially the meaning of *indigenous* and *native?* The dictionary, though an invaluable aid to definition, must be
used with discernment.

How can you work simple definitions smoothly into your developing thought? Several methods have worked successfully for experienced writers. The first way is by *the synonym*, allowing for the limitations mentioned in the discussion above.

▶ He then goes on to show that Agememnon too is guilty of the crime of *hubris*, of offending against the gods by excessive ambition.

F. Roy Willis<br>
*Western Civilization: An Urban Perspective*

Second, by *direct explanation:*

▶ This spontaneous and loyal support of our preconception — this process of finding "good" reasons to justify our routine beliefs — is known to modern psychologists as *"rationalizing"* — clearly a new name for a very ancient thing.

James Harvey Robinson<br>
"On Various Kinds of Thinking"

Henry Jones was more than an instructor; he was a *choreographer* — a true master in the art of designing the dance.

By *indirect explanation:*

▶ Trance is a similar abnormality in our society. Even a mild mystic is *aberrant* in Western civilization.

Ruth Benedict<br>
*Patterns of Culture*

▶ John was a *voracious* reader with an insatiable appetite for westerns.

By *the simile:*

▶ He was a *stolid*, unimaginative man, in appearance and intelligence much like a dumb ox.

The island was as *inaccessible* as a medieval fortress.

By an *analytic or formal definition:* In using this method, a writer defines by placing the word or term in a class (*genus*) and then identifying it with characteristics that show how it differs from other members of the same class.

Term ──────→ class ──────→ differentiate

▶ A dog is a carnivorous domesticated animal (*Canis familiaris*).

A fox is a flesh-eating mammal of the dog family, smaller than wolves and noted for craftiness.

A wolf is a large doglike carnivorous mammal of the *genus canis*, yellowish or brownish gray with coarse fur, erect, pointed ears, and a bushy tail.

▶ A republic is a form of government in which the power resides in the people (the electorate).

An aristocracy is a form of government in which the power resides in the hands of the best individuals or a small privileged class.

In organizing the simple definition, avoid the following mistakes:

1. Do not use the expressions "is where" and "is when" in beginning the main part of the definition. The verb *is* (a linking verb) should be followed by a noun, pronoun, or an adjective, not by an adverbial clause introduced by "where" or "when."

▶ A stadium *is* where they hold sports spectaculars.

A stadium is a structure in which sports spectaculars are held.

▶ Socialism *is* when the ownership and operation of the means of production and distribution is vested in the community as a whole.

Socialism is a theory or system of social organization which advocates the vesting of the ownership and control of the means of production, capital, land, etc., in the community as a whole.

The American College Dictionary

2. Do not use the "circular definition" — a practice of defining a term with the term itself.

> ▶ Dictation is the act of dictating.
>
> Communism is an economic system practiced by communists.
>
> An aristocracy is a form of government ruled by aristocrats.
>
> A depository is a place in which something valuable is deposited.

3. Define a word or term in simpler language than the original.

> ▶ The word *surreptitious* as a synonym for *clandestine* isn't really too much help; *secret* is a simpler synonym.
>
> The words *servile, obsequious, sycophantic* are not very helpful in explaining the meaning of *subservient; fawning, cringing,* and *slavish* are better.

The following explanation of the term *dialectical materialism* seems to be somewhat complicated:

> ▶ The theory of reality affirming continuous transformation of matter and dynamic interconnectedness of things and concepts, and implying social transformation through socialism toward a classless society, which was advanced by Karl Marx and Friedrich Engels and adopted as the official Soviet philosophy.

Webster's Seventh New Collegiate Dictionary

4. In using the analytic or formal definition, follow these few suggestions:

   a. Make the class broad enough to include all the members. *Sports* is broad enough to include all the activities in that group: football, tennis, baseball, and so forth.

▶ Literature is a broad enough class to include both poetry and prose works; *poetry* or *prose* is not broad enough.

b. Do not make the class too broad.

▶ *Entertainment* is too broad a classification in which to place an individual sport; there are too many kinds of entertainments which are not sports: motion pictures, musicals, plays.

c. Make sure to differentiate the members of different classes.

▶ Biology is a branch of knowledge.

Biology is a branch of knowledge that deals with living organisms.

▶ A sheriff is a law enforcement officer.

A sheriff is the chief executive officer of a state or county who is responsible for law enforcement in those areas.

5. Remember that examples are excellent for clarification in the process of defining; they are not definitions.

▶ The *gill fungi* include many species such as *mushrooms* and *toadstools*.

Political conservatives are men like Barry Goldwater and William Buckley, Jr.

## EXERCISE 3    Dictionary Definition

Study the dictionary entry below. Answer the questions that follow it. Answers are at the end of the chapter.

> **in·dig·e·nous** \in-'dij-ə-nəs\ *adj* [LL *indigenus*, fr. L *indigena*, n., native, fr. OL *indu*, *endo* in, within (akin to L *in* and to L *de* down) + L *gignere* to *beget*] 1: produced, growing, or living naturally in a particular region or environment 2: INBORN, INNATE **syn** see NATIVE — **in·dig·e·nous·ly** *adv* — **in·dig·e·nous·ness** *n.*
>
> *Webster's Seventh New Collegiate Dictionary*

1. In the sentence below, what are the best meanings for *indigenous*? That kind of cactus is *indigenous* to the Mohave Desert.

   (a)............................(b)...............................

2. What do the words **syn** see NATIVE mean?

3. Into how many syllables is the word *indigenous* divided?

4. *Indigenous* with its various forms is used as how many different parts of speech?

5. To what two languages may the word *indigenous* be traced back?

6. On what syllable is the accent given?

## EXERCISE 4    Dictionary Definition

Study the dictionary entry below. Answer the questions that follow it.

¹**na·tive** \ 'nāt-iv\ *adj* [ME *natif.* fr. MF, fr. L *nativus,* fr. *natus,* pp. of *nasci* to be born — more at NATION] 1 : INBORN, INNATE 2 : belonging to a particular place by birth 3 *archaic* : closely related 4 : belonging to or associated with one by birth 5 : NATURAL, NORMAL 6a : grown, produced, or originating in a particular place or in the vicinity : LOCAL b : INDIGENOUS 7 : SIMPLE, UNAFFECTED 8a : constituting the original substance or source b : found in nature esp. in an unadultered form 9 *chiefly Austral* : having a usu. superficial resemblance to a specified English plant or animal — **na·tive·ly** *adv* — **na·tive·ness** *n.*

   *syn* NATIVE, INDIGENOUS, ENDEMIC, ABORIGINAL mean belonging to a locality. NATIVE implies birth or origin in a place or region and may suggest compatibility with it; INDIGENOUS applies to species or races and adds to NATIVE the implication of not having been introduced from elsewhere; ENDEMIC implies being peculiar to a region; ABORIGINAL implies having no known race preceding occupancy of the region.

*Webster's Seventh New Collegiate Dictionary*

1. How many meanings are given for the word *native*?

2. What are some synonyms for the word (words that have nearly the same meaning)?

3. When would you use meaning 3?

4. How is meaning 5 limited?


5. To what word in Middle English does *native* go back?


6. How does *indigenous* differ from *native*?

## Extended Definition

An extended definition is the organization and development of the meaning of a word or term beyond the limits of the simple definition. It may be a paragraph or two or even an entire essay in length. Writers develop meanings of words and terms more extensively because the devices effective in the simple definition are not adequate for making the meaning of many terms and words in our language clear. Words and terms like *socialism, school spirit, correct English, democracy, power, personality, symbolism, prejudice, conformity, ethnocentrism, affluent society* cannot be defined adequately with a word synonym or a few lines of explanation. In addition, many writers feel that accepted definitions do not define the word or term as they are using it; therefore, they write definitions of their own. In the following model, the writer admits that there can be no absolute definition of "correct English," discards the traditional conceptions, and then presents his own definition.

> ► If we discard the authority of rules and of "reputable" writers, to what can we turn for a definition of "correct" English? At the outset it must be acknowledged that there can be no absolute, positive definition. "Correct English" is an approximate term used to describe a series of evaluations of usage dependent upon appropriateness, locality, social level, purpose, and other variables. It is a relative term, in decided contrast with the positive nature of (1) *reputability*, the determination of good usage by reference to standard authors; (2) *preservation*, the obligation to defend and maintain language uses because they are traditional, or are felt to be more elegant; (3) *literary*, the identification of good usage with formal literary usage. By discarding these traditional conceptions, and turning to the language itself as its own standard of good usage, we may find the following definition adequate for our present needs. *Good English is that form of speech which is appropriate to the purpose of the speaker, true to the language as it is, and comfortable to speaker and listener. It is the product of custom, neither cramped by rule or freed from all restraint; it is never fixed, but changes with the organic life of the language.*
>
> Robert C. Pooley
> "Teaching English Usage"

Except for the extended formal definition, you may organize and develop definitions by any one or any combination of the methods that you have studied. You will find the *question-to-answer* method a natural one for definition. Notice the simple organizational structure of the two model definition paragraphs that follow. Both begin with a question and follow with the answer. In the second model, however, the writer requires much more space to fully answer the question — in other words, to make the meaning of the word clear.

MODEL ONE:

▶ These arguments and debates led to the question, What is a volcano? It perplexed geologists for a hundred years. Now it is answered easily. A volcano is a hole in the ground through which hot gas, molten material and fragmentary products rise to the surface.

Rupert Furneaux
*Krakatoa*

MODEL TWO:

▶ What exactly is a tornado? The general picture is familiar enough. The phenomenon is usually brewed on a hot, sticky day with south winds and an ominous sky. From the base of a thundercloud a funnel-shaped cloud extends a violently twisting spout toward the earth. As it sucks in matter in its path, the twister may turn black, brown or occasionally even white (over snow). The moving cloud shows an almost continuous display of sheet lightning. It lurches along in a meandering path, usually northeastward, at 25 to 40 miles per hour. Sometimes it picks up its finger from the earth for a short distance and then plants it down again. The funnel is very slender: its wake of violence generally averages no more than 400 yards wide. As the tornado approaches, it is heralded by a roar of hundreds of jet planes or thousands of railroad cars. Its path is a path of total destruction. Buildings literally explode as they are sucked by the tornado's low-pressure vortex (where the pressure drop is as much as 10 per cent) and by its powerful whirling winds (estimated at up to 500 miles per hour). The amount of damage depends mainly on whether the storm happens to hit populated areas. The worst tornado on record in the U.S. was one that ripped across Missouri, lower Illinois and Indiana in three hours on March 18, 1925, and killed 689 people.

The tornado's lifetime is as brief as it is violent. Within a few tens of miles (average: about 16 miles) it spends its force and suddenly disappears.

Morris Tepper
"Tornadoes"

Frequently writers will define a word or term by a direct statement of the meaning followed by explanatory material, including examples to make its meaning clearer. The writers of the next model definition begin by defining the word *conformity*. They then present negative connotations using Hollywood as an example. They follow with an explanation showing that a society of nonconformists "is a contradiction in terms."

▶ **Conformity** can be defined as a change in a person's opinions or behavior as a result of real or imagined pressure from another person or a group. In common parlance, conformity usually has some negative connotations; to be called a conformist is to be called weak, a follower, a person who cannot or will not think for himself. This connotation is bolstered by the mass media; Hollywood, for example, consistently makes heroes of the nonconformist — the dashing figure who goes his own way in spite of tremendous group pressure. And yet, a moment's reflection should make it perfectly clear that if there is to be a society at all, there *must* be a significant degree of conformity to the laws and customs of that society. A society of nonconformists is a contradiction in terms. Conformity in certain cases may be weakness, but without a basic, underlying, and willing conformity to sensible laws and values, we would have chaos. There would not be enough policemen to protect us from the looters and the rapists; we could not trust our best friends. There are those who complain of the lack of law and order, but there is an interesting question on the other side too. Why is there any law and order in the first place?

Paul Mussen and Mark R. Rosenzweig *et al.*
*Psychology: An Introduction*

The writers' flow of thought in the above paragraph is from the generalization — the definition — through the particulars that further explain the meaning.

In the following model definition, Rachel Carson defines two kinds of tides — *spring tides* and *neap tides* — with a variety of methods. She begins with an explanation of the moon's action in causing tides. She then defines *spring tides* by explaining their nature and their etymology (origin or derivation of the word). "Spring tides" come from the Saxon *sprungen*, and "neaps" from the Scandinavian roots meaning "barely touching" or "hardly enough." In addition, she contrasts the strong, active movement of the "spring tides" with the sluggish "neaps."

▶ All through the lunar month, as the moon waxes and wanes, so the moon-drawn tides increase or decline in strength and the lines of high and low water shift from day to day. After the full moon, and again after the new moon, the forces acting on the sea to produce the tide are stronger than at any other time during the month. This is because the sun and moon then are directly in line with the earth and their attractive forces are added together. For complex astronomical reasons, the greatest tidal effect is exerted over a period of several days immediately after the full and the new moon, rather than at a time precisely coinciding with these lunar phases. During these periods the flood tides rise higher and the ebb tides fall lower than at any other time. These are called the "spring tides" from the Saxon "sprungen." The word refers not to a season, but to the brimming fullness of the water causing it to "spring" in the sense of a strong, active movement. No one who has watched a new-moon tide pressing against a rocky cliff will doubt the appropriateness of the term. In its quarterphases, the moon exerts its attraction at right angles to the pull of the sun so the two forces interfere with each other and the tidal movements are slack. Then the water neither rises as high nor falls as low as on the spring tides. These sluggish tides are called the "neaps" — a word that goes back to old Scandinavian roots meaning "barely touching" or "hardly enough."

Rachel Carson
*The Edge of the Sea*

Read the interesting model paragraph that follows in which the writer explains the origin of the expression *Jim Crow*.

▶ Thomas D. ("Daddy") Rice, a white entertainer, began around 1828 to employ a vaudeville sketch in which he blacked his face with burnt cork and sang a ditty that acquired the title, "Wheel About and Turn About and Jump, Jim Crow." Thus was born what later became the immensely popular minstrel shows, a burlesque by whites of black songs and speech mannerisms. The phrase "Jim Crow" from Rice's song soon came to be a slang expression for blacks and later for laws and practices that segregated blacks from whites.

James Q. Wilson
*American Government*

In addition to organization and development by the various methods with which you are already familiar — comparison, contrast, classification, process, cause and effect, and analogy — writers also develop definitions by presenting (1) the historical meanings, (2) the etymology (as seen in the Rachel Carson model), and (3) the negative meaning of a word or term. The following model stresses the historical and etymological roots of the word *personality*.

> ▶ Historically, the term *personality* has many meanings, ranging from the popular phrase "she has personality" to the profound theological usage found in the expression "personality of God" as expounded in the doctrine of the Trinity. Personality, thus, has come to have a great variety of connotations. When we examine the word etymologically we see that our confusion is only increased; for the Latin word *persona*, from which our term personality comes, as it has been translated into various languages, may signify nobody or no one when used with a verb in the French language, or it may mean a representative of a great body, as *parson* in English. These varieties of usage only emphasize the fact that personality is a generic term which has no specific meaning, universally accepted. Even animals are referred to as "having personality"; here the connotation is characteristic individuality.
>
> Of writers on the subject of personality, Allport (1937) has done the most adequate and comprehensive job of reviewing the historical meanings derived from the Latin *persona*. He distinguished fifty different definitions or meanings. Yet, as MacKinnon (1944) has pointed out, two opposed meanings stand out from the earliest to the latest of these definitions. On the one hand, personality is thought of as a mask, a mere shield of outward and usually superficial appearance; on the other hand, it is conceived as the inner nature, the substance of a man.
>
> Robert H. Dalton
> *Personality and Social Interactions*

The writer begins by showing the historical meaning of the word *personality*. From this analysis he arrives at the conclusion that the word "has come to have a great variety of connotations." He points out that an etymological examination of the word will only add to the confusion. Next, he mentions the fifty different definitions of the word accumulated by Allport. Finally, he states the two opposing definitions.

In defining, writers will frequently say what the word or term is not; then they will follow with the definition. Study the model that follows. Krutch defines "Lower Sonoran Desert" by telling his reader what it is not; then he describes what it is.

▶ "Desert" is an unfortunate word all around and most of its usual associations are inaccurate as well as unfavorable. In the first place the word doesn't even mean "dry," but simply uninhabited or deserted — like Robinson Crusoe's island. In that sense, the expanse about me is far from being a desert, for it is teeming with live things very glad indeed to be right there. Even in its secondary meaning, "desert," suggests to most people the rolling sand dunes of the Sahara. Something like that one may find in Death Valley; perhaps in parts of the Mojave; and especially, with an added weirdness, in the hundreds of square miles of New Mexico's White Sands, where the great dunes of glistening gypsum drift like snowbanks, one can hardly believe they are not. Most of my Lower Sonoran Desert, however, is not at all like that. The sandy soil is firm and hardpacked; it supports life, less crowded than in wetter regions but pleasantly flourishing. Nature does not frown here. She smiles invitingly.

Joseph Wood Krutch
*The Desert Year*

Complete Exercises 5 and 6 to review the different methods of definition.

## EXERCISE 5    Definition

Read the model paragraph unit below. Answer the questions that follow it. Answers are at the end of the Chapter.

▶ The concept of the frontier as a factor in history was developed in the United States and has been applied primarily to American history. Though the word appears in similar form in nearly all European languages, it has a meaning and a set of connotations in the United States entirely different from those which obtain elsewhere. As used in Europe, it means the boundary between two nations and it is represented on the map by a thin line. That line is one to approach with caution, equipped with passports and permits. It is a place to stop at or to pass at national peril — "the sharp edge of sovereignty."

In America the word frontier is hardly used to indicated the nation's limits. No American would refer to the line separating the United States from Canada or from Mexico as a "frontier." The American concept holds that the frontier lies *within*, and not at the edge of the country — not a line to stop at, but an area inviting entrance. In Europe the frontier is stationary and permanent; in America it was (note the past tense) transient and temporal. It is this American idea which we shall be concerned with, and which we shall apply to the enormous region that may be called the Great Frontier.

Walter Prescott Webb
"Ended: 400 Year Boom"

1. Where was the concept of the word *frontier* developed?

2. By what method is the word mainly defined?

3. By what method of contrast does the writer show the differences between the meaning of the word in Europe and in the United States?

4. What are some differences in the use of the word?

## EXERCISE 6    **Definition**

Read the short excerpt below. Answer the questions that follow it.

▶ What is prejudice? Its characteristics and origins have by now been carefully studied by psychologists and sociologists so that today we know a good deal about how it is transmitted from one person to another.

Prejudice is a false generalization about a group of people — or things — which is held onto despite all facts to the contrary. Some generalizations, of course, are true and useful — often needed to put people and things into categories. The statement that Negroes have darkly pigmented skin and nearly always curly hair, isn't a prejudice but a correct generalization about Negroes.

Ignorance isn't the same as prejudice, either. Many people believe that Negroes are basically less intelligent than white people because they've heard this and never have been told otherwise. These people would be prejudiced only if they persisted in this belief after they knew the facts! Well-documented studies show that when Negroes and whites are properly matched in comparable groups, they have the same intelligence.

Prejudiced thinking is rarely, probably never, confined to any one subject. Those prejudiced against one group of people are nearly always prejudiced against others. Prejudice, then, could be said to be a disorder of thinking: a prejudiced person makes faulty generalizations by applying to a whole group what he has learned from one or a few of its members. Sometimes, he doesn't even draw on his own experiences but bases his attitudes on what he has heard from others. Then he behaves toward a whole group as if there were no individual differences among its members. Few people would throw out a whole box of strawberries because they found one or two bad berries at the top — yet this is the way prejudiced people think and act.

Ian Stevenson, M.D.
"People Aren't Born Prejudiced"

1. How does the writer begin his definition?

2. How many paragraphs make up this short piece of writing?

3. What is the function of paragraphs 2 and 3?

4. In what paragraph does the writer actually define *prejudice*?

5. What is the writer's definition of the word?

6. With what kind of material does the writer make clear the meaning of the word?

Before writing your own definition paper, study the model essay that follows, paying particular attention to the various methods of development that the writer uses in defining the word *socialism*.

▶ SOCIALISM IN ECONOMIC TERMS

**Peter M. Jones**

*Introduction*

*Developed by:*
*Analogy*

*Contrast*

**Parable of the Isms:** *

**Communism:** *If you have two cows, you give them to the government and then the government gives you some milk.*

**Capitalism:** *If you have two cows, you sell one and buy a bull.*

**Socialism:** *If you have two cows, you give one to your neighbor.*

— Anonymous

*Analysis*

Though obviously oversimplified, that statement provides a neat little comparison of major economic systems. And most Americans would probably agree with the first two definitions.

*Use of guide phrase*

All systems that identify themselves as Communist, *for example*, do enforce strict controls over people's freedoms, particularly over economic freedom.

*Contrast*

Capitalism, *on the other hand*, is seen by most Americans as a system under which the individual is free to do what he or she wants with his or her property. Part of that freedom is the opportunity to increase one's wealth as, in this case, by breeding more cattle.

*Topic sentence*

*But the one "ism" definition that many Americans might disagree with is the image of socialism as a benign and sharing kind of economic system.* In a way that mystifies millions of people in other nations, a great many Americans have almost always equated socialism with dictatorship. At best, many people view

*Analysis of the misconceptions of*
*the word*

---

* *The American Treasury* 1455–1955, Harper and Row, 1955.

socialism as an economic system that denies opportunity, stifles innovation and tries to bring everyone down to the same level. At its worst, they view it as taking on the character of brutal Communist regimes.

What seems especially puzzling to socialists in other nations, however, is the fact that while socialism is rejected in the U.S., many elements of socialist economics are already part of American life and are accepted and even demanded by American citizens.

*Thesis statement: question-to-answer development*

*But what, exactly, is socialism? Who believes in it? Where did it come from?*

*Use of comparison*

Socialism, like any other economic system, is one approach to using natural resources and human talent — the bases of wealth — to produce goods and services for people. *Socialism differs from capi-*

*Statement of contrast*

*talism* in that it uses central planning and government intervention to determine how the available natural resources and human talent should best be used.

*Statement that the writer will provide historical background*

*Socialism as an economic and social philosophy had its origins near the end of the 18th century.* Coming from an English movement of thought and belief called the Enlightenment, from the ideas of the American Revolution, and later the French Revolution, the idea spread that each person has *natural rights* — rights that government cannot violate. These included the belief that government should not control the economic system in a society. (See "Capitalism — Out of Date?" SENIOR, Mar. 6, '81.)

*Origin of the word*

*Development by causes and effects*

*Around the same time, as a result of various inventions and developments,* large industries capable of mass-producing goods appeared. This was the beginning of the Industrial Revolution, as it is now called. And that revolution brought enormous exploitation of natural resources and of human resources, particularly in

England. Smoky factories and ugly mines scarred the land. And men, women, and children labored long hours, under dreadful conditions, for very low wages in those factories and mines.

*More causes and effects*

*The appalling conditions under which most people worked and lived in the early industrial age produced a reaction* — a competing idea — *to the belief that government should not interfere in economics and that industrialists were free to run their businesses as they saw fit.* The competing idea was socialism.

*Discussion of the origin of socialism*

A number of individuals, who were distressed by the exploitation of workers by the owners of industries, proposed a new kind of society — a society "based on association, harmony, and altruism." And, according to American sociologist Daniel Bell, the idea caught on.

*Explanation of the word as used at that time*

*"By 1840, the term* socialism *was commonly used throughout Europe,"* says Bell. *What the socialists meant,* what they wanted to create, was an economic system in which major industries — mines, factories, etc. — should not be owned by private individuals for their own profit. Rather, these were to be owned by the people as a whole and run for the benefit of all.

*Changing meaning of the word*

This idea spread to virtually every corner of the globe. *And in the process it was changed and modified to suit various local conditions.* Today, there are socialist governments or socialists in government in countries as wildly different from each other as Iceland and Tanzania, or Cuba and Israel.

*Discussion of the spread of socialism*

"Rarely in the history of the world has an idea taken hold so deeply and dispersed so quickly," writes Bell. "One would have to go back to the spread of Islam, in the century and a half following the death of Muhammad, to find a comparable phenomenon."

One result of that spread to all parts of the world is that socialists in one country may have different ideas about economics and government than socialists in other parts of the world. And the reason for that, of course, is the difference in their histories, cultures, populations, access to natural resources, or various other factors. *Socialists, in other words, like Christians in different parts of the world,* do not believe exactly the same things or behave in exactly the same ways.

In Western Europe and Israel, for example, socialists compete in free elections to win seats in their governments. Personal liberties, including freedom of press and religion, are deeply rooted in those systems. And the role of government in the economy is open to parliamentary debate the same as anything else. The Socialist International, an organization of socialist parties, bans membership to any socialist party which does not permit other political parties to participate in their government.

*However, not all socialists are democratic.* The governments of such countries as Cuba and the Soviet Union advocate socialism as an economic system but they are a long way from permitting the personal freedom and personal parties advocated by the Socialist International.

*But if socialists differ so much among themselves, what do they agree on?*

Whether or not they practice what they preach, socialists everywhere hold certain economic ideas in common:

(1) *Government ownership of productive resources.* This means a government take-over of such things as steel plants, mines, and railroads. *In recent years, however,* many socialists have edged away from outright seizure of these industries. Rather, they now seek greater worker control over the various industries.

*[Margin notes:]*

*Comparison*

*Use of an example to develop main idea*

*Statement of contrast*

*Development by examples*

*Question introducing a new phase of the discussion: an analysis of what socialists agree on*

*Use of figures to help reader understand the nature of socialism*

*Contrast*

(2) *Planning.* Instead of letting industry rise or fall according to the demands of the marketplace (what consumers will buy), special committees will decide what and how much is to be produced by the nation's industries according to the needs of the society.

(3) *Redistribution of income.* The goal here is to reduce the gap between the rich and poor. Among the ways to do this: limiting the amount of money people can inherit and the leveling of stiff taxes on high incomes. Income taxes, plus money earned from the state-run industry, is expected to pay for such things as free medical care and education, social security, old age pensions and decent housing for all.

Of course, just as socialist countries differ in their political systems, *they also differ in the degree to which they apply their socialist ideas to economics.* In Sweden, which many Americans see as the ultimate democratic socialist state, more than 90 percent of the industry — including Volvo automobile manufacturing — is in private hands. In France, a nation viewed as predominantly capitalist, the Renault automobile company is government-owned.

In Tanzania, where industry is government-owned, the country is so poor that people do not have access to government-supplied health, education, and welfare programs that are taken for granted in many capitalist countries.

*Even in wealthy socialist nations with deep traditions of democracy, life is not endless bliss.* In the Scandinavian countries, for example, where living standards are high, people have learned that government benefits are far from free. It is not at all unusual for an average citizen of one of those countries to pay 50 percent of his or her income in taxes.

*Critics of socialism argue that this* type

*Statement of contrast*

*Use of examples*

*Statement of a new phase of the discussion: disadvantages of socialism*

*Use of an example*

*Additional criticism*

of taxation is an invasion of personal liberty. They also say that socialist governments, no matter how democratic, can be costly, inefficient, wasteful and unnecessarily interfering with people's lives.

*Refutation of those claims by the backers of socialism*

*Backers of socialism contend that without socialist ideas,* there would be few attempts in industrialized nations to protect and support the sick, the old, and the powerless, and that enormous gaps would exist between rich and poor.

*Change in the writer's flow of thought indicated by the guide word* however *followed by the conclusion*

In the end, *however*, there is no such thing as a totally socialist system, just as there is no totally capitalist system. Like life itself, economic systems in all countries are a mix — no matter who owns the cows.

## Suggested Topics for Writing Simple Definition

Define one of the following words:

assassin
precocious
adversity
prestidigitation
clairvoyant

## Suggested Topics for Writing an Extended Definition

| | | |
|---|---|---|
| myth | ivory tower | husbandry |
| coup d'état | sportsmanship | manners |
| Common Market | colonialism | etiquette |
| cartel | chivalry | customers |
| habeas corpus | totem pole | ownership |
| delinquency | climate | ruthlessness |
| friendship | combustion | school spirit |
| integrity | parity | courage |

## Combining

In the preceding pages of this book, we have discussed separately the various patterns of developing thought. Most writers, however, combine the different patterns and shade them so smoothly one into another that the reader is seldom aware of the form that dominates. Thus, combining or using more than one method to develop your flowing thought is the most common pattern of written expression.

You have probably also discovered this to be true in your own writing. You realize now that a writer's purpose is the main determiner of the form that will dominate. But you know also that the kind of material will determine the kind of development as your thought progresses to the end of the paper. You may have written a paper to explain the causes of juvenile crime in your town or city. But in the process of fulfilling that purpose — to explain the causes of juvenile crime — you may have developed thought by definition, classification, and narration because the material lent itself to that particular kind of development. You defined the term *juvenile crime* at the beginning of the paper so that the reader would understand how you were using the term. You broke down crimes by juveniles into types in order to give order and meaning to a number of crimes committed by juveniles. Finally, you told some stories of crimes by juveniles to hold reader interest and illustrate your purpose.

The model essays that follow are examples of development by a variety of methods. But they are worth your time and study for a number of other more important reasons. They are, of course, structurally interesting and can become valuable models for your own themes. They illustrate also the variety of subjects that can become essay material if properly handled. But above all, they are interesting, informative, and enjoyable reading, which is the purpose of good exposition. They prove the point that expository writing need not be dull and uninteresting.

The first model essay, "New York: Revisit to a Shady Lady," is mainly a narrative with considerable description and some contrast. The writer tells of revisiting New York City after an absence of several years. As he walks about the city, he describes the places, the people, and the changes that he sees. On the surface, then, the essay appears to be a somewhat interesting account of the writer's return to that famous city. But the writer's informal style, his comparing the city to a "shady lady," careful selection of memorable incidents, and his delightful humor make reading the essay an enjoyable as well as an informative experience.

▶ NEW YORK: REVISIT TO A SHADY LADY
**Don G. Campbell**

[1]NEW YORK — Coming back to New York City, where you have once lived and worked, after an interval of several years, is a little like making an assignation with a lover you haven't seen in a decade.

[2]There's the dread that the two of you have grown so far apart, that you'll end up spending the afternoon in the lobby of the Algonquin exchanging snapshots of the kiddies.

Not to fear. What outsiders always forget is that New York City never really changes — face lift after face lift she's the same pouty, surly sexpot who drove you up the wall, and out of her life, many years ago.

**Blank-Faced Lemmings.**   Nothing really changes. She's still a city populated by blank-faced lemmings with a psychotic fear of finding themselves with nothing to eat. Thus, there is always the comfort of knowing that if you should topple over from hunger you will, of course, fall into the entrance of a restaurant or — should you fall short of the entrance — there'll be a sidewalk hot dog, pistachio nut or Sno-Cone vendor at your elbow for emergency treatment.

Eat. Eat. Eat. Walk. Walk. Walk. After a couple of years in Los Angeles it is interesting to rediscover your legs and recall that they have other functions besides pumping an Exercycle.

And, both then and now, the conviction remains that Manhattanites walk as much as they do not because they enjoy the exercise, but because they are perennially lost, thanks to a street-numbering system that, in the 18th Century, was drawn out of a Bingo bowl.

**A Mile and a Half.**   If the Chrysler Building is at 330 Lexington, and the address you want is 710 Lexington, then it follows that it should be an easy four-block walk, right? Try a mile and a half instead, which puts 710 Lexington on a direct line with the 1300 block of Third Avenue, just a block to the east. Looking for 310 Madison Ave.? Try looking for it on 42nd Street, a good half block west of Madison. There is no 310 Madison Avenue — not even a side entrance to the 42nd Street address.

Walk. Walk. Walk. And figure on a good third of it being in the middle of the street because of construction barricades. Once sufficient grime accumulates on the windows of mid-Manhattan buildings, they are automatically earmarked for demolition — to be replaced by even taller ones with even more glass to get dirty.

On 42nd Street, between Lexington and Grand Central, the once elegant old Commodore Hotel has been disemboweled and replaced by the new Grand Hyatt, all bespangled and bejeweled with doormen in gray frock coats and matching top hats. It's all very Grand, indeed, but there's a twinge of nostal-

gia for the down-at-the-heels Commodore where you had to lift
your feet cautiously to avoid getting snagged in a lobby carpet
that had more holes in it than the street outside had potholes.

And mourn the loss at the "Gentlemen Only" massage par-
lor that, in its final days, was such a delightful incongruity
behind the fluted and graceful columns of the mezzanine. And
where are the hookers who lounged under the rubber plants
around the outskirts of the lobby and, in deference to the Commodore's one-time grandeur, merely chewed — without pop-
ping — their bubble gum?

**Swank Newcomer.**   And, a half block away, abutting the
Daily News Building, an equally swank newcomer to the hotel
scene, the new Harley Hotel, is scheduled to open soon. It's
more dignified but promises to be a far duller neighbor for the
News than the previous tenant: the Central Commercial High
School, fondly known to News staffers as "The Wharton
School of Mugging," graduation from which — so went the
story — was dependent on the student's demonstrated ability
to penetrate the News' security system (not too great a feat in
itself — a publicity agent once sneaked a baby elephant up to
the newsroom without detection), disassemble a Linotype machine and then reassemble it in front of his Advanced Filching
class.

You have to be a little saddened by the upgrading of the
neighborhood, in a way. Will it mean the end of episodes like
the annual Santa Claus visitation in the lobby of the News
Building in 1973 when one of the little tykes passing across
Santa's lap managed to lift the kindly gentleman's wallet without getting caught? (It was the same week, in a department
store several blocks removed, that two proud fathers, their
children in tow, got into a scuffle over their place in Santa's
line that ended with one knifing the other to death.) Where else
but New York?

Where else such a seemingly endless supply of warped
characters acting out their fantasies with such a flair? Such as
the mustached and dignified foreign diplomat type — bundled
against the cold — who was quietly sipping his drink in a 1st
Avenue tavern, two blocks up from the UN one clear, winter
day. After paying his bill, the gentleman rose from his bar
stool, smile benignly at the bartender and said, "I have something for you."

And then solemnly reached into the breast of his expensive
overcoat, extracted a full-grown cat, dropped it gently over the
bar at the startled bartender's feet and quietly walked out.

"I think he likes you," another patron noted as the frenzied cat raced in circles around the bartender's feet.

Where else would you find the well-dressed, elderly gentleman who is wont to carry on deep, philosophical discussions with the lamppost at the corner of Lexington and 5th? Or the haughty lady who, one day, stared studiously at the Sperry and Hutchinson Building at Madison and 42nd and then walked purposefully over to it and planted a resounding kick on its cornerstone? Frustration at some past S&H Green Stamp injustice?

Or there were the two matronly and elegantly dressed suburban types who stepped out of an East Side tearoom one rainy afternoon only to watch in dismay as the only available cab on the street was successfully hailed by a harassed young mother struggling with a preschooler and a babe-in-arms. And then watched in apparent sympathy as the young mother, having got the cab door open, was frustrated when the baby dropped her doll into the gutter.

*A Kick in the Gutter.*   Helpfully, one of the fur-clad matrons stepped over to the dropped doll — just out of the mother's reach, and gave it a resounding kick 10 feet farther down the gutter. At which point, their social chatter never having missed a beat, the two ladies climbed into the cab and sped off, leaving the young mother racing down the gutter for the doll.

You live in New York, day after day — and shoulder-to-shoulder — with people who can, alternately, be the most charming and helpful mortals this side of an old Barry Fitzgerald movie, or the most sullen predators since Alaric sacked Rome.

There is the mystery of living, for almost two years, next door to an apartment that is obviously rented to someone but which remains devoid of all furnishings. And devoid of any tenants, too, except that occasionally through the adjoining wall there is the 2 A.M. sound of a viola being played softly and beautifully. But by daybreak the apartment is once again empty.

There are the mysteries of New York City apartment living, and then there is also the haunting feeling that you are being held captive by the jolliest crew that ever terrorized the Spanish Main. Where you shake hands with your doorman in a horizontal, rather than vertical, grip because his palm, of course, is frozen in an upright position.

And, before Christmas, receipt of the standard mimeographed greeting card that is designed to chill you to the bone: "Merry Christmas from Your Apartment Staff," with a meticulous, name-by-name listing of all those faceless people who — when it suits their fancy — come up and kick your plumbing for you.

***Second Notice.***  There is the apocryphal story of the tenant who received his usual staff Christmas card, absent-mindedly shoved it into his pocket, and proceeded to forget about it.

Until, a few days before Christmas, another envelope surfaced in his mailbox: "Merry Christmas from Your Apartment Staff, Second Notice."

Greedy, pushy, self-centered, uncaring, snobbish, bigoted and vicious. All come easily to mind as you lie, 3,000 miles away, on a California beach, soaking up the sun and recalling that it's been weeks since anyone blatantly demanded a tip from you — longer than that since a cab has deliberately swerved three feet out of the line of traffic to splatter you with mud. New York? Who needs it?

But then you fly back to her, and, sure enough, she's had another face lift but she's leaning against the same old lamppost with the same short skirt slit seductively up on her hips and the sultry, come-hither smile is as dazzling as ever.

And never mind that the polish doesn't quite cover the dirt under the nails.

Read the next essay; then study the annotations that accompany it.

▶ Holding Court for Canines
**Susan K. Fletcher**

| | |
|---|---|
| *Introduction: paragraphs 1–3* | [1]Until a run-in with a mail carrier, "Roman" seemed a well-adjusted family member. "Sasha" wound up on probation after standing trial for night howling. "Brucie" was arrested for hunting sheep out of season. |
| *Interest getter* | |
| *Thesis statement* | [2]Roman, Sasha, and Brucie are canine criminals, a breed apart from your everyday mugger or thief. *Yet dogs are increasingly likely to go through the same legal system as their human owners, complete with arrests and witnesses,* |

*courtrooms and lawyers, convictions and sentences.*

[3]"We'd like people to settle their dog problems out of court in a neighborly way," says Portland, Oregon, District Court Judge Joseph Ceniceros. "But often they're like the Hatfields and the McCoys, so we have to step in." So often, in fact, are canine issues appearing that Portland justices devote two days each month to doggie delinquents. Honolulu officials covertly compile tape-recorded evidence of illegal barking. The Santa Barbara, California, city attorney's office offers professional mediation to help resolve dog-related disputes, and New York City has at least one lawyer who specializes in canine law.

[4]If the prospect of eminent court justices weightily deliberating Fido's fate seems ludicrous, *consider the magnitude of the problem.* Humane Society statistics put the number of dogs and cats in the United States at 70 to 110 million; they have a birth rate of 2,000 to 3,500 animals per hour. In some urban areas the dog density reaches Malthusian proportions; Baltimore once claimed 450 strays per square mile. Dogs bite more than a million people each year nationwide. In New York City dogs deposit more than 125 tons of embarrassment on private lawns, public parks, and sidewalks daily.

[5]The result has been an unmistakable trend to put the legal bite on disobedient dogs and their owners — and in the process to create more clamor than a bulldog in a china shop.

[6]*Dog "doo" debates threaten the peace of even the most complacent neighborhoods, and animal-control officers are frequently the objects of guerrillalike attacks.* Threats were made on the life of an Oklahoma dog catcher. In Seattle a lone doggie defender struck, throwing an

*Topic sentence: first phase of discussion, the magnitude of the problem*

*Causes*

*Effect*

*Cause*

*Effect*

animal-control officer to the ground and urging a leashless dog and its owner to flee (they did).

Another phase: confrontations

[7]*"It's like the confrontation we used to have in the Old West between the ranchers and the farmers,"* says Oregon's Ceniceros, who has presided over numerous dog-court sessions in Multnomah County. "Even when people move out to the rural areas, they have to leash or pen their dogs. They resent it a lot. Usually the neighbors only complain after a dog has really crossed the line — and then everybody's up in arms against the owner."

Example

[8]*Confrontations occur in room 120 of Multnomah County Courthouse every second Tuesday and third Thursday of the month.* The day begins with ceremonious dignity as all rise for the judge, and the first witnesses are sworn in. After that anything can happen. Some days 50 to 100 dog owners appear for arraignments. On other occasions a single trial lasts all day, complete with high-powered lawyers and as many as a dozen witnesses.

Transition to courtroom

Discussion of procedures in court: paragraphs 8–11

[9]*The atmosphere is contentious,* to say the least. According to Mike Oswald, chief field supervisor for the county's animal-control department, the courtroom ambience has all the decorum of a professional wrestling match. "There's a rowdy crowd that's really got its hackles up," he says. "Only here the attacks are personal; it's character assassination. One guy accuses his neighbor of not being married to the woman he's living with, that sort of thing."

Further discussion of confrontations

Examples

[10]*Judges often put up with disorderly conduct because it's a safe way for people to vent their frustrations.* But they won't put up with dogs in the courtroom — not since one judge allowed an elderly woman to bring her pet so he could see for himself

whether it was vicious. After only a few minutes in court, the dog was ordered destroyed or removed from the county. It had tried to bite the judge.

[11]*Even with the dogs absent, animal court poses particularly difficult dilemmas for judges.* Ceniceros explains:

*Judge's views*

"When you have half the neighborhood in court, and you know that they're taking the day off work and probably losing money, there is pressure. You feel the tension in these people. And you feel, 'If I don't do something, they're going to take the law into their own hands.'

"You don't want to issue a decision that's going to leave a lasting scar. So, except in vicious-dog cases, I tell them, 'This is your neighborhood. I want you to be able to go there and relax. I want your neighbor to relax. I'm going to put your dog on probation now, and if it happens again, we're not going to have another trial. A neighbor will come tell me what he saw. If I believe him, I'm going to order your dog impounded.' With that approach, I haven't had many cases come back," concludes the judge.

*New phase of discussion: community approach*

[12]*The canine crises seem to require a nontraditional approach* — both in and out of the courtroom. Some communities have come up with surprisingly resourceful ways of coping with *four principal canine crimes: barking, running loose, "littering," and biting.*

*Analysis by structure*

*(1) Nocturnal barking*

[13]*While nocturnal yapping* may not be one of the more lurid crimes, it can play havoc with a neighborhood. There's always the problem of evidence — proving that this particular dog was barking in that particular place at such and such an hour.

*Discussion of (1)*

[14]Honolulu has a "barking dog" ordinance with teeth in it. Canines may legally yap for 10 minutes steadily or for a half-hour intermittently. That's it. The Humane Society has seven roving animal-

*Enforcement of ordinance*

control officers on call to enforce the ordinance. Seconds after headquarters receives a complaint, a dispatcher radios one of the officers. Equipped with tape recorders, citations, and the authority to use them, the officer shows up at the scene of the crime prepared to nab the wayward barker and prove the state's case in court.

*Discussion of (2)*

[15]*The running-loose category includes everything* from strays and dogs not contained by their owners to hardened motorcycle chasers or garbage-can diggers. Solutions to the problem of stray animals run the gamut and are often controversial. According to a *New York Times*

*Examples*

article, in an Indiana town police were authorized to shoot strays when the dog population became unmanageable. Another article told of the plight of an Oklahoma city where the mayor ordered the pound emptied of its residents when the city was faced with making extensive repairs to the pound to satisfy health standards.

*Leash laws*

[16]In most parts of the country there's a *definite trend toward more leash laws*, stiffer fines, and stricter enforcement. Increasingly, citizens are finding themselves in serious trouble when they ignore a "doggie at large" rap. Ceniceros recalls:

"We had a quite a to-do here when a lot of socially prominent matrons were given

*Enforcement of law*

animal-control citations to come to court on a certain day and they weren't doing it. So the judge in charge issued bench warrants for their arrest."

Says Cheri Ruiz, the animal-control officer who served the warrants: "Imagine a bunch of impeccably coiffed matrons in designer clothing, frantically calling everyone in the neighborhood to scrape up bail. They came up short, so we hauled them downtown and had them booked and locked up."

*Discussion of (3)*

[17]*Perhaps the most widely publicized as-*

pect of leather-collar crime is the litter problem — a euphemism if ever there was one. When New York City's infamous "pooper scooper" law went into effect in August, 1978, some metropolitan newspapers made a bigger to-do about dog doo than about current events in the Middle East.

[18]Apparently the law is working. Observers contend that New York's sidewalks and parks are a lot less treacherous these days. Still, enforcing the law isn't easy; last year the city raised the $25 fine to $50 and installed a computer system to track down frequent offenders.

*Enforcement of law*

[19]According to Dr. Alan Beck, director of the Center for the Interaction of Animals and Society, other canine-waste laws have been passed in Los Angeles, Minneapolis, Phoenix, Denver, Washington, D.C., and numerous small communities. "Scoop laws are all the vogue," says Beck.

*Examples of other cities with canine-waste laws*

[20]*While all areas of canine crime may stir up wild controversy, the vicious-dog problem is deadly serious.* Some experts call it an unrecognized epidemic — a far greater threat to life and health then the much publicized litter situation. As Beck puts it, "We've been focusing on the wrong end of the dog."

*Discussion of (4)*

*Seriousness of the vicious dogs*

[21]The end of the dog in question causes $100 million a year in medical expenses when it comes in contact with humans. More than half the victims are children.

*Cause and effect*

[22]For mail carriers, the classic butts of dog-bite jokes, the situation gets less funny every year. They can only fight back by refusing to deliver, but the courts have begun to retaliate more forcibly against owners. In the past most states operated under the theory that a dog owner was not to blame for the first bite inflicted; the pet got one free. Under new stricter laws that first bite could cost thousands in victim compensation. The

*Discussion of the dog that bites*

key is the owner's prior knowledge of the pet's vicious tendencies. Posting a "Beware of Dog" sign or even keeping the dog chained can constitute evidence that the owner knows the dog is vicious — even if the animal has never bitten before.

*Enforcement of the law*

[23]What's more, many judges go beyond levying fines or assessing damages when a dog bites. "I will probably get rid of the animal right away if it is truly vicious," says Ceniceros. "The great fear is if you don't do something, the dog will hurt or kill a child."

*Conclusion: recommended action*

[24]In the future the law may clamp down even harder. Some groups favor banning dogs from cities altogether; others recommend the European custom of training dogs to use toilets. But Lesley Agard of the Hawaiian Humane Society advocates licensing owners instead of pets. "There are no canine crimes — just human crimes," she says, *"We need to train people to be responsible pet owners."*

Read the following essay. Be prepared to answer questions on its organization and development.

▶ GUIDING LIGHTS

**Elizabeth Pierce**

[1]Julius Caesar took time out from his pursuit of Cleopatra to admire the view. So did soldiers from Carthage and sailors from Sicily. The gleaming lighthouse on the island of Pharos in the harbor of Alexandria was lit some 2,000 years ago, and for more than 500 years beckoned sightseers as one of the Seven Wonders of the World. The lighthouse, which was destroyed by an earthquake in the Thirteenth Century, remains a lodestone for legend.

[2]The coastal beacons of North America, like their ancient ancestors, have sparked the imaginations of many. Long the subjects of legends and prose, lighthouses today stand as mementos of the country's seafaring past.

[3]Boston Light, the first beacon tower in the American colonies, was erected in 1716 on a spit of land outside Boston

Harbor. Within two years a violent storm swept over the island and the lighthouse keeper, his wife, and daughter were all lost in the pounding sea. A local lad was moved to write a ballad about the incident. "The Lighthouse Tragedy" was set in type and peddled on street corners at a penny a copy by its creator, 13-year-old Ben Franklin. From that time on, lighthouse legends have become practically an American art form.

[4]The original Boston Light was destroyed by British sailors in the final weeks of the American Revolution, but its replacement, erected in 1783, still stands. The 90-foot tower, the oldest functioning lighthouse in the United States, is clearly visible — day and night — not only to mariners but also to planes flying in and out of Logan Airport. The light has shone almost continuously for nearly two centuries (the only significant interruption occurred during World War II when the light was extinguished for security reasons).

[5]The New England coastline has a slight edge as a lighthouse legend maker. New England settlers were among the first to foresee the maritime destiny of their new land, and the jagged rim of the shores made navigational aids a must. By the close of the Eighteenth Century, there were lights shining at Plymouth, Gloucester, Cape Ann, Natucket, Martha's Vineyard, Newburyport, and Bakers Island in Massachusetts; Portsmouth in New Hampshire; Portland and Seguin Island in Maine; Beavertail in Rhode Island; and New London in Connecticut. Some of these storm-buffeted oldtimers, built when American sailing vessels were first beginning to make their presence felt in the trading centers of the world, are still standing.

[6]The big boom in lighthouse building on the southern coast, including Chesapeake Bay and the Gulf of Mexico, came during Andrew Jackson's presidency. The strong beams from the Fresnel lens (capable of concentrating fragile oil fires into powerful beams) were visible for many miles at sea, guiding clipper ships on their way south. The light at South Pass at the entrance to the Mississippi River southeast of New Orleans greeted ships from Europe and the West Indies bound for the Mississippi River. The original 1851 light was replaced in 1881 by a 105-foot iron-skeleton tower, typical of Gulf Coast lights. These derrick light structures can be seen all along the Gulf Coast from Florida to Texas.

[7]When the 1849 gold strike in California enticed a rush of sailing ships to the ports of the Pacific, the continental circle of lights was complete.

[8]The modern lighthouse era began in 1939 when President Franklin Roosevelt brought an end to the old civilian light-

house service and transferred all the navigational aids in U.S. territorial waters to the jurisdiction of the Coast Guard. This move, and the turn to automated lighthouses, marked an end — with a few exceptions — to the time-honored tradition of family lighthouse stations.

[9]But the darkening and dismantling of many of the old lights also brought a heartening development for lighthouse buffs. In response to the growing public interest in the seaside sentinels, many lights on the Coast Guard's "Seacoast List of Lights" now have visiting hours. Others on the retired list now are maintained by local historical societies as museums. A number have been completely refurbished.

[10]One of the first things students of lighthouse lore learn on their guided tours is that nothing about lighthouses is a matter of whim. The colors and designs serve very important identification purposes. At night each lighthouse can be distinguished by the color of the light beam and its duration or flash pattern. By day, navigators rely on the shape of the buildings and the paint designs. For instance, Montauk Point Light on the tip of Long Island is white with a broad middle band of brown, while Georgia's famed Tybee Light looks something like an elongated black-and-white checkerboard, and Virginia's Assateague Light is red and cone shaped.

[11]The heaviest concentration of lighthouses is still along the New England coast, where more than 70 are strung along the shoreline from West Quoddy Head near the Canadian border to Whaleback Light near Portsmouth Harbor in New Hampshire. For information of specific lighthouses call the local Coast Guard office.

[12]What the California, Oregon, and Washington lights lack in number, they compensate for in surrounding scenery, accessibility, and hospitality. There are more than a dozen open to visitors in California alone.

[13]San Diego's old lighthouse at Point Loma is a good example of the trend toward preservation. When it was built in 1855 it was the southernmost light of the West. For more than three decades it was also, at 462 feet above sea level, the highest in the country, a dimension that caused its downfall since the beacon was often obscured by low clouds. The present Point Loma Light, a tall skeleton tower built nearly 90 years ago, is nearer sea level. The original lighthouse has been preserved and is furnished as it might have been by the family of a Nineteenth Century lighthouse keeper. It has a magnificent view and serves as a popular vantage point for observing the annual gray-whale migration.

[14]In San Francisco there are nearly a dozen lighthouses, both

old and new. A favorite of tourists is Fort Point, a quaint 112-foot iron structure atop the old fort beneath the Golden Gate Bridge. From the vantage point of the Fort, now a national historic site, five still-functioning lights are visible, including the one at Alcatraz.

## QUESTIONS ON    **Guiding Lights**

Answers are at the end of the chapter.

1. What is the function of paragraph 1?

2. In what paragraph does the writer state her thesis?

3. What is the subject matter discussed in the paragraph unit consisting of paragraphs 3 and 4?

4. What is the topic sentence of paragraph 5? Of what does the supporting material consist?

5. Paragraphs 6 and 7 have an implied main idea. What is it?

6. What was the immediate effect of the action by President Franklin Roosevelt in 1939?

7. Explain the cause and effect relationship in paragraph 9.

8. What do students of lighthouse lore learn?

9. Around what main idea do paragraphs 11, 12, 13, and 14 revolve?

10. Does the essay have a conclusion? In your opinion, is a conclusion necessary? Why? Why not?

Read the final model essay. Note that a brief analysis follows it.

▶ SEEMS TO ME

**William B. Mead**

I know people who are afraid to eat food from the supermarket, drink water from the tap, or breathe air in the city. I would like to dismiss them as sissies, but I fear they are trend setters. Look out.

Pollution no longer has much to do with these attitudes. The government could pipe in air from the Alaskan wilderness and certain people would still detect a fume — and be admired for it. *Phobias of this kind have become fashionable, signs of discriminating taste. They are the 1980s version of the little finger lifted from the teacup handle.*

You might ask what these people eat, drink, and breathe. Well, they make a show of shopping at health-food stores, preferably co-ops, where the employees are in their 20s and wear lots of denim and leather, and the customers try to look like the employees. Many of the shoppers have master's degrees and discuss agriculture with scholarly confidence. Their degrees are in psychology, and the oranges that they buy are small, black, and cost 50¢ each.

Milk is no longer delivered on our block but bottled water is. It comes in huge, unwieldy jugs that could crush your foot, a lesser risk, apparently, than drinking plain water. As for the air, I have friends who jog at dawn, even on weekends, to avoid auto exhaust. They do not have asthma; they have style.

These people represent the cutting edge. Most of my friends plod along the middle ground of fashion. Here in Washington, D.C., the hemlines of fashionable dining can be discerned from the writings of Phyllis Richman, restaurant critic for the *Washington Post*. In an annual review of restaurants not long ago, Richman wrote that Washington was trending away from red meat in favor of seafood. I already knew it, but it made me sad to see it in print.

It isn't that fish suddenly tastes better than it used to but rather that beef is out of fashion. Heart doctors who bewail the alleged refusal of Americans to cut down on their consumption of fatty meat should sit down to dinner with some of my friends. They haven't cut down on beef, they've about cut it out, and most of them have forgotten why. These are nice people, folks you would like between meals, but they would reject an invitation to a good steak house as stiffly as Jackie

Onassis would decline one to the Darlington 500, and for the same reason.

It used to be that a bad meal could be improved with good whiskey, but that's getting harder. Among the things that fashionable people do not do, besides eating good food, is drinking good liquor. They all drink white wine.

White wine is not just the preferred drink; it is the symbolic potion of the upper monoculture. Washingtonians of the right social class gather over white wine like Indians over a peace pipe. Some hostesses offer nothing else, not even a beer. I still lay out a pretty good bar when we entertain, but it is an exercise in nostalgia, like displaying baby pictures of our teen-age children. The women went to white wine in a rush several years ago, and the men have been succumbing one by one, like the gourds that gradually replaced all the people in *Invasion of the Body Snatchers*.

I could live with the changes so far, but the future scares me. We are undergoing a paling of the populace, a modern version of drawing-room delicacy, designed as always to distinguish the upper classes from those beneath. My own apprehension is of the gut variety. The people who now drink Perrier and eat raw fish were the first into wine and away from sirloin, and I fear that the future is theirs. I am keeping an eye on my wife and volunteering to do more of the grocery shopping, but it is a rear-guard action and I am watching the signs. Among our close friends, three whiskey drinkers remain, including me. If the night ever comes when Larry and Mike ask for white wine, I will flee into the darkness, the last survivor of a discarded species.

The writer uses an informal, lighthearted tone and style to express his feelings concerning tastes and trends in fashionable society today. Write a paragraph or paragraph unit defending his approach to his subject or recommending a more serious, even militant, approach to fulfill his purpose. Use details from the essay to support your viewpoint.

## Answers: Chapter 9

### Exercise 1

1. The subject of the classification is bees.
2. The writer breaks bees into three classes: (1) queen bees, (2) worker bees, and (3) drones.
3. The characteristics are the following: (1) sterile female, (2) nonfunctioning ovaries, (3) never lays eggs under normal conditions, and (4) excels in female virtues.

### Critics of American Vietnam Policy

1. The writer discusses problems in classification, such as simply dividing critics of American Vietnam policy into "hawks" and "doves." Such simple classifications are sometimes not very illuminating.
2. The three divisions are the following:
    a. Older citizens and persons with little schooling
    b. People who initially supported the war or were indifferent to it became opposed to the war because it seemed pointless and endless.
    c. Individuals who opposed the war because it violated their political ideology.
3. The classification is based on opinion polls.
4. The writer states that support for the war was greatest among younger persons and college graduates.
5. Such tactics deeply offended most citizens and may very well have prolonged the war.
6. The following groups:
    a. Older citizens and persons with little schooling — group 1
    b. Individuals who believed the war violated their political ideology — group 3
    c. Group 2
    d. Most citizens, including those opposed to the war
    e. No group — a separate minority

### Exercise 3

1. (a) growing/(grows); (b) lives naturally
2. Under the entry *native* in the dictionary will be listed synonyms for *indigenous* and also *native*
3. Four
4. Three — adjective, adverb, noun
5. Latin and French
6. Second syllable

### Exercise 5

1. It was developed in the United States.
2. The word is chiefly defined by contrast; that is, the definition of the word in Europe is different from the definition in the United States.
3. He uses the alternating or point-by-point method.
4. In the United States, *frontier* has these meanings:
    a. It is an area inviting entrance into a country.
    b. A frontier lies *within* the country.
    c. One approaches it with a spirit of adventure.
    d. It was transient and temporal.

    In Europe:
    a. It is a boundary between two nations.
    b. A frontier lies at the edge of a country.
    c. One approaches it with caution and fear.
    d. It is stationary and permanent.

### Guiding Light

1. It introduces the essay by presenting an example from history.
2. Elizabeth Pierce states her thesis in paragraph 2: "Long subjects of legends

and prose, lighthouses today stand as mementos of the country's seafaring past."
3. Information concerning the Boston Light.
4. The New England coast has a slight edge as a lighthouse legend maker. The supporting material consists mainly of examples — places where lighthouses were built.
5. It is a continuation of the listing of places where lighthouses were built — but in other parts of the country.
6. This move, and the turn to automated lighthouses, marked an end — with few exceptions — to the time-honored tradition of family lighthouse stations.
7. The darkening and dismantling of many of the old lights (cause) brought a heartening development for lighthouse buffs (effect).
8. They learned that nothing about lighthouses is a matter of whim.
9. General information about lighthouses in various sections of the country.
10. Individual choice by student. I feel that it requires no conclusion — everything has been said that is needed.

# Index

2 3 4 5 6 7 8 9 0